SCANDINAVIANS

IN SEARCH OF THE SOUL OF THE NORTH

SCANDINAVIANS

IN SEARCH OF THE SOUL OF THE NORTH

ROBERT FERGUSON

THE OVERLOOK PRESS
NEW YORK, NY

This edition first published in paperback in the United States in 2018 by
The Overlook Press, Peter Mayer Publishers, Inc.

141 Wooster Street
New York, NY 10012
www.overlookpress.com
For bulk and special sales please email sales@overlookny.com,
or write us at the above address.

Cataloging-in-Publication Data is available from the Library of Congress.

Typeset by Adrian McLaughlin
Maps by Jeff Edwards

Manufactured in the United States of America

ISBN: 978-1-4683-1667-4

1 3 5 7 9 8 6 4 2

For Nina

Contents

Preface

AS SOMEONE IN THIS BOOK OBSERVES, THE COUNTRY THAT I moved to in the winter of 1983 was not the real Norway. It was a nineteenth-century dream of Norway, the creation of a remarkable handful of artistic geniuses: Knut Hamsun, Henrik Ibsen, Edvard Munch and Edvard Grieg, all of whom in varying degrees I admired. It was these giants of European and world culture who first drew my attention to this tiny community in the far north of the world. That was over thirty years now, and a digitally-driven globalization means the best-kept secret in Europe is a secret no more. A brilliant but obscuring cultural layer has gradually been overlaid by the slow-motion tsunami of change.

As of this writing, Norway is one of the richest nations on earth following the discovery of North Sea oil in the 1960s, and as a result of a canniness both rural and Lutheran in investing the profits from the state-owned industry that extracts it into an investment fund currently worth in the region of 6,650 billion kroner, or 1.3 million kroner *per Norwegian*. This is a society so wealthy that by the early twenty-first century its indigenous working class has all but disappeared and it has been obliged to import one to build and repair its houses and flats, drive its public transport and taxis, keep its hospitals and old people's homes open, and sweep and wash the staircases of its communal apartment blocks. Back in 1983, when I first came to live here, the housekeeping was still done by the tenants themselves according to a rota system, and woe betide you if you forgot, for the local *nabokjerring*, a sort of socially responsible old battle-axe-cum-gossip, would come knocking at your door and more or less drag you out by the ear to do it. Today's tenants farm the work out, and the last decade has seen a boom in cleaning agencies. Most of them are run by immigrants from Poland, Latvia, Estonia, bringing with them a Roman Catholicism that has been more or less absent from the country since the Reformation – so many of them that Catholic churches struggle to cope with the demand for seats on Sundays. My morning newspaper, which was once delivered at the crack of dawn by a Norwegian schoolboy saving for his first bicycle, now comes courtesy of a mournful-looking Eritrean who is going grey at the temples. Huge numbers of young Swedes, too, have arrived in Norway over the past decade, looking for work in the numerous Starbucks-cloned coffee bars that have sprung up all over the country, 55,000 of them in the catering trade alone. They comfort themselves by making ironic comments about their 'only being here to take the country over again', while the Norwegians exult at finding themselves finally, after a thousand years 'below stairs', living upstairs in their own version of *Downton Abbey*, their menial needs attended to by this army of Swedes and other immigrants.

Things have changed, and before they change out of all recognition I have felt an increasing desire to look back and see if I can in some way trace the outlines of a more permanent manifestation of Scandinavian identity, or spirit, or soul or heart, whichever of those unsatisfactory terms seems most appropriate, and allow myself to ponder freely questions that I have been too busy living to ponder before, such as: Is social democracy really Lutheranism disguised as rationalism? Why are Scandinavian prisons so luxurious? Why are their prison sentences so short? Are these examples of weakness, naivety, or are they the best way forward? Why have the Swedes been neutral for the past two centuries? Is it principles, timidity or the future of mankind? Why are the social services in Scandinavia so generous? Is it wealth, decency, guilt or a combination of all three? And what, in a historical sense, has been the inner dynamic of the relationship between Danes, Norwegians and Swedes over the centuries? Greater minds than mine have addressed such matters. The nineteenth-century Norwegian playwright Henrik Ibsen once attempted to define the difference in status between the three peoples: 'Between us, Swedes, Danes and Norwegians, we possess all the qualities needed to form a spiritually united, single people: Swedes are our spiritual aristocracy, Denmark our spiritual bourgeoisie, and Norway our spiritual lower class.' How valid was Ibsen's analysis? How valid is it today? Who *are* the Scandinavians?

*

The sixth-century Gothic historian Jordanes saw in *Scandza*, by which he meant Scandinavia, the cradle of human life, 'a hive of nations and a womb of peoples'. In the 'Ynglingasaga' chapter of the thirteenth-century *Heimskringla*, his history of the kings of Norway, the Icelandic chieftain, poet and historian Snorri Sturluson writes of a tribal emigration northwards led by the great chieftain Odin from the coast of the Black Sea in the time of the Roman Empire. European Christians such as Alcuin and Asser knew the Scandinavians only as Vikings – as terrorists, barbarians, thieves and conquerors; the more anthropologically objective contributions of the Arab travellers and scholars who encountered the Vikings on their travels include the observations of a fourteenth-century Syrian geographer, Shams al-din al-Dimashqi, who wrote of a 'Frozen Ocean that lies beyond the Qibgaq-deserts at a latitude of sixty-three degrees. Its length is an eight-day journey and its breadth three days. A great island is located in this ocean, inhabited by tall people with white skin and fair hair and blue eyes.' The seventeenth-century Spaniard Baltasar Gracián, in his categorization of the differences between the three peoples, drew particular attention to a fondness for cruelty among the Swedes. Montesquieu found in the cold climate a scientific explanation for the alleged superiority of the Scandinavians in intelligence, ethical standards, and sheer intellectual and physical energy. In the *Lettres sur le Nord* published in 1840, the Frenchman Xavier Marmier rebuked his fellow-countrymen for the way all their knowledge of the north failed once it reached the dim fogs of the Baltic.

As the nineteenth century progressed, democracy in the Scandinavian countries took root slowly and in a more stable and less dramatic fashion than in other parts of Europe. The absence of feudalism in Sweden and Norway meant that political tensions between the social classes were fewer, and the idea of a flat and egalitarian structure a less unnatural one. Mary Wollstonecraft, in her letters home from her Scandinavian travels in 1795, praised the generally high level of education in all three countries compared with her native England. She also found that Norwegians, in the midst of what many of Norway's own historians continue to refer to as 'the four-hundred-year night' of dependence on Denmark and Sweden before the achievement of independence in 1905, seemed to her to 'enjoy all the blessings of freedom' and 'a degree of equality which I have seldom seen elsewhere'. A 'sensible, shrewd people,' she called them, 'with little scientific knowledge, and still less taste for literature,' but who appeared to her to be 'arriving at the epoch which precedes the introduction of the arts and sciences'. The inhabitants of the double monarchy Denmark-Norway seemed to her 'the least oppressed people of Europe'. The Swedes she found to be courteous, but with a courtesy bordering on insincerity, the effect, she maintained, of a spirit softened rather than degraded by wretchedness. A nineteenth-century visitor, Captain Charles Frankland, noted that he 'never saw anything yet to equal the laziness of those Swedes; they seemed to be as stupid as the Danes and twice as insolent'. Writing of a trip to Sweden in 1847, the novelist Selina Bunbury was more empathically inclined, but still effortlessly convinced of the superiority of the British way of doing things. She noted the primitive nature of the agricultural methods she witnessed, and 'could not help thinking what a mutual-advantage system it might prove if English or Scotch farmers were encouraged to settle in this agricultural country'.

But gradually those outside Scandinavia began to see the advantages of the egalitarianism practised in the north, in which neither the traditional power of the aristocracy nor the power of new industry ever became too dominant. The high level of literacy and an ethic of hard work, diligence and responsibility created a revised image of these countries as notably progressive and, by the end of the nineteenth century, there was almost uniform agreement in the writings of travellers and visitors that Denmark, Sweden and Norway were, in very similar ways, outstanding examples of peaceful and prosperous societies. The admiration continues into the twenty-first century. Perhaps oddly, none of these travellers made particular mention of the melancholy that has always accompanied, shadow-like, the other image the outside world now has of Sweden, Norway and Denmark as clean, well-lit places. Yet, especially in literature and film, this trope is never far from the minds of observers of the region and its people. In time, the enormous success of such bright and shadowless entities as IKEA and Abba, and the explosion of interest in Scandinavians as writers of crime-fiction and television drama may put an end to the characterization; but for now it persists, and it is one of the myths I want to look at more closely as I embark upon what isn't, strictly speaking, a history so much as a journey, a discursive and digressive stroll through the last thousand years of Scandinavian culture in search of the soul of the north.

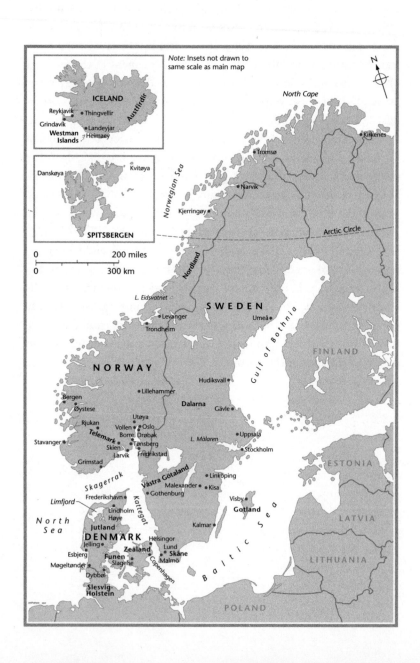

Note: Insets not drawn to same scale as main map

ICELAND

Reykjavik
Thingvellir
Austfirdir
Grindavik
Landeyjar
Westman Islands
Heimaey

Danskøya
Kvitøya
SPITSBERGEN

0   200 miles
0   300 km

North Cape
Kirkenes
Tromsø
Narvik
Norwegian Sea
Kjerringøy
Arctic Circle
Nordland

L. Eidsvatnet
Levanger
SWEDEN
Umeå
Trondheim

Gulf of Bothnia
FINLAND

NORWAY

Bergen
Øystese
Lillehammer
Hudiksvall
Dalarna
Gävle
Rjukan
Utøya
Vollen
Oslo
Telemark
Borre
Drøbak
Uppsala
Stavanger
Skien
Tønsberg
L. Mälaren
Stockholm
Grimstad
Larvik
Fredrikstad

ESTONIA

Skagerrak
Västra Götaland
Linköping
Malexander
Kisa
Gothenburg
Visby
Gotland
Frederikshavn
Kattegat
Limfjord
Lindholm
Høye
Kalmar
North Sea
Jutland
Baltic Sea
DENMARK
Helsingor
LATVIA
Jelling
Zealand
Lund
Esbjerg
Funen
Skåne
Møgeltønder
Slagelse
Malmö
LITHUANIA
Dybbøl
Copenhagen
Slesvig-Holstein

POLAND

Prelude

A Season in Hell: Copenhagen 1969

IN THE LATE AUTUMN OF 1969, WHEN I WAS TWENTY years old and still thought polar bears roamed the streets of Stockholm and that Henrik Ibsen was an Englishman with a funny name, I was working as a machine operator at Quinton Hazel's factory in Dock Road, Lytham, churning out silencers for motor vehicles at a leisurely rate for seven shillings and sixpence an hour. One day the foreman came by and announced that the company was introducing piece-work for all and compulsory overtime. After lunch at the fish-and-chip shop on the corner of Dock Road that same day I did not return to the factory but instead took a long and leisurely walk all the way down the seafront to Fairhaven Lake, where my friend Kevin was working as a gardener. After searching around for several minutes I discovered him weeding a large circular flower bed over by the sea-front car park at the far end of the lake. I immediately put to him the vaguely formed plan that had come to me during my walk along the Promenade whereby I proposed that the two of us leave Lytham St Annes at once and head off somewhere in pursuit of adventure and real life. As I was speaking Kevin picked up an earthworm from his spade and dangled it in front of his eyes, study-ing it in fascinated wonder. Before responding he spat on his fingers and then carefully washed its purple body clean before placing it gently in the grass. Then, still without speaking, he laid the spade down on the grass and we set off walking across the putting green in the direction of the Fairhaven Arms to discuss the matter further.

It was December by the time we left the town. To this day I have no idea why we decided to head north, for Sweden, which was my idea, rather than opt for Kevin's much more sensible idea that we try sunny Spain. Perhaps my wife is right and I was Scandinavian in a previous life and thus only responding to the blind and irrational promptings of my former incarnation. Or perhaps I was destined to be a Scandinavian in a future life, and this was by way of being a trial run.

We took the night ferry across the Channel from Dover to Dunkirk and hitchhiked north. When the rides ran out, we spent most of the little money we had on train tickets to get us up into Germany and caught the ferry from Travemünde to Malmö, on the southern tip of Sweden, disembarking at about ten in the morning on a bitterly cold day. Other than trying to get to Stockholm we had no plans at all and for the next five hours stood at a roundabout on the outside of town with our little rucksacks and tried to hitch a lift northwards, along the E4. No one stopped or even looked like stopping. Kevin was wearing a black, double-breasted overcoat that reached to his ankles, with shiny buttons and Civil Defence epaulettes, and for a long time I was convinced that this was the reason we weren't getting any lifts. He looked like Withnail and I looked like I. One driver who did slow down as he passed us pulled a mocking face and, pointing at his head, made scissoring gestures with his free hand to indicate that we needed haircuts. Finally, about mid-afternoon, a car did stop. Two tall and unsmiling policemen stepped out and demanded to see our passports. They searched our pockets, made us unpack our rucksacks and went through our belongings. As they drove off afterwards, the driver nudged the nearside wing into Kevin's thigh. It was already almost dark and the traffic was thinning out. All in all it was turning out to be a very disheartening start to our great adventure. Not long afterwards we got into conversation with a Danish hippy who had been dropped off at the roundabout. Hearing of our disappointments he urged us to forget Stockholm and instead take the Malmö ferry the short distance over the water to Copenhagen.

Denmark seemed like a different world. It was vibrant with people, noise, chance, life. Our plans for the trip had been almost puritanically inadequate and neither of us had packed even a sleeping bag. It meant that for the first few nights we spent fitful half-hours sleeping in bus and train stations before being woken up and moved along, and one entire electric-blue night on the floor of a city-centre nightclub. By day we roamed the streets of central Copenhagen selling a hippy newspaper called *Superlove*. It was a Danish version of the British *International Times* and it specialized in extravagant and provocative headlines such as 'Free Charles Manson'. We had to surrender our passports to the publisher and hung onto 50 øre from every copy of the paper we sold. We kept mostly to the Strøget, the shopping street that runs through the heart of the city, where the big department stores like Illums were. Kevin and I would meet there at pre-arranged intervals to use the toilets and stand beneath the giant hot-air fans in the entrance, putting some warmth into our freezing backs and hands. Each new edition of the paper sold well for about two days, but then everybody who wanted to buy it had already done so; and after that came days on which you would be lucky to sell as many as three copies. Neither of us had the salesman's touch.

Soon, with the lack of sleep, food and money, we started talking about giving up and going back to England. We were regularly getting duped by strange, mentally disturbed people, quite often Americans, who said they could help us out with places to sleep through the freezing cold nights. I remember in particular one who said he was a member of Elvis Presley's backing singers, the Jordanaires. He said he owned a large house in the city and we were welcome to sleep there: meet me here at ten tonight. He was tripping on LSD throughout this encounter but in our desperation we chose to believe his idiotic claims and duly made our way to Dronning Louises Bro, the bridge that divides Copenhagen's city-centre lakes. We waited for him there until past midnight and of course he didn't show. We ended up taking turns to sleep, curled up on the stone floor of a telephone booth in a nearby side-street.

Then one day we got lucky. A real hippy stopped to buy a copy of the latest *Superlove*. His name was Poul Rasmussen, he was about eighteen years old with waist-length chestnut hair, and he worked in a kindergarten. He said he had a little flat on Korsgade and invited us back for coffee. It turned out to be a two-room basement. The door opened onto a step-down kitchen with an impacted dirt floor and a door-space into a bedroom on the far wall. He said we could sleep on his floor.

A few years ago I found myself back in Copenhagen for the publication of a Danish edition of my biography of Henry Miller. During one free afternoon I set off out of curiosity to see if I could find that old place. It wasn't easy. Everything on Korsgade had been rebuilt or refurbished. A sign announced that the whole area was a Nuclear Free Zone. I walked past the site of a rock club where, one hallucinated evening, Kevin and I went to a concert featuring Family, an English rock group whose singer had a vibrato so piercing it struck terror into my fragile heart. I located the rundown old arts cinema where we saw *Antonio das mortes*, a film by the Brazilian director Glauber Rocha. High as I was on 'charge', as we used to call marijuana then, in imitation of Kerouac's characters in *On the Road*, I had no idea what the film was about. It seemed that the audience spent the whole time walking about, eating, talking and shouting across the auditorium in a way that recalled to me the cinema at St Nicholas Hospital in Newcastle-on-Tyne, the mental hospital where my father used to work and where, seven years old, I would sit in the gallery along with four or five other staff children every Friday evening trying to ignore the bubbling pool of weirdness from the patients below, the muttering, the bursts of song, the sobbing, the masturbating, the sudden weird cries rising up like something out of a Gesualdo madrigal, as we watched Mario Lanza in *The Student Prince* and tried to work out why on earth everything came to a stop every so often and he would burst out singing.

Before those days at Korsgade 68B finally came to an end Kevin and I found ourselves having to negotiate some strange ethical boundaries in our struggle to keep going. Shortly after inviting us to share the flat with him our Danish hippy saviour moved in with his girlfriend and handed over the keys of the basement to us. We took turns at sleeping in the bed, though the comfort of this was offset by the burden of being responsible for the rent. It wasn't much but it had to be paid. We carried on selling *Superlove,* but our luck was running out, until a time came when we couldn't see any option but to steal the food we needed. We took turns at it. A lump of cellophane-wrapped cheese. A packet of spicy salami.

One day, acting on an obscure piece of advice, we took a bus out to the suburbs and the studios of Rodox Films, a major producer of pornographic films in the burgeoning sex-film industry in which, at that time, Denmark was the undisputed world leader. The headquarters turned out to be a dark brick building with bars on the windows and a metal plate nailed over the front door. The man who let us in was somewhere in his thirties, with John Lennon glasses and a frizz of solar curls around his head and a sad, Sgt Pepper-type moustache. He introduced himself, said his name was Mogens, and led us through a short labyrinth of corridors into a brightly-lit office. A song by Savage Rose, Denmark's biggest group at that time, was playing on the Bang & Olufsen transistor radio standing on a shelf of videos behind him. Mogens asked how he could help us. We told him we wanted to make money being the man in a Rodox sex film. He gave a pitying smile and shook his head. We don't sell men, he said. We sell women. I have a list of men who are willing to *pay* to be in my films. He briefly lifted the edge of a sheet of yellow A4 paper on his desk as though this were the list in question. Unless you're *bøsser*? No, we weren't *bøsser*...

There was a video case on top of the photocopier next to his desk. The cover showed a black and white photograph of a pretty girl wearing a cowboy hat and not much else. She was squatting next to a black labrador, one arm dangling on its neck. The dog's front paws were wrapped in blue duct tape. Mogens turned his head to see what I was staring at.

'That's Bodil,' he said.

'Why does the dog have tape on its paws?'

'To protect her skin,' he answered.

'She has sex with her dog?'

'Yes. And with other animals too.'

Was I shocked? Probably not. Nothing seemed to shock me back then. I had no idea that Denmark that same year had legalized every form of pornography except child pornography.

About a week later, as I lay on the bed listening to my stomach growling and squawking like an Albert Ayler track, the door to the flat burst open and Kevin stumbled down the steps. He was followed by two burly men wearing raincoats. He'd been caught in a supermarket with a wedge of cheese hidden under his long black coat. The manager had called the police. We stood watching in silence as they searched the flat, looking for drugs inside the wood stove, the terracotta bread bin, the coffee jug and under the mattress. After about five minutes they exchanged a few words in Danish and then told Kevin to come with them. Halfway up the steps he stopped and asked what was going to happen to him. They told him he was going to be deported back to England.

As soon as the door closed a feeling of great calm descended on me. It always does when something bad happens. Had I known Kierkegaard's writing back then I would have understood why. The background drone of *angst* was gone. The dreaded thing had happened. I didn't need to dread it anymore. And the very next day the postman knocked on the door with a sign-for letter addressed to Kevin. The familiar blue wax-crayoned cross scratched over the address told me that there was money inside and I opened it without a second thought. It was from Kevin's brother in Cardiff. I almost fainted with relief at the sight of the two £10 notes tucked inside the covering letter. I opened the door and stepped out into the street. A soft, warm light in the air gave the faintest hint that the long hard winter we had all endured was almost over and spring was just around the corner. For the first time in weeks I felt like washing my hair. And I was hungry. I was extremely hungry for a specific kind of Danish bread that I knew the shop on the corner sold. A soft loaf with a sweet, salty, almost primrose-yellow flesh within the framing of pale golden crust. All the time, as I was washing my hair, as I was changing my pounds into kroner at the bank, as I was heading back along Korsgade towards the baker's, all the time I was agonizing over the question of whether to smother the first slice in a clear film of acacia honey or instead coat it in a swampy layer of crunchy peanut butter. Afterwards I made my way down to the docks and bought a ticket for the DFDS ferry to Harwich.

That evening, as the ferry pulled away from the dock and I watched the city slowly recede, I leaned over the stern rail and struggled against an obscure sense of defeat. I felt almost as though I had been sent to Copenhagen for a purpose but had failed to discover what that purpose was. The sense of failure gave way presently to a wonder at the strange dance-steps big ships seem to enact as they navigate their way out of docks, shunting around backwards, drifting sideways, turning in circles, as though the captain has no real idea what he's doing and we'll never get there. Recalling that departure dance now reminds me of one of Kierkegaard's most remarkable and subtle observations, that life can only be understood backwards but must be lived forwards. I think it means you have to turn around and start walking backwards, facing the past, if the present is going to make any sense at all.

A Note on Scandinavian Languages

ONE OF THE LAST JOBS I HAD BEFORE BECOMING A full-time student was serving behind the counter at Solosy's two newsagents shops, at the Trafalgar Square end of Charing Cross Road. When things were quiet in the shop I would often take down a book we stocked called Hugo's *Teach Yourself Norwegian in Three Months*. Browsing through it I came across words like *barn* (child), and *kirk* (church), that I had heard my Scottish grandparents use. I found *gate* (street), a word I remembered from probably the first song I ever learnt, 'The Keel Row', which begins 'As I came by Sandgate, by Sandgate, by Sandgate...'. These words turned out to be linguistic remnants of the Viking settlements in Britain that began early in the ninth century and continued for some three hundred years. Visitors to York today will find street names like Coppergate, Stonegate and Fossgate, from a time when the city was the centre of the Viking kingdom of York. Even our names for the days of the week derive from the same source and time: Monday (*Måne dag* – 'moon day'); Tuesday (*Tyrs dag* – 'Tyr's day', named for the god Tyr); Wednesday (*Odins dag*); Thursday (*Thors dag*); Friday (*Freyjas dag*). From all of this I quickly realized I had one foot in the door of the language. It was a tremendous encouragement to go ahead and learn it properly, as was the realisation that knowing any one of Danish, Norwegian and Swedish gives good access to the other two.

All Scandinavian languages derive from the varieties of 'Old Norse' that were spoken across the Scandinavian peninsula during the Viking Age and beyond. In the case of Norwegian, Swedish and Danish they remain mutually comprehensible, although largely for reasons of national identity and pride novels and textbooks are routinely translated between the languages. Written Icelandic remains closest to Old Norse and has retained the distinctive characters of *thorn* (Þ) and *eth* (ð). The former is a voiceless 'th' sound as in English 'think'. Thus, a name such as Þorgeir Þorkelsson is typically anglicized as 'Thorgeir Thorkelsson'. The voiced version, the *eth*, is pronounced like 'th' as in 'father', and is never used at the beginning of a word. It is often anglicized in writing as a 'd', so that Austfirðir may be anglicized as 'Austfirdir'. Both the *thorn* and *eth* appear in the pages to follow, for a sense of Iceland's distinctiveness.

Modern *written* Norwegian is complicated by the parallel existence of two official forms. *Bokmål* ('Book Language') grew from the Dano-Norwegian that developed during the centuries of Danish dominance over Norway. It is the language of the city, and the spoken and written form favoured by the overwhelming majority of Norwegians today. As in Danish, the alphabet retains æ, ø and å after z. *Nynorsk* ('New Norwegian') is an artificial construction from the mid-nineteenth century that attempted to bring the written language into line with the Norwegian spoken in more rural parts of the country. It is often the preferred language of poets.

The Swedish alphabet adds *å*, *ä* and *ö* after *z*. On account of the French roots of the House of Bernadotte, which has ruled in Sweden since 1818, Swedish retains a small but distinct French element which is entirely absent from Danish and Norwegian.

These historical complexities make it virtually impossible to translate place and personal names into English with any consistency. In the pages that follow I have preferred a subjective approach, mixing old and new and variant forms of the originals rather than imposing an illusory standardization on their exoticism.

1
Stones

ROUNDING A BEND IN THE COUNTRY ROAD THEY CAME
into view again. I could not take my eyes from them. I was riveted.
I felt as if I had personally discovered them. As if I were the first
person to have seen them in over a thousand years. There was a farm
on the same side of the road, and access to the field involving walking
up about fifty metres of muddy lane past the farmyard. Going up
that lane I was struggling to hold back a strange and annoying timidity that always seems to afflict me at the prospect of committing even
the least infraction while visiting a foreign country, even something
as harmless as this trespass. At any moment I expected to hear, and
then see, the farmer's ragged black Alsatian barking and straining to
get at me on the end of its very long chain. I started going through in
my head what I would say to the farmer when he appeared, with his
shotgun, beside the dog. Best to speak in English. Confuse him. But
I got to the end of the lane and turned left through the gate into the
field unchallenged, and set out on the long trudge through the snow
towards them.

They stood further apart than they had appeared from the bus, with
maybe fifteen metres separating them. Both were much taller than I
had expected. Both were distinctly phallic or mushroom-shaped.
I walked between them and squatted down in front of them, first one

then the other, and stroked the little fringe of rubble that surrounded them above the snow at the base. I stood on tiptoe before them and touched as high up on their faces as I could with my fingertips. I slid my palms up and down their narrow edges. I breathed on them. I whispered to them. I walked around and around them. I studied them and photographed them from every angle and was only mildly disappointed to find no trace on either one of a Viking longship or a band of runic carving. And when there was no other possible way I could think of to engage with them I closed my eyes and just stood there in front of them for a moment or two and glowed with happiness.

I had just met the Bro stones. They stand about a mile (2 km) north-east of Bro Church, about a half-hour bus ride out from the medieval town of Visby on the Baltic island of Gotland. According to tourist legend, these were two women who began arguing on their way to church one Sunday whom God had turned to stone as a punishment. But that's a post-conversion explanation and a good example of the way the early Church tried to give God credit for everything. Those Bro stones have been standing in exactly the same place in exactly that same field for at least the last 1,400 years. They're 'blind' stones. That's the general term used for Gotland picture-stones on which the images and all narrative trace of whatever story they once told of forgotten heroes and dead gods, lost epics, obsolete religious prac-tices and arcane beliefs has been obliterated by the weathering of the years. Walking away from the stones, over and over again turning back to look at them, I made a deliberate attempt to impress upon myself the significance of what I had just seen. Man-made things. Artefacts of huge significance to those who made them and to those who passed them by. But meaning what? Here, I said to myself, is an image of the silence in which most of Scandinavian history, not to say human history, is enshrouded. Do they symbolize phalluses? Are they massive erections, bursting up through the earth's crust in search of congress with the upper air? Are they from a time when people thought the earth was male and the sky female? Or did their shapes represent gateways through which one might gain entry to another world? If so, I thought, they are gateways to a world we can never enter, made by a people with whom we can no longer communicate.

I had been on my way to see the famous stone at the museum at Bunge, in the north of Gotland, when I spied these two from my seat on the bus and on impulse pulled the stop cable. The Bunge stone is richly and intricately illustrated and is deservedly one of the most famous picture-stones in the world; it was first on the list of stones I intended to see during my two-week stay on the island. These Bro stones were different. They moved me in a different way. The Bunge stone was kept under lock and key in an open-air museum. The Bro stones had been taking their chances out in the field since long before man's invention of linear time. To me, it was like the difference between domestic and wild animals. By the time I reached the gate I had even decided to be glad there was no trace of storytelling left on either one of them. It was an honest and truthful silence. So few things in this world are secret anymore. Their silence, and the fact that it could never be broken, pleased me greatly. As I closed the gate behind me and headed back down the muddy track towards the road, I saw the young farmer busily coiling up a bright yellow hosepipe in front of an open barn door. He glanced up momentarily from his work and gave me a cheery wave. The dwarf schnauzer beside him cocked its head on one side and looked at me.

⋆

Even where the iconography and runic inscriptions on the picture-stones and runestones have survived in legible form, as on the Bunge stone – or the mysterious Rök stone in Östergötland or the Sparlösa stone in Västergötland on the Swedish mainland – the very nature of the form means that what is communicated is telegrammatic and unadorned. The result, reinforced by the fact that the outside world's first dramatic experience of the Scandinavians as a tribe came with the eruption of the Vikings into Christian Western Europe, is that the earliest history of the Scandinavian people was written by their enemies, and by those whom they had tormented with their restless violence; and these writers were usually Christian monks.

Among the most famous of these early records is a reference made to the Viking raid on Lindisfarne in 793 by the Anglo-Saxon monk Alcuin, in a letter to Ethelred of Northumbria, king of one of the five or six independent kingdoms into which England was then divided. 'We and our fathers have now lived in this fair land for nearly three hundred and fifty years,' Alcuin wrote, 'and never before has such an atrocity been seen in Britain as we have now suffered at the hands of a pagan people. Such a voyage was not thought possible. The church of St Cuthbert is spattered with the blood of the priests of God, stripped of all its furnishings, exposed to the plundering of pagans.' For many, Alcuin's lament sums up the entire history of the Scandinavian people during the three centuries or so of the Viking Age (c.800–1100), but even at the start of the period it is clear that while Scandinavians might band together in large mercenary forces as Vikings, to go raiding in the Christian West and the Muslim South, they operated with distinct tribal identities as Danes, Swedes and Norwegians, associated with distinct geographical regions of the Scandinavian peninsula not greatly different from what we know today as Denmark, Sweden and Norway.

The Lindisfarne raiders were men from Norway's west coast who had probably already colonized Shetland and the Northern Isles, as they would later colonize the Hebrides, the Isle of Man and most of the north-west coastal fringes of the British Isles. The 'Great Heathen Army' that arrived on England's east coast in 865 and within thirty years had established dominion over the whole of the eastern seaboard, from York down to East Anglia, was largely composed of Danes. From this tribal base, in which their own Scandinavian law known as the Danelaw obtained, they carried out over the next 120 years a long, slow process of conquest, which culminated in a Danish king being crowned King of England in 1014. At its height, this North Sea Empire of the House of Jelling comprised England and the Northern and Western Isles of Scotland, as well as Denmark, Norway and large parts of southern and western Sweden. It faltered on the death of Cnut the Great in 1035 and was almost obliterated from English historical memory by the more lasting effects of the invasion of William the Conqueror in 1066.

The most familiar names from this stretch of early Scandinavian history are Ragnar Hairy Breeches, Ivar the Boneless, Bjørn Ironside – semi-legendary warrior figures with no human personality discernible at all beyond their violence. Probably the first actual Scandinavian we get to learn about as an individual is a Norwegian trader and farmer called Ottar, from Hålogaland, high on the northwest coast of Norway, in his own words 'the furthest north of any who live in the north'. Ottar turned up in Winchester in about 890, at about the same time as King Alfred's English forces were engaged in a desperate struggle to hold onto the kingdom of Wessex against Viking invaders. In the middle of all this, he quietly sat down and offered Alfred and his courtiers a detailed account of the part of the world from which he came, encompassing his life, his work, his finances, his home, his travels and his plans. It was all noted down and added as an appendix to Alfred's translation of Orosius's *Histories Against the Pagans*.

From the form in which the information is recorded it sounds as if Ottar, or Ohthere (as the Anglo-Saxons rendered the name), was answering questions put to him by a circle of interested courtiers. One can almost see the scribe, quill pen in hand, noting down his reply to a question about a trade route from his home in the north down to Skiringssal, a great market centre now vanished but located then about 3 miles (5 km) south-east of today's Larvik, in the south of the country: 'Could you make the journey from Hålogaland to Skiringssal within, let's say, a month? If you had the wind with you?' And writing down what Ottar tells him, that no, you couldn't make the journey in a month, not even if you took shelter every night and had a favourable wind with you every day. Questions about his economic and social status come up, and he tells them that he's a wealthy man, owner of 600 reindeer, including 6 decoys used for trapping. He goes further and tells them that he's one of the most powerful men in his country. The courtier, or maybe even Alfred himself, isn't convinced. He notes doubtfully that the man owns no more than twenty cows, twenty sheep and twenty swine, and that the little bit of land he farms is ploughed with a horse. Ottar seems to sense that his audience needs convincing and goes on to say that his *real* wealth comes from the tributes paid to him by the nomadic Sami people, each according to his means, in the form of hides, feathers, whalebone and ropes of whaleskin and sealskin. The farming land in his country is poor, Ottar concedes: 'The parts of it that can be used for grazing or ploughing all lie along the coast. And even that land is rocky in places. There is mountain wilderness to the east and the north, all along the cultivated land.' He tells them that the country he comes from is 'very long and very narrow', which is pretty much how you would describe geographical Norway today.

On reading through Ottar's lucid account one is struck by the clarity with which he distinguishes between the different peoples living in Scandinavia. 'Norwegians', 'Danes', 'Swedes' and 'Sami' are all identified as such, and he is just as clear about which king owns what in the region. From later and more extensive sources we learn the extent to which geography determined the main theatres of operation of the different branches of the tribe. For the Swedes, it was natural to head eastwards across the Baltic to the Gulf of Finland that gave them access to the Volga and the Dnieper and the great dangling network of rivers that would take their longboats raiding and trading as far away as the Black Sea. On 18 May 839, a group of envoys from the Byzantine emperor, Theophilus, turned up at Ingelheim in Germany and presented themselves at the court of the Holy Roman Emperor, Louis the Pious. They'd come to confirm a treaty of 'peace and perpetual friendship and love' between the two emperors. Arriving with them was a separate band of men who presented Louis with a letter from Theophilus asking for safe conduct through his territories on their northward journey home. Louis sent a cautious reply to Theophilus. He said that he would detain them for a time while he carried out some investigations. If these turned out to be satisfactory he would offer the help asked for; but if he found something he didn't like, he would be sending the men back to Theophilus for the emperor to deal with as he saw fit. Louis was taking no chances. Fifty years into the Viking Age, travellers from the north had acquired a firm reputation for violence and treachery. This tale is told in the French *Annals of St Bertin*, and it ends without our ever finding out what happened to the travellers. The annalist records that they identified themselves as 'Rus', from Roslagen, the name for the coastal stretch north of Stockholm from which they originally hailed. It was Rus warrior-aristocrats who founded the Old Kievan State that became Russia. It's the first time their name occurs in the written record, and it wasn't a record they wrote themselves.

Hundreds of miles east of Ingelheim, at the remotest fringes of the Islamic Empire, tenth-century travellers such as the Arab Ibn Fadlan and the Persian Ibn Rustah also came across bands of Rus and wrote their own accounts of the experience which were more objective, anthropological even, than the black and terror-filled tales of violence told by Christian clerics in the West. Ibn Fadlan watched a funeral ceremony carried out by one travelling band of traders he met camped on the banks of the Volga in 921. Like the Christian Alcuin, and like almost everyone who encountered heathen Scandinavians in this period, he was convinced that his was the higher culture. But one Rus obviously did not agree. Ibn Fadlan noticed his interpreter conversing with this particular man and asked what they had discussed. The interpreter said they had talked about ways of dealing with the dead. The Rus told him he thought the Arabic way stupid: you take the people you love the best and respect the most and you bury them in holes in the ground to be eaten by the rats and the insects. We burn our dead, he said. An instant and they're gone and in the next world already.

In his account, Ibn Fadlan cannot hide his disgust at the way the Rus didn't wash after defecating, urinating and having sexual intercourse; but he owned that he had never seen more perfect physical specimens. 'Ruddy-complexioned,' he called them, and 'tall as date-palms'. Irish annalists of the ninth century also remarked on the physical characteristics of the Vikings, distinguishing between the rival factions warring for possession of Dublin as the *Finngail* (the 'fair foreigners', being Norwegians) and the *Dubgaill* (the 'dark foreigners', or Danes). But apart from al-Dimashqi, no other chronicler mentions the fairness of skin and hair typically associated with Scandinavians. He added the observation that they understood no language but their own – a characteristic in which they differ radically from Scandinavians of today, among whom even primary school children speak a passable English.

Ibn Fadlan's sex- and death-drenched account of a Rus funeral is probably the most famous single document in all early Scandinavian history. In it, he describes in detail the selection of a slave girl to accompany her master into death, and the last few hours of her life, during which she is plied with alcohol before being lifted high by her late master's warriors to look over a raised bar and see into the next world; and he describes how she is then possessed by each of them in turn before being ritually strangled and stabbed to death by the Rus priestess.* The ceremony on the river bank, which ends in the burning of the chieftain's coffin-boat, has an air of improvisation about it, and reasonably so, because in the absence of any kind of heathen liturgy or central reference point equivalent to the Bible the beliefs and practices of pre-Christian Scandinavian travellers will have varied greatly from place to place and group to group. How common, for example, was this kind of human sacrifice among early Scandinavians? It's hard to tell, just as it's hard to gain any coherent picture of what they expected to happen after death. The upper section of the Bunge stone shows a small person, perhaps a child or a dwarf, prostrated across some kind of chair or block and obviously at the centre of an arcane and probably not very pleasant experience. Above the victim's head a *valknut* hovers, three interlocked triangles that mark the sacrifice as dedicated to Odin. The gods were paid in this fashion to help their believers. The deities of these early Scandinavians were not ethical beings.

---

* Michael Crichton's 1976 best-seller *Eaters of the Dead*, filmed in 1999 as *The 13th Warrior* (with Antonio Banderas as Ibn Fadlan), uses many of the description's most striking details.

Ethics was the province of man, and of the law. The Christian idea
of sin, and the notion that bad behaviour towards a fellow human

being, from cheating in a deal to cold-blooded murder, might offend
the gods, would only have struck them as absurd. The Old Norse
word for sin (*synd*) didn't appear in any Scandinavian literary
source until as late as 1030, a decade or so after the conversion of
the Norwegians, when the Icelandic poet Torarin Lovtunge in the
Glælognskvida, the 'Song of Peace', described the Norwegian saint-
king Olav Haraldson as having died a 'sinless death'.

*

I spent two weeks in Gotland visiting places of interest from the
Viking Age and from the earlier Vendel Period,* of which I remember most vividly, after the Bro stones, the almost African-looking
circular burial cairns at Trullhalsar (many of them edged with carefully laid chipped limestone), the wonderful giant 'man and wife'
picture-stones on the farm at Änge, the stone ship-settings and cairns
of Lilla Bjärs, and a large 'rock gong' I came across in a field, which
gave off a lovely ringing sound when you tapped it with a pebble.
What struck me forcibly during that stay was the importance

---

* *c.* 550–790. A period unique to Sweden that precedes the Viking Age. The name
derives from grave finds made in the Uppland parish of Vendel.

of stones to the early Scandinavians. It could be a great boulder wrapped up in rope, to anchor a longship or a 'knarr', the sort of stubby trading ship with deep central holds that Ottar would have sailed in; or to anchor the grave ships of the dead, like the one tethering the fabulous Oseberg ship inside the mound from which it was unearthed in Østfold in 1905, with a thousand years of mysteries still intact on board in the shape of bundled oars, buckets, a whole range of kitchen equipment, and a menagerie of slaughtered dogs, horses and oxen to feed its two dead passengers on their onward journey. Not the costly and glamorous sword and spear but the humble stone was the weapon of choice of the early Scandinavian. The library at the Baltic Writers and Translators Centre where I was staying had a whole shelf of Icelandic sagas, and I recall browsing through a copy of the *Saga of the Jomsvikings* and coming across a description of a sea-battle that took me completely by surprise. Two bands are fighting. A lot is at stake. A country, a kingdom. The fighting is hard and merciless. You might suppose the combatants would not dare not even for an instant to stop, for fear of getting an arm or a foot or an ear sliced off. And yet every now and then, in the midst of this life-and-death encounter, ships return to shore to stock up on stones. The commonsense banality of the interruption is breathtaking, as is the information that at a certain point in the battle the combatants stop, almost as though a whistle has been blown for half time, and remove some of their outer garments, because all that heavy clothing in the heat of the day has made the fighting *uncomfortable*. Comfort matters, even if your death is just ten minutes away. A detail like that can bridge the gap of a thousand years in a fraction of a second. In the words of the great Swedish poet Tomas Tranströmer, time isn't a straight line, it's a labyrinth. Press your ear up against the wall at the right place and you can hear footsteps and voices, you might hear yourself moving about on the other side.*

The picture-stone as an art form was more or less confined to Gotland. The runestone as an art form, with its twisting and meandering bands of text winding in and out of symbols and images, developed and reached its height in mainland Sweden, where almost 60 per cent of all the known runic inscriptions from before 1500 are found. Many of these messages are formulaic words in praise of the dead. Many are fragmentary. Some, like the Hillersjö stone in Uppland, have the same kind of historical and cultural importance as Ottar of Hålogaland's account; out of the fog of history an individual steps forward and for a few seconds a real human-being is glimpsed, someone with a name and a personal story, from a time when people looked to the flights of crows and not the flickering of screens in their search to understand life, someone who, but for the mysterious forces that rule such things, might well be us. 'Read the runes' the carver enjoins us sternly at the start of the Hillersjö stone's inscription. Germund married Gerlög when she was just a young girl. They had a son. But Germund drowned and not long afterwards the son drowned too. Then Gerlög married Gudrik, who owned the farm where these runes are being read. Gerlög and Gudrik had children. The only one to survive was a girl. Inga was her name. When Inga grew up she married Ragnfast from Snottestad. Inga and Ragnfast had a son, but Ragnfast died and the son not long after. Then Inga took over her son's inheritance. Later Inga married Erik, but then she died, and her mother Gerlög took over Inga's inheritance. The rune-master signs it off: 'Torbjörn the Skald carved the runes.'

* *New Collected Poems* by Tomas Tranströmer. Translated by Robin Fulton, Bloodaxe Books (1997). The lines quoted are from 'Answers to Letters', p. 136.

At the other end of the scale is the terse Kingittorsuaq stone, found in 1834 on one of the outermost of a line of skerries strung along the desolate coast of west-central Greenland. Flat, rectangular, a mere 10 centimetres (4 in) in length, all it tells us is that Erling, Bjarni and Eindriði reached this island on the Saturday before Rogation Day – 25 April in the Roman Catholic Church calendar. No year. Who were these three long-dead men? Scandinavian Greenlanders, most likely hunters following the walrus as they drifted south on the ice. Kingittorsuaq lies some 250 miles (400 km) north of the Western Settlement, one of the two Greenland colonies established by Icelanders in about 985. They endured into the fourteenth century, but by the time the Norwegian Ivar Bardarson sailed up the west coast of Greenland in 1350 there was nothing left of either of them but deserted farmhouses with collapsed roofs, crumbling walls, broken enclosure fences and wild cattle, goats, sheep and horses grazing through the ruins. The reasons for the failure of the Western and Eastern Greenland settlements are still unclear. The Medieval Warm Period was coming to an end, to be succeeded by the period of sharply falling temperatures that climatologists have dubbed the 'Little Ice Age'. As the temperatures fell, the ice sheet advanced and the meadows and wetland around the farms flooded, turning them into heavily sedimented lakes of no use to anybody. Ice then made access to the south and south-west coasts of Greenland difficult for ships from Iceland and Norway, and as these vital lines of contact failed the colonies suffered. The long years of the Medieval Warm Period had enabled the colonists to practise the animal husbandry of their homelands, and when it ended and the ice came, they proved unable to adapt to the hunting and fishing culture that enabled the Inuit, their aboriginal rivals for the territory, to survive.

*

In the summer of 2012 my wife and I planned to take the car over to England on the ferry from Oslo to Esbjerg, a journey that would involve a leisurely drive through Denmark to Fredrikstad and the DFDS ferry across to Harwich. A week before we were due to sail, the ship on which we were booked rammed into the dock in Harwich and all sailings for the next three weeks were cancelled while repairs were carried out. We had already booked to stay at a National Trust house in East Anglia. With no opportunity to cancel at such a late date, we had to change our travel plans. Instead of the ferry we took a Ryanair flight from Oslo to Stansted Airport, where we picked up a rental car. It was a ketchup-red Nissan, with muscles like a genetically manipulated toad and a rear-view window the size of a boiled egg. We took the A11 from Stansted, and after an hour stopped in pouring rain at a petrol station for sandwiches and a cup of coffee. I had parked in a sort of air-pump bay with a half-roof over it. Reversing out of this bay afterwards, straining to see through the ludicrously small and rain-smeared rear window, I heard an ominous scraping sound from somewhere behind us. I got out to take a look. I had reversed into a metal pole, about 3 feet high. It was painted black and white so that people wouldn't reverse into it. I stood there in the rain and ran my fingers up and down the glistening tower of scratch marks on the car, brushing the raindrops off, trying to decide whether the damage was highly visible or not visible at all. In the end, I decided it was highly visible. On we drove, and for the remainder of the holiday this incident more or less dominated my mind.

The pepper pot-shaped house we had rented was in the grounds of a stately home. The car was parked in the garden and at least five or six times each day I would get up from whatever I was doing in the house and go out and inspect the damage again. I pored over the terms of the hire agreement, in particular a long and densely worded section devoted to scratches, which grouped them according to their length and depth, each gradation incurring an ever larger surcharge the closer it got to bare metal. I had no faith in the human heart of car hire companies and spent a lot of time trying to accept the idea that the surcharge would run into hundreds, and possibly even thousands, of pounds. Very occasionally, if the light was right, I came close to convincing myself that only someone with the X-ray vision of Superman would be able to spot the scratches if they didn't know they were there in the first place. On a visit to Cromer market one day I fell into a long conversation with a stallholder selling a range of tinned car products that included touch-up paints for scratched bodywork. I was almost persuaded to buy a tin that seemed to us both a close match to the dark tomato of the Nissan's bodywork, and the only thing that stopped me was the absolute certainty that the paint would not be an *exact* match, so that on returning the car I would face the double distress of having to deny that I had reversed into the pole, and then admit it, and then admit I had tried to touch it up with this slightly wrong paint and in all probability incur a special surcharge for having tried to disguise the fact. Looking back now I cannot fathom the depth and persistence of the depression brought on by this incident. Sometimes I have thought that it had nothing at all to do with these scratches but was instead the expression of some profound, Kierkegaardian anxiety the real cause of which remained hidden from me at the time and has now happily vanished of its own accord.

We returned to Stansted in a burst of brilliant sunshine following more heavy rain, which had left a coat of glistening and bulbous raindrops all over the Nissan. At least ten other drivers were waiting impatiently to drop their cars off, buzzing around the despatcher, wiggling keys and waving documents at him, anxious to join their check-in queues. When it was my turn, he did a cursory five-second waltz around the Nissan, handed me a clipboard to sign and waved me off with a harassed cry of 'That's you, mate'. I walked away feeling a sense of tremendous but completely unwarranted pride, as though in some subtle but, even to me, incomprehensible way I had won a great personal victory over the system.

But the sense of a failed holiday remained. I had been looking forward to our drive across Denmark, and particularly the chance to stop off at Jelling in the south-east of the Jutland peninsula and spend a couple of hours studying the great Jelling Stone, raised by Harald Bluetooth in about 970 to mark the arrival of institutional Christianity in Denmark. My wife felt, too, that we should give the holiday we had planned a second chance. A week later, we took the ferry from Oslo to Esbjerg as originally envisaged, and in our own car set out on a wonderfully relaxed and enjoyable drive through the country. It began with a visit to the great Viking Age cemetery at Lindholm Høje in the north of the country, where we arrived early on a glorious weekday morning and had the entire field and all its stones to ourselves. It continued with a couple of hours walking along the ramparts of the enormous ring fortress built at Trelleborg by Harald; and it culminated at Jelling, where we would be able to see for ourselves this great stone that the Danes call their *dåbsattest*, their birth certificate.

Jelling is a small town. There is little about it to suggest that a thousand years ago it was the seat of royal power in Denmark. It's a sleepy place, and there's something dreamlike about the contrast between the magnificent pyramidal stone, actually the central part of a complex monument that includes the two truly enormous burial mounds flanking it north and south, and the car park right next to it, where we left the car. A hundred metres one way takes you into the Denmark of a thousand years ago; a hundred metres in the other direction, into a featureless but functional twenty-first century shopping mall.

I knew from my previous reading that the stone was in the grounds of Jelling Church, the oldest in Denmark, and that the original church had been rebuilt several times since Harald Bluetooth's day. In every picture of it I had ever seen, the stone was standing free just a few steps from the church doors; but on entering the churchyard, I saw at once that it had been caged behind slabs of thick, tinted glass. It turns out that in 2011 a deranged visitor had emptied a spray-can of green paint over it. Since this wasn't the first attack on the stone, the authorities decided the time had come to put it behind glass for its own safety. But the glass was so thick, and the sunlight so bright, that it was hardly possible even to see, let alone read, the banded letters and the magnificent biblical imagery that cover the stone on three sides.

Feeling an obscure need to apologise to my wife for the let-down I took her by the hand and as we made our way towards the cemetery gates I gave her as full an account as I could of the stone's history, beginning with the reports of an argument around the year 970 at the court of Harald Bluetooth over the respective powers of Christ and the gods of the Æsir. During this Christ's advocate, an otherwise unknown prelate named Bishop Poppo, voluntarily submitted to a form of ordeal known as 'throw-iron' that involved his carrying a lump of molten iron a specific number of steps before dropping or throwing it. Afterwards a thing like an oven glove was placed over his hand and the wound kept sealed for four days. The mitten was then removed and the wound examined: a clean wound would be proof of the protection and power of the ordealist's god; a dirty wound a sign of his failure. Though we had not time to visit the church itself, I told her, each stage in Poppo's ordeal can be identified in a series of seven gilded bronzes from the early thirteenth century that were found in 1870 at Tamdrup, in Horsens, nailed to the pulpit and covered in a thick layer of oil paint. The first shows Poppo and Harald together, the former urging conversion on the king, Harald declining. The second shows the iron being heated over the flames; in the third the bishop shows the king his hand after the removal of the mitten. The fourth shows Poppo's reward: he is baptizing Harald, who stands naked before him in a barrel of water. This is the occasion Harald commemorates on the Jelling Stone. In the *Gesta Danorum*, or 'History of the Danes', the thirteenth-century Danish historian Saxo Grammaticus tells us that on a beach in Jutland Harald came upon a massive red and black granite stone, crudely pyramidal in shape, weighing almost 10 tons and standing 2.5 metres (8 feet) high. He had it dragged on rollers all the way to Jelling by men whom he yoked to it like oxen, and at Jelling had it decorated with Christian imagery, inscribed with runes and painted. Translated, the inscription reads: 'King Harald had this monument made in memory of Gorm, his father, and in memory of Thyrwi, his mother; that Harald who won for himself all of Denmark and Norway and made the Danes Christian.' One side depicts a struggle between two animals: a fabulous creature that may be a lion, though its mane and head more closely resemble those of a horse, and a serpent with its tail in its mouth, coiled around the body. On the second side is a crucifixion scene; it is the first significant representation of Christ in Scandinavian art. The hands of two artists have been identified in the carvings, I continued, and it has been estimated that the decorations took them about a year to complete.

The suffering Christ had no natural appeal among those who formerly worshipped masters of violence like Odin and Thor, and from the beginning the focus of missionaries such as Poppo was on Christ's power and his warrior-like attributes. So the Christ of the Jelling Stone is a fierce-eyed warrior ready to jump down from his cross and do battle with the demons of heathendom. In fact, although Christ is depicted with outstretched arms, there is no visible cross to support him, so that it looks more like an exultant stretching than an execution. Instead, the arms and body are looped around with what some suggest are vine scrolls, in a stylization familiar from as far back as the fifth century as symbols of both Christ himself and the Church. Other scholars suggest that the carvers saw the cross as basically an optional background framing device and decided against it on aesthetic grounds. Still others prefer the idea that the design reflects the same sort of syncretic instincts that led the makers to transform the Christian lion into a Scandinavian horse and the Christian snake into the world-encircling Midgard serpent of Æsir mythology, offering familiarity as an enticement to acceptance in much the same way as designers of the first railway carriages in the nineteenth century deliberately designed them to look like horse-drawn wagons so that people would dare to step on board.

The ancient Danes coming to gaze at the stone Christ might almost have seen him hanging in the branches of a tree, which would have reminded them of the tale of the nine days and nights Odin spent hanging from the branches of the world-tree Yggdrasil as he waited for the chance to swoop down and steal treasures of knowledge from the kingdom of the dead. Knowing that the detail would please my wife, whose work as an editor had brought her into contact with some of the most celebrated Sami shamans in Norway, I added that, whether by accident or design, the iconography of the stone must have encouraged an acceptance of Christ by portraying him as a shamanic god engaged in a ritual with which viewers of the stone were already familiar. In contemplating the resonance the great stone must have had for contemporaries, I went on, it is useful to recall that the Jelling Stone, like most other runestones, must once have been decorated in bright reds, blues, yellows and greys, and in its meaningful prime been a thing of fabulous beauty. As a sort of postscript I added that in both Saxo Grammaticus and in Sven Aggesen's *Short History of the Kings of Denmark* we may read of how the great gesture backfired on Harald. Humiliated at being treated like oxen, the men who had dragged the stone back to Jelling for him refused to serve as warriors when he needed them. Instead, they offered their support to his rebellious son, Sven Forkbeard, and Harald was driven from the kingdom. Mortally wounded by an arrow, he wandered with a small group of men loyal to him until they came to the town of Jumne, at the mouth of the River Oder, and there Harald died in 987. His men stayed on in the region, and in time formed the nucleus of the legendary warrior cult known to history as the Jomsburg Vikings. Sven Forkbeard, as is well known, went on to found the short-lived Jelling dynasty in England. Crowned king in 1013 he was dead within three months and succeeded by his son Cnut, or Canute, as his English subjects called him, he of the waves that would not turn back.

From the churchyard we drifted across the street in warm sunshine to the café and souvenir shop, stopping to examine and photograph a waist-high copy of the stone, beautifully painted in the original pig-blood pinks and fawns with blue and grey highlights, which stood chained to the pavement. Inside we had a cup of coffee and a Danish pastry, known to the Danes as a *wienerbrød* or 'Vienna bread', and after several rounds of the shop and some pleasurable agonizing I bought two picture-postcards, a game of Pick Up Sticks in a tubular container, a 'Viking' teaspoon made of horn and a thonged leather 'Viking' bracelet, as well as a number of other items that I no longer recall.

2

The Conversion of
the Icelanders

INSPIRED, FOR ALL I KNOW, BY THE MISERY OF THE sojourn in Copenhagen in 1969, in the winter of 1970 I made a few trips to Iceland as a deckhand on a Fleetwood trawler named the *Kennedy*. Early one morning, after we had been fishing for about three days, and with the net still in the water, we ran into a storm. Ice built up on the rigging and wires, turning them into ghostly white cylinders. The *Kennedy* was a beam trawler, meaning that the net dragged from the side and not the stern, and as a matter of urgency the ice would have to be chopped clear or the weight would turn us over. We set about the job with our axes, working in teams in forty-minute shifts. During breaks I lay on my bunk below and tried to follow the thread of a paperback novel I had borrowed from the ship's cook, Martin Dibner's *The Admiral*, about the war in the Pacific. It was the only book on board, and I was reading it even knowing that the final third was missing, the pages torn out by someone who needed them for some other purpose.

The juddering of the ship made it hard to concentrate. I shared the berth with a deckhand in his sixties, a man named Norman Jinks who should have retired long ago but still needed the money. Every time the ship rolled I could hear old Norman cursing in the bunk below me. Suddenly there was a huge crash; the *Kennedy* stopped and shuddered like someone hit in the face with a hammer. The lights flickered. You could hear the wild racing of the engines as the propeller came up clear of the water. Norman and I jumped up and starting pulling on our boots and oilskins. From the corner of my eye I could see him doing this thing he always did when it was his turn to take the winch, or go on watch. He would drop into a disguised half-kneeling position by his bunk, his face turned back towards its warmth, his fingers clasped in a loose spire and mumbling something I could never hear but knew must be a prayer because it always ended with an Amen. I used to wonder why he did this in such a secretive and almost shameful way. The fishermen on those trawlers were as hard and unsentimental as the life demanded and in the end I decided it was probably because he had once shared a berth with someone who laughed at him for it.

Up on the bridge, looking down through the tiny circle of visibility in the window made by the rotating blade of the clearview, the deck was a mess. The wireless aerials had come down and the deck lights broken loose from the mast. They swayed from one side of the deck to the other in demented arcs above where the gutting pens had once been. The fish-washing machine had been ripped up by its bolts and tossed across the deck and lay clutching a stowed-up net like a giant spider. Chunks of ice the size of hay bales whirled and crashed about on the surface of the water surging across the deck. To begin with I couldn't work out where these came from, until I noticed Norman looking up. Following his gaze I saw that the wave had shaken the ice from the rigging. The sea had taken mercy on us. In the space of a few moments it had finished off a job that would have taken us hours more back-breaking work with the axes. It was too dangerous to haul in the catch and the skipper had ordered the gear to be cut, and with the net gone now there was nothing to do but head for shelter. We went below again, happy at the thought of a few hours' uninterrupted sleep.

The next morning, a deckhand named Billy Dingle woke me to say that the bosun had ordered us on deck to tidy up after the storm. We were anchored in a bay, and in the windless and pearl-grey mid-morning there wasn't a ripple on the water. It was hard to believe it was the same sea. Snow was falling, calm and dense, and while the daymen worked to repair the damaged fish-washing machine and rebuilt the gutting pens Billy and I got out a couple of brooms and began sweeping the snow and the tangled fish guts over the side. After a few minutes I stopped for a moment to look around. Dotted around us in the bay I could make out the faint smudges of five or six other ships that had also run for shelter. Beyond them, I saw the faint outlines of an island. I asked Billy if that was Iceland. No, he said, that's the Westman Islands.* Iceland's over there. He pointed in the opposite direction with his broom, and following the line I could just make out a sharp crescent of cliff rising starkly from what looked like a beach of black sand. The lower slopes of the cliff appeared to be black too, mingling higher up with snow as it sheered up into the puffy greyness of the clouds. As I continued to look and my vision improved I saw, high up on the slopes, the tiny shapes of

---

* Vestmannaeyjar in Icelandic.

sheep or goats with heads bent to the grass. I carried on looking at this scene for a long time, saying to myself over and over again: *That's Iceland. That is Iceland. I'm looking at Iceland*, as though I had never believed in all my life that I would ever get to see Iceland. And afterwards, after we'd swept the deck and Billy had gone off to play cards, sitting alone in the mess room with a big bowl of orange tea in front of me and listening to the loud, slow, ticking of the galley clock, I fell into a trance of contentment. Maybe it was the loudness and the slowness of the ticking that turned those moments into an epiphany for me. Maybe it was just the ecstasy of physical exhaustion. Whatever it was, I knew that I had seen true north and could never again unsee it.

The brake on one of the winches had been damaged in the storm, and the *Kennedy* had to put into Dýrafjörður, a tiny fishing port on Iceland's west coast, to get it repaired. All through those years there was disagreement between the British and Icelandic governments over the size of Iceland's territorial waters and British fishing rights thereabouts. It led to tensions between English fishermen and the local people when ships had to put in there, and even as we were docking ten or twelve of children lined up on the quayside started chucking things at us. Empty Coke cans, stones, plastic bottles. But when we came ashore, they followed us through the rutted little streets of Dýrafjörður, thinly clad children with star-white faces, asking for money, jumping up and hitting at our pockets. The bartender in the village pub wouldn't serve us alcohol and the company's local agent had to be sent in to buy the whisky for us. I didn't feel much like drinking, but English trawlermen get drunk, so when the bottle was passed round I drank my share. Everything about that time seemed magical to me. I kept wondering what I had done to deserve it all, who to thank for these adventures. Waiting for the winch to be finished we sat next to the ship, legs dangling over the quayside like children. Billy had a little Hohner Vamper harmonica with him and we sang Beatles songs. Behind us were Dýrafjörður's tiny pink and blue houses with their corrugated iron roofs, and beyond them the massive black mystery of the mountains.

*

I recall that particular trip whenever I think about the conversion of the Icelanders to Christianity in the year 999, which is a thing I have done many, many times over the years, convinced as I am that the story contains profundities and human truths it may take me a lifetime to understand. The tale of how that little group of Christian chieftains landed at a now-vanished settlement called Horgaeyrr on the Vestmannaeyjar, after the voyage from Trondheim, and spent two days there, putting up a tiny church, before making the short crossing to Iceland. In my mind's eye it is almost as though I can see them, the four chieftains who lead the mission – Hall of Sida, Gizur the White, Hjalti Skeggjason and Thorgils of Ölfus – standing on the black volcanic sands as they gaze across the water in the direction of Landeyjar and contemplate the task that lies before them, and the consequences should they fail.

They were not the first Christian Icelanders. *Landnámabók* (*The Book of the Settlements*), written in about 1200, names several Christians among the first people to settle the country three centuries earlier: Orlyg the Old, Helgi Bjola, Jorund the Christian (a woman), Aud the Deep-minded (another woman) and Ketil the Fool, so called by his heathen neighbours on account of his faith. Another, less foolish in their eyes, was Helgi the Lean, who believed in Christ but sacrificed to Thor whenever he put to sea, on the grounds that a god like Christ from a far-off land couldn't possibly have any knowledge of the currents and the winds around Iceland. But once these early converts were dead and gone, their children returned to the old faith and the rituals of sacrificing to Odin and Thor.

Nor were Hall, Gizur and the others the first to come to Iceland for the specific purpose of converting the inhabitants. Some fifteen years previously, an Icelander named Thorvald the Far-Traveller, a former Viking, brought a Saxon bishop named Fredrik back with him from his travels abroad, and together these two travelled about the country preaching the gospel. They soon found that Christian values and practices, especially the shaving of the beard, made them a target of ridicule. Mocking the Christian tradition of the godfather, local poets composed verses in which Thorvald and the bishop engaged in homosexual intercourse:

> *Nine children*
> *the bishop had,*
> *Thorvald father*
> *to them all.*

It was a deadly insult. Too much of the Viking he had once been remained in Thorvald, and in defence of his honour he killed two poets. He was duly outlawed and driven from the country. Olaf Tryggvason, who briefly ruled Norway between 995 and 1000, then sent an Icelander named Stefnir to see if he could succeed where they had failed. Once Stefnir realized that persuasion was not working, he turned to violence, riding about the countryside with a band of men and destroying places of worship and idols. It was in direct response to his activities that the Icelanders introduced legislation requiring the head of a family to prosecute any of its members who brought shame on his relatives by converting to Christianity. Stefnir was duly prosecuted by members of his own family under the new legislation and sentenced to leave the country.

Olaf Tryggvason sponsored a third mission under a Saxon priest named Thangbrand. Like Thorvald the Far-Traveller, he became the target of verses accusing him of homosexual behaviour that he too found unendurable. One day he turned up at the farm where one of his tormentors, a poet named Vetrlidi, lived, and killed the man while he was out cutting turf. Thangbrand killed a second man at Grimnes, in the south-west of the country, and was outlawed that summer at the Alþingi (Althing) Assembly. The Icelandic historian Ari the Wise tells us that when Thangbrand returned to Trondheim, he told the king it was 'beyond hope that Christianity would be accepted here', and that during the two years of his mission he had made only a small number of converts. Among these, however, were the nucleus of Olaf's next mission, the four chieftains Hall, Gizur, Gizur's son-in-law Hjalti and Thorgils of Ölfus.

As punishment for the Icelanders' treatment of his missionaries, the king had ordered that every Icelandic native in the royal capital of Trondheim be arrested and their property confiscated. On hearing of this, Gizur and Hjalti sailed to Norway to plead with Olaf to let them make another attempt to convert their people. Olaf agreed, but as insurance he held on to four hostages, one from each of the Icelandic Quarter districts, and each one related to a leading Icelandic chieftain.

Hall, Gizur, Hjalti and Thorgils, accompanied by a priest named Thormod, set sail the following summer, in June 999, aiming to address, at the end of the month, the great summer assembly that took place at Þingvellir (Thingvellir), some 27 miles (45 km) north-east of present-day Reykjavik. After landing on the Vestmannaeyjar and crossing to Landeyjar, a journey of about 62 miles (100 km) lay before them. The first stage of it took them east of the River Rangá and through territory ruled by Runolf of Dal, a powerful heathen chieftain who was passionately opposed to the introduction of Christianity. His son Sverting was one of the hostages being held by Olaf. Runolf forbade the farmers in his district from selling horses to the missionaries, so the travellers had to cross his lands on foot until they reached Háfr, in the area around Holt. Once they were there, they were able to buy horses from one of Hjalti's relatives. As they rode on towards the site of the assembly, at Þingvellir, they were joined by other Christians.

At the assembly meeting the previous year, Hjalti Skjeggjason had recited a blasphemous verse against Freyja, sister and wife of Frey and the most powerful goddess among the Æsir. All that remains of it is a brief and pungent couplet:

> I don't mean to bark at the gods,
> but Freyja seems to me a bitch.

For this blasphemy, Hjalti had been sentenced to the Lesser Outlawry, meaning a fine and three years' banishment. The missionaries saw no point in risking the anger of the country's lawful assembly by turning up with a convicted outlaw in their midst, so Hjalti was persuaded to stay behind with a group of men at a place called Laugardal while Gizur the White and the others set out on the final leg of the journey. That night they made camp by a lake within sight of the assembly ground. Late in the evening a messenger arrived from the assembly chieftains: unless they took part in the traditional hallowing ceremony that sanctified the proceedings each year, they would not be allowed to enter the site at Þingvellir. If necessary, force would be used to prevent them. On hearing the news in Laugardal, Hjalti decided the issue was momentous enough to justify breaking the law again; he and his men broke camp and rode to join Gizur and the others.

As the Christians – with Hjalti – approached the boundaries of the assembly site at Þingvellir, their provocation could hardly have been greater. But it may have been at this point that the heathen chieftains learned that the Norwegian king was holding some of their sons hostage. When the true complexity of the situation became apparent, tensions eased sufficiently for Gizur and Hjalti to be allowed to enter the hallowed ground and address the assembly from its focal point on a slope above the plain – a natural rock formation resembling a dais, known as the Lawrock.

Their arguments persuaded no one. Once the speakers had delivered their speeches and stepped down from the rock, a procession of men, some Christian, most heathen, queued up to replace them, each declaring formally their refusal to live under the same laws as the other. The Christians then raised the tension again by urging one of their own, Hall of Sida, to become their 'Lawspeaker' and to devise a separate law code under which the Christians could live. Hall, sensing the inevitability of civil war if he said 'yes', declined and passed on the request for a separate law code to the assembly's constituted Lawspeaker, Þorgeir Þorkelsson (Thorgeir Thorkelsson), a chieftain from the Eyjafjörður (Eyjafjord) region in the north of the country.

By this time, Þorgeir had been the Lawspeaker for fifteen years. He was the best legal mind in the country. It is an extraordinary tribute to the respect in which the Icelanders held their law that Þorgeir was not a Christian, and yet here were Christian Icelanders asking him to legitimize a division of their country into separate religious and administrative communities. No matter what he came up with, violence and the end of the commonwealth seemed inevitable. Þorgeir accepted the responsibility. He made his way back to his booth, the tent-like summer quarters housing those attending the Alþingi. When he got there he lay down on the floor and gave instructions that he was not to be disturbed on any account. Then, as both Ari the Wise and the unknown author of *Kristni Saga* tell us with peculiar precision, he wrapped his cloak around his head and began to think.

A full day later he emerged from his booth and gave the order for people to gather below the Lawrock to hear what he had decided. In his speech, he began by stressing the danger that faces any society when groups of people who worship different gods and observe different codes of law try to live side by side. He said such an arrangement could only end in violence on such a scale that their country would not survive it. Some of the actual words he used survived long enough in the minds of those who heard them for Ari the Wise to capture them in writing, some sixty or seventy years later:

> So this seems to me the wisest plan. That we don't allow those to prevail who are the most passionately opposed to each other. Instead, we will arrange things in such a way that both sides come away with a partial victory. So there will be one law here, and one religion. Because the truth of the matter is, if we tear our laws up now then we tear up our peace up too.

Near the end of his speech, Þorgeir directly addressed the leaders on both sides and asked them to swear that they would abide by his decision, no matter which way it went. And once he had their promise, he told them the decision he had come to: from that day on, the law of Iceland would be that everyone should be baptized into the Christian faith.

Of Iceland's population of 30,000, the vast majority were still heathen, and one can imagine the murmur of shock and disbelief that must have risen up from the crowd as he said these words. But even before it had died away, Þorgeir had gone on to add three important conditions that went back to the main point of his speech, which was that each side should come away from the deal with something. The first concerned a form of birth control that seems chilling now, but which reflects only the terrible demands of survival among the poorest members of the community a thousand years ago. When a woman gave birth to a child whom the family could not afford to feed, it had always been the law that the child could be taken outside and left to die. This practice, said Þorgeir, would be allowed to continue. His second ruling was that the eating of horseflesh would still be permitted. The exemption recognized that the communal drinking of a hot broth made from the flesh and the blood of a slaughtered horse was as firmly at the heart of heathen ritual as the bread and wine of the Eucharist was for Christianity. His third ruling was that people would remain free to sacrifice to the old gods should they wish, but they must do so in secret. Anyone caught doing it openly would face a fine and the three years' banishment of the Lesser Outlawry.

These concessions were enough to persuade the crowd, and before the assembly broke up that year most of those present had been baptized in the icy waters of the River Öxará that meandered across the assembly site. The exceptions were those from the western and northern quarters, who postponed the ceremony until their homeward journey brought them to the warm waters of the hot springs at Reykjalaug left behind by Hekla's eruptions.

★

It never ceases to impress and astonish me that a change of such magnitude should have come about without bloodshed. What a testament it is to the respect in which the law was held in tenth-century Iceland! And not only there, but throughout all Scandinavia. In their dealings with the Vikings, kings in England and Ireland – and successive leaders of the Holy Roman Empire, as it slowly fell apart after the death of Charlemagne – had learnt to be astonished by the democracy of the Viking leadership. Writing in about 1015, Dudo of St Quentin, the first historian of the Viking duchy of Normandy, reported the answer of the great Viking chieftain Rollo when asked by a Frankish emissary for the name of their leader: 'We have no leader. We are all equal. You will have to negotiate with all of us.' The Danish 'Code of Jutland Law', enacted in the time of Valdemar II in 1241, opens with the phrase *Med lov skal land bygges* ('With law shall the land be built'). The same phrase occurs in the contemporary Frostating, which was the law for the Trøndelag, the vast central-coastal region of Norway. It seems extraordinary that the same fidelity to the rule of law should have been as demonstrable among the heathen Vikings as it is today in the social democracies of Denmark, Norway and Sweden, surviving the sea-change of the arrival of Christian culture with its Bible, its Latin alphabet and what must have seemed to so many worshippers of Odin and the rest of the Æsir the bewildering inversion of all ethical instinct and commonsense in the Christian injunction to forgive your enemies and turn the other cheek. With their kingless commonwealth, the Icelanders continued to astonish the rest of Europe for the next three centuries. In his *Gesta Hammaburgensis* ('Deeds of the Bishops of Hamburg-Bremen'), the eleventh-century historian Adam of Bremen stated the oddity of it quite simply: *Apud illos non est rex, nisi tantum lex* ('Among them there is no king, there is only the law').

But if the status of law survived the arrival of Christianity in the north, there were casualties and repercussions that can be more or less directly traced back to the magnitude of the changes introduced. Poetry had a status close to divine in northern heathendom. Writing in the thirteenth century, Snorri Sturluson glossed the Icelandic word *skáld* as *frœðamaðr,* meaning a man who was learned, knowledgeable and possessed of essential information rather than simply a 'poet' in the modern sense of a maker of verse; and if the *goði*, or chieftain-priests, were responsible for the practical relationship between men and gods, it was the skaldic poets who were the keepers of the lore that lay behind the rituals. In both of Snorri's variant accounts of Odin's origins, the All-Father remains the inventor of poetry and the god of the poets. A special relationship existed between him and his poets, and it was the skalds who felt most keenly the threat to their culture and its ancient traditions from Christianity. The poets were the memory of the tribe, the guardians and celebrants of its lore and myths. They recorded the deeds of its great leaders and heroes in an elaborate poetic language of rigid metrical rules and wonderfully convoluted metaphor which depended for its success on a recognition by its audience of a world of disguised allusions to the stories, attributes and adventures of the heathen gods. The poets' patrons were kings, but once the Scandinavian kings converted to Christianity they would no longer allow themselves to be praised by blasphemous allusions to the gods whom Christianity had demonized. The art of the skald went into terminal decline.

From his episcopal see in Hamburg, hundreds of miles away, Adam of Bremen imagined an idealized state of affairs in Iceland after the conversion:

> They live in a holy simplicity, desiring no more than what nature offers them and echoing happily the apostle's words 'And having food and raiment let us be therewith content.' Their mountains are their towns, the bubbling springs their delight. Happy, I tell you, are such people, who envy no one in their poverty.

If this picture of life in post-conversion Iceland was ever true, it didn't last. After a period of relative stability, a power struggle broke out in the middle of the thirteenth century and propelled Icelandic society into decades of violent chaos. The *Sturlunga Saga* that documents the period tells of chieftains who had their enemies tortured, maimed, castrated and blinded and who killed the old as readily as the able-bodied; and of priests who abused their calling and openly took mistresses. Perhaps what lay behind this spiral into barbarism was the half-hearted abandonment of one set of ethical standards and the imperfect and unconvinced adoption of another and very different set, which led, over time, to a moral disorientation from which it proved hard to recover. In 1263, the exhausted combatants handed over control of the country to the Crown of Norway. Almost seven centuries would pass before Iceland regained its independence.

*

It might be hard to imagine a British prime minister or a US president going about decision-taking in the same way as Þorgeir, turning off his mobile phone, wrapping his shirt around his head and stretching out on the floor of the Cabinet Room or the Oval Office. But, leaving aside these accidentals of time and comfort, it is tempting to think of Þorgeir as much the same type of man doing much the same thing as any modern politician would do when faced with a truly important decision – analyzing, going over the pros and cons, trying to foresee the potential responses and outcomes, trying to work out which is the safest risk to take. A modern mind in an ancient man. In a word, a rationalist.

Some years ago the Icelandic scholar Jón Hnefill Aðalsteinsson wrote a doctoral thesis that offered a different explanation. He suggested that the reason Þorgeir wrapped his cloak around his head that evening was in preparation for sending his spirit on a shamanic journey to ask the gods for help in making the right decision, and that swathing the head like this, and forbidding anyone to disturb him, was an established ritual prelude to such journeys. If this is really what happened, then it was to Odin himself that Þorgeir went for advice, and it was Odin himself who advised him that he must choose Christ. This would explain why, in all their dazed disappointment, Odin's followers on the Þingvellir slopes understood and accepted the decision for, like the God of the Old Testament, Odin moved in mysterious ways. Enigmatic disloyalty and unfathomable unpredictability were among the All-Father's most familiar characteristics.

There is a strange and existential logic to such an explanation, for what could be more natural than that an old god, weary of the responsibilities of godhood, weary of his worshippers, weary of the endless imprecations of warriors and kings, poets and pretenders, weary of the useless sacrifices, and seeing the chance to hand these burdens on to a younger, fitter god, should at once reach out and seize it? It would give him time to concentrate on the things that really interested him. Like the God of the Bible, he had created a world. Unlike him, he had never felt that he understood his own creation. It is one of Odin's most compelling and even attractive qualities. It endowed him with a consuming curiosity about what he had made, why he had made it, and when it would all come to an end. Now, at last, he might have the leisure he needed to work all this out. Actually he would have to wait a little longer, for the Swedes continued to go on worshipping him for almost a hundred years after the Danes, the Norwegians and the Icelanders had given him up, until about 1090, when a Christian king named Inge was finally able to carry out the long-delayed destruction of the great heathen temple at Uppsala. But with that Odin was free to vacate his great world throne Hlidskjalf and begin his quest for understanding. We glimpse him sometimes as he wanders through the pages of Snorri's *Heimskringla*, a one-eyed old tramp, his face half-shaded by his wide-brimmed hat, telling stories to anyone who will listen, mischievously trying to slip a cut of horse meat onto a Christian king's menu, walking, wandering on, still trying to find out where we come from, what we are, where we're going, his powers slowly fading as the supply of faith that sustains him dries up until one day it's all gone.

*

The Cod Wars ended in 1976, and the Icelanders won the right to fish in a 200-mile (321 km) zone around their shorelines from which the British and others were excluded. Fleetwood collapsed. For over a century its men had gone to sea and its women to work in the canning factories and the net-making workshops and it took the town a long time to recover. On a trip to England about twelve years ago I hired a car and drove back up to take a look around.

It had become a museum of itself, selling a tale of how things once had been to tourists who strayed the four miles (6 km) up the promenade from Blackpool. There was even a museum ship, a distant-water trawler named the *Jacinta*, moored where the fish docks had once been. For £2.50, you could walk up the gangway and get a guided tour of the ship from a former trawlerman. I found myself unable to decide whether to take the tour or not and so just stood there, looking up at the ship for a long time and thinking for some reason of Odin.

3

Amleth, Luther and the Last Priest: The Reformation in Scandinavia

INSTITUTIONALIZED CHRISTIAN CULTURE ARRIVED IN Scandinavia in 1104, with the establishment of the see at Lund, geographically in southern Sweden but at that time part of the kingdom of Denmark. It was the first in Scandinavia. Up until that time, Scandinavian Church affairs had been run from the archbishopric of Hamburg-Bremen in Germany.

A linear conception of time and a new alphabet to replace the runic *futhark* were among the most fundamental changes the new religion brought with it. Odin and the rest of the Æsir were evicted and put to service outside church walls, as gargoyles to run off water from the guttering. The Christian monks in the monasteries who replaced the travelling skaldic poets of Iceland, Norway and Sweden as the historians of heathen culture did their work in Latin, and on parchment, not in Old Norse and orally. The combination of their ignorance and their disapproval led to the eclipse of vast tracts of knowledge about the customs and beliefs of their ancestors, among which the near-complete disappearance of the pre-Christian constellation names has always struck me as especially poignant. In particular the tale of how the star known to early Scandinavians as Aurvandil's Toe got its name provoked an unexpected disturbance in me when I began thinking seriously about the Reformation in the north and any possible impact this had in creating that melancholy and darkness of mind that has been, for so long and so strongly, the primary association the outside world has of the inhabitants of Denmark, Sweden and Norway. Shortly after reading the tale in Snorri Sturluson's *Prose Edda*, I came across Saxo's long and compelling account in the *Gesta Danorum* of the murderous intrigues at the Danish court in Elsinore, upon which Shakespeare based his *Hamlet*. In the course of the sixty pages that the narrative occupies in his history, Saxo describes a duel between two kings, Aurvandil and Koller, which ends with Aurvandil slicing off Koller's foot and Koller's bleeding to death. In gratitude, Aurvandil's ally, King Rørik, gives him his daughter Gurutha in marriage. The couple have a son, Amleth, or in Shakespeare's spelling, Hamlet. The killing of Aurvandil by his brother Feng, and Feng's subsequent marriage to his brother's widow, along with Amleth's response to it all, are described in Saxo:

Aurvandil, King of Denmark, married Gurutha, the daughter of Rorik, and she bore him a son, whom they named Amleth. Aurvandil's good fortune stung his brother Feng with jealousy, so that the latter resolved treacherously to waylay his brother, thus showing that goodness is not safe even from those of a man's own house. And behold when a chance came to murder him, his bloody hand sated the deadly passion of his soul. Then he took the wife of the brother he had butchered, capping unnatural murder with incest. For whoso yields to one iniquity, speedily falls an easier victim to the next, the first being an incentive to the second. Also the man veiled the monstrosity of his deed with such hardihood of cunning, that he made up a mock pretence of goodwill to excuse his crime, and glossed over fratricide with a show of righteousness.

Gerutha, said he, though so gentle that she would do no man the slightest hurt, had been visited with her husband's most extreme hate; and it was all to save her that he had slain his brother; for he thought it shameful that a lady so meek and unrancorous should suffer the heavy disdain of her husband. Nor did his smooth words fail in their intent; for at courts, where fools are sometimes favoured and backbiters preferred, a lie lacks not credit. Nor did Feng keep from shameful embraces the hands that had slain a brother; pursuing with equal guilt both of his wicked and impious deeds.

Amleth beheld all this, but feared lest too shrewd a behaviour might make his uncle suspect him. So he chose to feign dullness, and pretend an utter lack of wits. This cunning course not only concealed his intelligence but ensured his safety.

Every day he remained in his mother's house utterly listless and unclean, flinging himself on the ground and bespattering his person with foul and filthy dirt. His discoloured face and visage, smudged with slime, denoted foolish and grotesque madness. All he said was of a piece with these follies; all he did savoured of utter lethargy. In a word, you would not have thought him a man at all, but some absurd abortion due to a mad fit of destiny.

He used at times to sit over the fire, and, raking up the embers with his hands, to fashion wooden crooks, and harden them in the fire, shaping at their tips certain barbs, to make them hold more tightly to their fastenings. When asked what he was about, he said that he was preparing sharp javelins to avenge his father. This answer was not a little scoffed at, all men deriding his idle and ridiculous pursuit; but the thing helped his purpose afterwards.

Now it was his craft in this matter that first awakened in the deeper observers a suspicion of his cunning. For his skill in a trifling art betokened the hidden talent of the craftsman; nor could they believe the spirit dull where the hand had acquired so cunning a workmanship. Lastly, he always watched with the most punctual care over his pile of stakes that he had pointed in the fire. Some people, therefore, declared that his mind was quick enough, and fancied that he only played the simpleton in order to hide his understanding, and veiled some deep purpose under a cunning feint.

As I read this, the idea that Hamlet's father was in some mysterious way the same person as the dwarf whom Thor, the red-bearded God of Thunder, carried on his back across the celestial River Elivager, became entwined with the recurrence in both tales of an *injury to the foot*; until presently the whole thing froze into a bizarre but nevertheless organic certainty that Hamlet's father, referred to in Shakespeare only as King Hamlet to distinguish him from the son, and appearing only briefly and as a ghost in the opening scene, could now with absolute certainty be identified as a dwarf named Aurvandil. It was a thrilling discovery. I thought of the influence it might have on the way directors staged the opening scene. As a hint to the audience the ghost of Hamlet might be played by a very small actor who makes his entry carrying a basket beneath his arm. More to the point, I thought, by making this apparently irrelevant excursion in the book I was hoping to write on Scandinavian culture I could use the subject of *Hamlet* as the natural starting point for a discussion of the stereotype of the melancholic and brooding Scandinavian which came to succeed that of the bloodthirsty and Christian-hating Viking. It would also introduce the symbolically important site of the castle at Elsinore, or Helsingør as the Danes call it, on the north-east coast of Zealand overlooking the narrowest point of the sound that divides Denmark from Sweden, which re-appears with such surprising regularity and in so many unexpected contexts throughout the history of Scandinavia. Elsinore is not only Prince Hamlet's home but also the home of his treacherous friends Rosencrantz and Guildenstern. All three of them, along with Horatio, are students at the University of

Wittenberg in Germany, the place where Martin Luther nailed his 'Ninety-Five Theses on the Power and Efficacy of Indulgences' on the door of All Saint's Church: the crucible of the Reformation. Alas, the complexities of my idea began to give me a headache, and in the end I abandoned it. I switched off my computer and instead settled down on our living-room sofa to watch television. Norwegian State Broadcasting was showing a British series about Shakespeare's plays. My wife was away for the weekend at a book fair in Bergen and I watched this first programme in the series alone. As luck would have it, it turned out to be about *Hamlet*. The presenter was the Scottish actor David Tennant. At one point in the programme, Tennant travelled to Stratford-upon-Avon and was seen visiting the props department of the Royal Shakespeare Company. There the wardrobe mistress handed him a large cardboard box, which Tennant opened, and from which he produced a skull, holding it up in one hand and explaining to us that, in his own performance as Hamlet, this particular skull had been used for the famous gravedigger scene. He went on to reveal that it was in fact the head of a real person, a Polish pianist and composer named André Tchaikowsky, who had died as recently as 1982. Tchaikowsky had donated his head to the RSC shortly before his death from colon cancer at the age of forty-six, expressing the hope that it might, one day, be used as Yorick's. It seems that up until the time of the David Tennant production, directors of the play had avoided using Tchaikowsky's head because successive casts found the prospect disturbing. In terms of its effect on his performance, however, it was easy to believe Tennant when he spoke of the added intensity it gave to the prince's words on the brevity of all human life, knowing as he did that he was holding the head of someone who would, until quite recently, have been able to confirm them from personal experience.

Drifting off into an idle meditation on the general strangeness of the situation, I presently found myself once again, as so often before, distracted by the perennial oddity of the name 'Yorick'. This had puzzled me ever since the Friday afternoon double-English lesson at my old secondary school back home in England, when we had a class reading of *Hamlet*, and I dozed at the back of the classroom as the hot sun flooded through the windows on the long west wing of the school, on its way down over the wide and shining expanse of the Ribble Estuary, and I waited for the bell to end the interminable lesson and release us for the after-school kick-around in the Fairhaven Lake car park. Hearing Frith, the boy reading the part of Hamlet, suddenly stumble over 'Yorick' woke me from my doze. Even in those days, long before I had an interest in Scandinavia, I felt certain that 'Yorick' could not be a Danish name. But by the time I was fully awake it was too late. Our English teacher, a cherry-cheeked and wispy-haired man named Price, whom I have lately begun to confuse in my memory with H.G. Wells's Mr Polly, hero of another of our set books, had already offered some kind of explanation, and Frith, having knocked the hurdle down, was staggering on towards the next one.

For years afterwards, the singular oddness of the name remained lodged somewhere at the back of my head and did not surface again until the end of the motoring holiday my wife and I had taken in Denmark to see the Jelling Stone and Lindholm Høje. On our way back home, we spent the last night in Helsingør, before the twenty-minute ferry ride across the waters of the Öresund to Sweden in the morning for the drive up the E6 to Oslo. The castle was just a short walk from the Hotel Hamlet where we had booked in for the night. After a hamburger at the Restaurant Ophelia we strolled along to take a look at it.

I get little sense of place from old castles in which nobody lives. After a few minutes desultorily wandering through a series of large and bare rooms, I went outside and began walking along a high grassy embankment that ran out from the castle. Presently, my interest was attracted by a group of about a dozen middle-aged men and women who were gathered on the stony foreshore, just beyond the castle walls. The day was drizzly and overcast, and they were wearing anoraks with the hoods up and waterproof trousers. Most of them had either a camera or a pair of binoculars around their necks, and periodically one would lift the binoculars to his eyes and peer intently out across the water, or up into the sky. Curiosity overcame me and I made my way across and asked a woman at the edge of the group what it was they were waiting or looking for. They were birdwatchers, she told me, gathered because of reports that a rare type of falcon had been spotted in the skies above Elsinore. Had they seen it? I asked. No, she replied with a smile, not yet. But birdwatchers know how to be patient. As I turned away and headed back along the embankment towards the castle I felt a vague sense of disappointment. I don't know what I'd been hoping to hear, perhaps that they'd been looking for a Russian submarine that had reportedly been seen surfacing in the Sound. Back at the Elsinore souvenir shop, I bought a coffee mug rimmed with Shakespearean insults ('Anointed sovereign of sighs and groans', 'Quintessence of dust', 'Lump of foul deformity' etc.), a small tin horse on wheels that you pushed along with a handle attached to the back of it, and a book that examined the points of contrast between the castle (and its inhabitants) as imagined by Shakespeare and the castle as it appears in recorded history. Leafing through this book the following morning on the ferry over to Sweden, I learnt that 'Yorick'

was in fact Shakespeare's phonetic rendering of the common Danish name 'Georg'. Say 'Yorick' as fast as you can three or four times and you'll find yourself saying 'Georg'. A similar explanation resolved the enigma of the instruction given by the Gravedigger to his Companion in the play. Go, get thee to Yaughan, he tells him, Fetch me a stoup of liquor. 'Yaughan' is Johan, a name as common then and now in Denmark as 'John' is in England. At least three members of Shakespeare's own company, the Chamberlain's Men, previously belonged to a troupe employed at Frederik II's court at Elsinore between 1585 and 1586, and the incidental detail in Shakespeare's play, such as these names, may well have been acquired from them.

★

Over the years, and particularly after watching Kenneth Branagh's performance as Detective Inspector Kurt Wallander in the television adaptation of the late Henning Mankell's novels – which, on a scale of bleakness, lies several frozen degrees below that of either of the two Swedish actors who have played the part, Rolf Lassgård and Krister Henriksson – I have found myself wondering whether melancholy is a genuine Scandinavian tribal characteristic, or an artificial creation bearing as little relation to the real thing as, for example, the England of Roger Miller's old country-music hit 'England Swings', with its bobbies on bicycles two by two and the rosy red cheeks of its little children, bears to the real England. It might even be a combination of the genuine and artificial, in which melancholy became a self-validating diagnosis: everyone says we're gloomy, so we must be. I can't help thinking that 'the gloomy Dane' himself has played some part in creating this tribal identity, a 'Nordicism' analogous to the 'Orientalism' of which the scholar Edward Said complained some decades ago. Within twenty years of the appearance of Shakespeare's play, Robert Burton was philosophizing in his *Anatomy of Melancholy* about the restlessness of certain types of men, to whom the world itself seemed a prison, its seas as narrow as any ditch, who, when they had 'compassed the globe of the earth, would fain go see what is done on the moon'; but he excluded Scandinavians from his analysis on the grounds that 'all over Scandia they are imprisoned half the year in stoves, they dare not peep out for cold'.

The Norwegian playwright Henrik Ibsen, whose life I wrote a long twenty years ago in a biography that I now feel may have been a touch mean-spirited about the great man, was convinced that it was the *topography* of Norway that made its people so secretive, so brooding, so guilt-ridden and melancholy. Anyone who wants to understand me, he told an Austrian journalist, must know Norway. The magnificent but severe nature surrounding the people up there in the north, the lonely, secluded life, the farms miles from one another – they lose interest in other people and become concerned only with their own affairs. This is why they become introspective and serious, why they brood and doubt, why they lose faith. At home every other man is a philosopher. The long, dark winters come, he said, swathing the farms in dense fog, and oh how the people long for the sun. But Ibsen's theory wouldn't apply to Sweden or Denmark, nor explain the darkness of vision associated with an August Strindberg or a Søren Kierkegaard. Prince Hamlet could never have been a Catholic, any more than Brand, Gregers Werle or any one of a dozen other Ibsen characters could have been Catholics. Besides, part of what Ibsen was communicating in his characterization was the sheer *remoteness* of Scandinavia, and that includes an idea of its enormous distance from Rome.

So in the end I find I often return to the Reformation in Scandinavia as the only really significant common denominator to consider in any search for the heart of this historical association with melancholy. Its origins are complex and intricately bound up with the politics of the region over the five centuries that divide it from the end of the Viking Age. After the fall of the Jelling dynasty in England, the Viking Age rattled on for another couple of decades. Militarily, it came to an end with Harald Hardrada's failure to regain the English crown at the Battle of Stamford Bridge in 1066; culturally, it expired in 1104 with establishment of that first Scandinavian archbishopric at Lund. A sense of some kind of unifying tendency slowly began coming into focus. When the strife-weary Icelanders handed over the sovereignty of their country to the Crown of Norway in 1262, they were following a precedent set in the previous year by the Greenlanders. Kings and queens came and went, until quite suddenly, and more by the accident of early deaths and childlessness than any grand design, a unified Scandinavia emerged as a political fact in 1397 with the signing of the Kalmar Agreement, whereby Denmark, Sweden and Norway were united under a single monarch.

In its complete form, the Kalmar Union lasted just over 120 years, and the triangular marriage was never a happy one. The instigator of the union, Margrete of Denmark, was by far its most able leader, and for most of the time the Swedes chafed at their inferior status in the relationship. Following Margrete's death in 1412, she was succeeded by her nephew, Erik of Pomerania, who at once set off in pursuit of his dream of creating a Scandinavian Baltic empire, an enterprise that would involve him in endless wars against the German states. The crippling cost of these was met by heavy taxation in all three kingdoms, and only partially offset by his initiative in building the first castle on the site at Elsinore in the 1420s. This gave Denmark control of the entrance to the Baltic through the narrow Öresund which Erik and subsequent kings exploited to charge exorbitant tolls. He rarely visited Sweden, and alienated its native aristocracy by appointing Danes and Germans to the command of Swedish fortresses. Deposed in 1439, Erik made his way to Gotland, where he reverted to Viking ways and sustained himself as a pirate before returning to end his days in his native Pomerania. His nephew Christopher of Bavaria was elected to succeed him in 1440, but when Christopher died in 1448, without leaving an heir, the union began to falter. Over the next seventy-five years the three countries were agreed on a common king for only ten of them. By the time Christian II became king in 1513, Sweden was split between a Danish loyalist party, backed by the Catholic Church; and an opposition party under the leadership of a patriot, Sten Sture the Younger, resolved on full Swedish independence. In an effort to compel recognition of his rule, Christian invaded Sweden in 1520 and defeated a Swedish army at Åsunden, in Västergötland, fatally wounding Sture and capturing many of his most prominent supporters.

On 1 November 1520, Christian, already recognized as King of Denmark-Norway, was hailed as the hereditary King of Sweden. A week later, in an attempt to intimidate and subdue any further opposition, the city gates of Stockholm were locked and a purge of dissidents got under way, which subsequently became known as the 'Stockholm Bloodbath'. Eighty-two people were tried, found guilty of heresy and executed in torrential rain in Stortorvet, a square in the city centre, over the following two days. The names of the victims had been given to the king by three of Sweden's leading Catholic dignitaries, out of motives that were religious rather than political – Luther had already nailed up his Ninety-Five Theses in Germany and was on the verge of being excommunicated for heresy. To ensure their permanent exclusion from Heaven, the Protestant victims were denied Confession and the Last Rites before execution, and their corpses were burned afterwards. In a symbolic gesture, Sture's body was exhumed along with that of his infant son so that they could be added to the flames. On his way back to Copenhagen after the slaughter, Christian chose a route that took him through the heart of central Sweden, carrying out further barbarisms as he went.

Gustav Eriksson – the later Gustav I Vasa – was among those Sture supporters captured in the initial fighting. He escaped and fled to Lübeck, where he learned that his father, two of his uncles and several other relatives had been among those executed in the Stockholm rain. With financial help from the Hanseatic rulers of Lübeck, he returned to Sweden, gathered an army and rose against the tyrant Christian, defeating him and in the process gaining the crown of a newly independent Sweden for himself.

Gustav Vasa was able to harness the strong current of anti-Catholic sentiment in Sweden following the Stockholm Bloodbath. After his election as King Gustav in 1523, he actively nourished it by summoning the young radical Olaus Petri from his theological studies at Wittenberg to be secretary of state to the city's council, and by allowing him to preach Lutheran doctrine from the pulpit of

Storkyrkan, the most important church in Stockholm. He offered his very public support to Olaus Petri when the latter became the target of abuse from Catholics following his marriage in 1524. Petri's main opponent was Hans Brask, the Bishop of Linköping, who enjoyed the great advantage of having a printing press at his disposal. Once he became aware of this, Gustav ordered that the press belonging to the church in Uppsala be removed to Stockholm, thus giving the reformer a chance to defend himself against his opponents on equal terms. In due course, Olaus Petri also used the press to produce an Evangelical devotional book and, in 1526, a translation of the New Testament into Swedish. Fifteen years later, the whole Bible became available in Swedish in a translation known as the Gustav Vasa Bible, a cultural monument that acquired a status in Sweden comparable to that of the King James Bible in England, and one that endured as the standard Swedish translation until 1917.

In 1527 the new king announced his support for an open discussion between Lutherans and Catholics on the theological disagreements that had arisen in recent years. The revolt against Denmark had landed him in debt and his support for the reformers had this deeply pragmatic edge to it. Without access to some of the Catholic Church's wealth – it owned over 20 per cent of land in Sweden – the newly independent country would be unable to meet its debts. The leader of the Catholics, Hans Brask, refused even to talk to the heretics, and Gustav threatened to abdicate with immediate effect. The prospect of a constitutional crisis brought immediate dividends, with the Catholics promising him their financial support on condition that he did not interfere with the Catholic liturgy. An extensive programme of reclaiming church property and lands for the Crown and the aristocracy got under way.

From this artfully manipulated crisis, Gustav emerged as a curious throwback to pre-Christian times – a Protestant Christian *godi*, a king-bishop whose power over the new Lutheran Church was based on its newness, and on its dependence on him. Determined to avoid the mistakes of his Catholic predecessors, he was careful to keep the reformed Church as poor and as pure as its preaching advertised it should be. Yet like so many revolutionary leaders before him, Gustav craved the authority of what he had just overthrown in order to satisfy his sense of his own legitimacy. Alone among the Scandinavian countries, Sweden retained, as it does to this day, the doctrine of the Apostolic Succession, which holds that the only valid ministry is one based on bishops whose office has descended from the Apostles.

With the degradation of the Roman Catholic Church in 1536, a long period of intellectual and cultural barrenness ensued. Five centuries earlier, the arrival of institutional Christianity in Iceland and Norway heralded a cultural decline in which the arts and skills of the skaldic poets, so deeply rooted in heathen lore and heathen values, had all but disappeared; the almost equally dramatic changes entrained by the Reformation had a similarly negative effect on Swedish culture for much of what remained of the sixteenth century. For decades, no Swedish writers, poets, dramatists or composers of note appeared. Gustav allowed the Catholic schools, the centres of learning in the country, and the University of Uppsala itself, to fall into pitiful decline. There is an irony in the fact that it is Gustav himself who, in this cultural desert, emerges as one of the few interesting and memorable figures, an arrogant and vivid correspondent whose letters, even when dealing with matters of state, are always personal, trenchant and devastatingly to the point. When Hans Brask wrote to complain that Gustav was doing nothing to prevent the cloisters being used as military bivouacs, Gustav put him and all he stood for firmly in its place: 'Where you write that this took place in violation of the freedom of the Church and against the law which we have sworn to uphold, I know well enough that necessity breaks the law – not only the law of man but at times even God's law.' The king was as brusque in dealing with complaints from his lay subjects, reminding them of the bad old days under Danish hegemony and urging them to be grateful for the peace and safety he had brought them: 'Look to your houses, fields, meadows, wives, children, beasts of burden and cattle, and refrain from voicing your opinions on our political and religious rule.'

*

One might almost say that Protestantism was used by the rebels in Sweden as a tool in their struggle to break free of Danish domination within the Kalmar Union. The revolutionary element was largely absent from the Reformation's arrival in Denmark, where Luther's ideas entered the country from neighbouring Saxony almost through a process of osmosis. Christian II gave early indications of an interest in Protestantism when he invited a reforming priest from Saxony to preach in Copenhagen in 1521; but the manifestly incompetent way in which he had dealt with the revolution in Sweden and his autocratic behaviour at home alienated the native aristocracy and left his ability to carry through such a fundamental reform in question. As a young man, Christian had been his father's viceroy in Norway, and he had fallen in love there with a woman named Dyveke Sigbritsdatter whose mother ran a tavern in Bergen. He took Dyveke and her mother back to Copenhagen with him when he became king in 1513 and continued the relationship despite his marriage, in 1515, to Isabella of Austria. In what might almost have been a rejected sub-plot for *Hamlet*, Dyveke died in mysterious circumstances at the age of twenty-seven and was buried in the church of the Carmelite monastery at Elsinore. The grieving king vented his anger on a young nobleman named Torbjørn Oxe, whom he believed to have poisoned her with a gift of cherries, and had him executed for a crime of which he was almost certainly not guilty.

By 1523, a coalition of aristocrats and bishops had had enough of the king's excesses. They deposed him and offered the throne to his uncle, Frederik. Christian fled to Germany, where he tried to persuade his brother-in-law, the Holy Roman Emperor Charles V, to help him recover the throne. He then put his potential ally in an impossible position by converting to Lutheranism. Six years later, he realized the errors of his ways and converted back to the Catholic faith. This proved enough for Charles to help him land a small army in Norway, from where he hoped to begin a campaign to regain his throne. He was, however, soon tricked on board a ship with the promise of negotiations and then whisked away to the fortress at Kalundborg, where he spent the remaining twenty-seven years of his life in a civilized confinement, permitted to entertain, hunt and wander at his pleasure within the town boundaries.

His successor, Frederik, wisely avoided a too passionate involvement in the issues of the day. He did not openly break with Rome but regularly appointed Lutherans as his royal chaplains, and in 1526 approved the appointment of an archbishop who had been rejected by the pope, thus bringing the authority of the Roman Catholic Church in Denmark to a *de facto* end by rejecting the tradition of the Apostolic Succession.

In 1536 Frederik's successor, Christian III, inherited a country that was almost bankrupt. Christian applied to the Church – as owners of 40 per cent of all land in Denmark – for economic support, and when this was refused he took matters into his own hands. On 12 August 1536 he closed Copenhagen for the day and had the Catholic bishops arrested and confiscated their property, legislating for the end of a separate episcopal administration in Denmark and introducing a single, secular administration to control all affairs of state, including the Church: the state Church had arrived.

*

As an almost incidental result of this process, which also gives some indication of just how far behind Norway had fallen in what remained of the Kalmar Union, the legislation that made Lutheranism the state religion of Denmark also redefined Norway as simply another part of the Danish Crown, with the same provincial status as Jylland, Fyn and Sjælland. This marked the start of what Norwegians call their '400-year night', though many modern Norwegian historians dispute the implication that this was a period of unrelieved cultural and political exploitation. For the Danish Crown, the appropriation of Norway proved hugely lucrative, for the king's income more than doubled following the confiscation of Church estates there.

In Sweden, with the exception of Stockholm, religious reform had been an imposition of the passionate few on the contented many. The situation in Norway was similar. There were few signs of any vivid interest in the currents of intellectual and religious awakening sweeping across the rest of northern Europe, and no apparent desire for change. What the average Norwegian knew of the Reformation amounted to little more than the activities of the Hanseatic League, the German commercial elite centred on Bergen, who were allowed to hold their own Protestant services, in German, on the city's main docks. So unpopular was the practice that some kind of bomb was once placed under the house of their Lutheran preacher, and his life saved only when a disloyal shower of Bergen rain extinguished the fuse before the device could detonate.

The result of the Norwegians' indifference to the enforced ritual and liturgical changes imposed upon them from Denmark was that, for some time, very little observable change took place. Hans Rev, the Bishop of Oslo, was taken to Denmark, where he allowed himself to be rebranded a 'Superintendent', as Lutheran bishops were henceforth to be known, before returning to Oslo and resuming office, so becoming quite possibly the only man ever to have served successive terms as a bishop in both the Roman Catholic and Protestant Churches.

With familiar faces to comfort their congregations, and despite the Danish Ordinance of 1539 that fixed the order of service with Luther's catechism as its standard of doctrine, Church matters in Norway chugged along contentedly for the next twenty or thirty years, until the emergence of a new generation of priests to succeed those local pragmatists who had made the switch with an easy conscience. These young men brought with them a passion for liturgical reform that caused great offence to the conservative instincts of Norway's largely rural population. When the new minister at Jondal, in Hordaland, introduced a ban on the chanting of lauds and Hail Marys, and on the use of Holy Water in the church, and tried to prevent members of the congregation from kneeling before the altar with a cross, his flock grew so angry that they killed him. A number of other priests suffered the same fate for the zeal with which they tried to enforce Lutheran theology.

One notable effect of the overthrow of the richly traditional

Catholic Church in the Scandinavian north was a revival of belief in the Devil. This Devil was neither the imp of later Scandinavian folklore nor the half-comical monster created by the early Christian demonization of Odin and the rest of the Æsir. This was the much more sinister biblical creation, the force that competed with God himself for the worship of believers. And with Devil worship came the witch-hunt and the persecution of men and women who had become the object of the dislike or envy of the local population, and who might find themselves scapegoats for all manner of natural disasters, shipwrecks, sickness and accidents. Between 1560 and 1710, twenty-three men and women were tried as witches in Bergen, among them Anne Pedersdotter Beyer, widow of Absalon Pederssøn Beyer, the most famous and influential Norwegian Lutheran of the age and in his time a Wittenberg pupil of the great theologian Philip Melanchthon. At her trial, Anne found herself accused of the murder of six people by visiting fatal illnesses upon them. Elina, her maid, gave evidence to the court that her mistress had used her as a mount to fly to witches' covens at Lyderhorn and Fløyen. There, she had overheard her planning attacks on Bergen, to be disguised as natural disasters. Other witnesses spoke of having seen Anne consorting with a group of demons, including a creature with no head. Among the alleged victims was a child. Despite Anne pointing out that many children had died in the town, and that the death of a single individual could not be laid at her door, she was found guilty and burnt at the stake, on 17 April 1590.

In time, however, the new Lutheran liturgy became as much a part of the national cultures of Denmark, Norway and Sweden as the old Catholicism had been. In a step-like way that recalls the Icelanders' staggered replacement of the Ásatru, the heathen culture and heathen practices by Christianity six centuries earlier, the Swedes introduced a ban on Catholic worship in public in 1595 and made the faith itself illegal a few years later. Converts to the old religion were obliged by law to leave the country – a stipulation that at one point led, as we shall see, to a constitutional crisis – and the prohibition survived until 1860. The second paragraph of the Norwegian constitution of

1814, in flat contradiction of the claim in the opening sentence that Norway was a free, independent and indivisible kingdom, decreed that Lutheranism was the religion of the state, that immigrants were obliged to raise their children as Lutherans, and that Jesuits, monks and practising Jews would not be admitted to the kingdom.

In aesthetic terms, the result was a spiritual life that lacks the glamour and mystery of Catholic architecture and ritual, but offers instead the austere and simple beauties of the characteristic white wooden churches that the visitor to Scandinavia will observe everywhere, sometimes in the most appealing and isolated places.

An enduring effect of the Devil's return after the adoption of Lutheranism has been that religious swearing retains a force and power in the Scandinavian languages that it has completely lost in English. *Fy faen!*, *Helvete!* and *Jævlig* are all swear-words meaning, respectively, 'The Devil take it!', 'Hell!' and 'Devilish' – innocuous enough to English ears, and yet phrases that are still avoided in polite conversation among Scandinavians. Except in the harshest and most brutalized social environments the sexually based slang that has replaced it in English is rarely encountered. Of late it seems this has been experienced as a lack, and for an English visitor in the twenty-first century an unnerving feature of modern Scandinavia is the import into all three languages of the word 'fucking' as an adjective, usually with an 's' added and without the sexual specificity, as in *Hvem har tatt min fuckings blyant* ('Who's taken my bloody pencil?!'). Naturally, being just another foreign word, it has none of the taboo force it still – just about – retains in English. With an almost charming naivety the boy-band duo Robin and Bugge use the word more than twenty times in their 2016 recording 'Fuck You'.*
Not long ago, outside the National Theatre in the centre of Oslo, I saw a poster for a coming attraction, a new play by a Norwegian called *Fuck My Life*, which was going to try and explain to adult audiences 'what it is like to be a young person today'. And a few years ago I might, had I been so inclined, have visited the cinema

---

* Sung in Norwegian apart from the title. You can hear the track at https://youtu.be/igUq6EEuNCw.

complex at the Colosseum just over the road from where I live to see *Fucking Åmal*, a film by the Swedish director Lukas Moodysson about the boredom and futility of life in a small Swedish town. Weirdly but understandably, the title had to be changed for English audiences to *Show Me Love*.

The nuances of cursing remain enigmatic and hard to convey across the language barrier. Some twenty years ago English newspapers were delighted to be able to report that Norway's then Minister for the Environment, a bluff, genuinely working-class man named Thorbjørn Berntsen, in an exchange of views over England's Sellafield nuclear plant, had referred to John Selwyn Gummer, his opposite number in the UK, as a 'shitbag'. Berntsen found the press interest from the UK bewildering. 'Shitbag' is a literal translation of the word he used – *drittsekk* – but a literal translation renders the word far cruder and more aggressive than it is to the ears of a Norwegian, who uses it divorced from its semantic root in much the same way as the English might call someone a 'silly bugger' without reflecting on the literal meaning of the word bugger. Norwegian also has its share of unintended translingual puns. Long before I was ever interested in Norway, I remember a photograph of Harold Wilson in *Private Eye* looking very thoughtful with his pipe and his Gannex mac and captioned 'Full Fart', which some eagle-eyed English joker had spotted in a Norwegian newspaper. The actual meaning was 'Full speed'.

*

In the five centuries since the Reformation came to Scandinavia, there has never been rivalry between the Church and the state, for the simple reason that the Reformation made them the same thing, though the term 'state church' did not come into use until the middle of the nineteenth century. State-driven, rather than a protest from below, it enjoyed instant support as a monarchical project, and has ensured that the moral and legal codes remain identical. The roots of the 'Protestant work ethic' are to be found in the socio-religious ideology that appeared with the Lutheran Reformation, well illustrated

by the way in which Olaus Petri in Sweden managed to refine perceptions of the monastic system so that social disapproval was directed
not at the system itself but at the members of the Mendicant orders
– healthy and able-bodied adults who lived off 'alms' and were, to
Protestant eyes, no better than ordinary beggars. For centuries, the
idea persisted that everybody should work and pull their weight
in society. Begging as a crime was removed from the statute books in
Sweden only in 1964, by which time it was simply redundant, and
in Norway as late as 2006, for the same reasons. Drug-addicted beggars
and rough-sleepers were no longer seen on the streets of Oslo as the
hostel system provided beds for all who needed them, a magazine
to sell on the streets for those able-bodied enough to work, and the
protection and security of a generous welfare system for the rest. As
though the cosmos in some way objected to such an outstanding social
achievement, tribal families of Roma people with a way of life based
on begging, busking and collecting deposit bottles almost immediately
appeared on the streets of Norway and Sweden to replace the native
beggars, aware that they could not be moved on by law. The Danes
have no law against begging either, but the police have the right to
move people on, and a failure to do so when instructed is an offence.

The near-abolition of poverty in all three Scandinavian societies
might credibly be ascribed to the creation of the state Churches. The
fusion of Church and state made ethical obligations inescapably
a part of the duties of government. In doing so it also imposed a
requirement for a degree of social conformity that some found – and
still do find – oppressive. In his 1933 novel *En flyktning krysser sitt
spor* (*A Fugitive Crosses His Tracks*), the Danish-Norwegian novelist Axel Sandemose formulated ten propositions which he called the
Laws of Jante, and which he claimed summarized the indoctrination to which most Scandinavians willingly subjected themselves in
pursuit of the greater good of social harmony:

> *Du skal ikke tro at du er noe* / Don't ever think you are something.
> *Du skal ikke tro at du er like så meget som oss* / Don't ever think
>   you're worth as much as us.

Du skal ikke tro du er klokere enn oss / Don't ever think you are
   cleverer than us.

Du skal ikke innbille deg du er bedre enn oss / Don't ever think
   you're better than us.

Du skal ikke tro du vet mere enn oss / Don't ever think you know
   more than us.

Du skal ikke tro du er mere enn oss / Don't ever think you are more
   than us.

Du skal ikke tro at du duger til noe / Don't ever think you'll amount
   to something.

Du skal ikke le av oss / Don't ever laugh at us.

Du skal ikke tro at noen bryr seg om deg / Don't ever think anyone
   cares about you.

Du skal ikke tro at du kan lære oss noe / Don't ever think you can
   teach us anything.

These commandments are necessarily an exaggeration, and reflect
the fact that the societies involved are small by European standards, and have historically never had the kind of wealth such as
that which created permanent class differences in large countries
like France, Germany and Great Britain. But most Scandinavians
recognize there is an element of truth in them, that it is harder to
stand against the crowd in a small country than in a large one. This
may, in passing, explain why some of the most famous Scandinavian
writers, artists and filmmakers – those such as Kierkegaard, Ibsen,
Hamsun, Munch, Strindberg, Sigrid Undset, Ingmar Bergman and
Karl Ove Knausgård – have a tendency to be extreme figures, since
considerable personal courage and ethical conviction are required
if such voices are to survive disapproval long enough for people to
start listening to what they have to say.

But beyond these mere historical facts and generalizations on the
subject of Protestantism and its legacy in the north, I could not rid
myself of the thought that there was some more profound theological aspect to the whole thing that I had not quite got hold of, and
that would give me the sort of clear link between the Reformation

and Scandinavian melancholy that I was looking for. Accordingly, I sent an email to Geir Baardsen and arranged to meet him to talk about these imponderables. Geir had started out studying theology with a view to becoming a priest, but abandoned his studies a long time ago and was now a successful novelist.

We met at Oslo's Literature House, a large white building centrally situated near the royal palace, at the junction of Hegdehaugsveien and Parkveien, with a coffee bar and bookshop on the ground floor and conference and lecture rooms on the upper floors. The top floor is occupied by a large quiet room with individual desk-spaces, where up to forty writers and translators work in profound silence. We sat by an open window and, to the wheezing sounds of an old Roma woman playing, over and over again on her accordion, the same forlorn bars from Michel Legrand's 'Les Parapluies de Cherbourg', began to talk. I wasn't quite sure how to get our discussion going, but knowing that Geir was an admirer of the Swedish playwright Lars Norén and had written a couple of essays about him, I had jotted down some questions about Norén as a way of starting the ball rolling. I had read Geir's online review of a performance of *Hamlet* at Elsinore that Norén had directed, and I thought I would ask whether he thought Norén's attraction to this play at this time could in any way be connected to his involvement in the events that unwittingly facilitated the murders of two policemen at Malexander in 1999, an episode I intended to write about in some detail in my book on Scandinavian cultural history.* As far as I knew Norén had never expressed himself at any length about what happened at Malexander and I asked Geir whether he thought his wish to direct *Hamlet* might, on one level, be interpreted as a desire to re-examine the idea of self-doubt through the prism of the greatest play ever written on the subject.

Geir's response was that none of this had occurred to him, and that he really didn't know too much about the Malexander murders anyway. I felt the wind going out of my sails; but bringing up *Hamlet*

* See Chapter 14 for a full discussion of events preceding, during, and after the Malexander incident.

led him on to make some general observations on the subject of Scandinavian melancholy. He said that it was striking, and probably due to something deeper than just tourist enterprise, that the play has been performed at Elsinore many times, the first time as long ago as 1816, and that the first Nordic film of *Hamlet* was made there in 1910. Indeed, it was almost as though Scandinavians had embraced the cliché as a truth. I reminded him of Henrik Ibsen's idea that it was the landscape of Norway and the lonely secluded lives of the people that were responsible for their dark and brooding cast of mind. He said he thought Ibsen might have been onto something, but that he himself attached more importance to the role of a single element absolutely central to Lutheranism: the doctrine of *sola fide*, which distinguishes Roman Catholicism and northern Protestantism so essentially from each other, this idea that *faith alone* is the only road to salvation. I am talking, he said, about the essential loneliness and isolation of a mind that subscribes to this idea that salvation has nothing to do with good works, that it is only possible as a gift of God's grace and attainable only through the intensity and purity of one's faith in Jesus Christ. Consider what Shakespeare did in *Hamlet*. He took Saxo's story of incest, fratricide and double regicide set in pre-historical times and transposed it to a contemporary, post-Reformation setting. Nothing more clearly shows the visionary modernity of his mind than this artistic decision. 'To be or not to be, that is the question. Whether it is nobler in the mind to suffer a sea of troubles, or to take up arms and by opposing, end them': Hamlet's torment is intensified by the peculiarly Protestant fact that *he has no one to tell him what to do*. The responsibility to think the dilemma through to the end is his and his alone. There you have the essential *loneliness* of the Protestant soul. This goes for Ibsen's characters too. The sympathetic as well as the unsympathetic, they all suffer alone.

Over a second cup of coffee Geir went on to say that the associations excited by the themes and atmosphere of Ibsen's *Brand, Ghosts* and *Hedda Gabler* as being, in foreign eyes, typically Scandinavian in their darkness, fanaticism and melancholy had in fact been intensified, and probably deliberately so, by Ibsen's adoption in his later years of what amounted to a uniform of black suit, black frock coat and black top hat, which he habitually wore in public and which made him the most instantly recognizable literary celebrity across all of Europe in the last years of the nineteenth century. Geir smiled and said that you could say Ibsen was a professional Scandinavian; but the great thing about him was that he never lent his name to any cause nor allowed himself to be associated with any political party. His plays say everything important he had to say. He never tried to add to them outside the theatre walls. And don't forget either, he added, for emphasis wagging the thin wooden pin he had been given to stir his *latte* with, that there was a *fashion* for melancholy among Shakespeare's public. His audiences would have recognized Hamlet *at once* as answering, in his powers of articulation, in his acute mind, his rebellious and sensitive nature, his hatred of authority, his attraction to suicide, his uncontrolled outbursts of feeling, to the very image of the fashionable seventeenth-century melancholic.

I could see his point, but somewhere along the line I felt that my attempt to tie the Reformation in Scandinavia to the historical association with melancholy had failed. Perhaps the closest Geir had got to what I wanted him to say was his comment on the loneliness of the Protestant soul, and the weight of personal responsibility attaching to a relationship with God that was face-to-face, mind-to-mind, so that one was directly answerable to God for all of one's crimes and one's thought-crimes, and the whole thing was not rendered somehow symbolic and trivialized by the intermediation of a Catholic priest. Since I didn't really know Geir that well, I was a little stuck to know what we were going to talk about next. As my gaze flickered over the shelves and tables of the bookshop opposite where we sat, I noticed a copy of Niels Geelmuyden's book about the priest Børre Knudsen, a biography first published back in the 1980s when Knudsen was still alive. It had been reissued now to coincide with a documentary about him, which had just been showing at a couple of the smaller cinemas in town, and which went by the title *En Prest og en Plage* ('A Priest and a Plague'), a title that puns on the well-known saying in Norwegian that someone is a *pest og en plage*, a nuisance and a plague. When I came to Norway to live permanently back in 1983, the newspapers had been full of this man and his furious and lonely war against the expanding concept in Norway of abortion on demand. As far as I know, he was a figure unique to Norway in the passion of his opposition and the degree of uproar he caused; I don't think either Sweden or Denmark had anyone similar. Børre Knudsen was an object of horror and contempt to the radicals of the 1980s. I had seen the film recently and recalled suddenly a particular scene from it. Knudsen is on his knees in front of an abortion clinic, palms together in front of his face and singing psalms with an absorbed abandon. As usual he is alone and confronting a crowd who are as passionate in their support for abortion as he is against it. Now a woman steps forward from the chanting, baying mob surrounding Knudsen and clamps a hand firmly around his mouth. For a moment it looks as though he is going to pull her hand away, but then he lets his own hand fall back again. I can never forget the look of stunned horror that came into his eyes at that moment.

There's a famous novel by Johan Bojer called *The Last Viking*, and as I shook hands and said goodbye to Geir outside the Literature House the phrase 'The Last Priest' suddenly came into my mind. Børre Knudsen was the last priest. In Norway and quite possibly the whole of Scandinavia. Børre Knudsen, like something out of a Van Dyck painting with his thick white neck ruff, the wide dark spade of his beard and the clean-shaven upper lip, his anachronistic appearance and ancient passion the last fading echoes down through the centuries of the upheaval that was the Reformation slowly disappearing behind the hum and buzz of modern times. In the midst of this abortion furore he was invited to Rome to attend an expenses-paid pro-life conference. The delegates were granted an audience with John Paul II, and when his turn came Børre Knudsen did not hesitate. He approached the pope and requested, as a matter of urgency, that he lift the papal bull of excommunication against Martin Luther that had been issued back in 1521. John Paul gravely assured him that this was something the papacy was still working on. There's a last scene in the 2014 film, by which time Knudsen is old, his beard is white, and the battle against abortion on demand has long been lost. You've seen how the fierceness of his dedication to the cause cost him everything – his calling, his job, his home, even the love of his own children. Now he's walking down a leafy lane near his remote little country home in Balsfjord, singing in a loud, clear voice some darkly melodious psalm, quite probably one of the many he composed himself, his arm shaking and jerking with Parkinson's as he marches along, head held high, blazing blue eyes that could see through the sun, and his passion is so palpable that no matter where you stand on that issue you cannot but be awestruck.

Citizens of all three Scandinavian countries pay a Church tax of just under 1 per cent of their income, but the Danish Church is now the only one of the three that remains a state Church. The Swedish, the most radical of the three communities and still having the largest Lutheran Church in the world with over 6 million members, introduced the separation back in 2000. In 2009 its willingness to conduct gay marriage ceremonies led the Russian and Syrian Orthodox churches to end their co-operation with it, and for the same reason several African churches have stopped accepting financial support from the Swedish Church. Although it owes more to the sharp decline in Christian belief over the last sixty or seventy years and the administrative difficulties caused by the sudden and unexpected presence in the country of large numbers of Muslims and Catholics, the separation between Church and state enacted in Norway in 2012 probably owes much to the country's experiences with Børre Knudsen, and a recognition of the fact that the secularization and rationalization of society has moved so far since the time of the Reformation that the state and the Church can no longer be considered the same thing.

4

The King of the Past: Frederik VII of Denmark

AT BORRE, ON THE EASTERN ARM OF THE OSLO FJORD, not far from the ancient town of Tønsberg, there is a pre-Viking Age cemetery. I doubt whether I have ever come across a more peaceful resting place for the dead. In its leisurely forested depths, with its sleeping mounds and ancient rubbled cairns, it seems so much more suggestive of the idea of death as a rest and a freedom than the constricted allotments of our own cemeteries.

Once I discovered Borre I went back there many times – it was only a ninety-minute drive from Oslo. I remember in particular the first visit with my wife, to whom I had advertised the remarkable beauty of the place. It was a spring morning. There was a slight haze in the air that seemed to drift up from the fjord and hang through the branches of the trees. Presently we found ourselves wandering on separate ways along leafy paths, the more intently to savour the mood of the place, the more clearly to hear the rustling of the beech leaves, the more pleasantly to be surprised at rounding a mound and coming upon a small flock of ancient Jacob sheep grazing and dozing on its small slopes. Glancing across a stretch of open, glistening grass to a distant mound with six or seven giant oaks growing like antlers from it, I caught intermittent sight of someone between the swaying

boughs of a tree. The person was standing quite still on the top of the mound and leaning forward slightly, face tilted upwards, arms stretched out to the sides, palms downwards, as though about to take flight. After a few moments it dawned on me that they were trying to commune with whatever kind of force or remnant of the dead that might still be living within the mound. I thought at once of that remarkable vision described in the thirteenth-century *Eyrbyggja Saga*, of the shepherd out tending sheep for his master, the Icelandic chieftain Thorstein Codbiter, who sees the north side of a mountain suddenly swing open to reveal great fires blazing within and the sounds of drinking and feasting as the dead celebrate the news that Thorstein and all his crew with him will drown in the morning and join them inside the mountain; and then of Þórólfur (Thorolf) Mostrarskegg's beautiful and mystical injunction in *The Book of the Settlements* that none might look upon Helgafell, his 'Holy Mountain', with an unwashed face. It was not a response to the mood and mystery of Borre that had ever occurred to me, but it was one I instinctively liked. After decades inside rationalism's cramped little room I had long since ceased to find anything comical in this subjective way of relating to history. Half-hidden behind a tree, I watched the person for some time as she – from the build I could see that it was a woman – tried to pick up some fringed ripple of mystery from the earth, some kind of wave or pulse. Or perhaps she was waiting for the sudden jolt of a word spoken in a foreign tongue inside her head.

I had been looking for some time before the realization dawned that I was in fact looking at my own wife. When we later met back at the stone gateway to the park I made no mention of what I had seen. Hand in hand we strolled back up the tree-lined track to Midgard, the little museum and cafeteria dedicated to the site, where we bought postcards and coffee, which we took to a table outside. For a quarter of an hour or so we sat in the misty sunshine and listened to the singing of the birds mingling with the distant shouts and faint clattering of a half-dozen Viking re-enactors on the slope below us, practising fight scenes with realistically painted wooden swords and shields. Every so often one of the swordsmen or women would collapse with a loud grunt and the opponent stand astride the beaten duellist and finish the job off with a spectacular two-handed downward thrust to the heart. They were dressed in vaguely medieval clothing – leather pumps without soles or heels, leggings, cloth trousers gathered below the knee, belted tunics in dark reds and browns. None were wearing helmets, not the absurd and unhistoric horned helmets of the souvenir shops nor the leather skull caps that were certainly worn by real Vikings, nor yet the brimmed wooden helmets which may also have once been worn. Instead, most wore leather headbands to hold the long hair back from their faces. The exception was the last man standing, a youth in his early twenties with a haircut that reminded me of the singer from The Prodigy, a Mohican coxcomb running from the hairline to the nape of his neck, with a covering of dark blue stubble along both sides of his head.

The re-enactors rested from their exertions at the tables next to ours, laying their shields and weapons on the ground beside them. Falling into conversation with this particular youth, I learnt that Borre was hosting a Viking Festival that weekend. Thousands of visitors were expected. Re-enactors from all over Scandinavia, from Germany, Holland, even France, would be arriving and for three days they would dress like Vikings, live in tents like Vikings, eat Viking food, toil as blacksmiths at open forges, fight, fish, tell stories, make music, and get the chance to participate in an Ásatru ceremony of sacrifice and devotion for the most dedicated among them, those who had adopted in a slightly modernized form the ancient religion of the pre-Christian Scandinavians. It turned out there was a circuit of such sites across Scandinavia that took it in turns to host these gatherings. He told me that his speciality was a kind of Viking Age wrestling known as *glimma*. The way he described it, it sounded a lot like the Cumberland wrestling I had seen many years ago at the gypsy horse fair in Appleby, with a lot of holding and grunting and crab-like wheeling – a little dull for the casual spectator, but for the connoisseur no doubt offering a feast of intricacies and technicalities. I noticed his round wooden shield leaning up against the leg of the table. It was divided into quarters, with an illustration in each wedge. I recognized one as an image of the warrior-poet Egil Skallagrimsson, eponymous hero of perhaps the most famous of all Icelandic sagas. Bragi the Old, the earliest known skaldic poet, was depicted in another. There was an inscription in runic lettering around the rim of the young man's shield, and I asked him about it. Odin – that was his name – hesitated a moment before telling me that it was a verse from the *Hávamál* (*The Sayings of the High One*), the pre-Christian wisdom poem attributed to Odin, the verse that says cattle die, the family dies, you'll die yourself, but one thing that never dies is the name a man leaves behind him. It's probably the most famous verse in the whole poem.

My wife and I don't look like re-enactors of anything except what we did yesterday. I could see that my question had made him uneasy, and that he thought I might be about to say something he didn't want to hear. Sure enough, a few moments later he launched into an apparently irrelevant complaint about how young men like him who were proud of their ancestors and their history were always having to field accusations of being neo-Nazis. But it's our history, it's our culture, he said. We have a right to be proud of it. Since he was the one who had raised the subject I thought it was fair enough to make the point that in one way it was understandable that Scandinavians, and in particular the Norwegians and Danes who had both seen their countries occupied by the Nazis in the Second World War, should have developed an antipathy towards such expressions of admiration. The ceremonial calligraphy used by the Waffen SS, for example, was a deliberate and self-conscious attempt to appropriate the Viking past of the 'Germanic people' for their own propaganda purposes, and the aesthetic of Vidkun Quisling's Nasjonal Samling (National Unity) political party in Norway was based entirely on a similar return to a remote past, even down to Quisling's revival of the Old Norse word *hird* to describe his personal bodyguard. And yet even as I said this I could see the logic of his rebellion and of those like him, children and grandchildren of Scandinavia's radical 'sixty-eighters', couples with idealistic hippie values who practised a tolerance so extreme that it might well have made teenage rebellion impossible had their children not discovered the provocation that the cultivation of Scandinavia's Viking heritage could arouse. It also explained the passionate intensity with which young Scandinavian musicians cultivated different branches of what was once called Heavy Metal music, a name derived originally from William Burroughs' novel *The Soft Machine* but now moved far beyond that literary root into an elaborate sub-world of genres that includes Death Metal, Black Metal, Thrash Metal, Speed Metal and, of course, Viking Metal, in most of which Norwegian musicians have been the acknowledged masters.

We spoke a while about *The Sayings of the High One*. I told him I thought there were many good things in it, a lot of everyday commonsense as well as the mystical and the plain enigmatic, at which his bristles softened a little. Our coffee was long drunk by now, and as my wife and I stood up to leave he urged us to come back to Borre at the weekend for the festival. The *glimma* wrestling started at two in the afternoon, he said, and he would be defending his title. It turned out he was the All-Scandinavian champion in his weight class. I told him we couldn't, we had something else planned. He nodded, then added shyly that he was the youngest *jarl* in the whole country. The youngest what? He said it again. It was a simple straightforward

Norwegian word, *jarl*, 'earl'. I just hadn't fathomed the context. He was telling me he was the youngest *earl* in all of Norway. We said goodbye and as we crossed the cinder car park to our VW Golf my wife remarked rather witheringly that aristocracy and titles had been abolished in Norway long ago, way back in 1821. And yet, I thought, how interesting that, even in a controlled egalitarian paradise like Norway, there are some who don't feel right about it.

★

I'd almost forgotten about the incident earlier on that day, when I'd seen my wife apparently trying to commune with the spirits of the mound-dwellers. She was the one who brought the subject up in the car on the way home, mentioning the large V-shaped gashes she had noticed on several of the mounds, in some cases running from the crown almost down to ground level, and asking if I knew why these curious insertions had been made. I had been wondering about the same thing myself and felt obscurely defeated at being unable to provide an explanation. On the drive back to Oslo I had been trying to think of possible explanations. I knew one theory often mentioned in connection with the shafts dug into the mound that contained the famous Oseberg ship – just a ten-minute drive from Borre – was that the damage had been done by grave-robbers who knew or thought they knew that the dead had been buried with treasures in the form of swords, axes, spears and silver to help them make their way through the next life. But some of these mounds were 30 or 40 metres high and it took five minutes to walk around the base of even the smallest. Wedges or gashes that size would have required a lot of people, perhaps even a whole community, and would have taken several days of hard digging to complete. Not exactly a night's work for a Viking Age Burke and Hare. A second possible motive for so-called *haugbrott* ('mound-breaking') was that it might have been done to retrieve the bones of especially brave or powerful men – bones that could then be used in the forging of a weapon that would, in a literal sense, appropriate the courage and power of a dead hero. To the same end of enhancing the spirit of the sword or the spear, the bones of bears or wolves were used in the firing process. The blacksmith's is one of the very few trades explicitly mentioned on runestones, and beliefs like these might go some way towards explaining the blacksmith's high and sometimes almost mystical status in the Viking Age. A third possibility was that the tunnels had been dug specifically to disturb or even remove the remains of the dead so as to make it impossible for them to haunt and harm the living. Sagas like *Grettir the Strong* contain vivid accounts of the trouble that restless heathen mound-dwellers could cause the living after their death. A fourth suggestion was that those living in the Christian era had made the entries and removed the bodies of their heathen ancestors for Christian reburial, hoping it might be a case of better late than never for their souls. I liked this last idea. I had recently read, probably in *Skalk*, a Danish archaeology magazine to which I subscribe, that archaeologists excavating the old church at Jelling had come across what were almost certainly the bones of King Gorm the Old, founder of the Danish monarchy. Their theory was that Gorm had been disinterred from his original resting place in one of the two great mounds at Jelling by his son Harald, after Harald's conversion to Christianity late in the ninth century. There is a beautiful little old church right next to the burial park at Borre. Maybe the bones of Borre's original mound-dwellers lay buried somewhere beneath it?

Traffic slowed then came to a halt as we approached the little harbour town of Vollen, about 15 miles (25 km) out of Oslo. A lorry with Polish number plates had got a punctured tyre and was blocking one lane of the road. As the driver waited for the breakdown truck to arrive, for the next twenty minutes we sat and listened to a CD of Øystein Sunde's greatest hits. Sunde is a unique performer. He's not only a brilliant guitar player but also a unique lyricist, who, unlike many Norwegian performers, sings in Norwegian. He sings so fast, and his lyrics are so convoluted and pun-filled, that even Norwegians have to listen hard just to grasp what he is saying. By the time we eventually got back to our flat in Majorstua that evening, I had forgotten all about the gashes in the Borre mounds.

Not until a couple of years later was I reminded of that forgotten quest for a satisfactory explanation for those disfiguring wedges. While researching for a short book on the Vikings, commissioned by an Oslo publisher for the English-language tourist market, I was browsing through a paperback copy of the *Royal Frankish Annals*, a chronicle of events between 741 and 829 involving Frankish rulers. It seems that well before his death in 813, Charlemagne had plentiful experience of the new and troubling neighbour on his northern border, following his subjugation of the Saxons and occupation of their territory in the 780s. According to the annalists, the Danes were 'the most powerful people among the Northmen'. Of the three Scandinavian peoples, it is the Danes who, at all times in these early records, most resemble a coherent military power. Little is known of the administrative and social structures of Norwegian and Swedish society at the turn of the seventh and eighth centuries, but Frankish annalists convey a distinct impression that at the end of the eighth century a strong monarchy ruled over a Denmark that extended beyond the core islands of the archipelago to include Skåne, in the south of Sweden, and the eastern shore of the Oslo fjord that is now Bohuslän and part of Sweden. According to an entry in the *Royal Frankish Annals* for 813, a Danish army, led by two brothers who shared the kingship, crossed the waters of the Vik to the Norwegian Vestfold, 'an area in the extreme north-west of their kingdom whose princes and people refused to submit to them'. It was at this point in my reading that the memory of the forgotten quest returned to me.

Sensing that an explanation might be no more than two or three sentences away I rose from my couch seat in the living room, called out my wife's name, and realizing from her silence and certain unmistakeable hissing sounds that she was in the shower, I took the book with me into the bathroom. Leaning on the door jamb, now and then glancing up from my book at the diffuse whiteness of her outline behind the frosted plastic doors as she shampooed her hair, turning this way and that in the shower, I read the passage to her in a loud and authoritative voice, adding that it clearly showed that the purpose of the expedition was punitive. Mounds of the size of the Borre mounds were symbols of family power. They were built to be visible for miles around. And what is built to be symbolic may also be symbolically destroyed: those V-shaped defacements of the grave mounds were almost certainly the work of the army brought over by those two Danish kings in 813, to remind their Norwegian subjects of where the real power in the region lay and to persuade them to resume their tributary payments, or taxes as we would call them today.

'That's sounds pretty convincing to me,' I said to her as she shoved the plastic door half-open and reached out for a bottle of conditioner from the hand basin. 'What do you think?' 'Think about what?' she asked, then stepped back inside her warm, ethereal world and slid the door shut before I could answer.

*

With Gorm the Old as its first incumbent, the Danish monarchy is the oldest in existence in Europe. Stretching the definition of the word slightly, one might say that when Harald Bluetooth ordered Gorm's bones dug up it was an archaeological enterprise that made him the first in a long line of Danish monarchs with an interest in the study that continues to this day. The most recent exponent is Denmark's current monarch, Queen Margrethe II, Gorm's grand-daughter down twenty-nine generations, who spent a year studying prehistoric archaeology at Girton College, Cambridge. Her notable predecessors include Waldemar the Great, King of Denmark in the second half of the twelfth century, who, inspired by a local belief that a series of markings on the inner walls of a tunnel-like cleft in the ground at Runamo, in Blekinge, were actually runes describing the deeds of his legendary predecessor, King Harald Hildetand ('War Tooth'), despatched experts in the study of the *futhark* to Runamo to investigate. In effect, he was sponsoring the first official archaeo-logical expedition in Scandinavia. But the long rows of hieroglyphs defeated his experts. On their return his men told him the runes had weathered to the point of illegibility and could no longer be read.

The carvings continued to fascinate, and in the seventeenth century a priest and runologist named Jon Skonvig succeeded in making out the word 'Lund', the name of a town in southern Sweden, which was then part of Denmark. The rock was cleaned, more runes identified, and in 1843 a complete transliteration was made by the Icelander Finn Magnussen. He published a full account of his findings in a 743-page book. Alas, a further study carried out in 1844 by a young Danish sceptic named J.J. Worsaae revealed beyond any doubt that the mysterious markings were glacial striations – wonders in their own way but of no historical relevance to the Danish Crown. On hearing the news, Christian VIII, the king who had sponsored Worsaae's investigation, was greatly amused. He is said to have laughed uncontrollably for minutes on end, patting himself on the stomach and crying out over and over again: 'Oh the Scholars! The Scholars! And that enormous book on Runamo!'

Without doubt the most passionate, devoted and – in the primary and piteous sense of the word – *pathetic* royal exponent of archaeological investigation was Frederik VII, who ruled Denmark from 1848 to 1863. Two years into his reign he presided over the end of the absolute monarchy that had prevailed in Denmark since 1661, and the sheer intensity of his interest in the country's remote and golden past must strike one as the therapy of regret. At the time he made a melancholy little joke about it, *Nu kan jeg vel sove, så længe jeg gider* ('Well, now I suppose I can sleep as long as I like'); but for Frederik personally, the best result was that it gave him more time for his archaeological studies. He used it initially to study dolmens. In 1853, he addressed members of the Royal Society of Northern Antiquaries on the subject of how the ancients, with no technological devices at their disposal, had managed to raise the absolutely enormous stone caps that were used to finish off these burial chambers. In that first lecture he had assumed that the makers were limited in their choice of site by the occurrence of these stones in the landscape. By 1857 he had changed his mind and delivered a second lecture, in which he described in great detail and with appropriate illustrations a technique involving the use of rollers that would allow the giant stones to be moved about a landscape using people and oxen.

The revelation obviously owed much to Frederik's reading in Saxo's *Gesta Danorum* of how his remote ancestor Harald Bluetooth had used the technique to transport the gigantic wedge-shaped Jelling Stone from the Jutland beach where he first saw it to his court at Jelling. Frederik even quotes the relevant passage in his lecture.

On the tram to the National Library in Solli plass* a few weeks ago, I was reminded by an article I happened to be reading in *Skalk* of just how serious Frederik was about these things, and of how powerfully his interest seemed to express his impotent regret at the long, slow diminution in Danish power since those days. The article was accompanied by several drawings of the king, strangely affecting sketches that look like a small boy's dream of what a king's life must be like. One showed him sitting at a table with the Swedish King Karl XV, sharing a bottle of wine and smoking a pipe so long that its bowl appears to rest on the tabletop. Karl's servant John Panzio Toxon, who was technically the royal pipe-cleaner, hovers in the background, ready to serve a second bottle of wine. The meeting took place in June 1860, at Ljungbyhed in Skåne. Karl had invited Frederik over on the occasion of a military exercise being held there. King Karl was almost as keen on archaeology as Frederik, and one of the things they talked about may well have been the paper on dolmens Frederik had delivered three years earlier.

They may also have spoken again of one of triumphs of Karl's early years as king, and the vindication of ancient Swedish history when he organized the opening of one of the great 'Kings Barrows' at Old Uppsala, just north of modern Uppsala, the ancient capital of heathendom in Scandinavia. He had ordered the mound to be opened with the aim of refuting a theory advanced by a group of Swedish natural scientists that, far from being kings' graves, these barrows were merely naturally occurring phenomena in the landscape. He had a tunnel dug towards the centre of one of the mounds, using techniques familiar from mining operations, shoring up the walls and roofs with planking as he went along. Twenty metres (65 feet)

* *Plass* = 'place', 'plaza' or 'square'.

en tente cordiale

into the mound they came across the evidence: a pile of stones in the centre of which was a clay pot containing the remains of a cremation, as well as a number of finely wrought items made of gold from Sweden's Vendel Age.

A reminder of Denmark's golden past was what Frederik seemed in such desperate need of. For most of the time the nineteenth century had been another chapter in the kingdom's shrinking history. Although it tried hard to stay out of the Napoleonic convulsion, it was sucked in by the paranoias of war when the British convinced themselves that Napoleon planned to commandeer the Danish fleet and use it to replace his own, devastated at Trafalgar in 1805, to mount an invasion of Britain. The British response was to mount a pre-emptive strike against the Danes. The attackers used the occasion to experiment with the technology of the rocket as a weapon of war. Rockets had been tried before during a naval engagement in 1806 but had not reacted well to the vagaries of the sea and the wind. On that occasion most of the projectiles had landed harmlessly in the sea. With a target as large and stationary as Copenhagen, however, and a fine and windless week in September in which to demonstrate the technology's efficiency, rockets proved matchless as a weapon of terror. Over three days of intense bombardment, 14,000 pieces of ordnance, including metal balls, explosive and incendiary bombs from cannons and mortars, and some 300 rockets, rained down over the city, turning large sections of its centre into raging infernos. An added horror was that the flames proved resistant to water, making the fires effectively unquenchable. People took to the streets in panic, their possessions hastily piled onto handcarts. The object of the exercise was achieved, and the entire Danish fleet was confiscated by the British.

A less dramatic but more deadly feature of the war was the seven-year blockade of Skagerrak and the Kattegat maintained by the British between 1807 and 1814. Norway was, at the time, wholly dependent on the import of corn from Denmark, and presently most of the south of the country suffered a famine. Fathers in their desperation attempted death-defying crossings of the stretch of open sea to southern Jutland, with little or no chance of evading the patrolling British warships. Thousands were captured and imprisoned on their desperate journeying. Some died, some were exchanged, some fled, and some joined the Royal Navy. The crisis reached its height in 1809, with nearly 4,000 Norwegians held in British prisons for attempting to run the blockade. The corn never made it back to Norway. Estimates put the total number of deaths as a direct result of the blockade at 100,000 men, women and children – over 10 per cent of a population of almost 900,000.

The scars left on the Norwegian psyche were still visible to Henrik Ibsen when he went to Grimstad on the south coast in the 1840s, to work as a chemist's apprentice. Based on the stories of suffering he must have heard, which were still vivid in the memories of those living in that little coastal town, Ibsen's epic poem *Terje Vigen* describes the fate of one man who attempted to beat the blockade and feed his family. Terje makes the crossing rowing alone in an open boat, reaches Frederikshavn on the north-east coast of the Jutland peninsula and buys the precious corn. On the return journey he is captured by an English ship skippered by a humiliatingly youthful eighteen-year-old and sent to prison. After five long years he is freed, but by the time he gets home his wife and small son are both dead. *Terje Vigen* is Norway's national epic and, with the possible exception of the same author's *Peer Gynt*, Terje himself is a figure more familiar to Norwegians than any of the characters from Ibsen's more famous plays.

In an interlude of what seems like merciful light relief from all this, in 1809 a party of British traders led by a soap merchant named Samuel Phelps arrived in Reykjavik in the Danish colony of Iceland, lured by the legendary 'mountains of tallow' believed to exist there. The British carried licences to trade from the Privy Council but found their enterprise blocked by the colony's governor, Count Trampe, a Dane who loyally reflected the tensions and rivalries of the larger world by posting notices about the streets of the capital warning its 307 inhabitants that the penalty for trading with the British was death. Phelps promptly arrested Count Trampe, and within twenty-four hours had installed his Danish interpreter as the new governor. This was a man named Jørgen Jørgensen, one of a number of privateers used by the Danes to try to evade the British blockade of Danish and Norwegian ports, but who had been captured by the British and taken to England. There, his unusual personality and good grasp of English made him useful enough to be appointed to Samuel Phelps' small trading mission to Iceland.

Jørgensen took his sudden promotion to high office very seriously. The day after Trampe's arrest, he issued the first of two revolutionary proclamations. One announced that Denmark no longer had any claim over Iceland; the other asserted that henceforth only those documents carrying his personal seal were legally binding in matters relating to Iceland. He offered the Icelanders the prospect of legal separation from Denmark and a resumption of the democratic principles obtaining in the commonwealth before it had lost its independence to Norway five centuries earlier. There would be a new constitution reflecting the spirit of the French Revolution of 1789, guaranteeing an equal share of power between rich and poor; there would be freedom to trade and to travel; and schools and hospitals would be improved.

At a stroke of the pen, all debts owed by Icelanders to Danish merchants and the Danish government were cancelled. Furthermore, for the following year, until 1 July 1810, all taxes would be halved. The versatile Jørgensen even designed a flag for the new republic – three white cod swimming against a blue background – and promised to stand down once these measures were properly in place. In an *Ubu Roi* moment he appointed an armed militia consisting of eight men, several of whom had prison records, to protect his person and ensure conformity with his new laws. How pleasing to learn from William Jackson Hooker, in his *Journal of a Tour of Iceland in the Summer of 1809*, of the easy way the residents of Reykjavik responded to all this excitement: 'idling about', Hooker writes, and looking on 'with the most perfect indifference'.

Jørgensen's rapid emergence as a loose cannon meant that his Jarry-esque regime lasted all of five weeks, after which he was arrested by the captain of a visiting English warship, the *Talbot*. Trampe was released and reinstated* and Iceland, along with Greenland and the Faroe Islands, declared a neutral and friendly state under British protection and free to trade with whomsoever it wished. By the terms of the Treaty of Kiel in 1814, Denmark lost Norway to Sweden but was allowed to retain Iceland as a dependency.

As for Jørgensen, he was taken back to England, tried and sentenced to thirteen months in jail. He went back to jail many more times, usually on matters connected with his addiction to gambling, until finally a judge lost patience and had him deported to Australia. He died there a few years later, at the age of sixty-two, on the island of Tasmania. It brought to his life a strange symmetry, for as a boy-seaman in the British Navy Jørgensen had sailed to Australia on the *Lady Nelson* and been among those who established settlements at

---

* In *Journey to the Centre of the Earth*, Jules Verne tells us that one of the first things Professor Lidenbrock does on arriving in Iceland in 1863, to prepare for his descent into the volcano, is to hand Count Trampe, the Governor of Iceland, a personal letter of recommendation from Christian Jørgen Thomsen, 'Curator of the Museum of Northern Antiquities' in Copenhagen. The real Trampe died in 1832, the real Thomsen not until 1865, so Thomsen might just have had time to write Lidenbrock's letter for him.

Risdon Cove and Sullivans Cove in Van Diemen's Land, as Tasmania was then called.

*

In Kornerup's famous drawing Frederik sits in the royal armchair atop the great southern mound at Jelling, smoking his pipe as his attendants secure their top hats and cornices against the strong wind that sweeps across the wide flat landscape and up the sides of the mound. It is 1861. The king was on an extended tour of Jutland but

Kong Frederik den 7de lader bore i Gorm den Gamles Høi i Jellinge, den 3de August 1861.

keeping in regular contact by telegram with J.J. Worsaae, the operational leader of the opening of the mound at Jelling. Periodically, Frederik visited the dig himself. Inspired, perhaps, by his friend Karl's triumph over those natural scientists who would degrade the great King's Mounds at Old Uppsala into 'naturally occurring phenomena' he had decided to find old Gorm's bones and shake the firm hand of the far past. He may well have thought he needed the reassurance. Tensions over Slesvig and Holsten had flared up again.

The two duchies, which stretch as far south as Hamburg, had been Danish possessions since the second half of the fifteenth century, but at the cost of several dangerous ethnic and cultural anomalies: the inhabitants of Holsten spoke only German, those of

Slesvig a mixture of Danish and German. A tribal movement called pan-Germanism had emerged with the rise of the Prussian state, and in a confrontation in 1848, in the second year of Frederik's reign, the Prussians had provided active military support to the German-speaking rebels in Holsten. Denmark prevailed on that occasion, but tensions continued to simmer.

Perhaps, as Frederik sat there in his armchair, puffing on his pipe, he was thinking back to the military exercise he had attended with Karl at Ljungbyhed two years earlier, and wondering whether he could count on the Swedish soldiers he had watched drilling to come to Denmark's assistance in the event of a resumption of hostilities. Given the Danes' and Swedes' record of waging war with one another over the preceding millennium, the prognosis was not good. But under Oscar I, Swedish volunteers had fought side by side with the Danes to back Denmark's right to the duchies in the earlier skirmish (1848–51), and both Karl and Frederik may have felt there was potency still in the idea behind the Kalmar union.

The old dream of Scandinavian brotherhood had never vanished completely, though by the nineteenth century it was usually the Danes who were dreaming it. In the midst of the Napoleonic wars it made a bizarre reappearance when Frederik VI of Denmark, desperate to persuade Sweden to join him against the British, devised a plan that involved releasing a large number of balloons from the turrets of the castle at Elsinore. Beneath each balloon a small basket was suspended containing copies of an address entitled 'Stray Remarks on Sweden's Situation Summer 1808'. Readers of the document were told that the spirit of Kalmar was still alive, and that the failure of the union was the fault of the incompetence and personal frailties of its leaders. The time had come for the brotherhood of tribal loyalties to express itself again, once more under Danish leadership. Wind conditions delayed the release of the balloons several times, and when at last a favourable breeze did carry them across the Öresund, their progress was monitored by Swedish cavalry troops on the other side, who rode and scooped them up the moment they landed and burnt them on the spot.

The rise of the Prussian state and the ideal of a pan-Germanic racial union had spurred a rival pan-Scandinavianism among students in Stockholm, Copenhagen and Kristiania (Oslo). 'The time of our separation is past', declared the great Swedish poet Esaias Tegnér as he crowned the Dane Adam Oehlenschläger poet laureate of the whole of Scandinavia. Students from all three countries began meeting annually to toast each other and swear undying brotherhood. In such an atmosphere, King Frederik may have hoped that, past enmities notwithstanding, Sweden-Norway would indeed come to Denmark's aid in her hour of need when the tensions in Slesvig-Holsten flared up again. As verses from his poem 'A Brother in Need' made clear, Henrik Ibsen certainly hoped so too, though he had his doubts:

> *But you, my countrymen, safe hedged*
> *Within your snug terrain*
> *By virtue of a promise pledged*
> *And straight betrayed again, –*
> *Take flight, your ancestry disclaim,*
> *You steered a craven course!*
> *Flee port to port in Cain-like shame*
> *And forge yourself a foreign name,*
> *Deny that you are Norse!*
>
> *Conceal your home, your infamy,*
> *Your mother-tongue deny, –*
> *Else comes the whisper: 'Did you see?*
> *A Norseman scurried by!' –*
> *Don't ever to the top-mast tie*
> *The lovely triple hue;*
> *For any free man sailing by*
> *Will think that Norway's flag flown high*
> *Means that a plague-ship's due!*
>
> *It was a dream. Wake bold and brisk*
> *From folk-wide sleep to deed!*

All hands on deck! There's kin at risk!
Swift counsel's what we need!
Still may the saga-record go:
Danes, Danes own Tyra's hold!
Still Denmark's tattered flag can blow
Above the North's rich future, show
Its proud and rose-red fold.

(TRANSLATED BY JOHN NORTHAM)

But it wasn't a dream, and once violence flared it was apparent that the appeal of pan-Scandinavianism had never penetrated much beyond the bubble of the student world. Early in February 1864, an army of 57,000 Austrian and Prussian troops crossed the River Eider. The 40,000 Danes manning the Dannevirke, which protects the neck of the Jutland archipelago, made a tactical retreat to Dybbøl, and there, in the last battle ever fought on Danish soil, they were heavily defeated. The victorious Prussians and Austrians advanced and occupied Jutland as far as Limfjord, in the north of the peninsula. Negotiations in the late autumn of that same year gave sovereignty of the two duchies, along with Saxe-Lauenburg to the south (which had passed to the Danish king via Sweden some years before) to the Germans, a move that reduced the size of Denmark from 22,000 square miles (58,000 sq km) to 15,000 (39,000 sq km), and her population from 2.5 million to just over 1.5 million. Of the thousands of soldiers promised by Karl of Sweden-Norway, fewer than 150 volunteered and made their way to Dybbøl to fight.

Dybbøl was a national trauma for Denmark. It marked the end of her thousand years as a military and political power in northern Europe and the final shredding of that intermittent dream of a political and military union at the head of the two other Scandinavian-language tribes. Frederik, as though the impending humiliation was too much for him to bear, had slipped away weeks before the invasion, dying unexpectedly in November 1863. One of Kornerup's sketches from the excavation at Jelling shows him conferring the Order of the Danebrog on his Master Engineer Møller, the man

in charge of the tunnelling. Following the informal little ceremony, Møller is shown saluting as the king holds out an imploring hand to him and, in Kornerup's caption, pleads with his engineer: *I maae finde mig den gamle Konge* ('You *must* find the old king for me'), as though the recovery of old Gorm's bones might somehow make everything right again. But when they reached its centre, the great burial chamber turned out to be empty.

5

The *Vasa* Ship: Sweden's Age of Greatness

WHEN OTTO III MADE HIS DESCENT INTO THE TOMB OF Charlemagne at Aachen, in the year 1000, the great emperor and founder of modern Europe had been dead for almost two centuries. On entering the mausoleum, the young man found Charles seated on a throne, a golden crown on his head and in his gloved right hand a sceptre. The fingernails had grown through the gloves and wrapped themselves like talons around the head of the wand. The hair beneath the crown had also continued to grow for some time after the onset of brain death, but the body was otherwise remarkably well-preserved, the only real sign of decay being the missing tip of the nose. The young man, having obviously been apprised of this by some previous and unrecorded reconnaissance descent, replaced it with a shaped nugget of gold. He also trimmed the corpse's hair and cut its nails. Before leaving and closing up the tomb, he removed a single tooth from Charlemagne's mouth, no doubt in the hope that it possessed some magical power that might work in his favour. Alas it did not, and less than two years later he was dead himself, the victim of a smallpox epidemic.

If Frederik's search for the earthly remains of Gorm the Old might – beneath a veneer of scientific archaeological interest – have been motivated by a similar hope that some tiny physical remnant would magically invert all the failing fortunes of Denmark then he was disappointed. A document that might have brought him some compensatory comfort did emerge in the year of his death; but it was too late and too far away for him to know of its existence. While restoring a volume of fifteenth-century devotional works a librarian named Albert Lemarchand, in the library of the town of Angers, in western France, came upon four quarto pages of parchment that had been used to pad its binding. The parchment was in good condition and the pages copiously annotated and corrected. They were not finally identified until 1877, when a linguist named Gaston Paris recognized them as an extract from the *Gesta Danorum*. Expert analysis indicated that these pages were from Saxo's original Latin manuscript and that the annotations were his own. Once their historical value had been realized, the pages became the property of the Danish state, in exchange for a French manuscript.

Regardless of the fluctuations in their status as a European power, the Danes had always held this great history book as evidence of their pedigree and past. Along with Harald Bluetooth's Jelling Stone, the *Gesta Danorum* was the second great pillar upon which the Danish state rested as a historical entity. The Norwegians had their *Heimskringla*, even though its author was the Icelander Snorri Sturluson. Snorri honoured the Swedish Yngling family in the 'Ynglingasaga' chapter of the *Heimskringla* as the dynasty from which all later kings in Scandinavia should claim descent if they wished to be thought legitimate; and yet the Swedes had no single great work of their own that could bear comparison with the literary monuments of their Scandinavian neighbours. The long and rich tale of the Swedish past could only be told by putting together the telegrammatic and often enigmatic inscriptions on the runestones and picture-stones scattered throughout the country, and the uncertain fictions of a handful of mythological-historical sagas like the *Hervarar saga ok Heiðreks* (*The Saga of Hervör and Heidrek*).

By the late seventeenth century, this lack of a respectable cultural monument had become pressing for the Swedes. In many ways, the

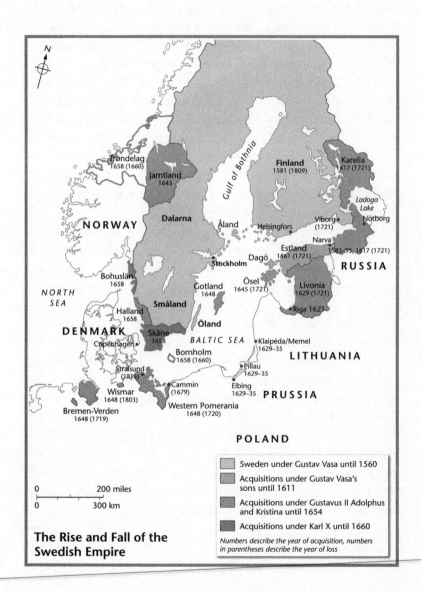

The Rise and Fall of the Swedish Empire

Legend:
- Sweden under Gustav Vasa until 1560
- Acquisitions under Gustav Vasa's sons until 1611
- Acquisitions under Gustavus II Adolphus and Kristina until 1654
- Acquisitions under Karl X until 1660

Numbers describe the year of acquisition, numbers in parentheses describe the year of loss

Map labels:
N

Trøndelag 1658 (1660)
Jämtland 1645
NORWAY
Dalarna
Gulf of Bothnia
Åland
Finland 1581 (1809)
Karelia 1617 (1721)
Ladoga Lake
Viborg (1721)
Nötborg
Helsingfors
Narva 1583–95, 1617 (1721)
Estland 1661 (1721)
Dagö
Stockholm
RUSSIA
Bohuslän 1658
NORTH SEA
Gotland 1648
Ösel 1645 (1721)
Livonia 1629 (1721)
Riga 1621
Halland 1658
Småland
Öland
DENMARK
Skåne 1658
BALTIC SEA
Klaipéda/Memel 1629–35
Copenhagen
Bornholm 1658 (1660)
LITHUANIA
Pillau 1629–35
Stralsund (1815)
Cammin (1679)
Elbing 1629–35
PRUSSIA
Wismar 1648 (1803)
Western Pomerania 1648 (1720)
Bremen-Verden 1648 (1719)
POLAND

0   200 miles
0   300 km

Swedish Empire that arose over the seventeenth century between 1611 and 1718, a period known as *Stormaktstiden* or 'Great Power Era', was a long-term result of the military energy unleashed in the process of breaking free from Danish regional domination. The Swedish revolt against the Kalmar Union that began in 1434 and reached a climax in the Stockholm Bloodbath of 1520, independence in 1523 and the break with the Church of Rome in the 1530s set in train a fierce rivalry for supremacy in the region. From a military point of view the Swedes faced a daunting task to assert themselves, ringed around as they were by Danish possessions in the Baltic, in Skåne, the southernmost region of the Scandinavian peninsula, the Jutland peninsula in the south, and in the west a border with Norway that was under the control of Denmark.

Control of the Baltic was the first essential of national security. The Swedes, building on their possession of Finland, emerged as victors in a three-way struggle between Sweden, Poland and Russia for possession of the Baltic states. Sweden's right to Estonia was recognized by the Treaty of Teusina in 1595.

Over the next few years there was a steady stream of military triumphs, strategic alliances and acquisitions. The balance of power began to tip during the reign of Gustavus Adolphus II (1611–32) and shifted decisively in Sweden's direction during the Thirty Years' War, the last great religious war in Europe, in which the historically Roman Catholic states ranged themselves against the newly created Protestant states of northern Europe, with Germany as the devastated battleground. His hand was forced by the series of defeats inflicted on Protestant Denmark by the Austrian Holy Roman Emperor, and by Emperor Ferdinand's Edict of Restitution (1629), which divested Protestants of all Church lands taken or acquired since the Peace of Augsburg in 1555, a move that seemed to presage the extinction of state Protestantism. Gustavus Adolphus's entry into the war gained him a reputation as the great defender of Protestantism, a kind of Lutheran equivalent in terms of political and religious responsibilities to the Catholic Emperor himself. As the long and bitter struggle twisted on into the middle of the seventeenth century, its various staging posts and treaties brought Sweden a foothold on the north German coast, east of the Jutland peninsula, a possession it was able to exploit to great tactical advantage in the Torsteinsson War of 1643, and again during the Swedish wars of 1657 to 1660.

Charles X, who succeeded Gustavus Adolphus's daughter Kristina when she abdicated in 1654, was able to respond to a Danish declaration of war in 1657 by bringing his army up through northern Germany to occupy Jutland, the continental-mainland element of the oddly dimensioned Kingdom of Denmark. He completed the rout of the Danes with a manoeuvre of extraordinary daring and imagination, marching his troops across the thick ice that had frozen the waters in the straits of the Lillebælt and Storebælt (the Little and Large belts) during that exceptionally cold winter to occupy Sjælland–Zealand. This piece of tactical boldness and brilliance paid the highest possible dividends at the Peace of Roskilde in 1658, at which Denmark was forced to concede Skåne, Blekinge, Halland and Bohuslän in the east of Norway, and the island of Bornholm. Emboldened by the almost shocking speed of these gains, Charles declared war on Denmark a mere six months later, intending this time to complete the conquest of the entire country. A siege of Copenhagen that showed no sign of succeeding indicated that things would not go so smoothly this time; and when Charles died suddenly and unexpectedly of natural causes in 1660, at the age of thirty-eight, the ambitious plan to unite all of Scandinavia under the Crown of Sweden was abandoned forever.

Charles's son and successor Charles XI, after thwarting a Danish attempt to recapture Skåne, devoted his energies to mending the royal finances, which had been greatly weakened following Gustavus Adolphus's cultivation of the Swedish aristocracy's support for the Thirty Years' War, a policy that had involved transferring ownership of a vast number of Crown estates into private hands. A programme known as the 'Reduction' reversed many of these grants, while the Swedish parliament further enhanced the king's power (and correspondingly reduced that of the aristocracy) by decreeing that the king need only consult the Council for advice if he felt the need for it. With further adjustments, the Swedish monarchy had become absolute by 1689, and the king ruled by the Grace of God alone. The power of the old, land-owning aristocracy was broken, passing instead to a new class of paid civil servants.

Charles's son and heir, Charles XII, presided over a gradual dismemberment of the Swedish Empire, and by 1718 it had shrunk to the smaller and more manageable size that a modest population could sustain. The enduring benefits for Sweden included the disappearance of the long-standing threat to its national security exerted by that arc of Danish possessions stretching up its eastern approaches, a development that also gave Swedes control of the entrance to the Baltic, and with it access to the markets in the east which their ancestors the Rus, the Swedish Vikings, had exploited to such advantage 800 years earlier. The territorial gains also gave Sweden control over the mouths of the great rivers of Germany – the Oder, Elbe and Weser – with the right to collect tolls from those who used them. Sweden, at the height of its Age of Greatness, was twice the size of the present-day country, with Stockholm at its centre and Riga on the far side of the Baltic as its second city. In territorial terms, it was the third-largest country in Europe, after Spain and Russia. But of all these rapidly acquired possessions, the most significant was the acquisition of Skåne. It guaranteed the geographical integrity of modern Sweden.

*

Much the most intriguing of Sweden's monarchs during this hastily assembled greatness was Queen Kristina, the only child of Gustavus Adolphus. She reigned under a regent from the time of her father's death in 1632 to 1645, and in her own right thereafter until her abdication in 1654. If her own father and the male relatives who succeeded her took care of the military responsibilities involved in the creation and maintenance of this northern European empire, it fell to Kristina to provide it with the cultural identity and attributes proper to a country that had, almost overnight, announced itself as a Great Power. An occasional actress herself, she cultivated the theatre, the arts, music and literature, and she worked consciously to makes hers a sophisticated European court. As a woman of questing intellect, with a deep interest in religion, philosophy and Greek antiquity, she was culturally ambitious for Sweden and keen to mark its new-found status. She must have been delighted when René Descartes, the most celebrated and controversial philosopher of the age, accepted her invitation to join her as resident philosopher at the court in Stockholm.

Hesitant at first, wary of finding himself reduced to a role as the queen's tutor, Descartes was relieved to discover, once he arrived in Stockholm, that Kristina was genuinely interested in hearing his response to the profoundly existential questions she had already raised with him in the correspondence that had preceded the appointment. They included: 'Which is worse, the abuse of love or the abuse of hatred?', 'What is love, and what are the effects of love and of its opposite, hatred, on a human life?' and 'What is the nature of the relationship between ordinary commonsense and religious revelation?' She also wanted to know whether a 'natural understanding' was sufficient for someone to love God; even before his arrival in Stockholm, the deeply modest Descartes had assured her that indeed it was.

By the time he arrived in the Swedish capital late in 1649 Descartes was, at sixty, already an old man by the standards of the day; but he was still pleased to wear a curly wig, embroidered gloves and the long, thin pointed shoes fashionable at the time. For much of his life it had been his habit to spend his mornings in bed, thinking, reading and writing, but this routine became brutally swamped beneath Kristina's own. As a queen in waiting, she had been disciplined from her childhood to spend ten hours a day in the study of religion, philosophy, Greek, Latin and several modern languages, including German, French and Italian. Happily for her, such discipline suited her temperament, and despite the wealth of new responsibilities that came with her coronation, these habits of study continued into her adult years. Poor old Descartes had to be fitted in somewhere, and that turned out to be 4am daily, in her library – unheated, in what was even for Stockholm an unusually cold winter. There it was his duty to be brilliant and revelatory in discoursing on matters that were, as it turned out, of quite exceptional importance to the queen. Descartes had no doubt been hoping for a more comfortable and less demanding sinecure, but he was sufficiently impressed by Kristina's obvious sincerity not to mention his personal discomforts. His passionate advocacy of doubt as the only intellectually honourable position possible for an individual in search of answers to the most profound questions changed her life and dramatically reshaped her destiny. As a queen, though, it ruined her and caused consternation and confusion among her countrymen, for as things turned out the daughter of Gustavus Adolphus, Lion of the North, Defender of the Protestant Faith, had somehow survived the childhood indoctrination of her Protestant tutors to find herself increasingly attracted to Roman Catholicism, a faith now so severely proscribed under Swedish law that conversion entailed the loss of all civil rights and automatic expulsion from the country.

These prohibitions meant that Kristina's journey to Catholicism was undertaken largely in secrecy, and the progress of her convictions is hard to plot. What is certain is that a crucial earlier influence was the French ambassador to Sweden, Pierre Chanut, a rational, civilized, learned and tolerant man, whose very attributes suggested to her that most of what her Protestant tutors had told her about Catholics was exaggeration, prejudice and propaganda. It was through her friendship with Chanut that she first came into contact with Descartes. Whether or not those icy early-morning encounters in the queen's library took the form of some kind of instruction or intellectual soundings of the queen's curiosity about Catholicism is an issue that has been much debated; but whatever it was they talked about, there must have been a peculiar intensity to their discussions, as the queen struggled with a growing realization of the impossibility of being the Catholic ruler of a Protestant people. Descartes must have impressed her in the same way as Chanut, exhibiting a brilliant intellect suffused with enough honourable doubt to concede that even rationalism has its limits, and that left him free to adhere rather than cling to his Catholic faith.

If indeed Descartes did have a crucial influence on the queen's thinking it was a final personal triumph. He suffered dreadfully from the rigours of Kristina's routine during their first full month as teacher and pupil, that bitterly cold January of 1650. By the time he arrived for their meetings, he would already be frozen to the bone by the coach drive to the palace, and as he walked the last few metres of the way across a little bridge, it seemed to him that in such extreme cold even men's thoughts must freeze like the water. Protocol required that he remain standing throughout their sessions, his head bare. By early February he was fevered, showing symptoms of pneumonia, and experiencing congestion of the lungs, which he gamely tried to treat with a medication of his own devising: liquid tobacco suspended in heated wine. As February dragged on, his strange concoction appeared to be having some effect, and one day he expressed a desire to get up from his bed and, with the assistance of his manservant Henry Schluter, sit for a while in an armchair. But even this mild exertion proved too much, and he fainted.

It seems he realized the end was close after regaining consciousness, and on 10 February a priest who had arrived to administer the last rites was given permission to proceed by a blinking of the eyes. The following morning, Descartes passed away. Kristina planned a state funeral for him, and burial at Riddarholmen among the kings of Sweden. As a temporary measure, he was buried the day after his death in the cemetery of Adolf Fredrik's church, with the idea that his body would be moved in the spring. Time and circumstance meant that nothing came of the queen's plans, and he lay there beneath a simple wooden monument for the next seventeen years, until eventually the body was exhumed and taken back to France. Perhaps his death served in some way to focus Kristina's dilemma. Within a year of his death, she had made her first documented contact with the Society of Jesus, sending a secret letter through an interpreter at the Portuguese embassy to the Superior General of the Jesuits' Order in Rome.

In February 1649, more than a year and a half before her coronation in October 1650, Kristina had announced that she was never going to marry and that, moreover, she did not propose ever to offer any explanation for her decision. Five years later, in 1654, she informed the Council of her intention to abdicate, and suggested that with their approval the throne of Sweden be offered to her cousin Karl. Perhaps only because she was a woman, Kristina's reign now – looked at from the perspective of Scandinavian societies that are characterized to an unusual degree by their promotion of traditionally feminine virtues and values, and in particular a distaste for violence – seems more predictive of modern Sweden than any of her predecessors' or successors' during the country's Great Power century. The quality that, for want of a better word, one might call 'civilized' was nowhere better illustrated than in the rituals of her abdication ceremony in 1654. To her own courtiers, advisers and diplomats, the abdication seemed supremely unnatural and tragic; and yet, realizing that there was nothing to be done about it, the situation was formalized in a ceremony of impressive dignity at the royal palace in Uppsala on 5 June. It was a mournful piece of theatre in which, item by item, Kristina was ceremoniously divested of her royal regalia. Everything proceeded smoothly until a courtier named Per Brahe, who had been a close friend to her late father and whose task it was to remove the crown from the queen's head, remained rooted to the spot when the moment arrived. Kristina flashed him urgent hand signals, beseeching him to step forward and play his part; but when even these failed to sway him, she lifted up her hands and removed the crown herself. The ceremony then continued with the coronation of her cousin as Karl X. Later that same day, Karl made an offer to marry her. It was an offer he had made earlier. Now, as then, she rejected it. Kristina left Sweden later in the summer. At Innsbruck in 1655, she formally converted to Catholicism and began the long, slow journey that would eventually lead her to Rome, where she would spend the remaining thirty-four years of her life.

Kristina had not been a cheap head of state for Sweden. In company with Axel Oxenstierna, the chancellor during her minority years, she had greatly expanded the Swedish aristocracy, handing out titles to barons and counts and selling off Crown lands to pay the appanages of these newly created nobles. Like her invitation to

Descartes, it may all have been part of an attempt to give Sweden the style she felt becoming for a major European power.

In the light of her father's elevation to the rank of Defender of the Protestant Faith, there is a huge irony in Kristina's conversion to Catholicism. In symbolic terms, I have sometimes thought it might express something close to an aversion to the rapidity of Sweden's rise from obscure northern nation to major player in the political affairs of northern Europe – a sort of Groucho Marx unease at being a member of a club that would have someone like her as a member. Gustav Vasa had shown a similar ambivalence about the triumphs of the Reformation when he retained the tradition of the Apostolic Succession in appointing bishops to the state Church in Sweden, hinting at a respectful admiration for the very antiquity, values and power which his revolution had overthrown. Was there, at some point in Kristina's dangerous attraction towards Roman Catholicism – if this is not too doggedly psychoanalytical a point – an expression of shock and regret at the temerity involved in rejecting the time-honoured authority of the Eternal City? Was this her quite private way of atoning for the Reformation? Or did she, with all the wealth of her princely education, become a victim of choice? Did she, like Kierkegaard in Denmark two centuries later, grow weary of the fashion to doubt everything as the default intellectual position? A fashion from which Kierkegaard, in his generalized contempt, gave honourable exemption to the man who started it all, Descartes? As Kierkegaard wrote in *Fear and Trembling*, quoting Descartes, we must keep in mind that the natural light of reason can be trusted only so long as nothing contrary to it is revealed by God. Above all, he wrote, we should impress on our memory as an infallible rule that what God has revealed to us is incomparably more certain than anything else.

Whatever possible truth there might be in such musings, there can be no denying Kristina's concern for her immortal soul and her objection to the fact of physical death. A four-page formula, devised by a German chemist named Johann Glauber, was found in her purse after she died. It turned out to be the recipe for an elixir of life, the 'Balsamo Mercuriale', to be applied by rubbing around the belly-button. In Kristina's case it turned out to be as little use as any other potion mixed for the same purpose.*

Kristina had been born with an unusually dense covering of lanugo hair that disguised her sex so effectively that Gustavus Adolphus was initially told he had fathered a son. When the error was corrected, he appeared not to mind, particularly as Kristina turned out to be a tomboyish daughter. In any event, as a princess who was being groomed for the throne she received an education and upbringing that took little account of her sex. Her determinedly unmarried status and the fact that she often dressed like a man and had a deep voice (remarked on many times by contemporaries) have, over the centuries, turned Kristina into a figure of mystery and fascination. In modern times, lesbians and transsexuals have laid claim to her as one of their own.

One early Swedish biographer, Curt Weibull, concluded that she might have been what is termed a 'pseudo-hermaphrodite', having normal female genitalia but a hidden chromosomal abnormality that complicated her sexual identity. So intense was the interest surrounding the issue that in 1965 an attempt was made to solve the matter. Her body was disinterred from its sarcophagus in the Vatican grotto in Rome, and a medical examination was carried out by Carl-Herman Hjortsjö, a professor of anatomy at Lund University. But as Hjortsjö himself conceded, the physical manifestations of ambiguous gender on the remains of a long-dead person are unidentifiable, and her body was returned to the sarcophagus with no one any the wiser. Kristina herself was aware of

---

* Just occasionally, such an intemperate longing to live forever produces unlooked-for benefits, as when an attempt by a Hamburg alchemist named Brand to make gold out of dried urine led, quite by chance, to the discovery of phosphorus.

these rumours about her sex, which must have been painful for her in their way. In old age, she wrote in her journal that she was 'neither male nor hermaphrodite, as some people in the world have pass'd me for'. Her life and enigmatic fate have been the subject of a number of novels and films. Strindberg wrote a play about her. Greta Garbo played her in a 1933 Hollywood biopic, dressed in men's clothing in certain scenes, in one of the film's few concessions to historical reality.

★

While Kristina spent much of her time as queen trying to create a golden present for imperial Sweden, a man named Olof Rudbeck was working equally hard to give it a golden past. Rudbeck had made his name at the age of twenty with the discovery of the lymphatic system, an impeccably modern contribution in the field of medical science which complemented William Harvey's discovery that the blood circulates around the body and the human heart is but a pump, a startlingly different understanding from ideas on the subject put forward 2,000 years earlier by the Greek physician Galen that had remained largely unchallenged since his time. Rudbeck's achievement brought his name to the attention of Queen Kristina and, until her abdication and the death in the same year of her chancellor, Oxenstierna, the statesman and the queen remained his enthusiastic patrons.

Rudbeck, a tall, well-built man with a full beard who wore his hair shoulder-length, was a universal genius of a type that Sweden has been particularly rich in. Emanuel Swedenborg and August Strindberg are well-known examples. In addition to his medical skills Rudbeck was a master fireworks-maker, an architect who designed and built the university's anatomy theatre at Uppsala, a civil engineer who provided the city with a plumbing system to bring water (via underground pipes) to the doorstep of many central Uppsala households, and a botanist whose *Campus Elysii* aimed to describe every known plant in the world. This latter task so often took second place to the demands of his other talents that the *Campus Elysii* was never finished; but even in incomplete form, it earned the praise of his fellow-countryman, the botanist Carl Linné (Linnaeus). Rudbeck was also the creator of a botanical garden intended to display some of the plants described in his book. It was an early example of the interactive approach – you've read the book, now visit the garden. His garden required copious watering and was one of the prime benefi- ciaries of his underground waterworks system. He lectured students in the art of ship-building, played a number of musical instruments, and for the coronation of Charles XI in Uppsala Cathedral in 1675 not only composed the music but sang it himself, with a passion reportedly loud enough to subdue the twelve trumpets and four kettledrums blaring and thrashing away behind him.

But of all these claims for Rudbeck's polymathic genius none can compare in its scope, its vision, its ingenuity and its sheer weirdness, no less for the Cartesian rigour which he brought to the field, with his discovery that Sweden was the location of Plato's lost continent of Atlantis, and Swedish the proto-language from which Greek, Latin and Hebrew all derived, just as the pantheon of Greek gods were later improvisations on the gods of Sweden's Atlantean antiquity – Thor, Odin, Loki, Frey, Freyja. These discoveries were presently embodied in four huge volumes, written in both Latin and Swedish, which appeared between 1679 and 1702. Rudbeck's strange theories and preoccupations on this subject derived ultimately from a long- standing interest among the Swedes in their Gothic roots, and in a theory proposed in the sixth century AD by the Roman historian Jordanes: that Scandinavia, which Jordanes called *Scandza*, was the home of those Ostrogoths and Visigoths who flooded south and west across Europe during the Age of Migrations and who, in 410, sacked Rome and brought the Roman Empire in the West to an end. At the Synod of Basel in 1434, the delegate from Sweden claimed the seat of honour, invoking his country's Gothic past to argue that of all the kingdoms represented, his was the most ancient, the strongest and the most noble.

It was the convulsions of the Reformation and Sweden's subse- quent rapid rise to the status of Great Power that gave real impetus to a revival of the myth that Rudbeck developed to such dizzy-ing extremes. As kings in a line with no historical past the Vasas encouraged any references to the country's ancient Gothic heritage. The military feats of Gustavus Adolphus in the Thirty Years' War seemed to echo the triumphs of Gothic kings of the fifth century such as Alaric, who led the sacking of Rome in 410. They were won against the same enemy, too, once Rome became the spiritual seat of Catholic Europe. In his public utterances, the king frequently invoked his Gothic roots and encouraged and sponsored his hist-orians to pursue the line in ever more detail. The very clothes he wore at his coronation at Uppsala in 1617 were in conscious imitation of those known to have been worn by the Gothic King Berik. Among the documentation studied by Swedish historians were a number of Icelandic saga manuscripts, acquired by the University of Uppsala. Although many of these were written no earlier than the thirteenth and fourteenth centuries, they were enthusiastically interpreted as reliable historical accounts by students of Sweden's Gothic past.

A scholar named Olof Verelius, who was preparing an edition of the *Saga of Hervör and Heidrek*, had asked his versatile friend Rudbeck to provide him with a map of the district around Lake Mälaren. The map was never delivered, for in the course of his work Rudbeck became at first distracted and then literally enchanted by what seemed to him remarkable similarities between the place-names and words he came across in the text of the saga, and the words already familiar to him from his knowledge of Greek, Latin and Hebrew. With a visionary rapidity these homophonous coinci-dences – of the same order as those that persuaded Snorri Sturluson that the Æsir, the Norse gods, hailed originally from *Asia* – became a revelation of the roots of a stupendous and fantastical tree, stranger by far than anything growing in his botanical gardens. By the time he had finished watering, nurturing, pruning and training it, he was able to use this extrusion to provide Swedes with incontrovertible proof that Old Uppsala was nothing more nor less than the true location of the lost continent of Atlantis of which Plato had written in the *Timaeus* and *Critias* dialogues.

In the summer of 1674, Rudbeck made the first of what would be countless field trips to Old Uppsala, taking with him twelve students whose task it was to carry out measurements of the site and contrast them with measurements of the size of the city and its distance from the sea as given in Plato. When there turned out to be a close correspondence between the two sets of figures, Rudbeck, in near-disbelief, ordered his students to carry out the measurements again. When the same close correspondences were again returned, it seemed to him that he had no choice but to believe. This first breakthrough into the realm of scientific proof was followed by others. He was soon able to give a location for the site of the horse-racing track mentioned in Plato, as well as the temple to Poseidon and Cleito, which he quickly realized must be the same as the one at Old Uppsala described by Adam of Bremen in the *Gesta Hammaburgensis*: a vast building, its façade framed by a fabulous linked gold chain, its interior walls decked in gold, from which enormous statues of Odin, Frey and Thor stared down at the worshippers as nine males of every species of animal were sacrificed to them in thanks and appeasement. In due course, Rudbeck located not the links themselves but fragments of the chain, embedded in the walls of the Uppsala Church, the oldest Christian church in Sweden. Anything found on the site became, axiomatically, another vital piece in the emerging picture of Sweden's Atlantean heritage. Presently he opened a museum, where delighted and astonished visitors could see for themselves Atlantean knives, axe-heads, pendants, spinning whorls, pins, nails and arrow-heads.

As Rudbeck's certainties grew, he moved beyond the realms of archaeology and philology into abstract speculation. By 1678 he was convinced that Sweden had been the home of the gods and demi-gods of antiquity and even offered precise correspondences: Heimdall, the watchman of the Æsir, had metamorphosed into Hermes; Balder became Apollo, Zeus Thor and Odin Hercules. Plato's statement that Atlantis was located near the Pillars of Hercules, marking the outermost limits of the hero's great voyage, was commonly held to be a reference to the mountain promontories flanking the entrance to the Strait of Gibraltar. Not so in Rudbeck's world. By now he was a man deep into the writing of a new kind of novel and had mastered the ability to weave everything, every encounter, every new fact unearthed, into the fabric of his great story. With a simple flick of understanding he moved these rocky pins to the Öresund, content that the translocation better answered Plato's intention to describe a place that marked the limits of the known world in his time. Consulting maps, Rudbeck found confirmation of his intuition in numerous place-names in the Öresund region that preserved elements of the name Hercules: Herhamber, Herhal and one close to Stockholm called Hercul.

The last of the four volumes of the *Atland eller Manheim* (translated into Latin as *Atlantica*) that documented all this was in the process of being printed in May 1702 when a great fire swept through Uppsala and consumed most of the town. Rudbeck's own house was badly damaged and his inventions, his instruments, his printing press and his cabinet of curiosities lost. Gone, too, were 7,000 completed woodcuts for the *Campus Elysii*, almost all unsold copies of the *Atlantica* as well as the partially printed copies of the fourth volume. Yet within a few weeks he was back at work, supervising repairs to the roof of his own house and his neighbours' houses, organizing the resurrection of the botanical garden, and drafting plans for a complete rebuilding of the town. In the midst of these endeavours, thoroughly burnt out himself, one might suppose, by a lifetime of superhuman dedication to the task of constructing, within the space of a few short years, a golden past worthy of Sweden's golden present and dismayed by this fiery proof of fate's brisk indifference to all his efforts, he fell ill and died in his bed on 9 September 1702. Although readers during his lifetime had included such luminaries of contemporary thought as Leibniz, Montesquieu, Pierre Bayle and Sir Isaac Newton, within twenty years of Rudbeck's death his whole strange balloon had collapsed and fallen back down to earth, and the Swedish Empire it had been launched to glorify and celebrate was gone.

For a time, Rudbeck's name came to be used as a verb to describe anyone engaged in reckless and uncontrolled speculation: *att rudbeckisera*, 'to rudbeck'. But history has not been unkind to him. The sixteen-page entry on his life and work in Volume XXX of the *Svenskt Biografiskt Lexicon* is respectful and sympathetic. Along with his real contributions to botany and medicine it stresses the intricate strangeness of the poetry he laid across his distinctive and thematically consistent world-historical tale of Sweden's gothic past, in which facts, dreams, myth and waking life, historical personages, biblical and mythological figures merge and flow and part in a mesmerizing drift that evokes in us the same sense of awestruck and uncomprehending wonder with which we contemplate the later writings of James Joyce.

★

Vast and ephemeral as it was, Rudbeck's *Atlantica* is too exotic, too strange, too resolutely the product of a quite different way of thinking, a wholly different attitude towards study, to serve as a symbol of Sweden's remarkable century as a European Great Power. In that context, the curious fate of the great royal ship the *Vasa* seems a more apt representation, though it took a while for me to understand this.

One's first impressions on entering the dark, vaulted museum home of the ship on the island of Djurgården, in central Stockholm, are overwhelming. The *Vasa* is 57 metres (187 feet) long, its afterdeck 17 metres (55 feet) high; the tallest of its three masts towers 49 metres (160 feet) above the keel. A lion leaps from the bowsprit, and the gaping heads of the rest of the pride surround the openings of the gunports, so that when the guns were fired they would seem to roar. The stem and stern are a riot of bright and intricate carvings. Twenty-three Gideon's warriors march across the upper gallery of the stern. There are mermaids, glaring cherubs, heathen gods and goddesses, musicians, more lions, more warriors – it is easy to see that, in every way, this was a 'king's ship', designed to be the pride of Gustavus Adolphus's navy. Its appointed task, in the political situation of the time, was to secure the Baltic against any German attempt to seize control of the waters.

She had a crew of 145 and space on board for 300 fighting men to see that the job was done. But they never got even close. On Sunday 10 August 1628 the *Vasa* was launched. Many of Stockholm's 10,000 inhabitants had made their way down to the docks to watch. Others took to the water in small boats intending to follow her out to the open sea. It was fine day. The wind from the southwest was so light that for the first few hundred metres, until she reached Tranbodarna, the ship had to be towed along. Finally, the moment came when the skipper ordered men aloft to set four of the *Vasa's* ten sails, a salute was fired, and she was off and sailing on her maiden voyage. Approaching Beckholmen she was exposed to slightly stronger winds and almost at once began to keel over to the left. She righted herself again, but passing the islet, struck by what Captain Söfring Hansson later described as 'just a slight gust of wind, no more than a breeze', she keeled over again and within a matter of minutes, before the astonished eyes of those watching from the shore, she vanished beneath the waves, sunk in 32 metres of water after a voyage of less than 1,300 metres. Fifty lives were lost; most of the survivors managed to swim to land or were picked up by the small craft following.

As soon as they reached shore, the *Vasa's* senior officers were arrested. It was assumed that the disaster was the result of some major act of incompetence, such as failing to secure the guns on the lower deck so that all of them trundled over to the same side. Suspicions of drunkenness were raised and quickly ruled out as the simple, dreadful truth emerged: for all her style, her beauty and magnificence, the *Vasa* was completely unseaworthy. The slight breeze that ruffled her sails as she approached Beckholmen had been enough to dip her down below the waterline and allow the water to come gushing in through the lion-head gun-ports, all of them open and less than a metre above the surface. She was too tall, too narrow, too top-heavy. Everyone on board either knew it or had suspected as much. No one said a thing. At the hearing, Shipmaster Jöran Mattson described a stability test conducted in the presence of the Admiral of the Fleet, Clas Fleming. Thirty crew members had been lined up and told to run from one side of the ship to the other and back again and the degree of list was then measured in plank widths. As the men were about to embark on a fourth crossing, the admiral stepped forward and raised both hands in the air, palms outward, to bring the exercise to a halt. By their rule-of-thumb form of measuring, the ship had listed a full plank for each time the deck was crossed. Had we carried on, Matsson told the board of enquiry, the *Vasa* would have capsized on the spot. He said he had tried to discuss the problem with Fleming but that the admiral's only response was that the shipbuilder had built ships before, so he must surely know his own business. Beneath his breath Matsson heard him mutter 'If only His Majesty were at home!' But Gustavus Adolphus was away in Prussia on military business and did not learn of the fate of his beautiful new flagship until two weeks later. When he did so, he too made an immediate presumption of incompetence or negligence and insisted that the guilty parties be found and punished. And yet, as successive witnesses could testify, the king himself had been a party to the ship's design and had approved it at every stage. Indeed, the unusually large number of heavy cannon on board had been at his specific instruction. 'Well then, whose fault it is?' asked a member of the board of enquiry. The lease-holder at Skeppsgården, a man named Arent de Groot, scratched his chin and replied that God alone knew the answer to that question. And since neither God nor the king

could conceivably have any fault in the matter, the board discharged itself without ever finding anyone guilty of anything.

Salvage operations began three days after the ship sank. A team led by the English expert Ian Bulmer succeeded in raising the *Vasa* to an upright position on the seabed on the first day at work, but were then unable to build on their achievement. A succession of adventurers, few of them Swedish, followed, contracted to attempt what was considered the most important part of the salvage, the recovery of the large number of new, bronze cannon, each weighing up to a ton, now languishing uselessly on the seabed. They were no more successful than Bulmer had been. Not until the 1660s, with Gustavus Adolphus long dead and Queen Kristina a private citizen living in Rome, was the problem of how to retrieve these guns eventually solved by two professional salvage experts, a Swede from Värmland named Albrecht von Treileben and his German business partner Andreas Peckell. At some point in their travels they had come across a new invention, the diving bell, and been sufficiently impressed by its potential to invest in one of their own.

It was this technological wonder that finally revealed to me, on subsequent visits, the sense and even the glory in the whole Vasa museum project, which had at first visit seemed such an odd celebration of incompetence and failure, as inappropriate as asking members of the public to admire the beauties of a raised and restored *Titanic*. A life-size copy of the diving bell is among the many sideshows in the museum's great hall. When I visit now I always head straight for it and am each time struck by the same rare sense of admiration for the ingenuity, the fortitude, the bravery and determination of the human race. Each time I contemplate it, I never fail to recall the remarkable account left by an Italian traveller named Francesco Negri, a priest travelling in Scandinavia who happened to be passing through Stockholm in October 1663.

Negri was staying in the city with friends, and in the course of their conversation he learned of the performance that was mesmerizing the whole of Stockholm that year: the sight of a man who was able to 'walk under the water'. Negri expressed an interest in seeing the miracle for himself and was duly taken to the site of the salvage operation at Strömmen. As their small craft approached the place of salvage, Negri says, they saw a small boat at anchor, an inelegant, battered, sturdy little vessel ringed around by a number of other small bobbing boats. This battered little craft had all manner of mysterious clutter strewn across its deck – thick cables, block and tackle, and several metal poles with hooks on the end that reminded him of shepherd's crooks. He learned, either first hand in conversation with Peckell or had the information conveyed to him by his hosts, that the divers were attempting to bring up the guns from the sunken ship, followed by all the ballast; after that, his informant believed, it would be a relatively simple matter to raise the hull itself. Pointing to the array of variously hooked and tipped poles, Peckell explained that the purpose of them was to rip away the planking around the gun-ports to make it easier to get at the cannons.

In his account Negri then goes on to consider the diving bell itself, which stands on a raft floating just next to the battered little vessel. This bell seems to him a remarkable invention. It enables a man to descend beneath the surface of the water and remain there for up to half an hour at a time. Although the design is not new – von Treileben introduced this fantastic piece of equipment as early as 1658, following a number of successful trials on the west coast – this is the first time it has been seen in use in the waters around Stockholm. Negri learns that the water in the east is not as clear or clean as it is off Gothenburg, but that the divers have such faith in their equipment that they are confident of success. He watches as one diver is readied for a descent, being helped into his diving gear as he sits on a stool. The outfit includes leather boots and a leather suit, both in double thickness. The tunic is sealed by iron rings and straps. A cap of ordinary cloth is placed on his head and he is ready to go down. The diver rises and in his awkward leather suit stumps a few paces to the side of the boat and contemplates the bell. It is, Negri notes, an anonymous and almost insignificant-looking creation. He estimates its height to be about one and a quarter metres. Its shape resembles that of a large church bell. Two men are needed to operate the block and tackle that is used to raise it from the platform.

As the bell slowly sways up into the air, Negri now sees the circular platform suspended on ropes half a metre below the skirt of the bell. He watches the diver's slow step up onto this, watches him stoop to receive the tools being handed to him by his assistants – tools that he will need to carry out his work 30 metres (98 feet) below the surface of the water. The most important of these, Negri is told, is the stout wooden pole, 2 metres long and tipped with an iron hook. The focus of the search is the ship's valuable cannons. Once the diver has located a gun, other specialist tools will be needed, including a large pair of tongs and a variety of grappling irons. For the actual raising of heavy items from the decks of the *Vasa*, a thick rope is used. The diver takes this

inside the bell with him. One end of it is attached to the raft, and his task after submersion is to secure the other end to the object to be salvaged. When he is ready to go the driver gives a hand signal.

Two men manning the block and tackle hoist the bell out over the surface of the water and Negri watches as it slowly disappears from sight. He describes the principle that now comes into operation. A pocket of air is trapped in the shoulder of the bell as it sinks under the waves, and for the next thirty minutes or so this is the diver's only supply of oxygen as he carries out his work in his thick leather suit, prodding about in the darkness with his hooks and grapples.

After about twenty minutes, rather less than the advertised time, the submerged man gives a tug on the rope that runs from the bell to the raft and he is hoisted back to the surface. On this occasion the haul is a heavy oak plank with iron fittings. Afterward Negri talks to the diver and learns that the truncated session was due to the unusual coldness of the water. It is, after all, late October. As he talks to the diver he notices that the man is shivering, despite his thick leather clothing. Then, like some twenty-first-century television traveller, Negri asks if he might be allowed to take a dive in the bell himself. The Swedes are impressed by his spirit as much as by this evidence of real interest in the work, but his request is rejected: the water is much too cold. Negri did not stay there long enough to see any cannons being raised, but he was told that the guns on the second and third decks had to be eased out through the gun-ports using a special technique, which its inventors declined to describe to him in any detail, fearing that it might become common knowledge and so harm their prospects of further salvage commissions. However it was done, it was notably successful: between them, von Treileben and Peckell's divers managed to salvage well over fifty guns from the wreck of the *Vasa*. Documents show that fifty-three of them were shipped to Lübeck in 1665.

And that, apart from the raising of one last cannon in 1683 in which no one appears to have shown any particular interest, was that. Soon, the *Vasa* and its strange fate and even its location had been all but forgotten. Matters remained so for the next 330 years, until 1956, when an amateur marine archaeologist named Anders Frantzen, who had developed an obsession with the sunken ship, finally managed, after several seasons of searching, to locate the wreck; and the long, slow process of raising and restoring the *Vasa* began.

The museum itself opened in 1990. Because it is situated just a short bus ride from the bus station in central Stockholm, where, when travelling to Gotland, I always had a wait of several hours for the connection to Nynæshamn and the ferry, I must have visited the Vasa museum five or six times – more often than either of my other two tourist options, the Strindberg Museum on Drottninggatan and the plaque at the junction of Sveavägen and Olof Palmes gata, marking the spot where Swedish Prime Minister Olof Palme was shot and killed on 28 February 1986. Usually when I travelled to Gotland it was in connection with the book I was working on about the Vikings, and one day as I left the museum and was making my way to the stop to catch the bus back into the centre the thought struck me that Rudbeck's theories of Sweden's Atlantean past, Gustavus Adolphus's great *Vasa* ship and the adventures of the Swedish Rus, those Vikings who travelled east across the Baltic and made their greatest mark on history over there, all had something in common as symbols of Sweden's brief century as an imperial great power. All three were:

1. Magnificent.
2. Ephemeral.
3. Impossible.

Magnificent, because all empires are in some way magnificent. Ephemeral and ultimately impossible, because Swedes in the seventeenth century, like the Rus in the ninth and tenth centuries, simply did not have the human resources to sustain the empires gained by their military prowess.

6

Abductions: The War Between the Danes and Algerians

IN 2015 I SPENT MOST OF THE MONTH OF APRIL SITTING at my desk in Forskersal 6 at Oslo's National Library translating the first chapter of a novel called *Kule* (*Bullet*) by the Norwegian novelist Jan Ove Fredriksen. The publisher wanted it done in time to take it with her to the annual Frankfurt Book Fair in October. At a certain point, my understanding stumbled over the following sentence: '*Historien er ikke alltid hva du tror den var,' sa Rank*. It was not so much the meaning of the sentence as something about the tenses that tripped me up in the middle of what had been, until then, a pleasurable ride atop Fredriksen's always amusing and inventive prose. The sentence came as a narrative comment on a passage in which the fictional narrator of the novel, Bart Rank, describes his consternation on consulting a volume (Volume 5) of *Den Lille Salmonsen*, a popular encyclopaedia in Norwegian and Danish homes, with the intention of reading the entry on Franz Kafka, and finding no reference there to the great writer but instead an entry on a German psychoanalyst named Gustav Kafka, author of several books on the psychology of animals. In an unbrained moment, Rank wonders whether Franz Kafka has already been forgotten, or perhaps not yet been remembered. The preoccupation with Kafka arises because Rank is at Oslo University studying *Litteraturvitenskap*, a self-confounding term best translated as 'Literary Science'. He has been asked to write a paper on Kafka's novel *The Castle* and, in despair at being unable to find anything interesting or original to say, has turned to this encyclopaedia. He then looks up the entry on Knut Hamsun, and finds himself similarly wrong-footed, for the article gives only the date of Hamsun's birth, 1859. But Hamsun is dead, surely? Only then does he check the date of publication at the front of the volume: 1938.

Perhaps it was mental exhaustion that brought me to a dead stop at what now seems a quite simple sentence, one that can easily and smoothly be translated into English: '"History isn't always what you think it was," said Rank.' Or an aversion to writing down a sentence that I did not understand myself, even though it appeared to convey a meaning. For whatever reason, I felt it necessary to talk to Jan Ove personally before continuing.

He lives not far from me, and when I called him up he readily agreed to meet and talk over a meal in the pleasant surroundings of Herregårdskroen, an open-air café overlooking the lake in the middle of Frogner Park. I was halfway through my first pint when I saw him approaching round the corner from the *pétanque* court, resolutely staring down at the impacted grass pathway as he passed between the rows of white wooden tables and chairs. As always, he was immaculately dressed, wearing a pale-yellow linen suit, collarless white shirt and hand-stitched tan leather boots, pointed, with Cuban heels. The waitress, a young Swede with a 'Z' shaved into the side of her head, immediately approached the table to take our orders: the restaurant's crispy French chicken for me, Herregårdskroen's own Hamburger Special for Jan Ove and a *hveteøl*, a wheat beer. It was not until we were onto our second pints and the food had arrived that Jan Ove, shy as usual, began to open up in the discursive way familiar to me from his novels, after I had explained to him the reason for our meeting.

'Rank suffers from the encyclopaedia problem,' he said. 'I do too. It's actually very dangerous for me to open an encyclopaedia, I should never do it. The problem is that the rigidly alphabetic ordering of the entries – and this is, incidentally, something that does not happen with Wikipedia, which I think may be a failing, but that's another story, but anyway, as you know, *Kule* is set in the 1970s long before the internet – the rigidly alphabetical ordering of the entries gives the impression of a strong sense of order which is almost always completely and even fiercely contradicted by the meaning and content of those same entries. You remember the puzzlement Rank has over the fact that the date of Hamsun's death is missing; in actual fact, if you'll recall, what he was looking up was the entry for Hamster, because the girl he's in love with owns a hamster and Rank intends to pose as someone who knows a lot about them as a way of getting to know her. But on his journey there he's distracted by the entry on Hamsun. It starts calling to him from one side of his field of vision. An entry on Hamsters dense with zoological terminology, Latin names, esoteric book lists, followed by an entry on Knut Hamsun on the same page. It's irritating, but at the same time very interesting. And that's just the beginning of it...'

Jan Ove took a long drink of his *hveteøl* and with a spreading motion of his fingers brushed froth from the tips of his well-maintained handlebar moustache. He squinted up into the afternoon sunlight falling through the elms along the shores of the lake. 'History isn't always what you think it was,' he said pensively, quite as though he had never heard the sentence before. He fell silent for a few moments, and when he spoke again I was expecting him to explain it, or expand on it, or even say that he no longer knew what it meant and perhaps we ought just to drop it. Instead, he returned to the subject of encyclopedias and the problem of the fluid nature of history that lay at the heart of the sentence.

'It's particularly interesting,' he said, 'when two encyclopaedias contradict each other. Factually, yes of course, that's in itself interesting. But what's even more interesting is when authors of different entries on the same subject take a quite different view of the subject. Take the case of the Norwegian Methuselah Christian Drakenberg. Look him up in Aschehoug's *Norsk Biografisk Leksikon*, Volume 3, from 1926, and you will find a date of birth, 18 November 1626, in

Blomsholm in the district of Skee, which was at that time part of the Norwegian Bohuslän that is now part of Sweden, followed by a two-and-a-half-page entry on his extraordinary life. How he served seven kings of Denmark-Norway as a seaman during the course of that interminable series of wars against Sweden. How he was captured by Muslim pirates in 1694 and spent fifteen years as a slave in Algiers and made a daring escape at the age of eighty-four and after all sorts of adventures got back home to Denmark. Lodging in a boarding house in North Jutland at the age of ninety-six he picks a fight with a Dutch visitor who has complained about the quality of his landlady's cheese; the Dutchman's friends join in and he gets beaten up so badly he has to walk on crutches for the next three weeks. In 1732 he's at a gathering in Copenhagen where he gets introduced as a phenomenon on account of his great age. He overhears some Frenchmen, unaware of his fluency in their language, openly casting doubt upon it among themselves and so he makes the long trip back home to Norway and returns with what appears to be documentary proof of it. The following year he has an unpleasant health scare when he finds that he has expelled a large worm from his bottom during a night-time visit to the toilet.

'In 1737 Drakenberg finally decides that it's time to settle down and marries a woman of sixty, a widow. She dies not long after the wedding. He tells his anonymous amanuensis that he caught a cold for the first time in his life when he was 124 years old, but then hastens to correct himself; he had almost forgotten, this was the second time, the first time was in Portugal, when he unwisely ate too many Portuguese sardines. Drakenberg gets into fights with people less than a quarter his age, he chases after girls; at 127 years old he falls in love with a farmer's daughter and asks her to marry him, but she won't have him and he falls into a grieving and inconsolable rage.

'His age starts to catch up with him. In August 1771 he notices his sight is starting to fade. He suffers constantly from a loud noise in his ears that sometimes seems to take the form of a choir of angels. On September 1772 – a Saturday – he experiences chest pains so severe that he vows on the spot to give up beer and spirits and restrict himself to tea, which he drinks in enormous quantities. Realizing he hasn't long to go, he has the last rites administered by a pastor named Middelbøe. He loses the power to make any kind of voluntary noise at all. Two days later, on 9 October, at Aarhus, he dies, 146 years old.

'All this you can read in Aschehoug's *Norsk Biografisk Leksikon*' said Jan Ove, prodding with his fork at the crust of his hamburger, as if he had only just noticed it on his plate and was wondering what it was. 'However, you look up that same life in Schultz's *Dansk Biografisk Leksikon*, Volume 6, from 1935, you'll find a single-page entry headed with the date of Drakenberg's death as being in the opinion of the writer the only reliable fact in the man's whole story, and the tone of the whole entry is one of doubt and even poorly disguised distaste. He refers to his 'semi-legendary memoirs' and with poorly disguised sarcasm talks about how Drakenberg had to 'put up with shipwrecks, imprisonment and fifteen years of slavery in Tripoli and other Mediterranean lands'. He mentions the trip back home to his birthplace to confound his French doubters, then goes on to describe how he made his own checks and found no trace of the priest who, Drakenberg says, baptized him nor any trace of the Pastor Cornelius Nicolai whom Drakenberg says copied out the entries from the church records for him in 1732. As far as he's concerned, he doesn't believe a word of it, and Drakenberg is just an old rogue. You look up Bonnier's *Biografiskt lexicon* from 1945 and he isn't even mentioned at all. It makes you realize, Robert, how hard it is to know what's true and what isn't.'

Jan Ove prodded again at his half-eaten hamburger. Suddenly he closed his eyes and an almost visible a cloak of silence settled around his shoulders. I saw that he had fallen into that state of unhappy and haunted distraction I have noticed before in the company of certain writers and painters, particularly the more successful ones, as though some kind of timer has rung inside them to say they should be somewhere else, preferably back home writing or painting. I was thus not greatly surprised when he presently, after the sketchiest of charades that included a harassed look down at his 'Rolex'* and a grunt of pretended surprise at the lateness of the hour, followed by a few improvised words about a forgotten appointment somewhere, stood up and shook my hand, leaving none of his beer but most of his hamburger, and slipped away between the tables, eyes glued to the ground, wanting to be looked at, needing to be invisible, disappearing into the trees along the side of the *pétanque* pit, reappearing briefly, heading for the main gates onto Kirkeveien.

*

I stayed on. I had finished my allotted number of hours on *Kule* for the day. It was a fine, mild afternoon, and because there is a special pleasure to be had in doing so in the afternoon in a large well-treed park in central Oslo, with the only sounds the faint thrum of traffic from Kirkeveien, the chirping of the sparrows and the distant shrieks and whoops of children playing in the open-air swimming pool on the far side of the park, I drank a third beer and began, in a sort of formal, now-let's-be-serious way, to relate Jan Ove's surprising account of the life and times of Christian Drakenberg, the 146-year-old man, to the subject of my question, the matter of the exact meaning of that particular sentence from the early pages of Jan Ove's novel which had puzzled me so.

Before long, however, in exactly the sort of 'encyclopaedic' way Jan Ove had been describing, I found myself thinking about the thing next to the thing I had intended to think about, in this case the peculiarly specific information that Drakenberg had been held as a slave by North African pirates for more than fifteen years. It seemed a surreal and scarcely credible fabrication. Walking home much later, and passing the Majorstua Always-Open Library, I punched in my code and twenty minutes later walked out again with several

---

* It was an imitation, which I knew he wore as a kind of private joke, since he had once told me the story of how he paid ten *yuan* for it from a man at a bus station in Chongqing who had another twenty of them for sale in the padded interior of his wooden display box.

back-numbers of *Skalk* and a copy of Vetle Lid Larsen's recent book on the subject of the Muslim enslavement of Christians in the sixteenth and seventeenth centuries, with particular reference to the Scandinavian experience.

That evening I learnt for the first time of the peculiarly and occasionally comically fraught relationship between Denmark-Norway and the Muslim rulers of North Africa throughout most of the seventeenth and much of the eighteenth century. When the Moors were driven out of Spain at the beginning of the seventeenth century, they settled along the 'Barbary' coast of North Africa in what are now the independent states of Algeria, Tunisia, Morocco and Libya. With their territories being largely desert, the inhabitants of these lands presently made piracy and slaving the centre of their economy. The natural field of activity for these piratical societies, of which Algiers became the centre, was the Strait of Gibraltar and the Mediterranean to which it gave access. Danish trading ships were regularly captured and towed into African ports, where their cargo was stolen and their crews sold into slavery. Between the middle of the sixteenth century and about 1830, the total number of Christians held in slavery in North Africa was in the region of 1.2 million, of whom an estimated 3,000–4,000 were Scandinavians.

Astounded as much by the very fact that such a state of affairs had ever existed as by the statistics, I placed the book down in my lap and for some reason thought again of Tranströmer's lines about time being more like a labyrinth than a straight line, and that if we press our ears against the wall at the right place we might hear our own footsteps and voices passing by on the other side. Is this, I asked myself, the same as saying that history repeats itself? That raid, for example, of which I had just been reading in *Skalk*, in which Barbary pirates descended upon the coast of Iceland in 1627 and which the Icelanders still call 'the Turkish Raid' – was it not, in surprising ways, similar to the first recorded Viking raid on the British Isles, at Lindisfarne in 793, which announced to the Christian world of Britain and mainland Europe the commencement of the Viking Age? And if that first Norwegian raid on the Christian monastery had seemed to its earliest historian, the Anglo-Saxon cleric Alcuin, a voyage 'not thought possible', then how much more extraordinary must the sight of those four pirate ships from far-off Algiers and Morocco have seemed to the Icelandic inhabitants of remote Grindavik, Austfirðir and the Vestmannaeyjar when they appeared over the horizon one summer morning?

After the end of the Icelandic commonwealth and its enrolment as part of the Crown of Norway in 1252, further change came with Norway's decline as part of the Union of Kalmar in 1397, and in the aftermath of the Reformation, ownership of the island had passed to Denmark. The great warrior-heroes of the Saga Age, the Egils, the Gunnars and Grettirs, the Bloodaxes and Ironsides were long vanished by 1627, to be replaced – in the European imagination at least – by that race of contented troglodytes whom Adam of Bremen praised in such blithe ignorance in the *Gesta Hammaburgensis*. Perhaps, it seemed to me, Adam was not far wrong after all to suggest that this community quietly savoured its remoteness and isolation from the rest of the world, somewhat as members of the tiny community that inhabited the island of St Kilda until 1930 were said to have done, formally shaking each other by the hand every day and treating each other with unfailing courtesy and respect. Against men as dedicated to violence as those Algerian pirates such people would have stood little chance. The local priest, Pastor Ólafur Egilsson, left a record of the response when rumours of the presence of the pirate ships first reached the Icelanders. When those in the Vestmannaeyjar first began talking about the pirates in the village of Grindavik, he wrote, there was no lack of big words and bold display, especially from those in authority. There was a lot of activity and building of defences, and these carried on until word came that the pirates had left the country, and that it might be a long time before there was a threat against the Vestmannaeyjar. At this, he noted, a sort of indifference descended on the people. They ceased their preparations and remained convinced they were safe and that nothing was going to happen.

On the morning of 16 July, which was a Monday, the pirates raided Grindavik, a community so poor that the only thing they found worth stealing were the inhabitants themselves: twelve Icelanders and three Danes. Frustrated in an attempt to make a further landing at Bessastaðir, they returned to Morocco to sell their captives. A second pirate ship under the command of a renegade Dutchman known as Mourat Rais had arrived in Austfirðir, in the south-east of Iceland, early in July and stolen cattle, sheep, horses, silver, as well as capturing 110 Icelanders. Moving south, the pirates reached the Vestmannaeyjar on 16 July, and for the next seventy-two hours rampaged and raided. Thirty-four people were killed, mostly the old, the sick and those who tried to resist them. Another 242 people, half the population of the island of Heimaey, were captured and taken back to Algiers and sold into slavery. Some went to good masters who treated them well, some to tyrants who kept them chained in underground dungeons, fed them little, worked them hard and punished them harshly. Some few agreed to be circumcised and converted to the Islamic faith.

The women, and some of the younger men, were sold into harems. Fair-skinned Christian women were especially valuable and in a raid on the Faroe Islands in 1629 women alone were abducted. With the kind of admiration that extraordinary tales of survival always excite in me, I read the story of one woman abducted in the Vestmannaeyjar raid, Guðríður Símonardóttir. By the time she landed in Algiers, slaves made up 20 per cent of the city's total population of a hundred thousand. The ransoming of slaves to the heads of European Christian states was another lucrative source of income, and in 1636, after nine years in the Algerian dey's household, Guðríður's freedom was bought back by the King of Denmark, and she was able to make her way to Europe. But the money was not enough to secure the release of her son, who had been two years old at the time of the raid and was now eleven; she had to leave him behind when the ship carrying her and other freed slaves sailed for Copenhagen. There, now aged thirty-nine, the former slave was given to the care of a young Icelander studying for the priesthood, Hallgrímur Pétursson, who was charged with the task of re-educating her and other freed slaves in the Christian faith, on the assumption that they had lost the understanding of it during the long years of their enslavement. Within a short time, Hallgrímur and Guðríður became lovers and she was pregnant with his child. This unexpected development was made still more problematic because, as far as Guðríður knew, she had a husband back home in Heimaey to whom she was still legally married. Enquiries revealed, however, that he had drowned some years earlier, so the lovers were able to marry and settle down in a village just north of Reykjavik.

Without abandoning his vocation, Hallgrímur went on to become one of his country's most famous religious poets, the George Herbert of Iceland, some of whose verses are still included in the Icelandic psalm book. God alone knows what remote regions of existential understanding Guðríður's experiences had given her access to. Perhaps she visited them on those occasions on Sunday mornings when her husband mounted the pulpit to preach his sermon, at which point people noticed that she would rise without fail from her seat and leave the church to sit on a bench outside. On the basis of this behaviour, some supposed she had converted to Islam during her enslavement. But how greatly we value the memories of who we think we are, and where we come from! How we cling to these memories, when the greater wisdom might be simply to understand and accept that *the past can change its shape.*

*

About three weeks after our meal in the park Jan Ove and I met again to go over his responses to my translation of the opening chapter of *Kule*. The weather was uncertain, with dark clouds approaching from the west over the dome of the Colosseum cinema complex, so we met indoors at Larsens Mat-og-Vinhus on Sørkedalsveien, a dimly lit, old-established and friendly bar just next to the side entrance to Majorstua metro station. Its most singular feature is an open wooden gallery about a metre high which runs across the top of the room above its three street-facing window-booths. This gallery is separated into three small rooms, each containing some tiny item of furniture, such as a table or a rocking chair, and inhabited by a family of celestial trolls: a bearded man, a hook-nosed woman wearing a headscarf and a cradle for the imagined baby.

I took a seat in the central booth, ordered a half litre of Hansa beer and spent the next few minutes studying the view through the window. It looks out directly onto one of the busiest pedestrian crossings in all Oslo. This view is one of Larsens' greatest attractions – for the solitary drinker in particular. Looking out through that large, clear rectangular sheet of glass is rather like being at the cinema and watching a film that has no main characters and no plot and yet is so full of a kind of bubbling moment-by-moment interest that in the end it is only with the greatest regret, and the fear that one is missing something of crucial importance the whole mysterious show has been leading up to, that one looks away. The human traffic grows denser as evening draws on, because this is the main route linking travellers on the metro with the six auditoria of the copper-domed Colosseum complex, its cupola just visible between the mirroring walls of the giant KPMG building, erected some fifteen years ago to replace a similar but much smaller building that was demolished to make way for it. The demolition attracted great media and television attention because the exploder in charge turned out to be a woman. There is also a line of shops that changes ownership and identity with the regularity of the seasons, neither car hire nor sushi firms nor bodybuilders' shops seemingly able to establish themselves for more than a few months at a time.

Jan Ove arrived, brushed a hand over his hair to shake off the light drizzle, gave his eyes a moment to adapt to the dim interior and then sat down on the other side of the booth. A few moments later the waiter, an unshaven and rather fearsome-looking Latvian wearing a dark blue cotton apron, appeared with his drink, an alcohol-free Clausthaler. From a newspaper interview I knew that Jan Ove observed a routine that consisted of two days' writing followed by a day's drinking, followed by two more days' writing, and deduced that today must be a working day.

We started on his comments on the translation. Scandinavian writers are usually so fluent in English that many assume their written English is the same. Mercifully Jan Ove was not one of them. I think our most extensive discussion was about the use of 'perhaps' contra 'maybe'.

And then we spoke of other things, including what we had been reading recently. As succinctly as I could I described the story of Guðríður's life and her strange fate, and ended by repeating the thought that had occurred to me – *the past can change shape* – adding that it had seemed to me, even as I was thinking it, to be quite close to the idea that he had expressed in *Kule*, the one we had discussed at our last meeting.

'This is a very interesting subject altogether,' commented Jan Ove, once I had finished my account. 'This whole subject of the relationship between Denmark and the pirate states of the North African coast in the seventeenth and eighteenth centuries has fascinated me ever since I was a small boy. The incident of which you speak, the Turkish Raid of 1627, was a rare example of the range of those pirates whom I, in my boyhood, always thought of as Vikings in reverse. I recall that it was my earliest ambition to run away to sea and join them, since I assumed they were still at it. As children it takes such a long time for us to understand that most of what we learn about is already ancient history. To this day I recall the huge relief I felt at the age of seven when an older boy at school reassured me that if another war broke out, the Romans would be on our side. So I wanted to be a Turkish pirate, the terror of the seven seas, wild-bearded and red-turbaned, with a scimitar sword stuck into the sash of my billowing red silk trousers.

'Any Danish ship that passed through the Strait of Gibraltar was likely to be attacked and towed into port in Algiers, its cargo stolen and the members of its crew sold off into slavery. The problem became so great that in the end, after long and intricate negotiations, the Danes and the Algerians finally agreed on a treaty that guaranteed the freedom of the Danish flag and promised that Algerian ships would never approach the coast of Denmark or its northern or southern colonies. In return the *dey* was to receive a large number of cannon, 4,000 bombs, gunpowder, bullets, and timber suitable for ship-building. Half of this one-off gift was to be re-given each year. I don't think the *dey* ever liked the agreement. They spent a lot of time looking for things to complain about so that they could get back to being pirates again. It was a very one-sided and costly arrangement. One year, the *dey* was compensated after he complained that the cannonballs delivered that year were *not round enough*. Another time, when the gift ship sank on the way out, the Danes hurriedly reassured the dey that he would receive a double settlement the following year.

'The Danes reached similar agreements with the other North African pirate states – Morocco, Tripoli and Tunisia. But Algiers remained the main problem. A courtesy observed with each change of ruler was that extra gifts would be presented to the new incumbent – gold watches, gold tobacco boxes, that kind of thing. But then there was one dey who didn't think it was enough and on top of all his other gifts demanded an annual present of jewellery. In 1769 this *dey* demanded an extra-large payment to leave the Danish ships alone and gave them three months in which to pay up. When the Danes plucked up the courage to complain, the *dey* accused them of lending out their privilege of passage documents to German traders from Hamburg. Not long afterwards, not even waiting for the three months deadline to pass, the *dey* declared war on Denmark. If it happened now you'd be astounded. You wouldn't believe it. You might even laugh. But I was a young boy when I first read about this, and Algiers declaring war on Denmark didn't seem surreal to me. Why would it? When you're a child you have no basis on which to distinguish between what is normal and what is surreal. And more and more it seems to me anyway that sooner or later all history seems surreal.'

Jan Ove paused and frowned, as though suddenly unsure of the meaning of what he had just said. As the waiter limped by I took the opportunity to place a silent order, two fingers of the right hand held up in a loose, v-for-victory sign, accompanied by a slight lifting of the eyebrows, all of which elicited a single nod, yes, he had understood my meaning and would be back.

'At war with Algeria', Jan Ove went on. 'Algeria declaring war on my country, Denmark. This was in 1770. How my loyalties were torn! I still wanted to be an Arab Viking, an Algerian pirate. But a declaration of war is different. It brings a new seriousness to things. Only countries declare war on each other. I was Danish. I knew I was Danish. And I wanted Denmark to win that war. I had to abandon my love of the Algerian pirates. But as things turned out the war was a disaster. A fleet left Copenhagen for Algiers. Two thousand sailors, five hundred marines. Four ships of the line, two frigates, two *bombardierfartøjer* – what is that in English? – and a troop ship.

'Not long after they left port there was an outbreak of typhoid on board. Men going down like flies. By the time the fleet reached Cadiz the hospital ship couldn't take any more. She was so overloaded she had to be towed along. And when there was a following wind the stench of putrid and rotting flesh was unendurable. At sunrise one morning a coffin was seen bobbing up and down on the waves alongside the hospital ship. It was the ship's priest. They hadn't put enough stones in his coffin to sink it. It was a farce', said Jan Ove, glancing his thanks at the waiter as he placed another Clausthaler on the table in front of him, another Hansa for me. 'The Danes didn't have enough men left alive to carry out the planned landing so they lay to and for the next ten days bombarded Algiers from what you might call a safe distance. It turned out to be the longest naval battle in Danish history. Of the hundreds of cannonballs that rained down over the rooftops of Algiers only one actually detonated. They gave up and went home. Next year they came back, but with different tactics this time, blockading the approaches to Algiers and forcing the *dey* to negotiate. A revision of the original treaty of 1746 was agreed on, although the terms were pretty much the same. And believe it or not that treaty remained in force until as late as 1830, when the French invaded and occupied the country in response to a diplomatic slight. The *dey* whacked the French consul over the head with his fan, something like that. So they invaded. It meant the end of piracy and having to pay what amounted over the years to a huge amount of what I suppose you could call "protection money".

'So it's who the writer *feels for* in history that determines the way it gets written', he said. This was after a long moment in which his attention appeared to be riveted by the sight of a beggar, neither an ethnically Norwegian drug-addict selling the latest edition of = *Oslo,** a Norwegian version of the *Big Issue*, nor a stout old Roma woman sitting on a cardboard box knitting woollen bootees for babies, but instead a story-book tramp of the type I seem to remember from my earliest childhood in England, with wild brown beard and matted dreadlocks. He was a man of indeterminate age, whom I had seen in various locations around central Oslo, always sitting on the pavement with his legs stretched out before him, his shoulders swathed in a striped, wine-red blanket, his feet wrapped in soiled bundles of cloth; a man from another lifetime of homelessness and begging, and still with a faded wisp of complete personal freedom hanging about him. He was on the opposite side of the road to us, his back leant up against the bright green bulge of one of the recycling bins outside Majorstua school, smiling often, at intervals beating the pavement in a series of rapid and hard blows with a stone held in his right hand that must have been painful. I had a conversation with him once. From what I could gather we were talking about language. With a strange intensity he maintained that he was a gifted linguist, capable of discoursing in many different languages, though even his Norwegian, coming as it did in long, disjointed salvoes, was hard to make sense of.

'Who you *feel* for,' Jan Ove repeated with emphasis. Returning his gaze to the tabletop and carefully drawing a circle with his finger in some spilt beer he said that throughout the century that saw the worst excesses of Christian enslavement by Arabs the Danes, too, had been slavers, carrying out abductions of their own, albeit few in number, and not for the purposes of slavery but in pursuit of what so easily seems to us now the crackpot and addled pursuit of a scientific understanding of our fellow human beings. 'On a number of separate occasions,' he said, 'Inuit Greenlanders were tricked on board

---

* The name means 'Like Oslo' or 'Equals Oslo', implying a complete identific-ation between the magazine and the city.

Danish ships and brought back to Denmark to see if they could be taught Danish and an understanding of the Christian religion. The first four were abducted in 1605. One was shot dead by the ship's captain for trying to escape and his body thrown overboard. The other three, whose names were Umik, Oqaq and Kigutikaaq, seemed at first to have resigned themselves to their fate with a genial good nature. Contemporary observers in Copenhagen reported that they smiled a lot and seemed cheerful. When unobserved, however, they spent their time secretly building a boat and one day made their escape. But, having very little idea of precisely where they were, they soon had to put ashore on Skåne, where they were held and in due course returned to the capital.

'All three returned to Greenland as part of a second expedition that set sail in May 1606 under the command of a Scot, Captain John Cunningham, the idea perhaps being that their presence would ease relationships with the natives. But Oqaq and Umik died on the outward journey, and the fate of Kigutikaaq is unknown. As before, Inuit were abducted, five this time, of whom one jumped overboard, two tried to escape in a kayak shortly after reaching Copenhagen, one was captured and brought back, the other was never heard of again. The three survivors all died within twelve years of their abduction. Of bewilderment and homesickness I shouldn't wonder.

'Actually,' said Jan Ove, 'I think another reason for bringing them back was to prove that the lost or forgotten colony of Greenland really had been rediscovered. An attempt was made to set up a Greenland Whaling Company by two ships that set sail in 1636. They were under orders to bring back native Greenlanders between the ages of sixteen and twenty, again with the aim of teaching them the fear of God, the Danish language and the art of reading, another of those bizarre ethnographic experiments. Two were captured this time. To prevent them escaping they were tied to the mast until the ships were well out to sea, yet the instant they were released both men rushed to the side of the ship and jumped overboard in a pitiful attempt to swim home.

'You might almost think', Jan Ove added with a mournful smile, 'that they knew what was in store for them. The last in the series of expeditions was in 1654. Another six Greenlanders were abducted. Same story. One jumped overboard. One old woman was set ashore. Four survived the trip back south – a twenty-five-year-old woman named Kabelau, her father Ihob, a middle-aged woman named Küneling, and Sigoka, a thirteen-year-old girl. Apparently they did learn to speak some Danish, but according to Thomas Bartholin, the doctor who attended them, the climate and the unfamiliar diet and way of life were too much for them and within five years all of them, including Sigoka, were dead. There's a portrait study of the four of them painted in Bergen when the ship put in there on its way down to Copenhagen. It's in the Ethnographic Collection of the National Museum in Copenhagen. Nothing ever came of the whaling company.'

He laughed – 'I dunno,' he said, 'Denmark and colonies, they kept trying. At the same time as all of this was going on they were trying to establish a colony in Trankebar,* on the other side of the world.'

'Perhaps all this colonial activity was the Danish response to Sweden's sudden rise to the status of European "Great Power",' I suggested hesitantly, although certain that I was right.

'I doubt it,' he said. 'I think it was more likely an attempt to keep up with the big boys of Europe. Spain. England. Holland. Portugal. All the Scandinavian countries have this, you know. This fear of being regarded as peripheral and insignificant, parochial even, because of the location and the small populations. It gave them a puff to have a few Danish names blinking away on the far side of the world. It was mostly about status; they stayed well clear of any big power conflicts in the region. They lost money on it. Never made any money out of it.'

Jan Ove turned his glass between his fingers and laughed.

'It's ironic,' he said, 'the most successful enterprise turned out to be, guess what? – piracy. Trankebar was tiny. Of a total population of three hundred only sixty-seven were Danes, and twenty-four of those were children. There was practically no integration, though the man who was probably the most able and successful of the governors,

* Or 'Tranquebar', today Tharangambadi in India's Tamil Nadu.

a semi-literate soldier named Kongsbakken, excited the disgust of the man sent out to replace him because he'd married an Indian woman. No, almost from the beginning they were trying to get rid of the place, but they couldn't, nobody else wanted it. They were stuck with it for over two centuries until finally they sold it to the British East India Company for £225,000 pounds. But now listen to this, you who are so interested in Scandinavians and what makes us tick – in the early 1950s the Danes established ties of friendship with the former colony with a commemorative sailing from Copenhagen to Trankebar. There was some scientific research purpose attached to it too, I forget what, oceanography I think. The Galathea voyage. There was another voyage in 2006. The plan was to call in at Trankebar again but they had to drop it for security reasons, after all the trouble over Kurt Westergaard's Mohammed cartoons in *Jyllands Posten* the year before. No, the sale of Trankebar in 1845 was just another chapter in the general history of the diminution of Denmark. But not a bad thing if you ask me. It's like people said after 1864 – *Hvad udad tabes, skal indad vindes*, how would you translate that?'

In Danish those words have a nineteenth-century pathos to them. One imagines them being spoken by a sad-eyed man with a heavy black beard, gazing off into the distance as he addresses a small gathering of similarly bearded men and offers them this enigmatic crumb of comfort. My first thought was something in the direction of 'What you lose on the roundabouts you gain on the swings.' Somehow, it didn't seem dignified enough for such a venerable and poetic phrase.

'What is lost without shall be won back within,' I offered.

Jan Ove looked at me doubtfully, from which I understood that he had not followed my reasoning in opting for this stilted and archaic formulation. Anxious not to cause him a crisis of confidence in his translator, I at once reverted to my original suggestion, and he nodded in contented agreement. 'Yes. What you lose on the roundabouts you gain on the swings. That is very good. Anyway, one result of it all was that the Danes began to take their own history seriously.'

He glanced at his watch. Not the fake Rolex today but a handsome self-winding Ingersoll. The merest flicker and dip of the eyelids.

I looked out of the window. It had started to rain, quite heavily. A wind had risen and was swaying the crowns of the beech trees in the schoolyard and I suddenly felt that this must be the first day of autumn. The old tramp still sat there, imaginary bluebirds still fluttering around his shaggy head. A cyclist, his oiled and shaven head glistening in the rain, had stopped to talk to him, or listen to him talk, a pleasant, fixed smile on his face. Periodically the harsh clacking of the stone he beat against the pavement sounded – as he seemed every now and then to remember about it – as though it was his job and the world would stop turning if he neglected it.

'What I mean,' said Jan Ove presently, 'is that we Danes realized the truth of what Henrik Ibsen wrote in *Brand: Evig eies kun det tabte.* "We possess forever only that which has been lost." Although I think Ibsen borrowed this idea from Adam Oehlenschläger. It's very similar to something Oehlenschläger says in his poem "The Horns". Do you know that poem?'

I shook my head. I knew of the huge influence the Danish poet had exercised on the young Ibsen, both as a Scandinavian, in terms of Ibsen's early enthusiasm for Oehlenschläger's National Romanticism; and as a dramatist and poet. But I had read little of him and nothing of his poetry, for there can be few genres that have aged more dramatically than the various national romanticisms of the nineteenth century.

'Well, Oehlenschläger wrote "The Horns" in 1803 following the theft of the golden horns in the previous year.'

Jan Ove then related how two curved golden horns of great antiquity and exquisite beauty had been found at Gallehus, near Møgeltønder in southern Jutland. They had been found separately, accidentally, in the same field, almost a century apart in time, less than 20 metres apart. The first, which was longer and heavier, was found by a farm-girl named Kirsten Svendsdatter, on 20 July 1639, the second by a tenant- farmer named Erik Lassen while working in that same field, on 21 April 1734. Suddenly, taking me completely by surprise, Jan Ove stood up and adopting a sonorous Danish baritone declaimed a verse from Oehlenschläger's poem:

Skyen suser,
Natten bruser,
Gravhöien sukker,
Rosen sig lukker.
De övre Regioner
toner!
De sig möde, de sig möde,
de forklarede Höie,
kampfarvede, röde,
med Stierneglands i Öie.

'I som raver i blinde,
skal finde
et ældgammelt Minde,
der skal komme og svinde!
Dets gyldne Sider
skal Præget bære
af de ældste Tider.
Af det kan I lære.
Med andagtsfuld Ære
I vor Gave belönne.
Det skiönneste Skiönne,
en Möe
skal Helligdommen finde!*

* The clouds are bustling,
The night blasts rustling,
Sighs are breaking,
From grave-hills quaking,
The regions were under
Thunder.
Of the mighty and daring,
The ghosts there muster,
Stains of war bearing,
In their eye star lustre.
Ye who blind are straying,
And praying,

Shall an ag'd relic meet,
Which shall come and shall fleet,
Its red sides golden,
The stamp displaying
Of the times most olden
That shall give ye a notion
To hold in devotion
Our gift, is your duty!
A maiden, of beauty
Most rare.
Shall find the token!

(TRANSLATED BY GEORGE BORROW)

In an interior corner of the dimly lit bar the only other patron, an elderly man with sparse long grey hair and a black violin case on the seat beside him, gave a slow and slightly overlong round of applause. Jan Ove responded with a solemn bow before sitting down. His eyes were glowing and it occurred to me that perhaps I had been wrong, and this was not a working day but a drinking day, and he had been drinking at home before coming out to meet me.

'Well of course,' he went on, 'in those days they didn't have the reverence for the past we do today. Historic buildings were knocked down and the stone and timbers used to make new ones. For centuries farmers in Norway, Denmark and Sweden have been lifting stones from Viking Age burial mounds to repair their walls and build their sheep pens. When the first horn was presented to King Christian IV he gave it to his son Frederik who immediately handed it to one of his goldsmiths with orders to turn it into a drinking horn. Only the pleas of Ole Worm, the court physician and one of our first modern historians, saved it. The horns were simply regarded as valuable royal possessions, things which an absolute monarch might do absolutely whatever he liked with. Of course at this time there was no national museum in Denmark. No scientific archaeology. No one had any real idea of the age of the horns, nor even of their original function. The present was a small, intensely lit room, the past a cavernous basement, rarely visited and filled with a swirling fog, a lumber room in which old objects were piled together of which they knew nothing save that they pre-dated Christianity in Denmark, but whether by a few years or a few hundred years they had no idea. So for decades the beautiful horns were stored in the palace's art chamber, and so flimsily protected that on the night of 5 May 1802 a man named Niels Heidenreich broke in using the key to his own front door and a home-made copy of a second key. In the dead of night he carried them through the streets of Copenhagen to the kitchen of his own house in Larsbjørnstræde. There he melted them down and transformed them into more easily saleable assets like brooches, earrings and 'pagodas', the small gold coins from Trankebar when the colony was briefly permitted to mint its own currency. Though these were rare enough in the mother country at the best of times – I think only eight examples are known to the Institute of Numismatics – Heidenreich unwisely decided to counterfeit them in large numbers. In fact, they were so unfamiliar that Heidenreich had no idea of the correct design and simply added details of his own invention. The theft was investigated but no progress made until about a year later when a goldsmith named Fridrich Regnell reported Heidenreich to the police for having sold him twenty pagodas that were underweight. Heidenreich was arrested, the coins examined and found to be counterfeit, and after three days of questioning he confessed and was tried, convicted, and sentenced to life imprisonment at the Tugt-Rasp-og Forbedringshuset, the city's House of Correction.

'It was his second offence. In 1789, he had been sentenced to death for forging banknotes, but had his sentence commuted to life imprisonment to mark the birthday of Christian VII. When Heidenreich was released after serving nine years of his sentence, he had documents to prove that while in prison he had studied as a watchmaker and a goldsmith, and earned the right to practise as both, as well as a loan towards the purchase of the glass-polishing machine that he would need if he were to set up on his own. But for whatever reason things hadn't worked out for him and he spent most of the rest of his life in the House of Correction and was released in 1840, seventy-nine years old, his three children dead, his wife long ago divorced from him and remarried. He died four years later. I remember reading somewhere that he spent a lot of his thirty-seven years in jail trying to square the circle, a pursuit not finally discovered to be futile until 1882. Not that it would have stopped him, I suppose. If you need to pass the time for thirty-seven years it's probably as good a way to do it as any.'

The drinker over in the corner rose from his seat, picked up the violin case and made his way between the tables towards the door. As he passed our booth, he and Jan Ove exchanged a nod.

'Do you know him?'

'That's Ludvig Eikaas. The painter. Have you never seen his masterpiece? It's just a page torn out of his notebook. With the word *Jeg* across it in biro.'

I tried to look suitably impressed but mostly I thought again about the oddness of having a three-letter word to mean 'I'. I asked if Eikaas could play the violin as well as paint. I knew from the shape of the case he was carrying there was a *hardingfele* inside it, a five-stringed violin mostly used for folk music. The fifth is a drone string.

'He's probably going round the corner to Valka with it. They let him play it there. They let anybody do whatever they like there.'

He was referring to Valkyrien, a nearby bar with valkyrie-themed paintings on its walls.

'But he *can* play it?'

'Yes, sort of,' he shrugged. 'Anyway, as I was saying, the horns were gone. Literally. No longer existed. Gold is probably the only thing you would do that with. Steal it then turn it into something else. What you're stealing is not the horns themselves, or what they stand for, you're stealing what they're made of. There was an exhibition about the horns at the Copenhagen National Museum back in 2004 that included two pairs of beautiful drop-earrings displayed in a glass cage. The descriptive note said that circumstantial evidence made it almost *certain* that these were among the pieces Heidenreich made with the melted-down gold. And I remember looking at them and thinking: what, exactly *what* am I looking at here?'

Jan Ove stopped and looked directly at me, as though I might know the answer. I was about to speak but then he resumed, and I realized the pause had been rhetorical.

'I think this is perhaps what you meant when you said that the past can change its shape. Because what was I looking at? Two pairs of golden earrings. You can see their like in the window of any jeweller's shop. Take a walk a hundred metres down the road from here and you'll see a pair just like them in Thune's shop window. Or at least in the lockup cabinet inside. But what history do they contain? Do you see what I mean? In the most profound sense those earrings contained nothing of the horns at all. Two pairs of earrings. And if Ole Worm hadn't made his beautiful and intricate drawings of the first horn we would never even have known what one of them looked like at all. God bless the astonishing versatility of that man.

I think the only sensible way to look at it is to realize that the Gallehus horns were fated to be lost. Someone made them a millennium and a half ago. They vanished. They reappeared briefly in the dirt of that field, they vanished again. Oehlenschläger understood this. In his poem he derided the archaeologists who descended on the site later and began digging the field up. They're blind, he says. They don't get the point.'

More discreetly this time, Jan Ove again recited lines from Oehlenschläger's poem:

Og hen de stimle
I store Vrimle,
og grave og søge,
Skatten at forøge.
Men intet Guld!
Deres Haab har bedraget;
De see kun det Muld,
hvoraf de er taget.*

He rapped his finger on the table and leaned intently across towards me. 'You see what Oehlenschläger is saying? His *poem*. That's what he's saying. His poem is the real treasure. The value lies not in the thing itself but in the memory of the thing. That which cannot be stolen. *Evig eies kun det tabte*. Only when the reality is out of the way can the mythology begin.'

He sat back and continued. 'The ludicrous ease with which the horns were stolen added to the unexpected sense of loss the theft brought, and with it the realization that a nation needs a heritage, and that a heritage needs to be actively maintained. Constant vigilance is required or else it will disappear as soon as it's dead. The theft of

---

* *Forth rush with gabble*   *But there's no gold!*
A countless rabble;   *Their hope is mistaken;*
The earth they're upturning,   *They see but the mould,*
For the treasure burning.   *From whence it is taken.*
                                                       (TRANSLATED BY GEORGE BORROW)

the golden horns was the direct cause of the establishment in 1819 of a National Museum, in the loft of Trinitatis Church, which opened its doors to the public for the first time so that people could see their Danish past for themselves, with the exhibits neatly arranged according to Christian Jørgen Thomsen's inspired classification of the past into Stone, Bronze and Iron Ages, the first time such a classification had ever been used. Technically speaking I suppose the horns occupied an Age all their own, the Golden Age that every nation that intends to endure through history needs to have somewhere in its past. The function of the horns remains unknown. Were they *lur*, for sounding notes? Or drinking vessels, as Prince Frederik seemed to assume? Or did they have a ceremonial function that placed them at the centre of some pre-Christian religious ritual? No one knows. No one has any certain idea of what the intricate swirls and disguised runic inscriptions mean. But released from a physical existence, their subsequent history becomes a delirious dance to the music of myth.

'Some years before the theft exact copies were made – two copies. One sent as a gift to an Italian bishop was lost when the ship carrying them sank on the voyage to Italy. Another was sent to the museum in Dresden and never heard of again. Sometime in the 1850s, the archaeologist king, Frederik VII, who, while not digging up the ground in Jelling and elsewhere in search of it, was moodily presiding over the breakup of what remained of the Danish Empire, ordered new copies of the horns to be made, in gilded silver. In the grip of the myth of history into which the theft had transformed them he instructed his goldsmith to make them slightly larger and still more ornate than the originals. These discreetly falsified horns are the horns I remember from my childhood visits to the National Museum in Ny Vestergade. Over the preceding 150 years they had *become* the Golden Horns. And so, naturally, when they were put on public display in 2007 at an exhibition celebrating Jelling's role in the history of Denmark, thieves broke into the gallery at night and stole them. The stolen copies were recovered a few days later and two young men apprehended. Both were given short jail sentences.

'So you're right,' he said. '*History never sleeps*. That is what you said, isn't it?'

I said I couldn't remember but it was something like that. He looked at me, then at his watch, quite openly this time, shaking it a few times, holding it up to his ear to check on the tick, as though he didn't quite trust the natural motion of his body to keep the main-spring wound.

'I have to get back,' he said. 'I'm in the middle of a paragraph.'

He stood up and shuffled sideways out of the window booth.

'You're English,' he said. 'Tell me, do they have Lurpak butter in England?'

I told him you would not find a supermarket in England that did not have a packet of Lurpak butter shining somewhere on its shelves.

He lifted his leather jacket off the peg on the back of the bench and shrugged it on. Halfway through, with one elbow still poking up towards the ceiling, he stopped and looked at me.

'Next time you're buying a packet,' he said, 'check the logo: *Lur* means horn. Those two curly things at the top, those are the Gallehus horns. *Ha det så lenge.*'

Momentarily taken aback by the abruptness of his departure, and in urgent need of some displacement activity, I immediately pulled out my smartphone and, for several seconds, gazed at the screen in rapt but empty absorption, until presently it occurred to me to Google 'Gallehus' and 'Lurpak'. Clicking on the 'Images' button of the results and peering closely at the logo on the Lurpak packet, it seemed to me possible that Jan Ove was mistaken. Certainly two horns were depicted; but both had flattened, trumpet-like openings that distinguished them clearly from the images of the stubby Gallehus horns. I checked the Lurpak website page on the company history but found no mention there of the Gallehus horns, only a reference to lurs as 'Bronze Age musical instruments that have become symbols of Denmark'. Pondering the oddness of Jan Ove's mistake as I put my phone away, I decided in the end that it might have been, in some obscure way, his final contribution to the subject of our discussion, which was, I think, the uncertain status of almost all historical fact.

7

The Short Sweet Rule of Johann Friedrich Struensee

IT WAS THE DANISH POET JESPER MØLBY WHO, AS WE walked around the walled town of Visby during a three-week visit to Gotland early in 2015, told me the incredible true story of Johann Friedrich Struensee. A German-born, German-speaking doctor living in Denmark, Struensee, for a brief period between 1770 and 1772, wielded absolute power in Denmark and used it to introduce a series of laws based on the reforming ideas of his two great heroes, Voltaire and Rousseau, which made Denmark the most enlightened country in all of Europe, and which included an ordinance of September 1770 giving complete freedom of expression to all Danes. The ordinance replaced an existing law of 1683 which punished anyone guilty of criticizing God or the King of Denmark by having his tongue cut out, his head chopped off and his body quartered. An almost bureaucratic part of the ritual – carried out before the physical punishments began – was the shattering of the condemned man's family shield. But the most grotesquely symbolic aspect of Struensee's own execution in 1772 was that his genitals were also severed and displayed separately to the crowd by the executioner, Gottskalk Mühlhausen. Struensee had been not only the trusted personal surgeon of the Danish monarch Christian

VII, but also the lover of Christian's wife, Caroline. For this act of *lèse-majesté*, his penis had to be punished.

The execution took place at Copenhagen's Fælledparken, on the site of what is now the home of the Danish national football team. I remember thinking, on hearing these details, how strange it was that it had never before occurred to me that a prisoner condemned to be executed and then quartered, on this occasion before a crowd estimated at 30,000 (just under half the city's population at the time), must first have been stripped naked to make the division of the corpse into parts easier, enabling them to be placed in a basket, which was then lowered to the ground where it was received by the executioner's apprentice. At Struensee's execution, this was a youth named only as 'Oswald' in the records. Like his master, Oswald was almost certainly drunk throughout the proceedings. Afterwards it was the joint responsibility of these two to thread Struensee's legs, arms, torso and genitals through and around the spokes of a large cartwheel, which was then placed on a pole and mounted upright in the ground. Such poles, intended to evoke both contempt for the

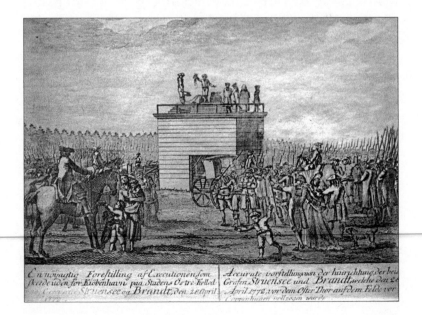

Cn nöÿagtig Forestilling af Execututionen som skeede uden for Kiöbenhavn paa Studens Oestre Fælled Grev Struensee og Brandt, den 28 April

Accurate vorstellung der hinrichtung der beiden Grafen Struensee und Brandt, welche den 28 April 1772 vor dem Oster Thor auf dem Felde vor Copenhagen vollzogen wurde

dead man and induce a fear of suffering a similar fate in those who saw them, might remain on display for months, and even years, in permanent and terrifying reminder of the price of offending those who possess the power and the will to go to such extremes against a fellow human being. On reflection, *of course* the victim had to remove his own clothes and stand naked before the show could begin – although we are told that in Struensee's case, his hands were so badly injured from the tortures inflicted during his incarceration, trial and subsequent attempts to cure him of his atheism that Mühlhausen had to unfasten the buttons of his tunic for him.

The event was well reported. Both Struensee and Enevold Brand, his friend and supporter, who was executed along with him for the lesser crime of biting the king's finger... but I'm getting ahead of myself here. Let me back up a little...

★

Impulsively cancelling my subscriptions to the two Norwegian dailies delivered to my doorstep each morning, *Aftenposten* ('Daily News') and *Klassekampen* ('Class War'), I went online and booked another trip to Gotland and the medieval town of Visby. Visby had become a place of refuge for me, somewhere in which I found it easier to ignore the crude and terrifying revelations of present-day history as it ceaselessly unfolded itself on all sides and wherever one looked or listened, distressing me in ways that were new and unfamiliar and leaving me with a dread certainty that all things I loved and valued about life were about to come to an end. It was the day after the *Charlie Hebdo* massacre in Paris on 7 January 2015. On that day, a woman who had just picked up her daughter from school arrived at the street entrance to the offices of the magazine where she worked and was about to punch in the entry code when two men dressed in black and carrying machine guns approached and threatened to kill the child unless she let them in. Once inside the building the men shot the receptionist before climbing the stairs to the first floor and entering a room in which the staff of the magazine were seated around a table for an editorial meeting. One of the gunmen produced a list of names which he went through one by one. As each journalist responded to the roll-call the other gunman moved around the table and killed him with a bullet through the head. Before leaving the men explained that they were religious, and that they reason they were killing the journalists was because the magazine had published certain drawings that had upset their religious beliefs. These and other similar acts of unspeakable cruelty and stupidity had started to penetrate even the sanctum of my dreams so that there were times when I dreaded going to sleep rather more than I did staying awake, subject as I was to a sudden and almost unendurable increase in the volume of that vague and constant background hum of unease about the very conditions of human existence itself that Kierkegaard called *angst*.

On the day of my arrival in Visby, 14 February, however, it was impossible not to hear the news that a youth in Copenhagen, influenced by the murderers in Paris and likewise claiming to be religious, had armed himself with a long-barrelled M95 Danish army rifle and fired numerous shots through the window of the Krudttønden café where Lars Vilks, the Swedish cartoonist of Mohammed, was among a group of people who had gathered to discuss the issue of freedom of expression. No one was harmed in the initial burst of fire, but the youth then killed a fifty-five-year-old man named Finn Nørgaard who had tried to wrestle the gun away from him. Later that day the same youth walked up to a Jewish man named Dan Uzan who was standing guard outside the doors of the synagogue in Krystalgade inside which people were celebrating a *bar mitzvah* and shot Mr Uzan through the head at point blank range. Mr Uzan was unarmed.

Having picked up my key from Lena at the Baltic Centre office and dropped off my suitcase in my first-floor room I strolled over to the low building that houses the centre's library, checked the names chalked on the residents board to see if anyone I knew was there, and then entered the kitchen, where I discovered that events in Copenhagen were the natural and even sole topic of conversation among the assorted group of seven or eight Swedes, Latvians, Estonians and Finns gathered around the large table that dominated the room. After exchanging greetings, I left as soon as possible, with the intention of returning later when things had quietened down.

At about ten o'clock that evening, as I was heating a fish pie in the oven, Jesper walked in. We shook hands and told each other our names. He was Danish, he told me, but had been living in Stockholm for the past fifteen years because he was married to a Swede who was a psychologist and who could only practise her particular branch of work in her home country. On the basis of this alone I felt a bond with Jesper. Both of us had made exiles of ourselves for love and condemned ourselves to the pleasures and tribulations of lives lived in a foreign language. I wondered if he, like me, had preserved a slightly old-fashioned form of his native language, the one we had with us when we first packed our suitcases for the journey. I liked his style too, his pale, thin unhealthy face and his slicked-back fifties' hairstyle. In Norway, I hadn't met many Danes. They're well represented in the building trade, but that isn't a world I move in, and in the service industries such as waitressing it's Swedes who are the dominant presence. Written Danish is almost identical to written Norwegian – Ibsen's plays are all written in Dano-Norwegian – but even Norwegians have trouble understanding Danes when they start to speak, so by tacit agreement Jesper and I spoke English from the start. He put his frying pan on to heat and began dicing vegetables. As a courtesy, and because he was Danish and it would have seemed perverse not to mention it at all, I offered him my condolences on the attack at the Krudttønden café and the synagogue, and was relieved to see that he did not seem to want to talk about this in any great detail. We spoke instead of other things. He told me he was working on a cycle of poems. I asked him if they were on a particular theme. With a directness that surprised me he told me they were about his wife. The story of his marriage, told in verse. He asked what I was doing and I told him I'd brought some notes for an idea I had for a book about Scandinavians. I told him it would probably be a road book, following the E6 all the way from its starting point near Trelleborg in Skåne in southern Sweden, up as far as the road-bridge over to Elsinore – Helsingør as you Danes call it – then taking a sort of leisurely spin around the Danish archipelago before driving back over the bridge and following the E6 up into Norway and all the way up past North Cape, past Tromsø to Kirkenes and the Russian border.

'The theme is going to be a quest for Scandinavian melancholy,' I said. 'The further north I get, the more strongly I'm going to feel its pulsing, until finally I reach the exact spot where its heart lies. At a place called Skellefteå, on the banks of the River Torne. The people there are proud of their melancholy. They've formed a club called the Friends of Darkness and the Cold. I was reading about it on the ferry over in *Svenska Dagbladet*. The membership currently stands at twelve. Their principal activity is competitive swimming in frozen water after chopping away a thick 50 cm (20 in) cap of ice to get at it. There was a photograph of them queuing up to get in. One was wearing a shark's head bathing cap with pointed teeth. In the Canoe Club changing rooms afterwards they talked about the liberating effects of the experience, the feeling of freedom, confidence and openness that comes afterwards, of problems suddenly put in perspective. They spoke of melancholy as a kind of religion. They're also planning a cultural anti-festival called the Melankoliade which will spend the winters touring the north of the country and promoting the virtues of melancholy.'

'You're talking about an exact spot on the ground? Like magnetic north?'

'Yes.'

'And you've already decided this? Even before you've got in the car?'

I explained that it was more of a literary device. That I would merely be pretending to find such a place.

'The Swedes and the Norwegians maybe, but we Danes aren't melancholic,' he continued as he moved over to the stove and scuffed the chopped onions and diced carrots into the pan with the blade of a bread knife and started prodding them about. I thought of mentioning Thomas Vinterberg's *Festen* as being on a par for bleakness with anything in either Ibsen or Bergman, but then doubted if bleakness was really the same thing as melancholy.

'Could be a problem,' he added.

'I know,' I said. 'I'll have to think of something else if I'm going to include the Danes.'

Later, sitting opposite each other across that wide table, inevitably, he raised the subject of freedom of expression: Did I know that the Danes were the first people in all Europe to have complete freedom of speech? No, I didn't know that. And, in spite of my best intentions I found that I was, after all, extremely curious to hear his elliptical take on this ancient problem and encouraged him to go ahead and tell me. And I listened while I made coffee for us as he told me about Dr Johan Heinrich Struensee and the two-year period of eighteenth-century Danish history during which, through the mere chance of his being physician to the mad King Christian VII – as well as being the king's most admired and trusted friend and the lover of the king's wife, the twenty-year-old English princess, Caroline Matilda – Struensee became the proxy absolute monarch of Denmark and introduced the first complete abolition of censorship in all Europe, in 1771. Jesper was about to get into the details of the story, having told me his wife was doing a Ph.D. at Stockholm University on the subject of Christian VII's madness and that he had become deeply involved in her studies, so I was very disappointed when he stood up as soon as he had finished his coffee and told me that he had to go back to his room and pack – that his stay was over and he was leaving on the mid-morning ferry the next day. I asked if we might meet and continue the conversation, perhaps take a walk before he caught the boat. He said he still had work to do on his poems and was hoping to get in an hour in the morning before the ferry left. I told him this would be a wasted hour and its results unreliable, because the hour or two before a long journey is always dead time. Even if he did work, he would only have to go over it all again once he got home. Better to get some exercise and some fresh air. He gave me a doubtful look and said he would get up early and do some work first. 'See you outside at eight-thirty.'

*

Jesper was already waiting for me when I opened the front door of
the dormitory building, in the act of stubbing out a cigarette beneath
his heel, the brown cord collar of his blue quilted jacket turned up
against a cold onshore wind. At his suggestion we set off in a northerly direction along Nygatan, following the rear wall of the city in
the direction of the Norderport, the north gate. He walked with his
head down and, after a minute or two, remarked on the mesmerizing
and almost nauseating way the kaleidoscopic pattern of the cob-
blestones defeated every attempt made by the eye to follow any one
particular row all the way from beginning to end – didn't I agree?

'Yes,' I said. 'It's very mesmerizing. Now please tell me all about
Christian VII and Struensee.'

'As a boy,' he began, 'Christian seemed bright and intelligent
though easily distracted and liable to, as it were, absent himself from
a conversation or lesson and engross himself minutely in some complete irrelevancy. Once, for example, in the middle of a lesson about
the thinkers of the French Enlightenment, his tutor Reverdil noticed
the prince digging his fingers into his stomach as hard and intently
as he could, so preoccupied in the activity that Reverdil had to call
out his name three or four times before Christian heard him. Possibly
as the result of an upbringing that was excessively attached to cor-
poral punishment, Christian had developed a desire to make himself
impervious to physical pain. His belief in the possibility of this may
well have been encouraged by his attention to the execution in 1767
of an army captain named Mörl and his servant Stutz, who had been
found guilty of the robbery and murder of another officer, Captain
With. This turned out to be a particularly intricate form of punishment that was spread over two or three hours and used five different
locations. At each new location a new and different torment awaited
them. Boiling oil poured over the skin. The squeezing of the flesh
with red-hot tongs. The ritual breaking of bones. That kind of thing.
Christian and a companion were following the execution party from
site to site, using an unmarked carriage to preserve their anonymity.
Throughout Captain Mörl kept up an almost continuous barrage of
noise, calling out to Stutz and urging him not to feel the pain, calling

on God for help and strength, continuing to do so even while his arms and legs were being broken on the wheel, and not falling silent until the final act of decapitation. Contemporary observers reported that the contrast between the articulate and almost superhuman bravery of the one and the screams and moans of the other were a source of both entertainment and wonder to those who had nothing better to do that day than follow the trundling wagon from site to site.

'By that time it had become obvious to the courtiers that something was seriously wrong with Christian. Apparently unaware that he was doing so he pulled strange faces in public. He would stretch his mouth wide in a grotesque grimace, thrusting out his jaw as far as it would go, his eyes screwed tight shut, his tongue poking out as though he was trying to vomit it out. He masturbated several times daily, often in public, so that one observer could note that he seemed to masturbate not in pursuit of pleasure but compulsively, performing the act mechanically and without passion. Now, the monarchy in Denmark had been absolute since the King's Law of 1665 which stated that "the Monarch shall from this day forth be revered and considered the most perfect and supreme person on the Earth by all his subjects, standing above all human laws and having no judge above his person, neither in spiritual nor temporal matters, except God alone."'

Jesper stopped for a moment to light a cigarette, back turned to the wind and shoulders hunched around his hands as he shielded the lighter. At the Norderport gate he headed down Silverhattan in the direction of the sea.

He continued: 'Naturally, a responsibility like this is an appalling and inhuman burden to place on the shoulders of a single individual. Sooner or later a king was bound to arise who would reject it with every fibre of his being. Christian's father, Frederik V, went some way towards doing so. On numerous occasions he would have to be carried back to his living quarters in the royal dwelling at Christiansborg because he was too drunk to walk. Christian took his rejection of the role even further. When an absolute monarch has no interest at all in ruling, the inevitable result is the appearance of people who do. In the years of Christian's minority it led to the rise of a group of prominent court officials who effectively ran Denmark, and who continued to do so following Christian's even more extreme rejection of the role once he was crowned king in 1766, at the age of seventeen. He made no secret of the fact – publicly announced it – that for the first two years of his reign he intended to live out the demands of what he called his *raseri*, his inner wildness. And he did. He embarked on a regime of debauched violence that, in its sheer relentlessness, seemed almost a calculated attempt to persuade the administration at court of the fatal flaws in their belief in absolute monarchy as the best form of government for Denmark.

'You know that the Danish monarchy is the oldest in Europe and the second oldest in the world? I think only Japan's is older. But in all that time, from Gorm the Old to Queen Margrethe, I don't think we've ever had a philosopher king. I suppose it's a contradiction in terms. An impossibility. Although I do remember, when I was about fifteen or sixteen, being fascinated by an English book that I found on my grandfather's bookshelves, in Århus, where I grew up. It was a very old book, with stiff, dark brown covers and a faint white cup ring on it. It was called *Curiosities of Literature*, by Isaac D'Israeli. Dozens, hundreds of short essays on all manner of things, with titles like "On the Custom of Saluting After Sneezing", and "Products of the Mind Not Seizable by Creditors", "Imprisonment of the Learned", "Men of Genius Deficient in Conversation", that type of thing. One essay was about the philosopher kings of Poland, and in particular one who suddenly disappeared. Courtiers and soldiers scoured the country for the missing king but could not find him anywhere. Years later, by which time most people presumed he was dead, his old chancellor happened to see a porter in a market-place walking along carrying a basket of apples on his head who looked familiar. Realizing it was the lost king he approached him. You are a king, he said. It is not right for you to walk along here among the common people carrying a weight like that on your head. The chancellor begged him to return to the castle and resume his throne. The king stopped just briefly. "Believe me,'" he said, "the burden I carry here is less by far than the burden I once carried as king.'" And away he walked. Disappeared into the throng. I know my wife thinks I'm romanticizing madness, but I still believe that somewhere beneath the ugly surface of his rebellion, beneath the crust of his distress and his unhappiness, Christian's early exposure to the ideas of thinkers like Voltaire and Rousseau and Cesare Beccaria had suggested the same thing to him, that there was something deeply wrong in the idea of a single individual wielding the powers of an absolute monarch, at the same time as he realized there was nothing he could do about it.

'I actually first became fascinated by this whole period of my country's history when I read P.O. Enquist's book *Livläkarens besök*.* They made a film of the story a couple of years ago. *En kongelige affære*.† With Mads Mikkelsen as Struensee and a Swedish actress playing Caroline. That's always seemed pretty funny to me, they cast a Swedish actress and trained her to speak Danish [he said it with a short first vowel, as though mentally spelling it with a double *n*] so that she could speak Danish to the Danish actor playing her lover. But Caroline was English, she couldn't speak Danish, and her lover couldn't speak a word of Danish either. He didn't have to. Copenhagen was a European centre of culture. But it was German culture, not Danish culture. Especially after Klopstock was invited to live there by Frederick V in 1751, on the suggestion of his German minister, Count von Bernstorff. Bernstorff was hoping Klopstock would finish *Der Messias* there. His masterpiece.'

We had been following the curve of the town wall and as it began to shape inwards towards the harbour Jesper turned down Gotlandsänget and headed us up in the direction of the botanical gardens. As he opened the wrought-iron gates of the gardens two cats emerged from some rhododendron bushes and approached him at a determined trot along the pinkish-grey gravel pathway. Jesper stooped to pet them, murmuring Danish endearments in a soft undertone. One of them had a crumpled ear. Pointing to the other, a white one, he drew my attention to its eyes. One was a milky grey, the other blue. When it looked directly at you the effect was unnerving.

*   *The Visit of the Royal Physician*
†   *A Royal Affair*

'They live here,' he said, 'they're wild. Do you know Klopstock's poems? The Odes?'

I shook my head and said that, like most of my countrymen, I was pitifully ignorant of German literature.

'Oh, you should read them,' he said, straightening up and moving on. 'There are some beautiful verses about his wife. He loved her dearly but she died after just four years of marriage. Klopstock suffered from melancholy. He couldn't write any more. Nothing seemed to make sense.'

Jesper's phone buzzed. He took it out, read the message, frowned, put it back in his pocket and stared for a long time over the chaos of Visby's low rooftops and ruined churches towards the ferry terminal. I felt another pang of guilt about keeping him from his work but was determined to keep him talking, for it might turn out to be a long time before I had the chance to converse with another Dane.

'You said something about the liberties taken by Enquist and the director of *A Royal Affair*,' I said, to nudge him back into his groove.

'Actually no,' he said. 'All I was going to say is that sometimes a novelist or a film maker will find a fact too insignificant or too undramatic to include in his story, and yet that fact might be crucial to a proper understanding of the unfolding of events. Christian's interest in philosophy, for example, is central to an understanding of how an obscure young doctor from provincial Altona came in the first place to the attention of the most absolute of all absolute monarchies in Europe. This, for example, is what the novelist or the film director doesn't have the patience to tell you: that Voltaire had written to all the crowned heads of Europe as well as other influential persons and aristocrats asking for their support in a case that preoccupied the whole of Europe's intellectual elite at that particular time, which involved a Huguenot named Jean Calas who had been tortured to death for allegedly killing his son because the boy had converted to Roman Catholicism. Voltaire was trying to raise money for a retrial and a posthumous pardon and he sent out this letter. Struensee was a great admirer. He translated the letter into German. Christian responded with a gift of money. It was probably Struensee's translation he read. Voltaire sent Christian a message of thanks. Called him a luminary. So this was the link. Although I doubt Voltaire would have called him a luminary had he seen Christian out on one of his *raseri*. His idea of fun was to wander the streets of Copenhagen at night masked and disguised with a gang of friends armed with staffs and cudgels, attacking people at random, picking fights with the city's patrolling night-watchmen and engaging in street brawls with them. Ferocious encounters between the upholders of the law and a gang of masked thugs led by the very man responsible for that law. How d'you like a king like that? Christian never revealed his identity unless the threat of a serious beating seemed inevitable. The night-watchmen for their part ran a great and unpredictable risk in taking on Christian and his gang because the king's status as absolute monarch made even the slightest assault on his person a capital offence. When Enevold Brand followed Struensee up the steps of the scaffold in 1772 he was paying with his life for the crime of having bitten the king's finger during a fight between the two men after a meal in which the king had pelted Brand throughout with food, including a lemon that hit him directly on the head. One should not laugh, of course. But what strange experiences these must have been for the night-watchmen! To go home to their wives at the end of their shift and explain the cuts and bruising and torn clothes as the result of the king having picked a fight with them. Of course everyone knew it was him but there wasn't much they could do. One night a group of street kids followed Christian back to the castle after he'd been out drinking and fighting and smashing up brothels. They were chanting "There goes little Christian," shouting out the name of his favourite prostitute, weaving about in front of him, obstructing him, pushing him as he stopped to urinate against a wall, knowing, as even the smallest child knows, that the big adult world they are about to enter is a joke, it's a bluff, it's all permanently out of joint. And that scene in the film, which actually happened, when Christian staggers up to the castle gates, and the kids hang back and watch the guards stand to attention and salute as he passes between them, a bottle dangling from his fingertips.

'The marriage was his courtiers' idea, to stop him masturbating, stop him drinking, get him to settle down and take up his responsibilities, but it made no difference, just like the birth of a child made no difference, none of it made any difference. Christian just carried on living like any trapped rock star, smashing up the furniture, throwing the pieces off the balcony. He was obsessed with a whore known as 'Støvel-Katrine', Katrine the Boots, from the high leather boots she always wore. He spent every night with her, paraded her quite openly in front of his wife, let her sit at the high table with him, let her sit next to him in the royal box at the theatre, the theatre being one of the few genuine pleasures in his wretched life.

'If there was nothing they could do about the failure of the absolute monarch himself, his courtiers could at least try to control these ritual manifestations of the failings of the institution itself. In their desperation a royal tour of Europe in 1768 was arranged during which he would be presented at the courts of Holland, England, France, Italy, Austria, Prussia and Russia, a *bildungsrejse* they hoped might turn this hopelessly unsuitable youth into a responsible monarch. The journey was private, as private as any journey could be when the party consists of fifty-five persons. It was planned to last a year.

'This hadn't occurred to me before,' said Jesper, 'but one purpose of the trip to England must have been to meet his brother-in-law, your George III, whose madness later became a literary trope to rival his own. In Danish we would call that *skæbnens ironi*, an irony of the fate. Probably the highlight of the whole trip for him was meeting the great Shakespearean actor of the time, David Garrick, a king whom Christian set far above any wearer of a round metal hat. He was granted an audience with the great man at his villa at Hampton on the Thames and proudly presented Garrick with a small gold casket. There was a dinner in Christian's honour at the French Academy, where he was feted as an Enlightenment hero for his gift of money to Voltaire. Voltaire himself wasn't at the dinner, but Christian had the pleasure of meeting Claude Helvétius and the encyclopaedist Denis Diderot. It seems that he was able to, how do you say, *tage sig sammen*? take himself sufficiently together on such occasions to act the part of a king. But the strain on himself and those travelling with him was intolerable. Uncontrollable rages. Smashing of furniture. Terrified fears that people were hiding in his room waiting for him to fall asleep so that they could cut his throat, fears that he himself had murdered someone the previous night and been given opium to make him forget it.

'Struensee was travelling with the party as one of the king's doctors. Christian took to him. It was always Struensee who was called on to search his room before he would go to bed at night. Struensee had a quiet firmness that seemed to calm the boy down. He didn't sycophantically pretend to accept the wilder claims of Christian's paranoia, and a relationship of intimacy and dependence built up between them. Christian trusted him. He thought of him as a friend he could say anything to. He would try to get Struensee to admit that he couldn't *possibly* be king, that he must be a changeling, that the true King of Denmark was out there mowing hay on a farm in some far northern corner of Jylland. He suggested to Struensee that the two of them run away together and join the army, cut all ties and vanish into the blissful anonymity of a soldier's life, like philosopher kings.

'Caroline, left behind in Copenhagen to nurse their infant son, spoke in just the same way to her maids and attendants. She used to ask them about their husbands and boyfriends, and tell them how much she envied them their freedom to marry for love, to submit to the power of true love, even forbidden love, to follow the loved one all the way though it lead to the scaffold, the wheel, to Hell itself. If ever she became a widow, she told them, she would marry only for love, no matter who it was.

'Two kids,' Jesper said wanly, 'and people were asking them to rule the world. Anyway, halfway through, the journey was cut short, and in January 1769 the party returned to Copenhagen. The film does that scene very well. Christian steps out of the carriage and goes straight to his dog Gourmand and ignores Caroline completely. You'd die for her then, the look of lost sadness on her face, Alicia Vikander, the actress. Actually people say she looks quite like my own wife. Look.'

Jesper pulled a small concertina wallet out of his pocket, opened the metal clasp and showed me. I saw a photograph of a blond-haired young woman with a side-parting. She had a friendly, warm face but was otherwise unremarkable, neither beautiful nor ugly. I had no idea how to respond and was on the point of saying that she had a lovely forehead, but then he seemed to regret the intimacy and with a few mumbled words closed the wallet and slipped it back into the pocket of his jeans before continuing.

'Seeing Struensee for the first time and how close he and Christian are, Caroline assumes he's just another sycophant exploiting the king's weakness for his own ends. But she turns out to be wrong. Struensee represents nothing and no one but himself. He's a genuine disciple of Voltaire and Rousseau. He heads no clique and he scorns the whole notion of networking. In fact, he's all set to return to his life as provincial doctor in Altona and his modest income of seventy *rigsdaler* a year until, out of the blue, he finds himself offered the job as Christian's personal physician. The politicians and courtiers around the king, the people actually running the country, have noticed the calming effect he has on Christian. They offer him a thousand *rigsdaler* a year. What choice does he have? He says yes.'

We sat on a bench in the botanical gardens below a circular and oddly Chinese-looking gazebo with slender red ochre pillars and a blue roof, and listened for a few moments to the ear-filling rush of the waves washing over the remarkable number of boulders and rocks close to the shoreline beyond the wall, some of them obviously deliberately placed there centuries ago as a defence against attack from the sea. Looking once again towards the ferry terminal, I saw a puzzling and alarming sight, a large dark fin-like shape heading towards the harbour with extraordinary rapidity. I watched its approach, spellbound, and presently realized that I was seeing the raked-back funnel of the arriving ferry sliding along the horizon, its redness drained by a faint morning mist which had still not cleared, the hull greyed to the point of invisibility against the grey of the sea. I thought again of how odd it was that after a mere three hours sailing on the ferry, the mainland vanished entirely below the horizon, so that on clear evenings the sun could clearly and incontrovertibly be seen to set in the water between Gotland and Sweden, an optical illusion which to this day can disturb my understanding of the physical world.

I wondered if Jesper had seen that fin-like apparition on the water and became selfishly alarmed that he might decide it was time to return to the Centre and make ready to leave before he had reached the end of his story. To distract him, and at the same time keep him focused on the subject of free speech, I began with no preamble at all to reminisce about the protest march organized by Muslim leaders in Oslo against the publication of a Norwegian edition of Rushdie's *Satanic Verses* back in 1987, three years after I went to live in the city.

I pointed out that the marchers were demanding a ban on a book that had not yet even been published in Norway, and which few, if any of them, could have had access to in any language. I described the slight drift of snow falling across Karl Johans gate that day and the peculiar and almost surreal sensation the event aroused in me, who had come to live in what was essentially a nineteenth-century dream of Norway, the Norway of Nansen, Ibsen, Amundsen, Grieg, Munch, Hamsun, at the sight of these marchers expressing a fear and an anger that was as baffling to me as it was to most Norwegians. I recalled standing watching outside Grand Hotel on Karl Johan with two journalist friends, and the heavy odour of crowd sweat that hung in the cold air as the marchers trudged by with their banners, men only, a straggle of women pushing prams bringing up the rear. We had kept pace with them, up past the Storting and down the slope from Egertorget towards the station. A scuffle that had broken out when two marchers tried to grab a banner held aloft by a Norwegian woman proclaiming the right to freedom of expression was quickly and efficiently dealt with by one of the marchers' own stewards.

On a Monday morning in October 1993, I went on, when most of those not directly affected by the *fatwa* issued by Ayatollah Khomeini against the novel's author, its printers, publishers, translators and stockists had all but forgotten about it, William Nygaard, the publisher of the Norwegian edition, had left his house in the fashionable Holmenkollen district, in the hills above Oslo, and crossed the gravelled parking space to his car to drive in to work. He had just got back from the annual Frankfurt Book Fair. At a drinks party in Frankfurt the night before he had left, there had been talk about the *fatwa*. Someone asked Nygaard if he was afraid. Nygaard said no, he had no fears for his personal safety. It seemed unlikely to the point of absurdity that violence of this kind might affect Norway, still in the minds of most observers a small, beautiful and orderly country outside the mainstream of world events with few, if any, genuine social problems.

On that Monday morning, as he approached his car, Nygaard noticed with annoyance that one of the Citroen's front tyres was flat. His son had been using the car and had dropped it off late the night before, and Nygaard felt a pang of irritation that he had neither dealt with it himself nor called in to mention it to his father before leaving. Nygaard reached out to open the door of his car to turn off the alarm prior to calling for roadside assistance and with the phone still in his hand felt a jolt of indescribable pain pass though him. He stepped back from the car and a second jolt hit him. Supposing that in some obscure way the phone or the electrics in the car had produced an electric shock, he was running towards an embankment at the rear of the parking space when a third jolt struck him and he tumbled down the slope. There he lay in agony for the next ten minutes, until a neighbour going out to her car heard his feeble cries for help and called the emergency services. Nygaard warned her to beware of some kind of powerful electric current operating in the region of his car. So sure was he of this that he even warned members of the ambulance crew who arrived to take him to hospital not to go too close to his the car, it was at the centre of an extensive and malignant force field. Only once his shirt was cut open at Ullevål hospital was it clear that he had been shot three times. Someone had tried to kill him.

It was the novelist Lars Saabye Christensen who told me what had happened. He arrived that morning at the work-room I had back then in Wessels gate to talk about the scripts we were working on for NRK's television series about Knut Hamsun. We both assumed immediately that the attack was directly connected to Aschehoug's publication of *Sataniske vers* back in 1989. But the police were not about to jump to any conclusions. At the first press conference after the attempted murder, a journalist asked the Chief of Police if, in the light of what had happened, Kari Risvik had been given an armed guard? A puzzled frown creased his forehead. Who is Kari Risvik? he asked. The journalist told him Risvik had translated the Norwegian edition of Rushdie's novel. He added that the book's Japanese translator, Hitori Agarashi, had already been murdered, and a failed attempt made on the life of Ettore Capriolo, its Italian translator. The police, however, either dreading an accusation of racial profiling or from sheer disbelief that a mere book could be the cause of so much violence, proceeded to spend the next few weeks interviewing Nygaard's friends and associates, examining his private life in search of some more mundane motive for the attempted murder.

'Even now,' I told Jesper, 'twenty-six years later, no one has ever been charged with the shooting. But can you imagine how that must have maddened Nygaard? To have the police plodding away looking for a mistress, or a jealous lover?'

Jesper shook his head and said he guessed so.

'How about Christian?' I asked. 'Did he know about Struensee and his wife?'

'Oh yes,' said Jesper. 'It was an open secret. He colluded in it. He wanted Struensee to take Caroline off his hands. It would leave him free to spend all his time drinking, fighting, hanging out with Støvel-Katrine, wrecking any brothels that were in competition with hers if she asked him to. Caroline had slumped into a depression. She never went out because she had nowhere to go and no one to go with. She started getting fat. Christian asked Struensee to call on her and see if he could help. Struensee did. He talked to her. He told her she should get out more. He recommended riding. It wasn't a thing respectable young women did, but Caroline was desperate so she gave it a try. She loved it. It was freedom. Struensee started riding with her. And I guess that's when it began. Out there in the fields and forests of Dyrehaven. Behind a fallen tree trunk. In some quiet hunting lodge. Everybody knows about it. But if the king doesn't care... And of course, there were people at court who *did* care. They had enemies. Caroline used to ride mounted like a man, with one leg on each side of the horse. One courtier wrote in his journal of seeing blood on the saddle after she returned from a ride. Not only has Caroline forgotten she is a queen, he wrote. She has also forgotten she is a woman. Now that's a dangerous kind of hatred.

'Struensee used a private rear staircase to get to the queen's room at night. The servants sprinkle powder on the floor and trace his footsteps in the morning. They put wax in the keyhole of her bedroom door and in the morning it's been forced. They fasten hairs across door-openings. And the king doesn't care so nobody cares. He thinks more of his dog Gourmand, a massive beast that reaches up to his chest. Gourmand has his own seat in the royal box at the theatre. When the king goes out riding Gourmand follows in a carriage of his own drawn by six horses. At the funeral of Christian's grandmother in Christiansborg Slottskirke, Gourmand is allowed to roam freely up and down the aisle. At one point the dog urinates on the coffin. It's the world turned upside down.

'Caroline gives birth to a child that is widely assumed to be

Struensee's, and she, Christian and Struensee carry on living together, like any twenty-first-century hippy family in the Christiania *fristad* in Copenhagen. And in the middle of all this, you can imagine, Struensee waking up and realizing that the road to absolute power lies open before him. The king is untouchable, infallible. But he owns the king's mind, and the king's wife. No one can stop him. He goes back to his Voltaire and his Rousseau. He makes out a wish-list, and one by one he starts drafting a series of democratic reforms that give the people of Denmark freedoms unparalleled anywhere else in the world. Freedoms *they didn't even know they didn't have*. Check: the abolition of torture; the abolition of that form of compulsory unpaid labour known as *corvée*; an end to the practice of preferring nobles for state offices; an end to special privileges for the nobility; the abolition of the rules of etiquette at the royal court; abolition of state support for unproductive manufacturers; introduction of a tax on gambling and luxury horses to pay for the nursing of foundlings; a ban on slave trading in the Danish colonies; the criminalization and due punishment of bribery; the re-organization of the judiciary to stamp out corruption; establishment of state-owned grain storages to end speculation on the price of grain; the assignment of farmland to peasants; a re-organization and reduction of the army; reform of the universities; and the introduction of complete freedom of the press. And all he had to do was hand the list across the table for Christian to sign and then present the reforms to the Privy Council as the *faits accomplis* of their absolute monarch.'

Jesper glanced again at his watch and a look of alarm flitted across his face. 'I have to get back. I haven't even packed yet.'

We stood up and exited the gardens into St Hansgatan, directly opposite a bar called 'The Black Sheep Arms'. A sign in ye olde writing on the door said it was an 'English' pub. Although it looked like something from about 1599 it was new since my last visit to the island and I made a mental note to check it out one day, just to make sure the barmen were Aussies and the music Irish. After another hundred metres the bright white front wall of St Maria came into view and we headed up Biskopsgatan into the cathedral gardens through a side gate and crossed in front of the main entrance, heading for the steep stone stairway that would take us back up to Uddens gränd and the Baltic Centre.

'Did his reforms survive him?'

'No.'

'None of them?'

'A tooth is what survived him,' said Jesper. 'It's the teeth and bones that survive a man. The hard parts. The tongue, the brain, the blood, the flesh, all the soft parts, they're what disappears. After fifteen months of what was effectively a *coup d'état*, Struensee's failure to create a network of support cost him dearly. A group of powerful and disaffected aristocrats gathered around the king's stepmother, Julianne, and with an almost childlike simplicity Struensee was arrested in his chambers early one morning, Caroline was subdued and her children taken from her, and Christian kept firmly out of the way and warned not to invoke the privileges of an absolute monarch. Real people had taken the country over again, and the whole thing turned back to shit.

'After the execution and the dismemberments, the body parts were taken in a wagon to a nearby site and mounted on wheels atop poles, with the head and right hand displayed on a pole of their own. An English traveller who passed through over two years later reported that the poles, with their macabre display, were still standing. And when they did finally keel over, a medical student named Marcus Kall took a tooth from each man's jaw as a souvenir of this strange interlude in Danish history. For some reason these teeth spent several decades in the keeping of the Theatre Museum, which some years ago donated them to the Medisinsk-historisk Museum.

In some ways the most depressing part of it all is that Struensee gave people freedom of expression, and for the most part all anyone did with it was compose endless vulgar and offensive verses directed at Struensee himself and his affair with Caroline. In his bright and visionary Denmark people had been set free to express exactly what they felt and thought, to educate one another, criticize one another constructively, to fearlessly challenge the high and mighty. What he got instead was a society of proto-internet trolls. *Shit. Piss. Fart. Willy. The king's a nutcase.* Just a year after the ordinance was passed, he had to introduce a modification which required the author's and printer's name to appear clearly on the front page of the publication, so that if people felt they were being libelled they would be able to prosecute a case under the law.

'Struensee was an atheist but a tolerant one. He didn't make any direct attack on Christianity as a factor in the public life of the state. His vision, however, was one in which the state interfered in the life of the individual as little as possible, and he introduced reforms to ensure that Christian morality and Christian prohibitions should only be applied to those who embraced them voluntarily. So, for example, under Struensee, sex between two people who weren't married was no longer a crime. Nor would he put up with religious intolerance. When it came to his attention that the university had refused to award a Jew a Ph.D., he told them it was the king's will that academic titles be awarded to those deserving of them, without regard to their religious beliefs. Everything was Struensee's idea and the king's will. All Christian had to do was sign the appropriate document.

'After Struensee's fall, and Caroline's death three years later of scarlet fever at the age of twenty-three, all his reforms were rescinded. But some kind of seed had been sown. The constitution of 1849 that abolished absolute monarchy gave Danes once again the freedom to say and print whatever they wanted, and banned censorship in perpetuity. We Danes still have a strangely ambivalent attitude towards Struensee. He exploited the king with the best of intentions, but it was still an exploitation. He was a member of the German cultural elite who ruled Denmark with so little respect for the culture and language of the Danes that among the ideas he didn't have time to put into practice was one that would ban the use of Danish in official contexts. It was as a direct result of the experience with Struensee that legislation was later passed reserving the right to hold high office in Denmark to native-born Danes. This legislation was tantamount to the introduction of citizenship and as such an important stage in the development of the concept of European nationhood. Before

Struensee, religious affiliation, along with talent, had been the deciding factor in appointments to high office. After Struensee it was not who you were, but where you came from that mattered.'

On the top step, Jesper paused to get his breath back, leaning on the railing and panting as he admired the view over the town. 'Some people think Struensee was a visionary. A Christ even,' he said presently. 'But he was too human for that. Plus, he was an atheist. I don't know if an atheist can be a Christ. But I think about him a lot, and this is what I think now: that there are certain crimes a state commits in its own name that are so hideous, so vile, so unforgiveable that they are tantamount to psychic suicide. In my view, the torture and execution of Struensee mark the end of ancient times and the beginning of modern times in Denmark. Even in 1772, the way he and Enevold Brand were executed was considered barbaric. Not the fact of the execution, but that barbaric package of secondary details. The sinning right hand that was chopped off first. The head, the genitals, the quartering. People say that as the show went on, the watching crowd fell silent, and when it was all over they left in silence. I think a limitless sense of shame was born on that April day in 1772, and shame is what turns societies around.'

Half an hour later, as we saw his taxi making its way up the cobbles towards Kyrkberget, the grassy knoll on which the Baltic Centre stands, and were saying goodbye to each other, Jesper laid his hand on my forearm and looked at me with an expression of such desolation in his pale eyes that I suddenly felt afraid for him.

'I haven't written a word while I've been here,' he blurted out. 'Four weeks and not one single fucking poem. I don't think I can do it anymore. It's just gone.'

For one terrible instant I thought he was going to cry. I wondered briefly why he was telling me, then decided it must be the hitch-hiker syndrome, where a man will reveal the most painful and private details of his own private struggle to a complete stranger, in the certain knowledge that they will never meet again. I patted him on the shoulder, which is about the most I can ever manage in such situations, and waved goodbye as the old rust-red Volvo did a three-point turn outside the Centre's library and trundled away along the cobbles. Going back into the dormitory block I met the Greek poet Ersi Sotiropoulos on her way down the stairs. She told me that the boy responsible for the Krudttønden attack and the murder at the Krystalgade synagogue had been shot and killed by the police in the early hours of the morning. I thanked her for the information and carried on up to my room. Sitting on the narrow bed, I navigated to Miles Davis's 'Flamenco Sketches' on my smartphone and put it on repeat, all nine minutes of it, placed the headphones over my ears and lay down and closed my eyes.

8

Taking God at His Word: Søren Kierkegaard and Olav Fiskvik

MOST SATURDAYS, AND ESPECIALLY IN THE AUTUMN AND winter, it was my habit to go along to Herr Nilsen's jazz pub in C.J. Hambros plass with my friend Eskil Nordlie, who taught philosophy at the University of Oslo, to hear the afternoon concert that started at four and went on till six. It was one of the few times I felt I was living in a big city, in that crowded little corner bar, with its heavy venetian blinds permanently closed and still with a brownish patina on their beige slats from the days before the smoking ban, all except those on the side where the windows had been replaced, blown in by the shockwave from Anders Breivik's bomb in 2011 as it swept down the long dog-leg of Apotekergata. Whenever I went there I would be reminded of a long-running programme on Norwegian State Radio (NRK) I tried never to miss called 'Studio Socrates', in which guest philosophers talked in a discursive way about the works and ideas of various writers and thinkers, breaking off every now and then to play a track by the featured jazz artist and towards the end of the programme trying to relate the thinker to the music in some unexpected way. I remember one broadcast featuring Henri Bergson and Chet Baker, another on Simone Weil and Jan Garbarek, another linking Knut Hamsun, his novel *Hunger* and the Stoic philosophers. It struck me as an original and inspired sort of combination and one that Eskil and I sometimes aspired to during those Saturday afternoons at Herr Nilsen's, often continuing at Burns' bar, opposite the National Theatre, to which we adjourned after the session finished. As this was a period when I had begun to read Kierkegaard, our conversations often turned, at my initiative, to a discussion of the man and his ideas. Among other things, I was trying to achieve clarity in my own mind about the continuing validity of one of the more prominent historical characterizations of the Scandinavian people as *melancholic* and *dark-minded*. On this particular Saturday afternoon I remember that as we took our seats in front of the little corner stage I said to Eskil that it was growing ever more clear to me that, under the influence of television and the internet, cheap air travel, and immigration on a scale unprecedented in the recorded history of the region, as well as changing perceptions encouraged by the international success of such basically cheerful phenomena as Abba, IKEA and a-ha, this handy characterization was becoming obsolete, and that I wanted to understand its historical roots before it disappeared completely.

'What do you make of Kierkegaard's possible contribution to this persistent association with melancholy? And if you doubt it, given that his writing did not become widely available in English until the middle of the twentieth century, then perhaps a case might be made for his influence through the work of writers and artists more well known than himself and over whom he is known to have exerted an influence, such as Henrik Ibsen, whose *Brand* after all is a dramatization of the pain Kierkegaard himself faced when he had to choose between his love for Regine Olsen and his work? Or better still Edvard Munch, who explored Kierkegaard's conception of *angst* in the cycle of paintings he called "The Frieze of Life: Images from the Life of the Modern Mind", which included *Scream, Vampire, Madonna, Ashes, Puberty, The Sick Child* and *The Dance of Life*? Surely Kierkegaard's identification with this conception of *angst*, so often translated into English as "anxiety", and not incorrectly so – and yet the English word seems to fail to capture the sheer *extent* of what Kierkegaard was trying to describe, that unfocused and diffuse fear that hums away at the back of the mind, at times so loudly one is completely incapacitated by it, and at other times so quietly one has to stretch one's hearing to almost unendurable limits in order to hear it at all. Surely... .'

At this point I broke off, having noticing the pianist glaring at me repeatedly over his shoulder, and resolved to wait until the musicians took their first break before asking Eskil for his response. 'Strayhorn', as they called themselves, were about fifteen minutes into their set before the pianist swivelled a microphone in front of his face and introduced the musicians. Four of the five of them were from Bø in Telemark, he announced. Norwegian local patriotism is a benign but enigmatic thing and for some reason this got a round of applause and some subdued, American-style whoops of approbation. With what I thought was rather perverse timing, Eskil chose that moment to turn to me and remark that I was wrong, Kierkegaard was not melancholy.

'Melancholy is impotent,' he said. 'It sits there with a cloak over its bowed head. Kierkegaard was passionate in his darkness. And you're quite wrong to suppose that Kierkegaard is important as a *thinker*. He is important as a story. As a terrible, cautionary tale. Let me tell you why.'

But now it was Eskil's turn to attract the beady eye of the pianist, and for the next twenty minutes we said nothing and simply enjoyed the music until the first break was announced. We asked the only other guest at our table, a bearded man wearing a pale biscuit-coloured suit with the widest padded shoulders I have ever seen, to save our places and, showing our blue-stamped fists to the youth on the door, stepped outside to the pavement and the fresh late afternoon air. Eskil sank into a seat by one of the three or four round smokers' tables that faced across C.J. Hambros plass, towards the impressive white façade of the Oslo District Court, and began talking about Kierkegaard. He told me that Kierkegaard was the youngest in a family of seven children, and that by the time he was twenty-two all of them, apart from one older brother, were dead. His mother too. According to Eskil, this profound personal experience of the brevity of life had led Kierkegaard to think of living as a preparation for death, and in its turn this awareness gave him a driven sense of the value of time. In fifteen years of active literary life, Kierkegaard's output was prodigious. On a single day in 1843 he published three books. Kierkegaard's father Michael rose from the lowest peasant class to become a wealthy importer of textiles. As a boy of fourteen, while out tending his master's sheep, he had looked up into the sky one day and cursed God for the unfairness of his fate. What happened to him subsequently – the sudden fabulous wealth, the succession of deaths in his family – seemed to him God's enigmatic response to this curse. He instructed Søren in a dark vision of Christianity that the boy resented for a long time, inducing a sense that he had had no real childhood at all. Later, Søren learnt to see the legacy as a chance to reinvent his own idea of what being a Christian really meant. On his father's death in 1838 he inherited a fortune that relieved him of the need to earn a living and enabled him to start in earnest on what he had decided would be his life's work: as a thinker and writer. In May 1837, at the house of a Copenhagen friend, Kierkegaard met and courted a precocious and talented young girl named Regine Olsen. When she was eighteen years old, in 1840, he proposed to her and was accepted, but a year later, in September 1841, he broke off the engagement. Shortly after that, he published the book that made him famous throughout Scandinavia and which is probably still the title most commonly associated with his name, *Either/Or*.

Eskil explained that these features of his early life – the intimacy with death, the enforced immersion in his father's world of guilt, the self-wounding decision not to marry the woman he loved – became the motor of all Kierkegaard's thought. He willed it to be so. His huge quarrel with the then dominant school of speculative philosophy represented by Friedrich Hegel was that the objectivity of such philosophy was pretended, and that universal systems of thought such as that offered by Hegel were flawed through a fatal overestimation of the power of reason. For Kierkegaard, reason was a useful tool for dealing with many of life's situations, but it was out of its depth when faced with the most profound existential questions: Who am I? Why am I here? What is death? He criticized Hegel for not living out the consequences of his own thought:

> A thinker erects a huge building, a system, one that encompasses the whole of life and world-history, etc. – and if one then turns attention to his personal life one discovers to one's astonishment the appalling and ludicrous fact that he himself does not live in this huge, high-vaulted palace, but in a store-house next door, or a kennel, or at best in the caretaker's quarters... Spiritually a man's thoughts must be the building in which he lives – otherwise it won't work.

Kierkegaard's objection to so-called objective, speculative philosophy was not merely that it was inauthentic and a falsification of the lived life; he saw real dangers in the prospect of its triumph:

> An epidemic of cholera is usually signalled by the appearance of a certain kind of fly not otherwise observable; may it not be the case that the appearance of these fabulous pure thinkers is a sign that some misfortune threatens humanity, as for instance the loss of the ethical and the religious?

Abstract philosophers favour the tidy crowd over the untidy individual. Kierkegaard was passionately concerned to develop a philosophy that was neither an abstract discipline nor a game with words, but something with profound relevance to the everyday life of the individual:

> I go about with the idiotic thought that everything should be done to

make people aware, with the thought that every individual person is a tremendous thing, that not a single one, let alone a thousand, should be wasted.

His gesture in breaking off his engagement to Regine was, in his view, an example of a sacrifice made in the name of being authentic and true to his beliefs – in this case that he could make neither her nor himself happy if he sacrificed the compulsions of his vision for the ease of married life.

Using himself and his own life as source material, Kierkegaard offered an analysis of personal development in a series of three stages – actually four, though the first of these, the philistine, is never referred to as a stage. Each constitutes an upward step from the one preceding. In the philistine stage, life passes in a state of complete unawareness. As philistines, we sleepwalk through our days. We may do so very successfully, hold high office, become wealthy and famous; but we are missing the point. The aesthetic stage ensues when we awaken to the realization that life is both larger and stranger than we had at first thought. It involves a stepping back from life, a realization that events and people can be manipulated. But the sole use the aesthete makes of this insight is to stave off the boredom that comes from seeing through everything, and the revelation that, seemingly, none of it matters much. The ethical person is the aesthete who has exhausted the pleasures of his lucid dreaming and come to understand that these involve no more than an endless chain of repetitions and meaningless choices that may well be damaging to those who are unknowingly manipulated. Kierkegaard captures the moment of realization in a bleakly hilarious rant:

Marry, you'll regret it; don't marry, you'll regret that too; marry or don't marry, you'll regret it either way; whether you marry or you don't marry, either way, you'll regret it. Laugh at the world's follies, you'll regret it; weep over them, you'll regret that too; laugh at the world's follies or weep over them, you'll regret it either way; whether you laugh at the world's follies or weep over them, either way, you'll regret it. Believe a girl, you'll regret it; don't believe her, you'll regret that too; believe a girl or don't believe her, you'll regret it either way; whether you believe a girl or don't believe her, either way, you'll regret it. Hang yourself, you'll regret it; don't hang yourself, you'll regret that too; hang yourself or don't hang yourself, you'll regret it either way; whether you hang yourself or you don't hang yourself, either way, you'll regret it. This, gentlemen, is the essence of all life's wisdom.

The aesthete finally realizes the terrifying nature of freedom, of being lost in this Hall of Mirrors and compelled to choose. It was this aspect of Kierkegaard's thought that so appealed to Jean-Paul Sartre and the Existentialists of the next century – the understanding that the freedom for which we so romantically long may, if we ever get it, bring on an unexpected and vertiginous nausea. The enlightened aesthete then starts to make ethical choices in his or her life.

The first and most important choice, Kierkegaard insists, is to choose oneself. To accept responsibility for our own lives as existing human beings. To accept that we are, for good and ill, the result of our own choices, and to do so in complete transparency and honesty. Only then can the ethical life begin, the life of choosing between things on an ethical basis.

What moves the ethical person to take the final step up, to the religious stage, is a shattering realization of the true nature of what Kierkegaard calls 'sin', which is the failure to have the courage to defy reason and to take the 'leap of faith' required to commit oneself wholly to the belief that Jesus Christ really was – and still is, in the eternal moment of his life – the incarnation of God on earth. For Kierkegaard, the opposite of 'sin' was not virtue but 'faith', a faith of almost inhumanly great dimensions, of which only a few have seemed capable. He thought long and hard about what he called the 'teleological suspension of the ethical', and made his obsessed wonder with the biblical story of Abraham and Isaac the subject of *Fear and Trembling*:

The ethical expression for what he was doing is that he was about to murder Isaac, the religious that he was preparing to sacrifice Isaac. The anguish that arises when confronted by such a dilemma would be enough to make anyone lose sleep; and yet without that anguish, Abraham is not Abraham. Or perhaps Abraham did not do what the Bible story says he did, perhaps by the standards of those times what he did was something completely different, in which case let us forget about him, for of what use is it to remember a past which cannot also be a present?... In removing the element of faith by reducing it to an insignificant factor, what remains of the story is simply that Abraham was prepared to murder Isaac.

Part of Kierkegaard's point was that the Christianity of the Danish state Church took all the power and danger and challenge out of a story like this, turning it into a myth with a happy ending. He wanted people to know that Christianity is a very hard discipline to follow.

Kierkegaard's Christianity is something many rationalists find hard to accept. The cynical suspect that some kind of intellectual dishonesty is involved; the compassionate see in it an exhausted mind finding refuge from the intolerable burden of thought. But his faith is what makes Kierkegaard so fascinatingly modern. He embodied the collision between the old religion, Christianity, and what he saw clearly was on its way to becoming the new one, Rationalism. Astonishingly rational and analytical himself, he nevertheless insisted that reason recognize its limits. He was the first to identify and explore the nature of *angst,* that drone of floating unease that seems to accompany us throughout so much of our lives. He believed in the power of prayer and wrote many prayers of his own. One seems to address the idea of *angst* directly: 'Teach me, O God, not to torture myself, not to make a martyr out of myself through stifling reflection, but rather teach me to breathe deeply in faith.'

Towards the end of Kierkegaard's life, his unease with the sort of Christianity promoted by the Danish state Church erupted into outright rebellion. Embarrassed that he might be guilty of the same failing for which he had once criticized Hegel and Schopenhauer – that of not living out the consequences of their philosophy – he launched a fierce attack on the Church, claiming that its priests were mere bureaucrats and that in the interests of inclusiveness and the stability of the nation state what they preached was a vapid Christianity that hardly deserved the name at all. In effect, he was calling for a second Reformation, so extreme at times that he was willing to contemplate doing without the Bible:

A Reformation that removed the Bible would now, basically, have just as much validity as Luther's removal of the pope. All this about the Bible has given rise to a scholarly and legalistic type of religiousness, sheer diversion. A sort of 'learning' in that direction has gradually found its way down through society and no human being now reads the Bible humanly. This causes irreparable harm; it becomes a refuge for excuses and evasions, etc. respecting existence, for there will always be something to check on first, always this sham that one must have the learning in shape before one can begin living – which means one never gets around to the latter.

Kierkegaard's death in 1855, at the age of forty-two, of a tentatively diagnosed tuberculosis, involved indignities beyond anything Samuel Beckett ever described. Doubly incontinent, and when not so, constipated, his rectum regularly flooded with soapy water, bedbound, with bedsores, his head dangling down onto his chest, the wasted muscles of his legs stimulated daily with electrical prods, his faith remained strong to the end. A visitor asked if he was able to pray in peace in the hospital.

Yes. And when I do I pray first for the forgiveness of sins, that everything may be forgiven; then I pray to be free of despair in death, and the saying frequently occurs to me that death must be pleasing to God; and then I pray for what I would so much like, to know a little in advance when death is to come.

As Eskil ended his account of the life of Kierkegaard as a cautionary tale, Strayhorn's drummer, a shaven-headed man of about fifty wearing a black polo-necked sweater and heavy-rimmed spectacles, stamped out a cigarette on the pavement and walked past us, and we followed him back inside, returning to our seats. We watched him step up onto the stage, his shaven head shining beneath the spotlights, spectacles glinting, sit down behind his drum kit and play a little here-we-are-again drum roll. The talking died down, and the pianist announced that the second set would be devoted to tunes from Dizzy Gillespie's *Groovin' High* to mark fifty years since the release of the original album. It was not music I had any particular relationship to, and I found myself, as one sometimes does, withdrawing from the moment and pursuing instead my own thoughts on the subject of Søren Kierkegaard and any possible significance his life and thought might have for an understanding of the Scandinavian character. My interest had been intensified by an article I had come across in the weekly *Morgenbladet* on the subject of a case of murder from the year 1721 that seemed so strangely predictive of a situation described in *Fear and Trembling* that my first assumption was that the story must have been what inspired Kierkegaard to write the book. In the 'Preamble from the Heart' section – which follows on from the opening accounts of the four different ways in which Abraham might have tried to interpret God's terrifying command that he sacrifice his only son Isaac on Mount Moriah – and the 'Speech in Praise of Abraham' section, Kierkegaard presents the following scenario: a priest preaches a sermon on the story of Abraham and Isaac in his local church one Sunday morning. With his low opinion of the institutional Church in general, and of its servants in particular, Kierkegaard imagines the members of the congregation dozing off during the sermon, all except one man, who hears the story in all its terrible detail and is so haunted by it he loses the power to sleep. A few days later, this man emulates Abraham and kills his own son as an offering to God. As soon as he hears the news, the priest rushes to the parishioner's home and bursts in on him. He denounces him with a greater passion than any he ever put into his Sunday sermon, cursing the man, calling him despicable, the lowest of the low, demanding to know what devil it was that possessed him and made him want to murder his own son; and Kierkegaard imagines the father replying that he has only done what the great Abraham did in the sermon the priest preached on Sunday.

Kierkegaard's point is that the priest was preaching, as it were, in his sleep, without listening to himself and with no idea at all what he was actually saying. The only person who had listened and tried to understand the story had been this parishioner. Of course he couldn't get it out of his mind. Who could? Knowing that in some mysterious way, one was supposed to admire Abraham. This is Kierkegaard's idea of real faith. That a man never questions the word of God – not even on something like this. The Bible has its happy ending for the father and son: an angel comes down and stays Abraham's upraised hand as he is about to kill Isaac, and then Abraham sees the ram with its horns caught in the thicket and realizes God wants him to sacrifice this instead. But in Kierkegaard's version, the parishioner isn't so lucky. No angel to stay his hand, no ram to take the place of his boy. The upshot of it all, according to Kierkegaard, is that such a man would either be executed or shut away in a madhouse. But was Kierkegaard right in his analysis? I wondered. Was his imagined killer copying only Abraham's outward behaviour, without any deeper understanding of the man? Granted, the killer assumed that the same sequence of events would occur for him as for Abraham: an angel would intervene, a ram appear, and all this would happen in the moment between lifting the knife and applying the knife to his son's throat, so that he was not merely miming the sacrifice but showing God he was willing to go the whole way. Only in his case, that's not what happened.

The group were now playing their version of 'Salt Peanuts' and, as the trumpeter launched into the solo, it occurred to me that Kierkegaard's parishioner was like those trumpeters in the Fifties who idolized Dizzy Gillespie, and who thought that if they bent the horn of their trumpets upwards the way Dizzy did that would somehow magically enable them to play as well as he did. Or like those Fifties' alto-sax players who took heroin because they thought that was the secret of Charlie Parker's brilliance.

The piece in *Morgenbladet* was based on a book by Erling Sandmo called *Mordernes forventninger* ('Expectations of Murderers'). Sandmo's book has nothing to do with Kierkegaard but concerns the subject of how and when the idea arose that a murderer might be insane at the time of the deed and so not be accountable for his or her actions. It was part of the discussion that filled the news media during the weeks and months leading up to Anders Breivik's trial for the bombing of the government buildings in Oslo and the shootings on the island of Utøya, which resulted in the deaths of seventy-seven people, the majority of them young political activists. The journalist used the case studies in Sandmo's book as a way of putting the question of Breivik's sanity into a historical context. One of the studies concerned a murder committed in 1721, in a remote farming community in Norway's Rendalen valley, by a man named Olav Tollefsen Fiskvik.

One Sunday, Fiskvik went to church and heard the priest deliver a sermon about Abraham's faith and devotion to God. Just like Kierkegaard's hypothesized parishioner 120 years later, Fiskvik was afterwards unable to get the story out of his mind. Four years passed. Then, on one Thursday in July, Fiskvik went off into the woods and took his seven-year-old son Halvor with him. He said he was looking for bark, and for wood to make a new handle for his axe. Fiskvik's wife Siri said there was no need, that she and the serving girl Gjertrud had just been out gathering bark. But Olav said he had to go anyway, and so father and son set off hand in hand through the trees. There was something in Fiskvik's manner that Siri found disturbing; she sent Eli, her daughter from a previous relationship, after them.

Not long afterwards, Eli came running back. She was very frightened and said her stepfather had chased her away with the axe. Then father and son walked on deeper into the forest, Olav still holding Halvor by the hand. When they came to a clearing, Olav stopped and began gathering wood, piling it up. He told Halvor to turn around and face the pile, and then raised the axe above his head with both hands and swung down at his son. Halvor fell forward across the woodpile. His father hit him again twice, to make sure that he was dead. Olav added more wood to the pile and tried to set light to it – but the wood was still green and the flame wouldn't catch, so he turned and retraced his steps back home. On his return, Siri asked where Halvor was, and Olav said something she didn't understand, that the boy's spirit was out walking. Siri told Eli to go out and find him, so that he wouldn't get lost. That was when Olav told her the truth, reaching out his arms towards her, saying: 'God will love us now, now we too are God's children.' He said that God had told him to sacrifice Halvor if he wanted to be loved. Gjertrud the serving girl said that God would never make such a demand. It was at this point that Fiskvik realized what he had done. He said he wanted to die. He agreed to show them where the body lay. Gjertrud told Siri to stay at home, as she would not be able to bear the sight, and it was Gjertrud who lifted the little body from the smouldering woodpile and carried it back to the farm.

In 1721 the idea that a killing committed 'while the balance of the mind was disturbed' might involve a mitigating circumstance had not yet been thought. The punishment for murder was quite simply death. But in this case something remarkable happened. The Rendalen bailiff made it his business to talk to those in the community who knew Fiskvik. He learned that Fiskvik had periods when his thoughts seemed to go astray and he would wander about the valley threatening and frightening people with his behaviour. When he was in the grip of these moods, his father and brothers would be contacted, and Fiskvik would be overpowered and held in a locked shed on his father's farm at Akre until the mood had passed.

The bailiff listened to all this before handing down his judgement on the case. He did not order Fiskvik's execution. Instead, he ordered that he be kept locked up by his relatives for the remainder of his life. And since his wife was too poor to keep him on their farm in this way, and lacked the physical strength to control him anyway; and because it would be an intolerable burden for her to see the killer of her son every day for the rest of her life, the bailiff ordered that Fiskvik's birth family should bear the responsibility. And that is how the matter was dealt with. Fiskvik stayed locked up on his father's farm until his death in 1751. It was care in the community. What else could you call it?

Reading the story it seemed to me a remarkable and even a peculiarly Scandinavian solution to an intolerably difficult situation, and not one that I could ever imagine a British judge of the period arriving at. Having offered Eskil a précis of the situation I said as much as we sat outside during Strayhorn's next break. Knowing already that Eskil thought I had a tendency to idealize Scandinavian societies, and that he sometimes spoke as if he were on a personal mission to cure me of sentimental delusions about them, I was unwilling to let all of my argument depend on the lenient treatment of Fiskvik, but challenged him to account for the very striking fact that Norway, Denmark and Sweden had all abandoned the use of capital punish-

ment several decades before the British did so. 'The last British woman to hang was Ruth Ellis in 1955,' I said. 'The Swedes stopped hanging women back in 1890: Anna Månsdotter, lover of her son and murderer of her son's wife. Look here.' I took out my phone and showed him the famous photograph taken in secret a minute or two before her execution, with Anna standing next to the priest and looking over at her executioner, the tall man standing to her right.

'And the last Swedish man to be executed was Alfred Ander, back in 1910, for a murder committed during an armed robbery. In Denmark, the last judicial killing took place in 1892. Norway stopped executing people even earlier,' I went on. 'In 1876.'

'I know who that was. It was Kristoffer Grindalen. A complete fucking bastard,' Eskil said without looking up. He was still studying the image on my phone, vainly trying to zoom into the woman's face with quick, flexing movements of his fingers before handing the phone back to me. A giant blue tram rumbled past the Oslo Courthouse on its way up Kristian Augusts gate. The pianist emerged, talking, with three or four other people. On the other side of the tramlines, hooded skateboarders clattered up and down the courthouse steps. Eskil had taken his beer outside with him. He nodded a greeting to Strayhorn's drummer, who sat down at the table next to ours. I realized now that he was actually the house drummer, I'd seen him playing at Herr Nilsen's many times before. He stretched out his legs, patted his pockets, couldn't find his cigarettes, smiled and pointed at the packet of Teddies glistening on the table in front of us. Eskil gestured expansively. Sure, go ahead. It was November, and cold. We smoked in silence for a few moments. A fine net of drizzle was falling through the warm orange light of the sodium street lamp on the corner of C.J. Hambros plass and Rosencrantz gate, and looking into it I felt a familiar rising ecstasy, as powerful and as irrational as *angst* and yet its polar opposite, a sensation of almost unendurable happiness, to be talking and talking about things I would never tire of trying to understand, and to be completely at ease with the certainty that I never would understand them, for who knows what the magpie thinks. From the open doorway of Per på Hjørnet, the bar next to Herr Nilsen, I heard the sound of a power trio, recognizing like an old friend the busy acoustic riff that opens Fleetwood Mac's 'Oh Well'. Just warming up, checking their sound, getting ready for the night. I became so lost in the joy of the moment that when Eskil next spoke it took me several seconds to remember what we had been talking about.

'You mean you see this as an early example of the advanced, liberal, humanitarian thinking that is typical of a precocious spirit of enlightenment among Scandinavians in the field of crime and punishment?' he said, smiling slightly, his brow creasing.

'Something like that, yes.'

'Well, I don't. I don't think the bailiff's procedures were necessarily psychologically advanced at all. Consider this: if he was being logically judicial about it, where did the ultimate responsibility for the murder lie? Following the religious logic of the time, it lay with

God. But you couldn't say that in 1721. You couldn't even think it. Somewhere along the line it must have occurred to the bailiff that perhaps Fiskvik *was* another Abraham, a 'knight of faith' as Kierkegaard called people of naturally limitless and unquestioning faith. Had he sentenced Fiskvik to be hung, he might well have felt that he was putting his understanding of human nature above God's. Which would be blasphemous.'

'Well, even granted that,' I said, 'What about the Scandinavians' record on capital punishment? Streets ahead of anyone else.'

'But how valid is that,' replied Eskil, 'when we executed Quisling and a whole lot of other collaborators after the war?'

'Treason is special,' I objected. 'And anyway, Quisling wasn't mad.'

'Are you so sure? Have you read *Universismen*?' Eskil described a book on which Vidkun Quisling had been working in desultory fashion throughout most of his life. Apparently Quisling believed himself to be a visionary, and to his political vision for his country he had added a religious vision he called 'Universism', which he wanted to see as the new state religion after the triumph of fascism. It was his own synthesis of Lutheranism, Confucianism, Buddhism, along with the thought of Goethe, Kant, Nietzsche, Spinoza, Schopenhauer and various others, and what he understood of quantum physics. He called it his *Antropokosmiske system*, his Anthropocosmic System. None of it is actually very exceptional, but being Quisling he thought it was all deeply original, a new teaching that was destined to sweep all others aside. Quisling worked on his Anthropocosmic System during the last few days of his life, trying to master the prospect of his own death. Sleep can't have come easily anyway, for the lights in his cell were always left on for fear he would commit suicide and cheat the executioners. Eight hundred pages of essays and notes written on hotel stationery, restaurant menus, the backs of train tickets and pages ripped from magazines. He tried to sum it all up in series of aphorisms written between 1 October and 6 October, which he packed up in an envelope and addressed to 'Maria Quisling, my beloved and faithful wife. In gratitude.'

Eskil stopped speaking suddenly and fumbled another cigarette out of the packet. I knew that his own marriage was in trouble, and I couldn't help wondering if, perhaps to his surprise, he had been moved by his own account of Quisling's last days and supposed mental collapse. That is the appalling truth, I thought, that even monsters can suddenly and unexpectedly appear before us as human, and we have to struggle against the temptation to feel pity for them. The last words of the Nazi Julius Streicher were a cry of love for his wife Adele, muffled by the executioner's hood pulled over his head but still audible. Even knowing the unspeakable cruelty these people inflicted on others, it seemed to me these sudden flashes of humanity can make life unbearably complicated at times.

'As it survived,' Eskil went on, 'Quisling's manifesto was incoherent and never attained a form in which it could conceivably have been published in his own lifetime. I read the edited and abridged version published by Juritzen a few years ago, and at the very least you would have to say Quisling was so odd in his general view of life, and of the meaning of life, and of the future of life on earth that modern forensic psychiatry would almost certainly have found him not fit to plead. Like the first two psychiatrists appointed by the court to assess Breivik, who diagnosed him as a paranoid schizophrenic who was in a psychotic state on the day of the killings and unfit to plead. But of course public opinion would have been outraged if Quisling and the twenty-four others executed with him had been found not responsible for their actions.

'Besides,' Eskil said, 'people *want* to be held responsible for their actions. It's one of the human rights. Look at what happened to your great hero Knut Hamsun. After weeks of incarceration and examination at the clinic in Vinderen and the Old Folks' Home in Larvik, the two psychiatrists in charge of assessing his fitness to stand trial, Langfeldt and Ødegaard, psychiatrists of the old school who wore white coats to work, submitted a report to the attorney general stating that throughout the war Hamsun had been suffering from *varig svekkede sjelsevner*, "permanently impaired mental faculties", and could not be held to account for things he wrote in the newspapers and said on the radio during the years of the German occupation of Norway. It's Stalinist. You don't like what the enemies of the people say so you declare them insane.

'To me this is the least attractive aspect of social-democratic thinking. A kind of asymmetrical paternalism in which the conception of victimhood has been wildly expanded, that refuses to recognize the existence of bad or even alternative thoughts and treats the thinker of them as a victim in need of treatment. It's well-meaning, but what it amounts to is an unintended assault on the dignity of the individual. Social democracies like ours are dependent for their successful functioning on a high degree of conformism that is, hopefully, voluntary. In my view, this is one of the main reasons most of the great Scandinavian artists – think of Ibsen, Munch, Strindberg, Hamsun, even Knausgård if you like – are always so ferociously individualistic and seemed to be fuelled by a kind of cornered anger. The art they produce includes this direct reflection of the huge struggle it cost them merely to be allowed to express it. Add Bergman to that list.

'The other side of it is the suspicion and even fear of great individuality and independence of mind. This is what Kierkegaard devoted so much of his fabulous literary energy to attacking, especially towards the end of his life, when he launched that furious attack on the whole of institutionalized Christianity in Denmark. He wanted people to remember how *hard* Christianity is. It's something that can only be attempted at the level of the individual, with the individual accepting complete responsibility for his own life. The state Church was axiomatically a Church for everyone, a club with no membership requirements, and no demands on the members either. He wanted to remind people of the greatness and the mystery and the dread that constituted the essence of real Christian faith. And so, during those last few months of his life, when he almost literally worked himself to death writing and publishing *Øyeblikket*, 'The Moment', his mouthpiece for all this, many of the people he attacked believed in all honesty that he must, of course, have lost his mind. What other explanation could there be?'

Eskil stood up as he said this and flicked the stub of his cigarette out past the canopy into the drizzle. A tiny shower of sparks and then gone. 'But enough of my *tvisyn*,' he said, with a little laugh. 'I think you call it playing the Devil's advocate in English. Or judicial vision, something like that. If people really listened to Kierkegaard and tried to follow him, the world would spin off its axis altogether. And I find his refusal to condemn Abraham personally distasteful. In fact, I find his whole idea of the teleological suspension of the ethical distasteful. The pianist's just gone back inside. Shall we?'

As the group members stepped back up onto the stage, the pianist already bent over the keys and leafing through the sheet music on the stand, I felt moved to make a last defence of my understanding that the Scandinavians were among the first Europeans to institutionalize human kindness in their approach to crime and punishment, and I challenged Eskil again to give me a rational and objective explanation of the gap of decades that separated the abolition of the death penalty in our two countries. He shrugged and said that perhaps it was simply part of the difference between running a big country and a small country.

'In small countries like ours, everyone is still an individual. That's a luxury they don't have in big countries like the USA or the UK. Everyone is family. Even a Breivik. Even Breivik deep down is regarded as someone whom *we* as a society have failed in some way, whom we failed to prevent from taking the wrong path. Criminals and murderers are people who have got lost in the wilderness and need to be helped back to the way. You have to realize,' said Eskil, 'that law in the Scandinavian countries has always involved a strong sense of community. Under the laws of the old Norwegian Gulathing and the Frostating punishment of criminals was a communal responsibility. A thief convicted of a petty offence had to run a gauntlet of stones and turf. The thirteenth-century Bjarkøyretten in Trondheim even stipulated the fine to be paid by anyone who failed to throw something at the thief. We're all in it together. Always. So shame is a historically powerful factor in small communities like ours. A seventeenth-century French traveller in Sjælland wrote of his surprise at seeing men hanging from gallows by the roadside with the corpses of wolves dangling next them. It was an established practice among the Danes; Saxo mentions it in the *Gesta Danorum*. The presence of the wolves, he discovered, was to increase the dead man's shame.'

For their final session, the group was joined onstage by a girl singer. Stylish, in a red dress, with short blonde hair and no make-up, she looped her hand around the back of the microphone, the pianist counted the group in and she began an achingly sad version of 'You Don't Know What Love Is'. The Norwegian language doesn't have a voiced 's' and in some inexplicable way the refrain was rendered still more poignant by the way she treated the final 's' as voiceless, *You don't know what love iss*. As an audience we were not used to having a singer onstage at Herr Nilsen, and were unsure whether to applaud her each time she sang a verse, as though it were a piano or a tenor solo, or to save our applause to the end. It was oddly nerve-wracking. Sometimes we clapped in the middle of the songs, sometimes afterwards.

Strayhorn, with guest artist, closed the final set with 'My Foolish Heart', a song made famous by Billy Eckstine. I watched Eskil watching the singer. His marriage to Gry had broken up about two years earlier. She had moved away and taken the children with her. He hadn't wanted it to happen. But I knew he had met someone else recently, a woman who worked as a children's book editor at a publishing house in Drammen, and that he really liked her a lot. As I watched him, I was hoping she liked him a lot too. He moved his lips, mouthing the words now and then, nodding his head in a slow and decided way, as though he had written the song himself and the singer was singing it just the way he thought it should be sung. Then I fell out of the moment and began worrying again about whether or not I had upset the pianist by talking too loudly. There seemed no way of knowing for sure. Did he really glare at me as he went back inside after the break? Or had I just imagined it? And since I knew the whole inner discussion was both absurd and completely irresistible, exactly what kind of Kierkegaardian *angst* was I suffering from? Was it the *substantial* or *prototypical angst* of Mozart's Don Giovanni? Hardly. Or maybe the *tragic angst* he discovered in Antigone? Or the *psychopathic angst* that tormented Nero? In the end, I decided it was none of these, but rather the form explored at length in *The Concept of Anxiety* – the background hum of anxiety about nothing at all, that knows it's about nothing at all and is therefore absurd, and so searches the immediate vicinity for a peg, however ridiculous, on which to hang itself. Having surrendered completely to this explanation, as soon as the musicians laid down their instruments I placed myself at the head of the queue that formed in front of the stage to buy their latest CD, the oddly titled *Strayhorns and Posthorns*, some forty or fifty copies of which were now displayed inside an open brown leather suitcase, it was to, as it were, *apologise* to the pianist, and if at all possible encourage him to reassess the low opinion he may have formed of me as an impolite man with no interest in jazz who had simply wandered into the bar in search of a drink. I bought two copies and gave one to Eskil. About 10 o'clock that night, waiting for my tram home at the National Theatre stop, I realized I had left mine at Burns'. On the off-chance he was still there, I called Eskil on the mobile, recalling, as I waited for him to pick up, an anecdote he had told me earlier in the evening, which he called a 'joke', about how Kierkegaard was chased down a Copenhagen street one day by a group of small boys throwing stones at him and jeering: *Hin enkelte! Hin enkelte!* – The individual! The individual!

9
The Loneliness of the Long-Distance Explorer

I MET ERLING JONSRUD ABOUT THIRTY YEARS AGO, NOT long after I first came to Norway. I had got into the habit of going to the Film Club showings at Filmenshus in Dronningens gate in downtown Oslo as many as three or four times a week, not so much out of interest in the films themselves as because I suspected I was starting to drink too regularly in the early evening hours between finishing my day's studying at the University Library in Solli plass, and my future wife's return from one of the two or three yoga classes she attended each week to the rooms we shared in Kringsjå student village, so that we could eat our evening meal together. Going to the cinema was a harmless and sometimes interesting way of passing that waiting time alone.

I enjoyed the ritual purity of those Cinemateket showings, the intimacy of the two small theatres, the atmosphere of dedication which meant that the showings always began precisely at the appointed hour, with occasionally a brief introduction from the director, or from an actor, now old and grey, who had made a brief appearance in the film at the start of his career; the way there were no advertisements, no trailers for forthcoming attractions, no buckets of popcorn and no coffee, nothing extraneous to the experience we were about to have, only the quick dimming of the lights and the hushed swish of the plush red drapes as they opened. Most of those who attended regularly were men, usually on their own. I guessed they were film buffs, unlike me, and for a long time, until I got to know him well enough to ask him to be best man at my wedding, I assumed that Erling also had a particular interest in film as an art form.

The Flight of the Eagle was showing that night, a Swedish film from 1982 directed by Jan Troell and based on a best-selling novel by Per Olof Sundman from the 1960s, about Salomon August Andrée's attempt to fly a hydrogen balloon to the North Pole in 1897. On a July morning that year, Andrée and two young companions had lifted off from Danskøya, an island off the north-west of Spitzbergen, and drifted away towards the horizon, never to be seen nor heard from again. The part of Andrée, usually known as Engineer Andrée, was played by Max von Sydow. Göran Stangertz played the expedition's physicist and photographer Nils Strindberg, aged twenty-three, and the Norwegian actor Sverre Anker Ousdal was Knut Fraenkel, twenty-seven, their strong man and mathematician, who was preparing for a career in the army when the chance to join Andrée's exhibition came up. Andrée was forty-three.

As the film ended and the house lights went up members of audience rose to their feet in a staggered silence, men bending to pick up their coats and scarves and gloves and woollen hats from one of the vacant seats on either side of them – the club was not very well supported and the theatres were rarely more than a quarter full – and shuffling out towards the aisles in a pensive silence. All save on my row, which until moments before the film started I had had to myself until a latecomer pushed through the swing doors and sat down in the first available seat, which happened to be at the end of my row. And he remained seated now, watching the white words rise up the screen, until finally he and I were the only two people left in the auditorium. I glanced at my watch. Six forty. She would still be at her yoga so I was in no hurry to get back to Kringsjå, and I stayed in my seat, waiting until the figure at the end of the row decided to leave. Minutes passed, however, and he showed no signs of moving, and finally I felt constrained to loom over him. I remember that he gave a slight start of surprise as he became aware of my presence and looked up at me, and that his eyes were glistening with unreleased tears as he made a remark, quite as though we had been watching the film together – which, of course, in a way we had – the gist of which was that it was a strange thing to immerse oneself in failure on such a grand scale, *without that failure necessarily even being heroic*. He said these last words, speaking in that italicized way I came to know as habitual, as he got to his feet, apologetically fumbling for a thin and faded yellow scarf, which he knotted around his throat, and in a quite natural way we fell into conversation as we exited into Dronningens gate. Turning right onto Tollbugata he came to a halt outside Original Pilsen and announced that he was going in for a drink, would I care to join him? Like a man on a strict timetable I glanced at my watch, hesitated as though conducting an inner debate about whether or not I had time, and then, acting a sort of irritated resignation that might have puzzled him had he noticed it, said yes, I had time, but it would have to be a quick one.

We ordered our drinks at the bar, a beer for me, a beer and an aquavit in a tulip-shaped glass for him, and sat down at a table by the wall next to a pool table. I had never been in the Original Pilsen but knew of its reputation as a bar frequented by prostitutes and drug addicts, very often the same thing in those days. This was some years before the appearance in central Oslo of large numbers of Nigerian prostitutes, most of them travellers from Italy, who briefly turned the Egertorget area around the Storting government building into a red-light district, and whose energetic hustling was a main cause of legislation introduced shortly afterwards that made it a criminal offence for a man to pay for sex. The exuberant self-advertisement of these big and healthy-looking Nigerian women was in stark contrast to the pallor of the scrawny little drug-addicted Norwegian girls one used to see on street corners in the old business district of the city around Akershus fortress back in those days, huddled against the cold in their tattered anoraks, tottering forward on high-heeled boots and bending to lean in through the windows of the cars that crawled to a halt by the kerb.

We started talking about the film. Erling seemed to know a lot more about the expedition than the story told in the film, something I remarked on later in the evening and which he explained by saying that he had also recently seen a documentary film made by the same director, Jan Troell, about the expedition and its fate.* 'The Swedish government organized a search for them but called it off after a couple of months,' he went on. 'They assumed something must have gone wrong with the balloon, but they had no way of knowing where the men might have landed. And then for the next thirty-three years, nothing. Until one day in 1930, a little Norwegian walrus-hunting ship, the *Bratvaag*, put a party of men ashore on a remote island in the Arctic called Hvitøya.† Two young deckhands from Tromsø were sent off to look for fresh water. They walked along the flat, rocky beach heading for a stream. One of them found an aluminium lid among the stones. And on the far side of a stream something that looked as if it might be man-made showing through the melting ice. They crossed to take a closer look, scraped away some of the coating of snow and ice and realized that it was a small boat. Two boys not even born at the time the expedition went missing. Perhaps they'd never even heard of Andrée's expedition. Or thought the boat might have something to do with Roald Amundsen, who had vanished without trace two years previously while taking part in the search for another missing balloonist, the Italian Umberto Nobile.

'Anyway, they made their way back to the camp and told the *Bratvaag*'s skipper what they'd found. They led the skipper and the other members of the landing party back to the spot. After a quick search of the terrain they came across what looked like two piles of blackened rubbish. On closer inspection these turned out to be human remains. One was leaning against a rock. There were boots on its feet. The head was missing, the bones in disarray. The body was still partially clothed, and opening the jacket they saw a large monogram,

---

*   You can see the film at https://youtu.be/dJM62aIN.
†   White Island.

'A', from which the skipper deduced that, after thirty-three years, he was looking at what was left of Engineer Andrée's expedition. A little later, they found a third body, carefully covered with stones and wedged into a wall of ice. It turned out to be Strindberg. He must have been the first one to die. They had tried to bury him. That's what people do. They bury their dead. Killed by a bear according to the film. That was a very well-done scene where he gets mauled to death by the bear, wasn't it? I wonder how they did that?'

Erling raised his head and peered at me with his pale blue eyes. I was getting used to his face. There was a troubled melancholy about it that reminded me of David Janssen, the actor who played the lead in a 1960s' television series, *The Fugitive*, about a doctor on the run, wrongly suspected of murdering his wife, whose strongest card in trying to get people (women, usually) to help him was a lost and haunted look, which, as a fifteen-year-old schoolboy, I spent a lot of time trying to make my own. Erling, like Janssen, wore his hair short, neat, parted on the left. His cheeks were almost painfully clean-shaven and glowed with the false health of alcohol, for – despite his obvious intelligence and the coherence of his speech – I knew already, from the dense wall of alcohol that surrounded him even at this early stage of the evening, that Erling was a man devoted to drinking. He emptied his shot of Gammel Oppland aquavit, chased it with a long mouthful of beer, caught the eye of the Pakistani waiter, and gestured briefly with split fingers at the two empty glasses in front of him.

'It's only when people close to you die that death becomes real. Your parents die, but they're supposed to die. It's different with a brother or a sister or a close friend. When a friend dies it's like death jumps down and stands beside you. Once Nisse was dead, killed by a bear or however it happened, only then did Andrée and Fraenkel realize that *of course* they were going to die too. It was just a question of in what order. They realized, if they hadn't realized before, that the whole thing, the whole expedition, had been a sort of salon dream from start to finish. Did you see how they planned to cook? On a primus stove suspended seven metres below the gondola? They were going to use mirrors to help them. *Mirrors*. And a *pole*.

You would think, the very first time Andrée brought up this idea of cooking with mirrors, that Strindberg or Fraenkel, one of them, would have said to him: "Look, this is insane, let's drop the whole thing now, before it's too late."

'Andrée worked at the Patent and Registration Office in Stockholm. I've often thought about the significance of that. If you look at the expedition details, the idea of going in a balloon itself, those thick ropes dangling from the gondola that were supposed to drag along the ice below and help them control their speed through the air; that "steering sail" mounted at the front that would enable them to sail at a thirty-degree angle to the direction of the prevailing wind; this dangling cooking arrangement; the idea of using homing pigeons to carry messages and progress reports to the people back home, the whole stupid idea, it was all an absurd dream in the mind of a man whose every day was spent in the company of madmen who visited his offices trying to take out patents on things like perpetual motion machines. A man came in once with a sack containing hundreds of little bits of wood and cogs and emptied it on the floor of Andrée's office. "Has it ever worked?" Andrée asked him. "Yes," said the man, "it worked once. One night it just started up rotating, all by itself. But it made such a tremendous racket my landlady came running up the stairs and starting banging on the door and threatening me with eviction if I didn't turn it off." Which he did. He switched it off and the thing exploded, pieces of it flying all over the room, he told Andrée. And it's never worked since.'

He fell silent momentarily as the waiter put his two drinks on the table and then headed off to another corner of the bar without taking any money. I still couldn't get used to the way Norwegians didn't pay for their drinks until the evening was over. It seemed very trusting to me. Erling rearranged the drinks so that the aquavit glass was closer to his right hand than the glass of beer. He took a sip of the aquavit, moved his hand in the direction of the beer glass but then changed his mind and let it rest on the table.

'This was the kind of person Andrée was spending his time with. Maniacs. Madmen.'

Since Erling seemed to know so much about the story, I asked him something that had been on my mind throughout the film: the expedition's photographer Nils Strindberg, was he related to the playwright? My impression was that Strindberg wasn't a common surname in Sweden.

'Nisse was the son of Strindberg's cousin,' he said. 'When the Swedish papers first started writing about the expedition, August Strindberg's wife thought he was the one who was going up in the balloon with Andrée. They were separated, so she didn't know any better. Strindberg says in his diary that she wrote him a hysterical letter telling him she still loved him and begging him not to go, not to commit suicide, which more or less shows you what she thought of the whole enterprise. That was in 1896, when the *Eagle's* first attempt to take off had to be abandoned after they'd waited weeks for a favourable wind that never came. In July the next year, Strindberg was walking along with a friend of his, a man named Axel Herrlin. Two pigeons flew over their heads, he says in his diary, and Herrlin pointed up at them and said "Look, there are Andrée's pigeons."

'The next day, writes Strindberg, he was woken by a scream which seemed to come from somewhere above him. It sounded "like the mocking of a dying man," he wrote, and he says he thought straightaway of Andrée's balloon. This was only six days after the balloon took off, three days after it came down 118 miles (190 km) north-east of Danskøya. Nobody could've known about it. So maybe Strindberg really was psychic.'

He broke off, dipped into the pocket of his sheepskin jacket, draped over the back of the chair, pulled out a cigarette-rolling machine and a small rectangular packet of dark tobacco, fed a leaf of paper into the side of the machine, and then began separating the tobacco out into strands and arranging it evenly in the tiny cloth hammock suspended between the rollers.

'The pigeons were Alfred Nobel's idea,' he went on. 'Nobel was a friend of Andrée's boss at the patent office. That's how they met. Nobel took a great interest in the expedition, especially after he put 65,000 kroner into the 1897 attempt, which amounted to half the cost. He'd already put money into the Ljungström brothers' plan to build an ornithopter, a flying-machine that was supposed to work by imitating the wing-strokes of birds. He also advised Andrée to coat the balloon with a special type of French varnish that would stop it leaking so much. It was leaking a lot of air through the seams. But Andrée wouldn't listen. It must have been one of the last projects Nobel supported. He died in the winter of 1896. Andrée went to his funeral. I bet he was standing there thinking how glad he was it wasn't him that was dead. Nobel was only sixty-three years old, he was probably thinking, well, I hope I get to be older than that. I'm glad he gave me the money before he died. That's the way people think. There's nothing wrong with it.'

Erling lifted the cigarette from its cradle, licked along its adhesive edge, conjured a ragged flame from his Zippo lighter and lit it, inhaled, looked upwards and blew out a cone of smoke. The ceiling was stained a speckled brown, the colour of the upstairs on double-decker buses in England before smoking was banned.

'Are you sure you won't have another?' he asked, as the waiter passed our table again. I thought about it. I looked at my watch. Seven o'clock. Probably still too early to go back. Okay. I ordered another beer and a glass of peanuts.

'You know why they were trying to be the first men to reach the North Pole?' Erling resumed. 'Why it was so important to them? This is interesting for you, if you're trying to understand Scandinavian culture: *it was because they were Swedes.* Norway, little Norway, was way ahead of Sweden in the field of Arctic exploration. A tiny country but in terms of polar exploration we were a superpower. We had Fridtjof Nansen, famous all over the world. The Swedes had nobody. Well, Adolf Nordenskjold, but he wasn't in the same class. When the British and the Americans wrote in the newspapers about polar exploration it was *us* they wrote about. The little brother was outshining the – do you say that, outshining? – the big brother. And don't forget, this was just eight years before independence. The tensions between Sweden and Norway were very, very high. No one had ever reached the North Pole. You saw in the film how the crew were treated in Sweden. All that feting and celebrating. Dining with the king. The women looking at them, wanting to be with them. Treated like heroes before they'd even set foot in the gondola. You know how many times Andrée had been up in a balloon before this? Nine, maybe ten times. He was an amateur. And this great hero was going to do this wonderful and futuristic thing that no one had ever done before. A few hours in a balloon. Above Paris,' he added witheringly, as if flying a balloon above Paris made it even worse.

'That scene as they were boarding the train at Stockholm station. The people crowding the platform, wanting to touch them, shake their hands, get autographs. The flags. You can bet they wanted to put the Norwegians in their place. But I'll tell you the worst thing about it: Andrée was so dishonest. A person should always know when to give up, don't you think? Don't you think that that is the most basic requirement any human being should be able to make of himself? Don't you think that there is nothing more contemptible than a man who is so afraid to disappoint people, who is so afraid of disappointing himself that he would rather die? And let others die too?'

He stopped talking, stopped smoking, and peered at me with such a peculiar intensity that for a moment I thought he actually wanted me to answer. I was about to say that probably there were things more contemptible than a lack of self-insight, but before I could do so he was off again.

'Strindberg was just a boy. Twenty-three years old. Andrée was nearly twice his age. And I don't think he really wanted to go, not the second time, because in that intervening year two things happened that changed his life.'

He opened his left palm and stared intently down into it, as though he had a note written there, and then tapped it with the index finger of his other hand.

'One, there was originally a different third member of the party besides Andrée and Strindberg, the one Fraenkel replaced. Nils Ekholm was a meteorologist. He was a mature man. Nearly the same age as Andrée. He knew the balloon was leaking air at the seams through the eight million stitch holes, and that it just wouldn't be tight enough to make the trip unless they did something about it. They tried all sorts of things. Layers and coatings on the inside and outside. Patches. But afterwards, when they did tests with some kind of litmus paper, to see if hydrogen was still escaping, the air still came whispering out, the paper turned black. After that, you know what Andrée did? He went to the balloon hangar on his own, secretly, seven times, and ordered more air to be pumped into it. *Seven times.* Not a word to the other two about it. Andrée was a man who wouldn't listen. He thought faking the evidence didn't matter because he was right anyway. Ekholm saw through him. When he discovered what was going on he dropped out, and that's when Fraenkel came in. I always liked Ekholm. He trusted himself, and his reward was another twenty-six years of life.

'And two,' he went on, looking back into his palm and now tapping with two fingers: 'Andrée's mother died in 1897, just a month before they left Stockholm. Andrée had no wife, no children, his father was dead. They give him a secret lover in the film but I don't think so. Andrée's mother adored him. She was his biggest fan. He could do no wrong in her eyes. When he was trying to describe what it felt like to lose her he said he'd lost *the only reason he had to go on living.* Two weeks later he boards the train from Stockholm and it's up, up and away in his beautiful balloon and off into the cold white sky, taking those two boys along with him, waving goodbye to a world in which he felt he'd lost *the only reason he had to go on living.'*

Erling was telling his story with such empathic intensity that I found I was getting caught up in it, and when he suggested we move on to another bar I readily agreed. We headed along Dronningens gate, turned left and walked up past the shops along Karl Johans gate, past the cathedral. As we walked, I told Erling the story of Donald Crowhurst, with which Andrée's tale seemed to share similarities.

Crowhurst was a participant in a round-the-world single-handed yacht race back in the 1960s, when there was great interest in these competitions following on from the triumph of Sir Francis Chichester who made the first solo circumnavigation of the world in *Gipsy Moth.*

Crowhurst appeared to be on the final stretch of the journey and looking likely to win, heading for the eventual glory and prize money that would save his little Cornish boatyard from bankruptcy, when he suddenly disappeared from the airwaves. Some days later, his catamaran, the *Teignmouth Electron*, was found drifting with no-one on board. Crowhurst's body was never found.

I told Erling about the log-books found on board the *Teignmouth Electron*. The fictional one meant for public consumption, which described his triumphant circumnavigation of the globe; and the true one, which revealed his disintegrating mental state as he realized his boat had never been adequate to the task, and which showed that within days of setting out he had made secret trips ashore to have it repaired, so desperate to win the race and be a hero that he hatched his plan to hide in radio shadow in a remote bay off the Leeward Islands and then to triumphantly reappear on the airwaves weeks later as one of the race leaders. Tormented by loneliness and by the possibility of his deception succeeding, in the end Crowhurst forced his mind to believe it had discovered a secret of Einsteinian proportions, a revelation so vast that it could only be communicated in BLOCK CAPITALS, how to carry out a circumnavigation of the globe using only the imagination.

My point was that from *The Strange Voyage of Donald Crowhurst*, one of the few books I have ever sat up reading all night, when I was twenty, I took a chilling warning about starting something you cannot complete. Something you know to be beyond your abilities. The importance of never being afraid to say you were wrong about yourself. Never being afraid of disappointing people. I thought Andrée, too, probably realized he could never succeed, no matter how much he wanted to, no matter how many well-wishers they had. He was just not cut out for great things. He and Crowhurst both were not as exceptional as they wished they were. And they could not accept it. They couldn't disappoint themselves or their supporters.

We passed through the four-way pedestrian junction of Egertorget, the high point of Karl Johan, from where you can see both the palace at its western end and the railway station at the eastern end, where a vertical signboard alongside the main entrance, long since replaced, advertised 'GOD MAD', an old spelling of *god mat* ('good food') that always made me smile. Snow was starting to fall. Leaning over the railing of the first-floor balcony, a waiter from the Mona Lisa was having a smoke. He looked cold in his white shirt and waistcoat. I said to Erling that in my view he was being too harsh towards Andrée. I was moved by a sentimental and empathic sense of the general tragedy of the whole affair, thinking not of the isolated and individual failures of judgement and foresight that led the three men to their early deaths but rather of the nobility of daring to dream such a grand dream. Whether they succeeded or not, I said, to me they were heroes. 'After all,' I objected, 'they were risking their lives. They knew the risk of failure was great.'

'Aha, but did they?' Erling interjected. 'I don't think they did. Andrée was quite literally up in the air from the very moment he thought of the plan. In his dreams he was floating to the North Pole in the relative comfort of his balloon. Instead of all that hard physical slogging across the ice he was going to complete the journey in a few days and do it the smart, modern, clever way. It was all going to be a breeze.'

He smiled at me as he said this, proud of his word-play, as though it demonstrated his mastery of the language. In much the same way, I had once thought it must be astonishing to be named *Torbjørn*, meaning 'Thor Bear', or *Øyvind*, meaning 'Island Wind' – both of them quite common male names – but could never persuade any Norwegian so named to share in my astonishment. Puns and the literal meanings that delight the linguistic tourist simply do not register with native speakers.

'Listen,' he said, holding up his palm to me, as though I had been talking all evening and not listening. 'Within minutes of lift-off, two things happened. One, three of the four of those 'patent office guide ropes' came unscrewed from their sockets and fell off the gondola while the ground crew still had their hats off waving goodbye. The balloon dropped like a stone towards the surface of the water and they had to toss out valuable ballast left right and centre. Clothes. Food.

Although not the champagne! Oh no. And that silly buoy-thing he was going to drop onto the North Pole as they passed over it... .'

Here I had to interrupt again, for as it happens I had that very morning been reading Hugo Hamilton's *Hågkomster*, a political memoir from 1928 that was of interest to me for its references to Alfred Nobel; and there I came across a question that had occurred to me as we sat watching the film earlier that evening, namely: how would the balloonists, from their position aloft, know when they had reached the North Pole? It appears that at a gathering of the expedition's main backers – besides Nobel, King Oscar II had put up a lot of the money – the Swedish king had asked exactly this question. Before Andrée could reply, Nobel had offered his explanation. The position of the Pole will be self-evident, he told them. Consider the speed at which the earth must be rotating at the precise polar point, he continued, and that it has been doing so for millions and millions of years. 'Obviously large amounts of terrestrial matter must be continuously ejected from this point, so there will undoubtedly be a large hole there clearly visible to you from the gondola.'

Hamilton says that the king stared at Nobel in some surprise and then asked Andrée what he made of the idea. Andrée, looking slightly embarrassed, muttered that it was certainly one theory. Maybe so, said the king, and changed the subject.

Once, writes Hamilton, when he and Nobel were gathered at a dinner party, a guest recalled a previous meeting at which Nobel had mentioned a project that involved buying a row of houses on a Parisian boulevard for some obscure purpose, and asked Nobel whether anything had come of the mysterious project? Nothing came of it, Nobel replied. It's a disgrace that something like that could happen in the most civilized country in the world. I have often wanted to do something for the people of Paris, he said. They have been very friendly and helpful to me on many occasions. And in thinking of some way in which I might repay their kindness the odd fact occurred to me that in Paris, the most civilized city in the world, people often commit suicide in the most repulsive and degrading surroundings. Now, it is the duty of any civilized society to ensure that any among its citizens who wish to depart this life should be able to do so in a dignified manner, and not condemned to cut their throats in some miserable alleyway, or have to throw themselves into the Seine, polluting the water for their fellow-citizens. Nobel said that this was a problem he had been thinking about for a long time.

In due course he had involved two acquaintances, an architect and a doctor, and put to them a plan that he was certain people would find very attractive and which, should it be successful, might prove inspirational to the rest of the world. Along one of the main boulevards in Paris he proposed to build a number of small and tastefully designed villas in which anyone wishing to kill themselves would be able to lodge while obtaining the assistance necessary to do so in a pleasant and pain-free fashion, certain in the knowledge that their dead body would be respectfully dealt with and their dying wishes properly observed, since legal as well as medical expertise would also be provided. When the guest asked why Nobel's plan had come to nothing, Nobel responded in great exasperation that the Parisian police had forbidden it. He had protested furiously and arranged meetings with all sorts of influential people, to no avail. So in the end he abandoned the plan, consoling himself with the thought that the future would have a better understanding of what he had been offering.

We passed the Storting and Grand Hotel, then took a right along Rosencrantz gate and entered Original Nilsen, so-called to distinguish it from the larger Herr Nilsen on the corner of C.J. Hambros plass. Gone now, Original Nilsen was a small bar with black walls and ceiling, and at the far end a Sonor drum kit with bass drum, cymbal-stand and a snare drum with black glitter surround, which glinted faintly in the dimness. It was a Tuesday night, not a live-music night, and there were just a handful of drinkers in the bar. We sat at a small round table next to the tiny stage and as Erling took a first sip of his third or fourth aquavit – and I a sip at my first, a Gammel Oppland he had insisted on buying me since I was new to the country and the culture and 'had to learn about such things' – he returned to the subject of the doomed Andrée expedition. I couldn't help noticing that on several occasions he had referred to it as 'suicidal'. He seemed to use the term literally, not just as a way of underscoring the dangers involved.

'You keep describing Andrée's voyage as *suicidal*? But what about Nisse and Fraenkel? They didn't want to commit suicide?' To me one of the most successful and beautifully treated themes in Troell's film was the way the thought of his fiancée waiting for him was what kept Nils Strindberg going.

Erling looked at me, sensing perhaps a vague disapproval behind my question. Taking a last drag on the frail rag of his roll-up, he squashed it in the ashtray with a twist of his thumb.

'A lot of people who commit suicide don't care who else dies with them. In fact, I believe they probably even think they're doing them a favour. They believe they've seen deeper into the heart of human suffering than others, and that they know better than other people what they want. Of course Nisse didn't want to commit suicide. He had someone. He loved someone and she loved him. Nisse was the nicest and sweetest boy, you can tell from his diary, from the heartbreaking sweetness of his letters to Anna Charlier. And the pictures he kept on taking, that lay undeveloped in his camera, the technicians were able to recover ninety-three of them. The spirit in that. The hope. You can feel it yourself. The idea that if you keep on photographing what's around you then somehow you're still in charge and it's all still a sort of adventure. A very difficult and demanding holiday, but something you will be able to talk about afterwards. Here we are, standing with our rifles over the first polar bear we shot. Or Andrée and Fraenkel standing next to the basket. That black polyp flopped on the ice like a fucking dinosaur. I'll bet they gave it a few kicks. Get up you fuck. You shit. Get up and fly.

'Next year, or the year after, once it's over and a trove of rich and unforgettable memories, Nisse, with Anna at his side, now his wife, will travel the world with a lecture and a slide show and show all these photographs. People will marvel at his photographs, at the fact that they really did fall out of the sky and lived to tell the tale. And here, ladies and gentlemen, is the fork Andrée made for Fraenkel. How we laughed!'

'So you believe Andrée committed suicide?' I asked. 'And persuaded himself that Nisse and Fraenkel wanted to die too?'

'You're being too literal. Everybody wants freedom from the fear of dying. Even happy people. That is the suicide's gift to those who die with him. He takes away their fear by giving them the thing they fear most.'

A big, hulking, badly dressed man passed, hands clasped behind his back and walking with hurried, tiny steps towards the door to the toilet, which was painted black like the walls. He stopped at our table, and he and Erling exchanged a few words before he continued his journey. I hadn't understood anything of what they said and told Erling so. He laughed and explained that Rune was from the same town as him, Øystese in Hardanger. 'We have to change the way we speak when we're in Oslo, otherwise no one would understand us.' I remarked that no one in England would do that. A Geordie or a Scouse would think it shameful to change his accent so that Londoners could understand him; but Erling said there was nothing shameful about it in Norway, it was just practical.

'You're being too literal,' he said again. 'Some people just can't stop doing the thing they know will kill them. Andrée didn't poke a hole in the balloon. He wanted to die without noticing that he was dying. Collecting plants. Making scientific "observations".

Hoping he would just fall asleep in the middle of making a scientific "observation".'

I couldn't really see much difference between Andrée's continuing to collect samples and make observations and Nisse's carrying on taking pictures with his camera, but I said nothing. Erling seemed to have taken an almost personal dislike to Andrée.

'Not like her,' he added, with an upward flick of his eyes.

I followed the direction of his gaze. He was looking intently at the photograph of a woman, one of the gallery of black-and-white portraits that lined the upper part of the walls in a frieze. I recognized some of them – Miles Davis, John Coltrane, Jan Garbarek – but not this one.

'Who is she?'

'Radka Toneff. And that's Jon Ebersen. Terje Gewelt. Arild Andersen. Jens Wendelbo. Pål Thowsen.... .' He identified them all, finger dipping from picture to picture, as though they were well known and I should have heard of them. My gaze returned to the portrait of the dark-haired young woman. She seemed hardly more than a child.

'What did she play?'

'She was a singer. Pretty good singer. I heard her many times. Here, and at Club 7. Radka Toneff, she did it with her eyes open.' He told me she'd killed herself over an unhappy love affair. Drove out to the Bygdøy peninsula on the outskirts of Oslo on a bitterly cold winter's day and parked in a car park there. Took an overdose of pills, washed them down with whisky then left the car and walked away.

'How old was she?'

'Thirty, thirty-two, I don't know. Anyway, she did it properly.'

I sensed he was talking half to himself, and hardly even cared whether or not I knew what he was talking about. But everything about the country and the culture was new and exotic to me. I was still thrilled beyond measure at this unexpected bonus that came with learning the language. A complete parallel cultural universe had opened up to me at the same time, with composers like Fartein Valen,

Geir Tveitt, David Monrad Johansen, Øystein Sommerfeldt, poets like Rolf Jacobsen and the Swede Tomas Tranströmer, and a film industry with its own pantheon of stars, who appeared in almost every film made – Sverre Anker Ousdal, whom I had just seen playing Knut Fraenkel in Troell's Andrée film, the beautiful Kjersti Holmen, Helga Jordal with his rumpled face and his thick Bergen accent; and footballers with nicknames like racehorses – Sverre 'Brandy' Brandhaug, Jan Ivar 'Mini' Jacobsen. Artists and writers and sportsmen largely unknown to the outside world. Yet, once you penetrated below the superficial level of local, good-natured deference to the global celebrity enjoyed by the stars of American and British culture, these names were dearer and closer to Norwegian hearts and minds than any of them. These were family.

'I shouldn't have said that,' he said after a few moments. 'She didn't do it properly. It was a stupid and thoughtless thing to say. She took her own life. That's all. That sweet little feather took her own life.'

He was a chain smoker. He'd stopped rolling his own now and started on a packet of Teddies. He tapped another cigarette out of the soft blue and white packet and lit it with his Zippo.

'One mistake can be enough. The world turns dark. You think it'll never brighten again. Or maybe it will, if you drink. So you take a drink. But instead, each day you wake up is blacker than the one before until finally one day you can't face another one. You've had enough. You can't go on.'

Jimmy Giuffre's 'The Green Country' was playing softly in the background. A man with shoulder-length grey hair and huge, drenched eyes, almost comatose with drink, was being helped towards the door with exquisite tenderness by a taxi driver.

'They had opium. Andrée kept giving it to Fraenkel every time there was something wrong with him, did you notice that in the film? You've got a sore foot? Here, have some opium. Diarrhoea? Have some opium. Nisse dies and they wedge his body into that wall of ice, they took his jacket and his trousers. Andrée takes the locket with Anna Charlier's hair curled into one half of it and her picture in the other, and, probably very weak, just piled stones on top of the body. I can imagine the two others returning to the tent. Maybe making a cup of coffee on the primus. And then after that, what? Because really, there is no next. There's nothing to do but wait for nothing. Fraenkel says he's not feeling well and asks for some opium. Andrée says no, still trying to maintain his position as leader. Fraenkel ignores him and takes it anyway. And not long after him, Andrée too. They weren't found inside the giant sleeping bag they all slept in for warmth. No one was inside it when they found it. They knew they wouldn't feel the cold. They were ghosts already. They'd turned into their own ghosts long before they died.'

From above the cloud of smoky chatter a woman's voice floated down.

'Listen,' said Erling, touching the back of my hand. 'This is Radka Toneff.'

I strained my ears to hear. The voice was diffuse and faint, like a ghost's voice, the song a ballad with a strikingly melancholic refrain – *the moon's a harsh mistress, the moon can be so cold...* *

'I asked the woman behind the bar to play this for you. I told him you were an English visitor who wanted to hear some of our

---

* Hear it at https://youtu.be/XtgIxU8TCyY.

Norwegian jazz singers.' Resisting the urge to remind Erling that in fact I wasn't a visitor but had come to Norway to stay I said again: 'So – you do think it was suicide?'

'Who knows what it was? Drink up,' he said, suddenly brisk, standing and shrugging on the sheepskin jacket that I later learned was the only jacket he possessed, 'I want to show you something.'

*

We paid and left the bar. Outside in Rosencrantz gate the snow was still falling, as it seemed to fall all the time during those first four or five winters in Oslo, with evening temperatures always well below freezing, the cold air chilling and tightening the skin, pinching the insides of the nostrils in a way that made me think of the trips to Iceland all those years ago.

We turned right along Karl Johans gate, passed the corner of Universitets gate and the coffee bar that I knew – from my memories of reading *Hunger* – had once been the site of Cammermeyer's, in the 1880s the only bookseller and publisher in the city, and far too small an operation to publish giants such as Ibsen and Bjørnson, or Alexander Kielland and Jonas Lie: *de fire store*, the four Norwegian greats of the era, who took their plays and stories to Copenhagen to be published by Gyldendal.

We crossed Karl Johan and slanted over in front of the National Theatre, between the plinthed and greening statues of Henrik Ibsen and Bjørnstjerne Bjørnson, and then up Drammensveien, with the royal park on the right and on our left-hand side the first-floor apartment on the corner of Arbiens gate where Ibsen had lived after returning from his twenty-seven years of exile in Italy and Germany, with the palace and the royal family as his neighbours across the road. I gathered that Erling was talking about another explorer, a Norwegian named Hjalmar Johansen, and that this man, of whom I had never heard, was well known as the only man to have travelled with both Fridtjof Nansen and Roald Amundsen on their polar expeditions; but I was so enchanted by the black night and the mysterious beauty of the royal gardens in the overspill of cold white light from the streets lamps we walked between that I realized I had missed some important narrative link connecting Andrée with Hjalmar Johansen and had to ask Erling to recapitulate for me.

He patiently began to explain it once more, slowing with each step as he spoke; and I knew, since he had already done it several times during the course of what had turned into a pub crawl through the centre of Oslo, that he would shortly come to a complete halt and turn to face me while continuing to speak. I had tried once or twice to subvert the manoeuvre by simply turning my head in his direction and nodding slowly and deeply several times, clearly signalling that he had my complete attention even if, as on this occasion, it was not quite true, and that there was no need for us to stop walking.

'Andrée's and the other bodies were never given proper autopsies when their remains were brought back to Stockholm in 1930. And after the parade and the services, they were cremated. A glove, a mitten, they don't know whose it was, was found on Hvitøya. It's in the Andrée museum up in Grenna now. They found shards of finger-nails inside, enough to do tests on. One theory was that they died from lead poisoning from all the tinned foot they ate. But the tests proved nothing, they hadn't eaten the tinned food long enough, and the diaries show no evidence of the derangement that is one of the symptoms of lead poisoning. However, they did eat enormous quantities of...'

He stopped in mid-sentence to stare with transfixed wonder at the snow whirling around in the light from a street lamp on the far side of the road, mouth slightly open, as though he'd never seen such a thing before, the way the flakes seemed to swirl upwards towards the light as though seeking it out, moving so swiftly it was hard to see how they would ever reach the pavements and the parks and railings and lay themselves across the rooftops and the trees, the parked cars, the statues and frozen fountains, across the ships moored in the dark-ness down by Aker Brygge and onto the head of the tall, swallow-thin statue of Håkon VII, the first king of modern Norway, in 7 Juni plass.

'What was I talking about?' he asked, suddenly looking at me, and causing me to wonder how drunk he was.

'About a connection between the Andrée expedition and this other explorer, the one who...'

'Yes, yes, that's right,' he interrupted impatiently, 'Hjalmar Johansen.'

The act of recall jolted Erling into motion again and he led us on up Drammensveien, crossing the road to pass the elegant façade of the Nobel Institute where, with a casual flick of his bony wrist, he brought to my attention the stone head of Alfred Nobel on a plinth in the gardens outside the front entrance. We crossed Inkognitogate, a street name which to this day fills me with a sense of mystery and enchantment, and headed on up Sommerogate into Solli plass and the heavy stone cube of the university library, which I had already visited several times in connection with my studies.

'The most widely held theory about the cause of their deaths is that they suffered from trichinosis. It's a form of food poisoning from eating too much polar bear meat. Although not the liver – it's clear from Andrée's diary that he was aware of the danger of poisoning from eating too much vitamin A. But the meat they ate must often have been almost raw. They had the primus, but Andrée mentions several times the problems they had in getting it to work properly. And by the time they reached Hvitøya early in October, which is when the diary entries more or less stop, and were faced with the prospect of spending the months of the Arctic winter there, with only woollen clothes, they had no furs, always menaced by the bears. And wondering how many more of them they would have the good fortune to kill and eat. So they kept these chunks of raw bear meat and seal meat. And ate every piece of it. The tongue. The brain. The blood, which Fraenkel made into pancakes. The bone marrow. But no fish. They never managed to catch any fish. Andrée did rig up a line out of hooks and safety pins, but they never caught a thing. That's up in the museum too. Can you believe it? Going off on a trip like that, with the flags and the champagne and the caviar and the special buoy to drop onto the North Pole, but no fishing line?'

We passed a narrow banked strip of parkland that ran parallel with Sommerogate. A cloaked and huddled stone figure with a white cone of snow on its head stood holding what looked like an enormous key in his hand: a study by August Rodin for his *Burghers of Calais* group.

'But I don't believe that it was food poisoning,' said Erling. 'Just the year before the balloonists, Nansen was travelling in that same region, with *Fram*. His great idea was that he would let the ship be frozen into the ice and then let the polar drift carry her across to the top of the world to the North Pole. But, as time went by, he realized it was going to take much longer than expected. Five, maybe eight years. So in March of 1895, he decided to leave the ship and try to reach the Pole on foot, taking one other man with him. He chose Hjalmar. Hjalmar was the best dog-handler of the crew and the fittest of them as well. They reckoned they had to cover an average distance of about 11 miles (18 km) a day.

'Things started off well enough, but soon they found out, just as Andrée would, that the fantastic distortions and endless walls on the surface of the ice slowed their progress to a fraction of that speed, and early in April Nansen decided to abandon the attempt and try to get back to Franz Josef's Land. They spent the next eighteen months exclusively in each other's company. Nansen was Norwegian upper class. Johansen was a janitor's son from Bodø, away up in the north. Big class difference. They probably told you over there, your Norwegian teachers, that there's no class system here in Norway. They probably boast about how we abolished the aristocracy back in 1821. Not true, my England man. There are classes here, upper class, middle class, working class, just like there are everywhere. Old money, new money and no money. There are no titles but there's an aristocracy of names. Politicians, painters and writers, journalists on television and radio, you find the same names down through the generations.

'For months on end, Nansen and Hjalmar slept together like man and woman. Shared the same double sleeping bag for warmth. They saved each other's lives, countless times. They ate their way through a zooful of seals, birds, dogs. They ate nineteen polar bears. It was what you might call a brutal intimacy. And not until they'd been living like this for *ten months*, on New Years' Eve of 1895, Nansen turns to Johansen, in that tiny shelter they built themselves out of the bones and skins and sinews of whales and seals, Nansen stands up, big man, tall man, couldn't stand up straight inside it, and he says to Johansen: "Don't you think it's time we started saying 'Du' to each other?" It's like he was saying "Listen, we've been living like this for quite a while now, maybe it's time we started *calling each other by our first names*." After all those months. Just the two of them.'

He came to a halt, and in a gesture with which I would become familiar over the years to come, clutched his forehead with the spread fingers of his big right hand as though trying to control the raging of his thoughts.

'Throughout that whole time they had been observing the formalities, the what do you call it in English, *the social niceties*. Eating pancakes made from bear's blood, still *observing the social niceties*. Your queen would have been proud of them. *He* would have been proud of them.' Erling gestured across the road in the direction of a verdigrised statue of Sir Winston Churchill pugnaciously leaning on his stick outside Industriens- og Eksportens-Hus, a block of offices people just called Indexhuset.

We were walking now through the small park directly opposite the entrance to what was then the university library and now houses the National Library. Distantly I heard the City Hall bells chime eleven, and with the snow and the strangeness of the night and my intense and voluble companion my thoughts turned again as they so often did during those early days, particularly at night and in the winters, to *Hunger* and Hamsun's homeless, vivid and hungry narrator in his ceaseless wandering through the streets of old Kristiania. I knew my future wife must be wondering where I was, and that soon I would have to manufacture a break from this walking and from Erling and get back home to her. At the end of the park that is nearest to Drammensveien and the library a dark rectangular slab commemorates those executed during the Nazi Occupation for their involvement with the illegal free press. A few paces on from it was a large shallow pool with a low, surrounding wall. The water was frozen. Two magpies pecked at something on the ice. Erling brushed snow from the wall, sat down and crossed his legs and pulled a small flat bottle from his inside jacket pocket. Its lower half was encased in what looked like zinc, a thin, hand-stitched black leather coating protecting its upper half. Norwegians call such flasks a *lommelerke*, a pocket lark that sings to you. He unscrewed the metal cap and took a long swig and offered it to me. I accepted. It was Gammel Dansk. With its hard, sweet, herbal tang and almost syrupy consistency it was not unlike a proprietary brand of cough medicine and the perfect antidote to the chill that was becoming extreme, the temperature now down to about minus eight or nine.

'This is where he shot himself,' he offered suddenly, stroking the air above the ice with the palm of his hand.

'Where who shot himself?'

'Hjalmar Johansen. Here in Solli Park. 6 January 1913. He put his service pistol in his jacket pocket and walked up here from his miserable little bedsit in Egertorget, sat down on one of these benches and put a bullet through his head. Can you work that out? You go through all that. Struggle so hard to save your life, as though your life meant something to you, as though it was important to you, as though you liked it...'

He reached down and rapped on the surface twice with his bare knuckles. I had noticed earlier he wasn't wearing gloves. I was about to cough and look at my watch and enact a pang of distress at the lateness of the hour and say I needed to head off home immediately, but before I could do so, he spoke again.

'See, Hjalmar was a drinker. Only when there was some present danger of losing it, that's the only time life mattered to him. A bear. A wilderness. Fight and you stay alive. Don't fight and you die. Out there, death is never more than ten seconds away. It breathes on your neck, into your face. Like when he was attacked by a bear. Hjalmar was on his back on the ice, punching up at the bear's snout as it stood over him. You know what he shouted to Nansen? 'You better hurry up or it'll be too late!' He repeated it under his breath in Norwegian, as though it hadn't seemed real in English: *Nå får De nok skynde Dem, skal det ikke bli for sent.* Like characters out of a saga. But they were real people.

'Drinking took too long,' I said, to show I understood. 'So he shot himself.'

Erling put his head back and drained what was left of the Gammel Dansk without offering it. 'The terrors of ice and darkness,' he said with a bitter laugh. 'Ice blizzards, polar bears. They're nothing compared to whisky.'

He half-turned and with a flick of the wrist span the empty bottle across the ice. It skipped and skidded with a high, whining sound before sliding to rest against the wall on the far side. The movement caused him to lose his balance and he had to reach down to steady himself on the ice with his hand. Then he stood up and walked unsteadily around the perimeter of the pond to retrieve it. I took advantage of the distraction to call a goodnight to him and set off beneath the dripping chestnut trees of Bygdøy allé on the long trudge back to Kringsjå.

On the way I thought a lot about the evening and the conversation with Erling. I understood that he was a connoisseur of failure, that he was one of those people who feel a curious and powerful attraction towards failure. Somewhere along the line I had picked up that he was in the fifth or sixth year of a Ph.D. in biochemistry at the University of Oslo, and that the delay in finishing it was partly because he was also a painter. He had become fascinated – or perhaps obsessed is a better word – by the story. He had told me he was working on a series of paintings that he called his 'Frieze of Death', an echo of Edvard Munch's *Frieze of Life*, and that his inspiration for the series was the photographs Nisse Strindberg had carried on taking, almost to the very end, as he documented the little group's terrible and terrifying six-week trudge towards death and those piles of human rubble found by the crew of the *Bratvaag*. He seemed to feel a closer bond with these failed and unheroic explorers than with the success and rugged glamour of either Fridtjof Nansen or Roald Amundsen. Did he, I wondered, feel that the fate of August Andrée and Hjalmar Johansen epitomized something important about Scandinavians as a tribe that was obscured by the glories surrounding these two heroes? Was he trying to articulate a tension that existed between the profound individualism of the polar explorer and the sometimes oppressive communality of Scandinavian societies?

*

It was well past midnight when I got home. My future wife was already in bed and asleep. I wasn't drunk, the night had been too cold for that. But I knew I would regret the drinking in the morning and as I crept into bed beside her I made a determination not to carry on this way, now that I had been given, at the late age of thirty-four, this unexpected gift of a rebirth. I understood that my drinking was an expression of protracted adolescence, an unwillingness to concede the passage of time rather than the true sickness unto death of a real drinker like Erling. I made up my mind to avail myself of her fabulous commonsense, so that I could live close to it and learn from it every day, and the following morning, as soon as I woke up, I proposed to her. She said yes. That same afternoon I bought a grey suit from a Dressman store and two weeks later, at 11 o'clock on a Wednesday morning in the City Hall, we married each other. Erling was my best man. Apart from Mona, my wife's closest friend since the age of five, he was the only guest at the meal we ate afterwards at Grand Hotel on Karl Johan. A piano trio was playing. I remember it was the first time I ever heard a live performance of Thelonius Monk's 'Round Midnight'. That tune is almost impossible to whistle.

*

In the early days of our friendship, Erling drank more or less constantly without ever actually appearing to be drunk. He was a continual smoker too, occasionally trying to break the chain with the use of an old briar pipe, which, as I told him on several occasions, suited his dignified bearing well. But very shortly the pipe would be put away and the cigarette-rolling machine would reappear, or the soft blue and white cellophane pack of Teddys, lying between us on the tables of the bars and cafés we visited over the years.

He got married not long after I did and at about the same time he abandoned his biochemistry studies to devote himself to painting, drinking, talking and listening to music. To my astonishment, since he never spoke of it unless asked, I also learnt that he believed in the literal truth of the Bible. In his youth, he said, he had gone to bible school with the intention of becoming a missionary. His ability to read Hebrew involved him in so many semantic arguments with his teachers, he said, that in the end he was asked to leave the class. But he rarely spoke in a personal way at all and the little I knew of his upbringing came from sentences dropped here and there, late at night in the studio he had built for himself at the first-floor apartment in the neighbourhood of Storo, which he and Karoline moved into after they married, listening to the *St Matthew Passion* or anything by Glenn Gould, whom he adored, and surrounded by half-finished canvasses from his 'Frieze of Death'. His family came from Skien on the south coast of Norway, an area with a strong tradition of piety. Henrik Ibsen was from the same town and Ibsen's brother Ole and sister Hedvig joined a Christian revivalist movement started there by Gustav Adolf Lammers, which broke with the state Church in the 1850s and established its own free Church. Lammers denounced literature as the Devil's work and forbade the use of curtains on the grounds that everything a person did should tolerate the light of day. His women followers thought he was the returned Christ. The movement spread all along the south coast of the country and laid the basis for *sørlandspietism*, a tradition of austere piety that survives in the region to this day.

Erling had spent the first eight or nine years of his life in Argentina, where his step-father worked as a missionary. On the rare occasions he spoke of this man, it was with a passing and frightened bitter-ness that was out of character with his usually tolerant and benign indifference to people. Otherwise the experience of those early years in South America left him with a great fondness for the Latin temperament, which he said he greatly preferred to the Protestant chill of Norway. He spoke Spanish fluently, idolized the Formula One racing-driver Juan Fangio, hated pop music but made an exception for the Gipsy Kings, and always quietly but insistently referred to the Falkland Islands by their Argentinian name, Las Malvinas.

With the passage of time, Erling told me, he gradually lost the knack of going to sleep. Instead he would sit up all night in the studio drinking, painting and listening to favourite recordings like Olli Mustonen's doubling of Bach and Shostakovich's *Preludes and Fugues*. If he couldn't paint, which happened with increasing frequency, he found other ways of passing the time. Once, at about three-thirty in the morning, he decided to cut his hair. Somewhere between the blunt scissors and the hand-held mirror and the perceptual disturbances of the whisky he realized he had made such a mess of it that he saw no option but to scrape the lot off with a safety razor. Exhausted by the strains of the adventure he then crawled into bed beside his sleeping wife, and was sleeping soundly when he was awoken some three hours later by her screams of distress at the sight of what lay beside her. He told me the story as we sat over a beer in an upstairs corner of Justisen on Møllergata that evening. He seemed genuinely bewildered and even aggrieved by Karoline's reaction but had agreed to her demand that he wear a woollen hat until some hair had grown back.

It was at around this time that he got into the habit of making more or less incoherent phone calls late at night. I rarely, and latterly never, had the patience to listen to these rambles of his, which were almost always complaints about Karoline's unreasonable responses to his drinking. He was living entirely in his own world by this time and once complained bitterly of her fury when he had failed to return home for all of one night and most of the next day, having failed even to telephone home to warn her. His own explanation was the usual one: *he had been talking*. To him this justified everything, and he had no understanding at all of his wife's fears that something might have happened to him. Much as I liked Erling I could not bring myself to take his side against hers in these exchanges, and in the end bought a Caller ID device and, with an always guilty heart, let the phone go on ringing if the display showed his number.

I saw Erling for the last time in 2004, about a year before his death and fifteen years into our friendship. In the course of one of those late-night communications we had arranged to take a walk together in the Oslo *marka*, the dense belt of forest that surrounds the city on three sides. My wife and I had moved into an apartment in the eastern suburb of Lambertsæter by that time and I asked him to call on me there at ten in the morning, supposing that no one, not even Erling, would turn up drunk at such an hour. He arrived an hour and quarter late carrying an old-fashioned and battered little grey rucksack which contained only a quarter bottle of Dawson's whisky. He had been up all night. It was early spring but snow still lay thick in the forest above the lake at Sognsvann. It wasn't walking weather and we had to keep to the impacted snow in the centre of the ski tracks, cursed by skiers as they raced by. I remember that walk now with mixed emotions. My anger at him for his failure even to *try* to cure himself. The way he kept stopping to take a pull on his bottle of Dawson's. His disappointment and surprise at my refusal to join him. The pity and sadness afterwards, when we parted company in the metro station at Kringsjå, where he had taken a cleaner's job at the student village. It had been a long time now since I had heard any talk of the 'Frieze of Death' and I knew better than to ask about it.

A young mother was waiting on the platform with her son, a boy of about six or seven. Women always took to Erling, even shrouded in his cape of alcohol. They seemed to sense his decency and gentleness and his absolute unfitness to live in the same world as the rest of us. He engaged her attention with a few remarks about the new buildings that were going up all around Kringsjå to accommodate the ever-increasing number of foreign students arriving in Oslo to study. But when he bent to address the child there was something about him – the jerky uncertainty of his movement, the redness of his face, the washed-out blueness of his eyes, the poisonous blast of whisky from his open mouth – that terrified the boy. He stared into Erling's face for a moment then turned and ran to his mother and buried his face in her thigh.

During the walk I told him I had made a vow never to drink whisky with him again. It felt like the last good turn I could ever do for him. As things turned out I never drank anything at all with him again. Never even saw him again. Periodically, over the next few months, I heard news of him from our mutual friend Bjarne, a dentist who was part of my wife's crowd from her secondary-school days and with whom I had become friendly, and who, in due course, had become friends with Erling too. From Bjarne I learnt one evening that Erling had left Karoline and divorced her, and shortly afterwards married a childhood sweetheart, a woman of whom I had never heard him speak but who was, according to Bjarne, a highly successful biochemist who shared with Erling, in all its compelling and private intensity, a faith in the literal truth of the Bible. Bjarne said that the two of them sang psalms together at the breakfast table. No longer able to tolerate spirits Erling was drinking only watered wine. The risk of incontinence had become so great that he rarely left the house. One day a toothache necessitated a trip to Bjarne's to have a tooth taken out. At home that evening the cavity began to bleed and the bleeding never stopped.

In his oration at the densely Christian funeral the priest did not mention by so much as a word the part Brother Alcohol had played in Erling's demise; and yet for one of the very few times in my life I felt that a priest's words from the pulpit were a true and meaningful address to the body lying in the flower-decked white coffin below him. Erling's faith never wavered. He believed implicitly that he was bound for a better world than this. After the service we followed his coffin in bright cold sunshine as it juddered along a twisting path atop a metal, battery-driven trolley to the grave, and stood around watching as the box was lowered into the ground, and listened to the rattle of earth and stones on the lid. I don't remember feeling any grief, only how little dignity there is left in life. It's curious as I write this to reflect that Erling is still down there in that hole, still wearing his suit, perhaps even still remotely recognizable in some way. It makes me think of the words of that Swedish trader whom

Ibn Fadlan met on the banks of the Volga more than a thousand years ago. We burn our dead, the Rus told him. In a few moments they're gone and in the next world already.

★

Close to the end of Troell's film there is a scene in which the three explorers take turns at looking into a small mirror Nils Strindberg has unexpectedly found among his camera accessories. At first it seems fun to them, like a toy. Then, as the memory of who they once were returns to them, they fall silent. They act almost as though they wish Strindberg had never found it. The camera cuts to the scene of Nils Strindberg struggling beneath the polar bear and then abandoning his struggle. Knut Fraenkel takes off his boots and his gloves, helps himself to an overdose of opium and lies down to die. Max von Sydow, as August Andrée, stands alone on the rock-strewn beach and remembers the episode with the mirror. He listens to his inner voice as it reminds him again of how little of ourselves we are able to see. Just the front. Not the back, and not ever the face. Like birds, von Sydow's hands begin to flutter at his sides. They glide and flit about his body. He turns his head, watching them, his own hands, flitting about his body as though he has no control over them, as though they belonged to someone else. Follows their fluttering with the bewildered fascination of a child.

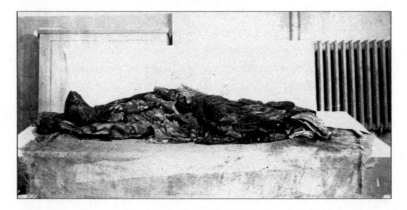

Interlude
Ibsen's Ghosts

IN LATE DECEMBER 1843, A FEW MONTHS SHORT OF HIS sixteenth birthday, Henrik Ibsen left Skien on the coastal ferry *Lykkens Prøve*, debarking four days later in Grimstad, a small town on the south coast of Norway. Winter that year was particularly severe – the newspaper in nearby Arendal reported temperatures of minus 10–11 degrees Réamur in his first week, and a north-westerly gale that brought with it 3 feet (1 m) of snow. Two ships sank off the coast with heavy loss of life. Ibsen had come to take up a post as assistant to the local apothecary, a man named Reimann. He was wearing his confirmation pontificalia and his luggage consisted mainly of a large number of books. His hopes at this stage were divided between the ambition to become a doctor and the dream of becoming a painter.

Charged with being Ibsen's surrogate father as well as his employer, Reimann was to prove a second unsatisfactory male role-model for the youth. Already heavily in debt by the time Ibsen joined him, during his brief, troubled period operating as an apothecary, Reimann had a tendency to escape from his problems into drink. Perhaps it was these early experiences of ineffective father-figures that contributed to the low opinion of men characteristic of so many of Ibsen's works.

His pay at Reimann's was poor, the food merely sufficient, the living accommodation cramped. The ground floor consisted of two rooms, the Reimann family's sitting room and the dispensary itself, which also functioned as a post office. Upstairs were three connecting bedrooms. The Reimanns and their youngest children slept in one, Henrik in the next with the three older boys, and the two household maids, Marie Thomsen and Else Sofie Jensen, in the third. The door between the two outer rooms was left open at nights in cold weather, as the maids had no stove of their own and needed to share the heat from the adjacent room. When the night-bell rang, Ibsen would attend to the customer, pulling on his dressing-gown and passing through their room to descend the steep staircase to the dispensary. For someone of Ibsen's reserved nature such a lack of privacy must have been distressing. Yet for the next six years he was compelled to live 'in the open' like this. The effect on his personality was profound. In time it turned the need for privacy into an incurable pathology.

Grimstad was in many ways similar to Skien, although with 800 inhabitants it was less than half the size. Most of its young men went to sea once they left school, and even the meanest wage-earner would invest some part of his savings in a trading ship. The streets were narrow, poorly lit and without sewage – the gutter ran down the centre of the main street. There was no mains water-supply, and water had to be drawn from wells, either public or private. During his first two years there, Ibsen's life was lonely and uneventful. He immersed himself in the work, spending his time preparing adhesive tape, heating up valerian root, and acquiring a basic knowledge of the medicinal properties of herbs. He had not initially been enthusiastic about the job; but with the coming of spring, he warmed to the task and wrote to his friend Poul Lieungh in Skien that he was 'extremely well content, and have never regretted coming here. Reimann is very good to me and does everything possible to encourage my interest in the work, which was not great to begin with'. During this period his pleasures were solitary. On his Sundays off he would either row out to nearby Maløya to collect herbs, or climb in the local hills with his paintbox and paint landscapes. At night he studied, hoping to pass the university matriculation exam which would allow him to take the so-called 'Norwegian' medical exam, a sort of university degree without Latin. Often he would stay up reading and writing until two in the morning.

Between working for Reimann and pursuing his own studies, young Ibsen remained an unknown quantity for the youth of Grimstad. On the few occasions on which he did venture out into company, he was obliged to participate in pastimes and amusements that cannot have brought him much pleasure. These included arm-wrestling and primitive weight-lifting contests with local boys. His solitary ways and introspective nature made him an object of suspicion for the young working class, and he was often ducked in the snow. The local girls nicknamed him Spætus, 'Tich'. He found the company of older people more congenial. One companion of this early period was Mina Wahl, a Danish woman nine years his senior, who worked as governess for the local parish priest and who shared with Henrik an interest in landscape painting. Another was Svend Fjeldmand, also an immigrant into the community, a serious-minded man in his late forties who helped out in the shop, chopping ingredients and washing bottles. He and Henrik sometimes walked over to the cemetery at Fjære on Sundays.

With the maids in the house, there developed an enforced intimacy. The kitchen maid, Marie Thomsen, remembered that in his unhappiest moments Ibsen would complain of his father's neglect, and lament that he felt he would never find his rightful place in the world. Such confidences aroused maternal instincts in the women. The nanny Katrine made him a dressing-gown. He clashed often with the sharp-tongued Marie Thomsen, but as quickly as the tempers flared they would subside again. Able to observe the youth at close quarters, the maids could see for themselves that there was substance to his claims to be different. His capacity for study impressed them, as did his artistic talent. The Reimanns too were impressed by his paintings and hung them on the walls of the house.

The other maid in the house was Else Sofie Jensen, known as

Sofie. At twenty-eight, she was ten years older than Henrik, and by the standards of the time an old maid. Like him, she was from a family that had come down in the world. Her grandfather was Christian Lofthus, a Norwegian landowner who, in the 1780s, had agitated against the exploitation of local people by the Danish king's agent and led a number of minor insurrections, which ended with his arrest and imprisonment in Akershus, where he died in 1797. Ibsen later tried to write a novel based on Lofthus's story. Whether as the result of a sustained relationship, or simply in an unplanned moment, Henrik and Else Sofie became lovers early in 1846. She fell pregnant, and in the summer went home to her parents' house in Børkedalen, east of Lillesand, where she gave birth to a son on 9 October. Ibsen never saw her again, nor did he ever see his son. Following a grudging admission of paternity, he was ordered by county resolution to contribute to the upkeep of the boy, christened Hans Jakob Henriksen, until he reached the age of fourteen. It was an obligation Ibsen struggled to meet. In his twenties, as his debts mounted, he was at one point sentenced to a term of hard labour in a debtor's prison in Kristiania (Oslo), a fate from which only the intervention of friends saved him.

No surviving letter of Ibsen's, nor any interview with his friends, contemporaries and family members, contains any reference to the existence of this son; nor was Hans Jakob mentioned in any biography of Ibsen until more than forty years after the great dramatist's death. The shame and the need to keep the incident hidden intensified an already secretive nature and nurtured that obsession with nemesis which became the chief characteristic of his greatest art. Much of the energy that fuelled his subsequent career as a dramatist came from the tension between a sense of having fallen from grace, and a fierce determination to prove that he had not fallen from grace at all. In its final manifestation it became a need to reform society, to provoke it into becoming the kind of society that would have punished neither himself, nor his lover, nor their son, with the burden of secrecy and shame that spoiled so much of the joy of life for all three of them.

Ibsen's Ghosts, the play that follows, uses Ibsen's own retrospective technique to describe what might have happened had these ghosts from his own past suddenly reappeared to haunt him at the height of his fame.

Ibsen's Ghosts

A Play in Three Acts

DRAMATIS PERSONAE

Henrik Ibsen, *the playwright*
Suzannah, *Ibsen's wife*
Henrik Jæger, *Ibsen's biographer*
Else Sofie, *an old woman*

ACT ONE

The scene is the Ibsens' apartment, Arbiens gate, Kristiania (Oslo), 1898. We are in the midst of the celebrations for Ibsen's 70th birthday.

A set suggestion: Henrik Ibsen's study in the apartment on the first floor. Heavy, dark Victorian furnishing. Ibsen's desk with papers on it, a globe. On the wall above the desk at centre is a large oil painting, gilt-framed, behind glass. This is the Swedish painter Julius Kronberg's three-quarter-length portrait of Ibsen, done in 1877, on the occasion of the award to Ibsen of an honorary doctorate from the University of Uppsala. He is wearing ceremonial robes, carries a scroll in his left hand, and a decoration on a red ribbon hangs around his neck. Like Hedda Gabler's portrait of her father the General, Kronberg's portrait is a constant and dominating presence throughout.

Further along the wall a rash of smaller paintings, mostly land-scapes. There is one other, smaller portrait. This is Ibsen's son, Sigurd.

There is a window with a mirror positioned in front of it. A black, wrought-iron wood-burning stove. Armchairs. A grandfather clock.

A small area set aside to represent the entrance to the apartment, with coat and hat stand, and a table. A second area representing the entrance to the room in which Jæger is staying.

In the middle of Ibsen's study, severely hampered in her move-ments by arthritis, SUZANNAH IBSEN is struggling to position a step-ladder beneath the Kronberg portrait. Once satisfied, she

slowly proceeds to mount the steps. She is carrying cleaning equip-
ment, with which she begins carefully to wash the gilt frame around
the portrait.

After a few moments, ELSE SOFIE appears in the doorway. She
is dressed in dirty, men's clothing. She coughs, to attract Suzannah's
attention. Suzannah does not hear her. She knocks timidly on the
double doors. Suzannah answers in a strong, declamatory voice:

SUZANNAH. Yes? Who is it? Who's there?

ELSE SOFIE. It's only me, ma'am. The ratcatcher. Excuse me ma'am
    but I wonder if I could trouble you for a bit of string? The bit I
    have is broke.

SUZANNAH. I don't understand. String?

ELSE SOFIE. Yes. To tie round my trouser legs. To stop the rats getting
    up.* I'm sorry to bother you only there was no one in the
    kitchen.

SUZANNAH. No. They're all off attending the investiture at the palace.
    Dr Ibsen is to be decorated with the Great Cross today.

She looks at the painting.

SUZANNAH. It's his seventieth birthday this year. I expect you've read
    about it in the papers.

ELSE SOFIE. Yes, ma'am.

SUZANNAH. Wait then. Just a minute.

With the same great difficulty she climbs down the steps. Else Sofie
does not offer to help, but—

SUZANNAH. That's alright. I can manage by myself, thank you.

She goes to a cupboard to get the string.

SUZANNAH: Tell me, are there many rats down there?

ELSE SOFIE. Oh yes there's quite a few, ma'am. Regular plague of
    them in Kristiania just now.

* See Interlude Note 1, page 255.

SUZANNAH. Yes. That was my impression. My husband doesn't seem
to mind. As long as they don't invade his study. But I won't have
them in the kitchen. It's not hygienic.

ELSE SOFIE. No, ma'am.

SUZANNAH. Will this be long enough?

Suzannah holds up a length of string.

ELSE SOFIE. Yes, ma'am that'll do nicely, thank you.

SUZANNAH. You're not from Kristiania, are you?

ELSE SOFIE. No, ma'am. Lillesand.

SUZANNAH. I thought I recognized the accent. You must excuse my
curiosity – Doctor Ibsen and I have lived abroad for many years.
We've been back for some time now, but it's still a pleasure for
me to spot an accent. Tell me, I'm curious to know, why is a
woman catching rats? I should have thought that was man's
work. Have you always done it?

ELSE SOFIE. Not always, ma'am. I was in domestic service once.

Only now does Suzannah offer the string to her.

ELSE SOFIE. Thank you kindly, ma'am.

SUZANNAH. Oh but you're bleeding! Here, let me have a look at that.

ELSE SOFIE. It's nothing. Just a nip. It happens all the time.

SUZANNAH. Did a rat do that? Oh how horrible! Please, let me wash
it for you.

ELSE SOFIE. Oh no, ma'am, I couldn't let you touch me.

SUZANNAH. Not touch you? Why ever not?

ELSE SOFIE. You mustn't be touching a dirty old woman like me.

SUZANNAH. Oh don't be ridiculous. Come over here with me.

*She leads Else over to a pitcher and bowl, pours water over her
hand and commences to wash the wounded finger.*

SUZANNAH. I really do, you know, I think it's quite scandalous that a
woman should have to do work like this.

ELSE SOFIE. Bless you for saying so, ma'am, but it's not because I'm
a woman that I'm doing it.

SUZANNAH. No? Then why do you do it?

ELSE SOFIE. Because I'm poor. That's why I do it.

SUZANNAH. Yes but at your age. Don't you have any children to look after you?

ELSE SOFIE. I have a son, yes. One son. But...

SUZANNAH. Well then, why can't your son look after you?

ELSE SOFIE. Perhaps he could, ma'am, but... Well, to be truthful, my Hans Jakob, he's not much of a worker.

SUZANNAH. What about your husband, the boy's father?

ELSE SOFIE. I never was married, ma'am.

SUZANNAH. Oh. I see.

ELSE SOFIE. That's right, ma'am. My Hans Jakob is a bastard. We grew up outside the law, as they say. It was in Grimstad. I was in domestic service there. You know the way of it in the southern towns, with the preachers and the religion.

SUZANNAH. I hope you don't mind my asking you this, but was your employer the father of your son? That is regrettably so often the case.

ELSE SOFIE. No he was not, ma'am. The father was a young man worked there, same as me.

SUZANNAH. This was... Grimstad, did you say?

ELSE SOFIE. Grimstad, ma'am. That's right. It was in Grimstad.

SUZANNAH. When was this?

ELSE SOFIE. Oh long time ago now. Long time ago.

SUZANNAH. My husband spent some time in Grimstad in his youth. Tell me, did you know my husband in Grimstad?*

ELSE SOFIE. Yes I did, ma'am. I knew your husband quite well.

SUZANNAH. And you were in domestic service you say?

ELSE SOFIE. That's right, ma'am.

SUZANNAH. Was your employer a chemist?

ELSE SOFIE. Yes, he was, ma'am. Reimann the chemist. Your husband was working there as his assistant. He had the room next to mine.

---

* See Interlude Note 2, page 255.

*Suzannah walks to corner of the room and looks out
the window.*

SUZANNAH. My husband has a son from… from his… from the time
when he worked in Grimstad.

ELSE SOFIE. Is that so, ma'am?

SUZANNAH. My husband is the father of your child, isn't he? Well,
isn't he?

ELSE SOFIE. Yes he is, ma'am. He is the father of my boy Hans Jakob.

SUZANNAH. I see. Tell me: did you know this when we… when I…
contacted you? To come here? About the rats? Did you know
that it was to Dr Ibsen's house that you were coming?

ELSE SOFIE. Yes I did, ma'am.

SUZANNAH. Does the doctor know that you're here? He does, doesn't
he? How does he know? Have you spoken to him?

ELSE SOFIE. Yes, ma'am. We had a conversation. Before he left for the
palace for his invesis … his invessist…

SUZANNAH. For the investiture, yes. Go on. Did you come here to
threaten him? I asked you a question.

*Else covers her face with her hands. She begins to rock on her
heels. Suzannah is moved. She touches her shoulders and guides her
towards an armchair to sit down. Else resists at the last moment.*

ELSE SOFIE. No, ma'am, I mustn't sit down on your lovely armchair!

SUZANNAH. Sit down. It's alright.

ELSE SOFIE. The dirt…

SUZANNAH. Sit down!

*There is a newspaper rack beside the chair, and Else, in an almost
comic moment, manages to grab a newspaper and get it onto the
seat beneath her as Suzannah forces her down.*

SUZANNAH. Now. I think you'd better tell me exactly what happened.
You threatened Ibsen, didn't you.

ELSE SOFIE. Yes, ma'am, I did threaten him. Or try to. But I didn't
mean it, I swear to you.

Else fumbles in her pocket and produces an envelope, which she holds out to Suzannah.

ELSE SOFIE. Here – you have it. I want you to have it. I don't want it anymore. I wish I'd never seen it, ever. I wish it didn't even exist...

SUZANNAH. What is it?

ELSE SOFIE. It's his birth certificate. Hans Jakob's birth certificate.

SUZANNAH. Your son's birth certificate. I see. You were going to blackmail Dr Ibsen with this?

ELSE SOFIE. No, ma'am! (*More thoughtfully*) Yes. It was his idea. Hans Jakob's. He put me up to it. I didn't want to do it. I didn't even want to take this job, not when I knew who it was. But he persuaded me and I just brought it along with me. I don't really know why, I wasn't going to do anything with it. And on my way down into the basement I saw Henr... I saw... Dr Ibsen, in all his suit and everything, and I...

SUZANNAH. And you introduced yourself? You told him who you were?

ELSE SOFIE. That's right. And then we had a conversation. Oh I don't know why I brought it with me, I just wish I hadn't. It was Hans Jakob – he said if I didn't he would, I don't know, he said he would do something at this thing this evening, this thing outside the theatre.

SUZANNAH. The unveiling of Dr Ibsen's statue?

ELSE SOFIE. Yes, the statue. He said he didn't care. He threatened he would make a scene there when they were doing it. Disgrace Henr... disgrace Dr Ibsen or something, if I didn't.

SUZANNAH. So you were going to blackmail Dr... blackmail my husband with this? Who were you going to show it to? Me? Could you possibly have imagined that I didn't know all about it? My husband and I have no secrets from each other. None. Do you understand that?

ELSE SOFIE. Please, ma'am, I wasn't going to show it to you.

SUZANNAH. Who then? The newspapers?

ELSE SOFIE. Oh no, not them. I don't know who I was going to show it to. I didn't think about it. I just put it in my pocket and came here. I said to myself, I was thinking to myself, maybe Dr Ibsen might be interested to see it. He's never seen it, you know. His own son's birth certificate. Never even set eyes on his boy, on Hans Jakob. Don't you think that's... Not once. I just wanted to... I was hoping he might help us. Oh not money, I wasn't thinking of money. But maybe a job for my Hans Jakob. I was thinking he would maybe help my boy to a job.

SUZANNAH. Well alright then: if not me, and if not the newspapers, then whom?

ELSE SOFIE. It's like I said, I hadn't really thought about it. But then, as we were talking a gentleman came in, he said he was looking for some papers he'd lost or something.

SUZANNAH. That would be Dr Jæger.

ELSE SOFIE. Yes, ma'am. And from something they said I got the idea this gentleman was writing a book about Henr... about Dr Ibsen's life.

SUZANNAH. That's right. Dr Jæger is writing my husband's biography. He's been staying with us for a few days.

ELSE SOFIE. And I don't know what came over me, but I spoke up and told this gentleman I was an old acquaintance of Dr Ibsen. So then after he'd gone, this, this...

SUZANNAH. Dr Jæger.

ELSE SOFIE. After he was gone it occurred to me: what if I were to say to Dr Ibsen that if he would be so kind as to help us, by helping my Hans Jakob to a job, because I mean, he's so rich and famous, and a man in his position must know someone who could give my Hans Jakob a job – then I wouldn't go and visit Dr Jæger and show him Hans Jakob's birth certificate and tell him about... tell him what happened in Grimstad. But I didn't mean it, ma'am. I swear I would never have done it. It was just a stupid plan. Here, take it. You have it. Do what you like with it.

Again she offers the envelope to Suzannah, who this time takes it.

ELSE SOFIE. There. So you see, fru Ibsen – your husband's secret is safe from Dr Jæger.

SUZANNAH. So he turned you down, did he?

ELSE SOFIE. Yes, he did, ma'am.

SUZANNAH. Thank you for this. But you should have realized, a man like Ibsen would never submit to blackmail. That was your mistake. You did not understand what kind of man he really is.

ELSE SOFIE. No, ma'am.

SUZANNAH. I have a son too, you know.

Suzannah hobbles to the small portrait of Sigurd Ibsen hanging on the wall.

SUZANNAH. Sigurd.* He's a diplomat. He speaks six different languages. He's a doctor too, like his father. A doctor of law. Once a journalist came here and asked to speak to Dr Ibsen. 'Which one?' I said. 'You'll have to be more specific, I have two Doctor Ibsens here!'

ELSE SOFIE. (*realizes this is meant to be humorous*) Oh! That's nice.

SUZANNAH. Tell me, your son, fru… ?

ELSE SOFIE. Jensen, ma'am. Else Sofie Jensen.

SUZANNAH. … fru Jensen – does he have any kind of training? Does he have a trade?

ELSE SOFIE. He's a blacksmith by trade.

SUZANNAH. Can't… what did you say his name was?

ELSE SOFIE. Hans Jakob, ma'am. Hans Jakob Henriksen.

SUZANNAH. Can't he find work as a blacksmith here in Kristiania? I should have thought there were plenty of opportunities for skilled men, with all the new tram lines and railway lines opening up.

ELSE SOFIE. Oh there's work to be had alright. Only...

SUZANNAH. Yes that's right. You said he wasn't a good worker.

ELSE SOFIE. It's a manner of speaking, fru Ibsen. My boy drinks. That's the long and short of it. But in my mind it's only because

---

* See Interlude Note 3, page 256.

of his disappointment. My Hans Jakob is clever too, like your son. He can't speak foreign languages, but he loves to read. History, geography, anything like that. He's read all of his fa... all of Dr Ibsen's plays. He's proud of being... proud of who his father is. Sometimes too proud, I think. His... his... Being who he is, I think it makes him think he's too good to work at doing heavy, normal work with his hands. That's why I have to do this.

SUZANNAH. But if he drinks, then what use would it be for Ibsen to help him find work? Presumably, if he did, he would fail to hold down also that job?

ELSE SOFIE. Yes, ma'am. Only I was hoping that maybe Ibsen might, I don't know, speak to him.

SUZANNAH. Speak to him?

ELSE SOFIE. Speak to him. Put him to rights.

SUZANNAH. Speak to him like a father, you mean?

ELSE SOFIE. Yes, ma'am.

SUZANNAH. You do realize, of course, that Ibsen could never, under any circumstances, act as a father to your son? You do understand that, don't you? I could not allow it.

ELSE SOFIE. Yes, ma'am. I don't know what came over me, I'm sure, I let myself get carried away by the coincidence, I suppose, of this being his house and I thought maybe it might be a sign or something. I shouldn't've come. But now I'm glad I did because I gave you the birth certificate and you can do what you like with it and now I must go and get on with my work, thanking you for your great kindness and patience to an unworthy person.

She gets up from the chair. The newspaper is still beneath her, on the cushion.

SUZANNAH. One moment, fru Jensen. Before you go, there is something I want you to know.

Else Sofie stops in the doorway.

SUZANNAH. Later this afternoon, when Ibsen returns from the palace, I shall speak to him. I shall tell him about this conversation of ours, and I think he will know what to do.

ELSE SOFIE. The police? Oh not the police, ma'am, please don't call the police. I gave you the birth certificate. You have it now. It was a mistake... a mistake. We didn't mean any harm to the doctor, I swear it.

SUZANNAH. No, I'm not talking about the police. This evening, at 6 o'clock in front of the National Theatre, a statue of my husband is to be unveiled. Ibsen will make a speech there, and in that speech, in front of the whole world, he will acknowledge the existence of both you and your son. No more than that. But I promise you, he will acknowledge your existence. It is enough.

ELSE SOFIE. Oh no, ma'am, please, he mustn't do that. It's fate, I understood that all along. Hans Jakob and I, this is our fate. You and Dr Ibsen, you have a different fate. That's the way it is. It's the Lord's way. It's how things are.

SUZANNAH. Fru Jensen there is no such thing as how things are. How can we ever expect to improve society and advance as human beings if we go around talking about 'how things are'? How shall women achieve justice and equality in society if we are to be fatalistic and blame our ills on 'how things are'? All it takes to wipe out injustice is a few courageous individuals. Let me tell you this: what an Ibsen believes today, tomorrow a whole world will believe. You have shown your good faith by entrusting us with this birth certificate. In return I have made you a promise. Ibsen will acknowledge your existence. In both of your names, Ibsen will demand an end to society's cruel observance of the double standard whereby unmarried women and their wholly innocent children must endure a lifetime of ostracism and shame for something which in a man is considered no more than a youthful folly. If indeed that.

ELSE SOFIE. I know you mean well, ma'am, but you mustn't think of doing it. You can't know what it's like. The shame and the disgrace. You don't know how cruel people can be. We're used to it, my Hans Jakob and me. Please don't do this, ma'am.

SUZANNAH. You underestimate my husband, fru Jensen.

ELSE SOFIE. Do I, ma'am?

SUZANNAH. Yes, fru Jensen. I assure you that you do.

ELSE SOFIE. Yes, ma'am. I'm sorry.

SUZANNAH. My husband is no stranger to the hostility and abuse of the ignorant. We knew it after *The League of Youth*, after *A Doll's House*, we knew it after *Ghosts*. It was nothing to us, nothing. As I told you before, fru Jensen, you do not know Ibsen. My husband thrives on adversity. Where the cause is just he is utterly without fear for his name. You will see. This evening, in front of the world, you and your son will receive your just rehabilitation in society. And one other thing: I want you to know that your story will be told in Dr Jæger's book after all – not because of your threat of blackmail, but because Ibsen himself will have it so.

ELSE SOFIE. Yes, ma'am. Thank you for the string, ma'am. I must get back to my work now.

SUZANNAH. I think, on reflection, that you had better leave. I'll get someone else to do the rats.

ELSE SOFIE. Yes, ma'am.

Else goes out. Slowly Suzannah returns to the step-ladder in front of the portrait of Ibsen and begins to climb it. Halfway up she changes her mind and slowly climbs down. She hobbles across the room and picks up the envelope containing the birth certificate. She crosses to the stove with it. She waits. She opens the stove-door and is about to throw the envelope in. But she changes her mind again, closes the oven door, puts the envelope back on the table and returns to the ladder. At the foot of it she looks up at the portrait.

SUZANNAH. Ibsen will do it. He *shall* do it.

She climbs up the ladder and resumes her cleaning.

ACT TWO

The study, later that afternoon. SUZANNAH sits knitting as IBSEN and JÆGER return from the investiture at the palace. They remove their coats. Ibsen's medal is hanging on a coloured ribbon around his neck.

SUZANNAH. Well? And how was it?

JÆGER. Oh, fru Ibsen, it was wonderful! You should have heard them! When Dr Ibsen was called forward to receive his medal the applause just went on and on. I thought it would never end.

IBSEN. Dr Jæger exaggerates, of course. Still, if they don't know how to do such things at the palace then I should like to know where they do. The lunch was magnificent. I brought the menu for you to have a look at.

Ibsen hands Suzannah the menu, then pours himself a drink.

IBSEN. Like a drink, Jæger?

JÆGER. No, thank you, I really must get along and do some packing. But what a day. You must be absolutely exhausted, Ibsen!

SUZANNAH. Yes he is, so off you go now and give him a chance to get some rest before the unveiling this evening!

JÆGER. Alright! I can take a hint! Joking apart, fru Ibsen, you must be very, very proud indeed of your husband.

SUZANNAH. I can assure you I am, Dr Jæger. But there again, as I have told you before, I knew from our very first meeting in Bergen what a remarkable man Ibsen was.

JÆGER. Indeed, indeed. Well thank you, doctor, again, thank you.

IBSEN. Thank you for what, my dear Jæger?

JÆGER. Why, for today. For letting me be part of history. And when my book... oh, by the way, the old lady who was here this afternoon, that old acquaintance of yours – do you know where I might contact her? I would so like to interview her about the old days in Grimstad before I leave Kristiania.

Ibsen ignores this completely.

JÆGER. No? Oh bother. I did so want to speak to her. No idea at all where I might get hold of her?

Suzannah puts aside her knitting.

SUZANNAH. No, Dr Jæger. We have no idea at all of how the woman may be contacted.

JÆGER. Dash it. Ah well. The packing I think.

He stops on the way to his room.

JÆGER. Oh by the way, doctor – I hope you haven't forgotten your promise?

IBSEN. My promise?

JÆGER. Yes. A last interview this evening?

SUZANNAH. Now Dr Jæger, my husband really must...

IBSEN. No, I haven't forgotten. But will you have time?

JÆGER. Oh yes. The Stockholm train doesn't leave until ten this evening.

IBSEN. Then let's say here at eight-thirty, after the unveiling? Does that suit you?

JÆGER. Eight-thirty, fine.

SUZANNAH. Now off you go and get on with your packing, Dr Jæger!

JÆGER. (*laughs*) Alright! That's it! Done! Finished, I promise!

Jæger goes into his room and closes the door.

IBSEN. Jæger thinks knowing me makes him part of history.

SUZANNAH. Well, doesn't it? Anyone who knows someone as famous as you are becomes part of history. Dr Jæger knows quite well that if his name is remembered at all it will be for this biography of you he is writing.

IBSEN. Oh, come come.

SUZANNAH. It's perfectly true.

IBSEN. Well, who knows, you may be right. (*Pause*) So she's gone, has she, the old woman? The ratcatcher?

SUZANNAH. Yes, Ibsen. Fru Jensen has gone.

IBSEN. Ah. So you spoke to her.

SUZANNAH. She was bitten by a rat. I washed her hand for her.

Ibsen glances at Jæger's door.

IBSEN. Then you know who fru Jensen is?

SUZANNAH. Yes Ibsen. I know who she is.

Ibsen sits in an armchair.

IBSEN. For God's sake, Suzannah. The woman is threatening to tell Jæger all about that... that *episode* in Grimstad. She had the boy's birth certificate with her. She showed it to me. Tried to blackmail me. I told her to go ahead and show it to him, said I refused to accede to blackmail. But, oh, this afternoon! Suzannah, you have no idea! When King Oscar was hanging the cross around my neck I thought for one terrible moment that that... troll family of mine might come bursting in, causing some horrible commotion at the door, beating their disgusting tails on the floor and demanding to be let in. We must get hold of her somehow. Come to some kind of agreement with her. She wants me to find the boy a job of some sort. That shouldn't be beyond the bounds of possibility. Maybe your brother might have something for him at the bank.

SUZANNAH. So you propose to give in to her blackmail?

IBSEN. No, of course not. I just want to make sure she doesn't show that birth certificate to Jæger. God knows, I'm sure if he did get wind of the story Hegel would never allow him to use it in his book, even if he wanted to. But the thing would get out. In a little fishpond like Kristiania it would get out. And wouldn't my enemies have a field day then!

Suddenly gets up from his chair

IBSEN. There isn't an envelope out there addressed to Jæger is there?
SUZANNAH. No, she didn't leave anything for Dr Jæger.
IBSEN. Are you sure? How can you be so sure? What about the mail-box? Perhaps she put it in the mailbox.

He goes out into the hallway. Suzannah's voice detains him.

SUZANNAH. No, she didn't put it in the mailbox.
IBSEN. What did she do with it? Did she tell you?
SUZANNAH. Yes, Ibsen. Fru Jensen and I had a long talk together. And when we had finished, she gave it to me.
IBSEN. The birth certificate? She gave it to you?
SUZANNAH. The birth certificate. Her son's birth certificate.

*She picks up the envelope and holds it out to Ibsen.
Ibsen takes it.*

IBSEN. She gave this to you? She gave you this? But, Suzannah, that's marvellous. That's wonderful. I'm saved. How on earth did you manage it? Did you speak to Herman at the bank?
SUZANNAH. I didn't do anything. She gave it to me of her own, free will.

Ibsen opens the envelope and takes out the birth certificate. Studies it for a few moments. Laughs with relief.

IBSEN. That is absolutely the... that is wonderful.

He crosses to the stove, opens the door and throws the envelope and birth certificate into the fire. Then he closes the door. Then he sits down, on the chair with the newspaper on it.

IBSEN. Well, that's the end of that, thank God! What a load off my mind.

SUZANNAH. Yes. Dr Jæger need never know anything about it now.

IBSEN. No. And why indeed should he? What does such detail have to do anything? Jæger's biography is supposed to be about my life and work. My inner life. My spiritual development. That is the real story. This... this business, this was a youthful indiscretion, nothing more. The woman was a housemaid. Just a maid.

SUZANNAH. And what were you?

IBSEN. Me? I was lonely, Suzannah. I was eighteen years old, away from home, deeply and unendurably lonely. I paid, don't forget. For fourteen years, out of my pittance, I paid towards that boy's keep. I fulfilled my obligations towards him – and her. And now it's over. Finished. Done with.

He reaches down to the newspaper rack beside the chair.

IBSEN. Where's that damn newspaper? Why can't people put things in their proper place?

SUZANNAH. You're sitting on it.

Ibsen frowns. He turns and picks it up.

IBSEN. What's it doing on the chair?

SUZANNAH. She put it there. Fru Jensen insisted on putting it there before she would accept my invitation to take a seat. She was worried about soiling our furniture with her dirty clothes.

IBSEN. Oh. No need for that, I'm sure.

And yet Ibsen moves to the other vacant armchair in which to sit with the paper.

IBSEN. And how has your day been? I mean, apart from that? Quiet?

SUZANNAH. Yes. A quiet day. I cleaned the pictures.

IBSEN. You know, I've told you before, I do wish you wouldn't climb up and down those stepladders. A woman in your condition, you should let the maid do it.

SUZANNAH. Ibsen you know quite well that I don't allow anyone else to touch my pictures.

IBSEN. It's still a piece of nonsense.

He settles to his newspaper.

SUZANNAH. Tell me about the investiture. Did you speak to the king?*

IBSEN. Oh indeed. His Majesty persists in his high regard for writers, which is of course excellent news for us all. Although you know sometimes I wonder whether he really understands all that much about it.

SUZANNAH. What makes you say that?

IBSEN. Well, at one point he took me aside, told me how much he valued my work but informed me that I should not, under any circumstances, have written *Ghosts*. He appeared to prefer *Lady Inger*.

SUZANNAH. And what did you tell him?

IBSEN. I told him the truth, of course. Your Majesty, I said, I *had* to write *Ghosts*.

Suzannah looks radiant at this reply. This is her Ibsen. She approaches him from behind and lightly places her hands on his shoulders.

SUZANNAH. Ibsen...

IBSEN. Yes?

SUZANNAH. There's something I must tell you. This afternoon...

IBSEN. Yes? What this afternoon?

SUZANNAH. This afternoon I made someone a promise. On your behalf.

IBSEN. Made who a promise?

SUZANNAH. That woman. Fru Jensen. The mother. This afternoon, while we were talking, she told me about her life. Ibsen, she's had such a hard life, such a pathetic life.

IBSEN. All lives are hard.

SUZANNAH. Yes, but her life, it's hardly her fault now, is it?

* See Interlude Note 4, page 261.

IBSEN. Are you suggesting that it is my fault?

SUZANNAH. I'm saying that it was no more her fault than it was yours. That it was no one's fault. I'm saying that it is not fair that her life should have been... destroyed by this one mistake. That her reputation should have been ruined. While you...

IBSEN. Yes? While I what?

SUZANNAH. Well, look at us, Ibsen. Look at this apartment.

IBSEN. I deserve my success, Suzannah. I've worked hard for my success. You, of all people, should know that.

SUZANNAH. Oh I know it, I do know it, believe me I do. But didn't I work hard for your success too? Haven't I deserved your success too? *Our* success, as I sometimes think of it.

IBSEN. Yes, God knows, I couldn't have done it without you. But then, you wanted my success as much as I did. You shared all my views, my aims, my aspirations, my dreams, my desire to change things for the better.

SUZANNAH. That's right. I shared everything with you. I wanted you to be a great man. I knew what was in you.

IBSEN. And I am a great man! Why else have I been awarded this?

He indicates his medal.

IBSEN. Why else is a statue of me being unveiled outside the National Theatre in the heart of our capital city? It's not something *I* say. These things – the decorations, the statues, the honours – these are not *my* ideas. They come from the people. It is other people who decide who is to be called great, and who is not. And in this as in everything else, Suzannah, believe me, I am profoundly aware of how much your belief in me has meant – and will continue to mean. Continue to mean!

SUZANNAH. Then do this thing for me. Show me how much you appreciate what I have done for you by keeping the promise I made on your behalf today.

IBSEN. But, my dear, how can I give such an undertaking, when I don't even know what the promise is? Does it concern the boy? Is it this business about helping the boy to find a job?

SUZANNAH. No, it isn't that. This much I will tell you: if you do this thing, if you keep this promise, it will make you greater in the eyes of those around you than anything you have done before.

IBSEN. I am insatiably curious. What is it?

SUZANNAH. Do you trust me?

IBSEN. You know that I trust you more than any other human being on earth.

SUZANNAH. Then please – give me your word. Even before you know what it is I am going to ask of you give me your word that you will do it.

IBSEN. Good God! This means a great deal to you, doesn't it?

SUZANNAH. It means everything to me.

There is a silence. Then:

IBSEN. Very well, then. I give you my word. Now tell me: what have I promised?

SUZANNAH. I have given fru Jensen our word – your word – that this evening, at the ceremonial unveiling of your statue outside the National Theatre, when you stand to deliver your speech, you will not talk about the statue, or the theatre, at all. I have promised her that when you speak to the crowd you will take this opportunity publicly to acknowledge the existence of this woman and of her son. That you will tell them what happened all those years ago, and that you will demand social justice not just for her but for all such mothers and their children. That is all.

IBSEN. That is all?

SUZANNAH. Proclaim her right – and his right – and the right of all those like them – to the simple respect to which every human being under the sun is entitled!

IBSEN. Have you gone completely out of your mind?

SUZANNAH. The streets and the hostels of Kristiania are full of these tragic souls. Show that crowd you are not ashamed, Ibsen. Show them, the gossips, the petty-minded, the narrow-minded, show them how incomparably far in advance of them all you are!

Show them true greatness! Instruct them! Teach them! Change
the world, my darling husband! You did it once before, now I'm
asking you, please, do it again!

IBSEN. You cannot possibly be serious.

SUZANNAH. I was never more serious in my life.

IBSEN. It is out of the question.

*He gets up and walks to the side of the stage. They are now
on opposite sides of the stage, with the Kronberg portrait
between them.*

SUZANNAH. I have been thinking. There is something else I want
to say.

IBSEN. Something else? What might that be? Would you like me, for
a grand finale, to kneel down and ask the theatre manager to
chop off my head?

SUZANNAH. This secret of yours, Ibsen – of ours – this secret that
you brought into our marriage with you, that we never talk
about, at times it seems to me that it has wrapped itself around
the years of our life together like a winding sheet. It has stifled
our happiness. Think, my love, if we could free ourselves from
it! Think how your courage this evening could mean liberation
not just for the unmarried mothers and the bastard children,
but for us too!

IBSEN. You don't understand, Suzannah. You haven't thought this
through. What about the gossip? Have you thought of that? The
whispers. The heads turning. The insolent smiles. The fingers
pointing. Have you thought of that? What right does any man
have to ask his wife to expose herself to such… luridness… Such
humiliation?

Suzannah moves towards him.

SUZANNAH. Oh my great bear, surely you know me better than that!
This would be nothing to me. Less than nothing. The truth
laughs at such pettiness! Think of dear old Dr Stockmann. He
didn't care what people said, he didn't care what people thought,

all he knew and cared about was that he had justice on his side, justice and truth. It is enough. It is more than enough. You said it yourself, my darling – the strongest man in the world is the man who stands most alone!

IBSEN. I said that? I most certainly did not say that. Dr Stockmann said that. I can't be held responsible for all his ravings. You, as the wife of an artist, should know that better than most.

SUZANNAH. Yes, but, but your *sympathies*... Everyone knows where your sympathies lie.

IBSEN. Oh they do, do they?

SUZANNAH. Yes. It is obvious.

IBSEN. Is it? Is it indeed? Is it really so obvious? And has it never occurred to you that *everyone* might be wrong? It isn't so much what people *say*, Suzannah; it's what they *think*. What you read in their eyes when they look at you.

SUZANNAH. Yes, and what do you think that poor unmarried mother has been reading in the eyes of those around her these past forty years?

Ibsen pauses. He is beginning to be uncertain.

IBSEN. (*quietly, hesitantly*) No... No... Extraordinary notion. (*Louder*) But tell me, do you really think it's possible? At our age? Can people really change their lives, at our age?

SUZANNAH. Of course they can, my darling. All it takes is courage.

IBSEN. If only you were right, Suzannah.

Ibsen is agitated. As he paces about the room he catches sight of his own reflection in the mirror and stops. Then his gaze moves to the Kronberg portrait.

IBSEN. A life without secrets. Is such liberation possible? It's too much, surely.

SUZANNAH. No, Ibsen. You can do it. Do it! And when the world hears that the great Henrik Ibsen has refused to bow to the claims of false shame, think how much this will mean to others!

IBSEN. Perhaps you're right, Suzannah. Truth cleanses. Truth heals, truth perfects human beings. Once expressed, even the harshest and ugliest of truths bathes us in nobility. This is what I have urged over and over again in my work, the need for courage in the service of truth. But oh my God, how different it is, how very much more difficult it is, to take that same courage out of the sanctuary of one's study and carry it down into the dirt and noise and merciless vulgarity of the street! Say it, yes. Believe it, yes. But do it? And yet – why not? Why not? What is it, this thing, this name that one is so afraid of losing?

Ibsen turns to her. Suddenly decisive.

IBSEN. Suzannah, your divine madness is infectious! I *will* do it!

SUZANNAH. I knew it! I knew it. Oh my loved one! Oh my lover!

She stands with her arms outstretched, hailing him, radiating her love and admiration for him. He stands erect. She approaches him. They touch each other – awkwardly – for they are very unused to touching one another. They are interrupted by a ringing on the doorbell and Ibsen pulls away from the embrace.

IBSEN. My cab for the theatre. I must leave.

Ritually, Suzannah helps him on with his black morning coat and glossy top hat.

SUZANNAH. I'm so proud of you, Ibsen. So proud.

At the door, Ibsen turns, seeking strength from her. She clenches her fist to show him strength. He leaves, closing the door behind him. His footsteps can be heard descending the staircase. Suzannah hobbles to the window and looks down at Ibsen departing in the cab. Then she turns into the room, facing the great painting, exultant, her fists clenched at her chest. She closes her eyes.

ACT THREE

Evening. The apartment at Arbiens gate. Suzannah alone, waiting in a state of visible tension for Ibsen to return from the unveiling. There is a ring on the doorbell and she admits Jæger.

SUZANNAH. Ah, Dr Jæger. Isn't my husband with you?

JÆGER. Fru Ibsen. No, I expect he's on his way. I've never seen the streets so crowded. Quite amazing.

He removes his coat.

SUZANNAH. Well? And how was the unveiling?

JÆGER. I missed it! Of all the wretched luck. The horse – would you believe it? – the horse fainted. And by the time I managed to find another cab and get to the theatre the ceremony was over. Sinding's statue is, of course, magnificent. A masterpiece.

SUZANNAH. But the speech, Dr Jæger? My husband's speech? You must have got some sense of how his speech was received?

JÆGER. Oh I should say so! Everyone was talking about it! Huge success!

SUZANNAH. I knew it! I knew it, I knew it, I knew it!

JÆGER. Yes, indeed. A memorable day. A great day for all of us. For the whole country. But for Ibsen! Your husband has known many great days in his life, fru Ibsen; but this, this must surely rank as the greatest of them all.

SUZANNAH. Oh yes, Dr Jæger. This is, beyond the shadow of a doubt, our greatest day.

JÆGER. And the atmosphere! What an atmosphere! There was a crowd of, oh I should think it must have been several thousand gathered below the balcony.

SUZANNAH. Tell me, how did Ibsen look? How did Ibsen seem? Oh tell me, tell me, I want to know everything.

JÆGER. Dr Ibsen sat there as serene, as poised, as dignified and as perfectly composed as that extraordinary statue. Cheer after cheer after cheer. It was like the seventeenth of May! It was like National Day! Thank you.

Jæger accepts a drink from her and sits down.

JÆGER. Rather curious incident afterwards, though. On my way back here, as I was walking through Vika, I was approached by some madman claiming to be the doctor's son!

SUZANNAH. Someone claiming to be Ibsen's son?

JÆGER. (*Still laughing*) Yes!

SUZANNAH. Did you speak to him? This... madman?

JÆGER. Oh yes! I told him that if he really were Ibsen's son then he must come back here with me, because I'm sure his father would be delighted to make his acquaintance!

SUZANNAH. You invited him here?

JÆGER. Bless you, fru Ibsen, I'm only joking! No, I gave the rascal a *skilling* and told him not to spend it on drink, although as he was already almost totally incoherent I doubt if he even heard me. He was being egged on by a crowd of young students. I should think it was they who put him up to it. I saw them pointing me out to him, urging him to speak to me. They had dressed him up in evening dress – like the doctor – top hat, morning coat, the lot.* Even hung a fifty øre piece round his neck on a length of string. Pretty tasteless sort of joke really. Probably some poor vagrant they picked up in the course of the night's

---

* See Interlude Note 5, page 262.

drinking, and, noticing he bore a resemblance – as a matter of fact a quite marked resemblance – to the doctor, put him up to it. But what an extraordinary fantasy! Still, that's the price of fame, I suppose.

SUZANNAH. What happened to this man? Did you see what happened to him?

JÆGER. Indeed I did. The last I saw of him he was being frogmarched off into the meatwagon by two of our largest constables. An old woman was hanging onto their arms, yelling at them to let him go, that she would take care of him. The mother, presumably. Really the problem of begging and public drunkenness in Kristiania is getting out of hand.

SUZANNAH. So they locked him up?

JÆGER. Yes. And quite right too. This is a day of considerable civic and national pride. Of course one is sorry for such people, but one really can't allow drunkards and beggars to spoil it all.

SUZANNAH. Dr Jæger, that man will be released from jail this evening. Ibsen will arrange for his release as soon as he hears what has happened. And you shall hear this poor man's story for yourself.

JÆGER. Ever the idealist, fru Ibsen!

SUZANNAH. Oh, on the contrary, Dr Jæger! When our dreams come true we are no longer dreamers, and when our ideals are realized we are no longer idealists.

JÆGER. I'm afraid I don't quite follow you, fru Ibsen.

SUZANNAH. Had you been present and heard my husband's speech you would understand exactly what I mean. (*Skittishly*) However, as a punishment for your horse fainting you must now wait until your final interview with my husband this evening to find out!

JÆGER. Well, that seems a little harsh, I must say! And now, I wonder if you'll excuse me for a few minutes. I still have a little packing to do.

Jæger goes into his room, where he can be seen sorting through his papers. Suzannah looks up at the portrait of her husband, closes her eyes, clenches her fists in wonder. Suddenly she wants to throw the windows open. She crosses to the window and tries to open it. It is too stiff and will not open.

SUZANNAH. Jæger? Dr Jæger? Can you help me with this window?

Jæger comes in.

JÆGER. A little stiff is it?

But he too struggles in vain to open it.

JÆGER. Well, it's beyond me. Must have swelled up with all that rain.

He returns to his room. Suzannah continues to try to open it. She hears Ibsen return and makes one last attempt to open it before his entry.

SUZANNAH. Ibsen. My husband. My love!
JÆGER. (*from his room*) Is that you, Dr Ibsen?
IBSEN. Ah, Jæger, back already?
JÆGER. (*Entering*) Yes. And ready to take your last confession now – if you're ready to make it!
IBSEN. My confession? What on earth are you implying?
JÆGER. Why, nothing. 'Your last confession'. It's just a turn of phrase.
IBSEN. Of course. Just a turn of phrase. Suzannah, will you excuse us for just a little while, my dear – I gave Jæger my word that he should have a final interview with me before he leaves Kristiania this evening. We'll talk about the ceremony later and I promise you, you shall hear all about it.
SUZANNAH. Later then. Oh Ibsen, I'm so proud of you. So proud!
IBSEN. Yes.

Suzannah goes out, Ibsen and Jæger sit opposite each other, Jæger with a notebook on his lap.

IBSEN. Alright then. Fire away.
JÆGER. I'd like to ask you about your harem, Dr Ibsen. Your women.
IBSEN. I beg your pardon?

JÆGER. Your women. All your Noras, Rebeccas, Heddas, Ellidas. Why is it that so many of your major characters are women? What was it – what is it – that has led to your writing so many plays that both depict and deplore the plight of women in our modern society?

IBSEN. 'Depict and deplore'? I don't suppose I can persuade you not to use that phrase in your biography, can I, Jæger? I'm sure I don't know the answer to your question. Do my plays really 'depict and deplore' the plight of women in society, as you put it?

JÆGER. (*discomfited*) Well, the members of the Women's Union seem to think so. At the dinner they gave at which you were guest of honour on the occasion of your 70th birthday, which was, let me see...

He consults his notebook.

IBSEN. Yes, yes, I know when my own birthday is.

JÆGER. I meant the dinner.

IBSEN. I will repeat for you what I said to them on that occasion: that I have in my writing been more of an artist and less of a social philosopher than people like to think. It is not women as such that interest me. It is people. Individual human beings, whether they happen to be men or women. Does that answer your question?

JÆGER. Well, if you'll forgive me, not really, Dr Ibsen. Recently I interviewed fru Krog of the Women's Union about *A Doll's House*, for example, and she told me that in her opinion your play was the single largest factor behind the change in the laws relating to the rights of married women to own property and manage their own finances. As she pointed out, these changes took place within two years of the appearance of your play. Surely there's some connection there? Our women generally, not just members of the Union but women generally, regard you as their champion.*

IBSEN. No. I am nobody's champion. I belong to no Party and I am nobody's champion. I am an artist.

---

* See Interlude Note 6, page 263.

JÆGER. But surely, Dr Ibsen...

IBSEN. Very well, then. Since you insist. My wife. The influence of my wife.

JÆGER. I see. Your wife.

He takes this note.

JÆGER. The socialists in London – I'm thinking of the dramatist Bernard Shaw – are also claiming you as one of their own. May I ask how you respond to this?

IBSEN. I dislike it intensely, for the same reasons as I dislike being taken for a champion of women's rights.

JÆGER. But would you not agree that a great many of your ideals...

IBSEN. (*losing patience*) My ideals? What ideals? My ideals are my own. If my moral position on some issue or other happens to accord with a social-democratic principle then that is a fortunate coincidence for the socialists and nothing more.

JÆGER. I see.

Takes this note.

JÆGER. If you don't mind, I'd like to return to the subject of the women in your plays...

IBSEN. As a matter of fact I do mind. I'm tired of talking about women. I don't want to talk about women anymore. Either in my plays, or anywhere else for that matter. Is that clear?

JÆGER. Yes, but...

IBSEN. Are you watching your time, Jæger?

JÆGER. I beg your pardon?

Ibsen stands up, consults his watch – the 'interview' is over.

IBSEN. Your time, man. Your train.

JÆGER. (*pulling out his watch*) No, you're quite right, I mustn't miss my train.

He begins to pack his papers away into a case. The 'danger' is over for Ibsen, who now begins to pace the floor, talking calmly, as though to himself.

IBSEN. You've never asked me how I work. Would you like to know how I work? The material first, then the theme. First material, then theme. Never the other way round. I mull over the material for a long time before I set pen to paper. I'm not talking about days, or weeks, or months. I'm talking about years. Years. I take long walks, alone. Going over, in my thoughts, some experience from the past that I have not merely known but lived through. Do you see the difference? Not merely experienced, but lived through. And not merely lived through, but lived through and put behind me. Only when it is all absolutely clear to me, when the central problem has been digested in this fashion and become an abstract formulation, only then do I begin the process of committing myself to paper. I write a draft. Very crude. Very rough. Then I work on it. Changing it. Adapting it. Distancing it from the original, personal event and transforming it into a generally applicable experience.

Jæger, realizing he is hearing something interesting, leaves off packing and begins to note this down.

IBSEN. I have one inflexible rule. Invariably, at the end of each working day, I stop at a point at which I know exactly what is going to happen next. I have the lines ready in my head, I simply don't write them down. So the following day, when I sit down at my desk, there they are, still waiting for me. I write them down, and on I go. And, of course, I must be alone. Absolutely and completely alone. The only person whose company is even remotely tolerable to me at such times is my wife. My son, for example, is never allowed to be present when I'm working. Not under any circumstances. Do you understand?

Ibsen stops pacing. He rubs his face with both hands.

JÆGER. You look tired, Dr Ibsen.

IBSEN. Yes. This has been a long day.

Jæger resumes packing.

JÆGER. A long day, but a great day.

IBSEN. Yes, a great day. Shall I tell you something, Jæger? I envy you your train journey this evening. Do you travel much by train?

JÆGER. Why, yes. When I can. It's much the most convenient way of getting about in these modern times.

IBSEN. Very well put, Jæger. Nicely phrased. I'm too old to travel much now, but in my time I have travelled a great deal by train. It's an ideal way of looking at things. People, countries. You see it all through the windows. And yet it doesn't concern you somehow. It doesn't impinge.

*Ibsen is lost in his own thought as Jæger concludes
his packing.*

JÆGER. Well, Dr Ibsen, I'm afraid I really must rush off now if I'm to make my train.

IBSEN. Oh no, really? Must you go?

JÆGER. I'm afraid so.

IBSEN. Oh, that's a pity. Well, I hope you found your stay here with us fruitful.

JÆGER. You've been most helpful, Dr Ibsen, most helpful.

IBSEN. The inner story, that's the thing. That's what people want to read. Not a lot of vulgar tittle-tattle.

Jæger is slightly affronted.

JÆGER. I beg your pardon?

IBSEN. Oh, don't take it personally, Jæger, I'm not referring to your book. But can people ever really know each other? Even when we possess all the facts about a life, surely something is always going to be missing? Who knows, perhaps even the most important thing of all.

JÆGER. Well, as a matter of professional pride, Dr Ibsen, I feel bound to say that I hope there is nothing missing.

Jæger is now ready to leave.

JÆGER. Well, thank you again for your hospitality and your co-operation. You really have been most patient. That reminds me, I was speaking to Sinding the other day...

IBSEN. (*interrupts*) You were speaking to Sinding? What on earth were you speaking to Sinding for? Sinding knows nothing about me.

JÆGER. I happened to meet him in the street, that's all. It was quite by accident, I assure you. I congratulated him on the statue and I pointed out to him that we were both, in a sense, your biographers – Sinding has written the story of your life in stone, and I have done so in words. He told me that you were probably the best and most patient model who has ever sat for him.

IBSEN. And I should think so too. If there's one thing a writer knows how to do it's sit still for hours on end.

Jæger looks at him a moment: is Ibsen amusing himself? Then he proffers his hand.

JÆGER. Goodbye, doctor.

IBSEN. Goodbye. Good luck with your book. You will send me a copy when it comes out now, won't you?

JÆGER. Indeed I will. With a dedication!

IBSEN. Of course! Don't forget the dedication!

Ibsen ushers Jæger towards the front door.

JÆGER. Fru Ibsen. I must thank fru Ibsen.

IBSEN. I'll pass on your thanks to her.

JÆGER. But...

IBSEN. Look sharp now! Mind your time!

The door is open, and Jæger has gone. Ibsen shuts it behind him and lingers there, deep in thought.

SUZANNAH. (*calling*) Who was that?

IBSEN. Jæger.

SUZANNAH. (*enters*) Has Dr Jæger gone?

IBSEN. Yes, just gone. Had to rush for his train. Asked me to pass on his thanks and good wishes to you.

SUZANNAH. Did you tell him? He didn't hear your speech, you know, he missed it.

Ibsen doesn't answer. He sits down in an armchair.
Suzannah is staring at him.

SUZANNAH. Well, Ibsen? Tell me all about it! I want to hear all the details!

IBSEN. Details? (*Pause*) Oh *that*. No, I couldn't.

SUZANNAH. You couldn't?

IBSEN. I couldn't do it.

SUZANNAH. But you gave me your word...

IBSEN. (*angrily*) Yes, but what does that matter, when I simply *couldn't do it*?

He tries to speak 'reasonably'.

IBSEN. It isn't fair, Suzannah. You can't ask a writer to do more than write. You mustn't. It's his *writing* that matters. The statements he makes. The carrying out of it all, the practical application of it all, that's for society to take care of, that is *society's* responsibility. Does a general lead his army from the front? Of course he doesn't, of course not. The risks are too great. Suzannah, a more enlightened age is dawning. You know it, I know it, we both know it. It is very possible that the world will change. And perhaps, in this new world that is dawning, perhaps there a fru Jensen and her... and her son will someday find the... ease, the... . But not yet, Suzannah. Not today. It's asking too much of me, to do this today. (*He looks straight at her.*) It's the disgrace, you see. I simply couldn't bear the disgrace.

She turns away from him.

IBSEN. When I was a child, Suzannah, when I was a boy, from the front door of the house in Skien where I grew up, you could see the stocks on the other side of the square. And even though they stopped using them years ago, I used to dream about them. I dreamt about them many, many times. I felt as though those little arms were reaching out to me, calling me over, to embrace me. And do you know what? I still dream about them. Seventy years of age and I still dream about those stocks... and there's something else. Won't you listen to me? Please?

SUZANNAH. Go on then: what is this something else?

Turns to face him again.

IBSEN. I realized, as I sat up there on that theatre balcony waiting to make my speech, with all those thousands of people milling about below, I realized that I did *not even want* to keep my promise.

She half-turns away again.

IBSEN. No, please, listen! Listen! Looking at that sea of heads beneath me, I suddenly understood something I had never understood before: I understood just how much I needed it.

SUZANNAH. How much you needed what?

IBSEN. The secret, Suzannah! The secret itself. I realized that it is the secret itself that has kept me going all these years. It's been like some great underground engine, grinding away deep down inside me all through the years, digging up these plays, transporting them to the surface, despatching them to stages all over the world, play after play after play after play. The secret is my power, and I am its slave. I realized – freedom from secrets, freedom from guilt – these are not for the artist, Suzannah, these are for other people. Take the secret away from an artist and you take away his lifeblood.

Having said 'it', he begins to navigate his way away from it.

IBSEN. And then, of course, there is the matter of Sigurd's career to consider. Perhaps I could have lived with the disgrace; but it would be unfair to any son of mine to expect him to have to do so. Because, of course, a scandal like that would ruin everything we have struggled for – his prospects in the diplomatic corps, his career, everything. No, no, it was impossible. Impossible.

He has finished. He takes out his pocket watch and checks the time.

IBSEN. Oh my goodness, look at the time!

Ibsen goes to the big clock, checks it against his watch, winds it up. As he closes the glass door he catches sight of the reflection of the Cross hanging around his neck. He studies it, then turns to Suzannah.

IBSEN. Did you see it, my dear? (*He holds up the Cross.*) The Great Cross?

SUZANNAH. The window won't open, Ibsen. I tried to open it this afternoon while you were out; but I couldn't do it.

IBSEN. I'll get the caretaker to have a look at it tomorrow. Shan't need it open tonight anyway, it's freezing out.

Ibsen sighs heavily. He puts his watch back in his waistcoat pocket, sits down, reads the paper. Suzannah sits down too, takes up her knitting. The big clock ticks. Suddenly stumbling heavy footsteps are heard coming up the stairs. Ibsen lowers his newspaper, Suzannah stops knitting. The footsteps stop at the front door. There is a quick, loud knock.

IBSEN. Oh my God, who's that? It's not the boy, is it? Is it the boy? You don't suppose it's the boy, do you?

Ibsen stands up. The knock is repeated. After a while:

IBSEN. Has he gone? Who do you suppose it was? Do you suppose it was him?

SUZANNAH. You needn't worry about the son anymore, Ibsen.

IBSEN. Why not?

SUZANNAH. Because he's in jail. Dr Jæger saw the whole thing. This afternoon. On his way back here from the theatre. He was drunk, apparently. Telling anyone who would listen to him that he was Henrik Ibsen's son. No one believed him, of course. The police handcuffed him and took him away.*

IBSEN. Then perhaps it's Sigurd. (*He calls through the front door.*) Grimbart, is that you? Did you forget your key?

There is no answer. He opens the door. No one there.

IBSEN. (*calling into the darkness*) That you, old man? Grimbart? (*He steps out onto the landing.*) Jæger? Miss the train? (*He comes back into the apartment and closes the door.*) That's odd. There was no one there.

He shrugs, sits down, picks up his paper again. Suzannah knits. The clock ticks. After a few moments Ibsen lowers the paper.

IBSEN. A rather odd thing happened at the theatre this evening. I was watching from the balcony as they raised that... the what do you call it... the cloth that covers the statue. There was cheering, clapping, a band playing – tremendous noise. I couldn't take my eyes off the statue. It's enormous, you know. Absolutely enormous. I don't think I quite realized up until then just how big it is. It was cold, sitting up there. Very cold. And faces everywhere, all looking up at me. And suddenly a sort of confusion overcame me. And it was as though I couldn't tell which was which anymore. Which was the statue, and which was me. It only lasted a few moments, of course, and then it was over, and it was clear to me again, which was the statue, and which was me.

He sits motionless for a few moments, then raises his newspaper again. Suzannah has been looking at him. Now her gaze shifts to the Kronberg portrait. She sits forward and peers at it. She gets up and hobbles out. Moments later she reappears with the step-ladder and a cloth, opens it in front of the portrait and begins slowly to climb up.

---

* See Interlude Note 7, page 266.

IBSEN. I thought I told you not to do that.
SUZANNAH. There's a mark on it.

She begins to rub at the glass with her cloth.

IBSEN. Leave it.
SUZANNAH. But there's a mark on it.

Still rubbing the glass.

IBSEN. (*giving Suzannah a fierce bark that 'freezes' her*). I said
LEAVE IT!

Suzannah lowers her arm and remains standing as the light fades to blackout on this tableau.

———

Interlude Notes

1. 'To stop the rats getting up'

Rattus norvegicus is known as the Norwegian rat from an early misapprehension that it originated in Norway. Also known as the common, street, sewer, barn, brown or wharf rat. Where brown and black rats occupy the same habitat, in this instance an apartment block, the black rats will tend to live on the upper floors while the brown rats seek the lower levels. Brown rats were long thought to be a major source of bubonic plague and the probable cause of the Black Death. In Ibsen's 1894 play *Little Eyolf*, an old woman known as the Rat Wife arrives at the Almers' house asking if there is anything 'gnawing away in the house' and offering to lead the rats away to drown in the fjord. The Almers tell her they have no need of her services. Their crippled son Eyolf, however, becomes fascinated by the woman and is drawn to follow her down to the water, where it is he who drowns.

2. 'Tell me, did you know my husband in Grimstad?'

While living and working in Grimstad, Ibsen spent much of his free time painting. A watercolour of the local harbour is among the few survivals of this interest. He also wrote *Rypen i Justedal* ('The Grouse in Justedal') under an early *nom de plume*, Brynjolf Bjarme. Although he announced it on the title page as being in four acts, he never got further than the middle of the second act. The fragment is set in a remote part of Norway in the years immediately after the Black Death, which by the middle of the fourteenth century had wiped out over half the population of the country. It is based on a legend concerning a number of families in the Sogn district of central Norway who secluded themselves in the Jostedal valley, in an attempt to escape the ravages of the plague. Some years later a group of travellers passing through the valley found only dead bodies on the farms they encountered. At the most remote of these, they saw footsteps that led away and up into the mountains. Following them, they discovered the only surviving member of the community, a young girl who had reverted to a feral existence and could speak only three words: *Mor, vetle rjupa* ('Mother, little bird'). Nine years later he made another attempt to use the legend as the basis for a libretto to be called *Fjeldfuglen*, 'The Mountain Bird'. Only fragments of it survive. The tale of the feral girl contined to haunt Ibsen. The wild hermit girl Gerd, in his great breakthrough play *Brand* from 1866, sounds a strong echo of her.

Grimstad.

3. 'Sigurd. He's a diplomat.'

During their first year in Italy, in Ariccia, while Ibsen was working on *Brand*, his family were poor and lived an austere life, which in some ways reflected the domestic life of Brand, Agnes and little Alf that Ibsen was describing in his play. Suzannah was the disciplinarian in the family, ensuring her husband sat down at his desk for work each day, making sure that he was left undisturbed, and raising their son Sigurd herself, without the aid of a nanny. When she had to go out and leave the child on his own she would place a wad of cotton wool on the floor and tell Sigurd that he was on no account to pass beyond it until she was back. In later life, Sigurd Ibsen often recalled that wad of cotton wool, and how he would stare at it as though hypnotized until his mother returned and raised her spell.

The boy had something of his father's nature, a fierce mixture of the rebellious and the submissive. He would sometimes give way to impulses that called for him to push the pot plants off the window sill down into the street below. Once, when travelling with his parents, he was compelled to wear a sailor's hat which he detested. In the carriage taking them down to the harbour he threw it away; it was retrieved. On board the ship he threw it into the water; someone rowed out and rescued it. Completing the final leg of the journey by train, he was at last able to get rid of it by hurling it through the open window of the railway carriage.

Sigurd showed the same qualities of disciplined boldness in adult life as a diplomat in the Norwegian-Swedish Foreign Office based in Stockholm, and then later in Austria and the United States; but he became the object of resentment in certain quarters for the way in which his career seemed to profit from his father's great celebrity. Leaving the diplomatic service in 1890, he campaigned for the establishment of a chair in the new discipline of Sociology at the University of Kristiania, and towards the end of the decade he delivered a series of lectures on the subject that were well attended but failed to convince the university board of his fitness to head the new department. He was instead made Director General in the country's Department of the Interior with responsibility for building up a Foreign Office. This was at a time when the Norwegian campaign for independence from Sweden, which had been gathering pace over the last two decades of the nineteenth century, began its final acceleration towards the drama of 1905.*

Norway's independence finally brought to an end the associations and separations set in train 500 years earlier by the Kalmar Union, in 1397. During the nineteenth century, from the chaos surrounding the end of the Napoleonic Wars and the transfer of sovereignty in Norway from Denmark to Sweden, the Norwegians had emerged with a constitution of their own that gave its parliament powers of self-regulation very similar to those handed to the devolved parliaments of Wales, Northern Ireland and Scotland in the United Kingdom in the late 1990s that were intended to kill nationalism 'stone dead in the water'. Norway in the 1890s enjoyed all the freedoms of independence except a Foreign Office and consular service of its own. Sigurd Ibsen's brief was to build up a Norwegian Foreign Office, with the establishment of an independent consular service as a secondary demand. He wrote articles for the newspaper *Dagbladet* highlighting the failings of a joint diplomatic service, and was opposed by supporters of a continued union, both sides using the newspaper columns as a forum for debate in a way that remains characteristic of the Scandinavian way of doing things, with all aspects of important public matters being extensively articulated and discussed on the way to reaching a conclusion.

Very often the contributors to these debates were prominent writers. Having abolished the aristocracy in 1821, Norwegians in the nineteenth century turned increasingly to poets and writers as leaders of opinion. The first of these *dikterhøvdinger*, or poet chieftains, was the poet Henrik Wergeland, whose long campaign to remove the opening paragraph of the constitution that prohibited Jews and Jesuits from entering Norway finally succeeded in 1851, six years after his death at the age of thirty-seven. The mantle then passed to the playwright, short-story writer and poet Bjørnstjerne Bjørnson, Ibsen's great friend, rival and almost exact contemporary, a

---

* In the twenty-first century the Norwegian example has been used by the Scottish National Party as a blueprint for its own campaign for independence from the United Kingdom.

more extroverted and charismatic orator and public man than Ibsen, whose greater ethical power made itself felt through work rather than through speeches. The value of these *dikterhøvdinger* was that their insight and intelligence were respected without being binding in the old way of a formal aristocracy.

Sigurd Ibsen was in favour of an independent Norway, but not fanatically so. He was a cosmopolitan who had lived most of his life abroad and been educated at the universities in Munich and Rome. His daily exposure in Germany and Italy to the colonies of expatriate artists, writers and thinkers from Denmark, Norway and Sweden resident in these cities made him a natural pan-Scandinavian, with little of that mixture of aggression and patriotic fervour with which most of his fellow-countrymen, less well-travelled and experienced in the ways of the world, viewed the prospect of life as an independent nation. In 1903, at a time when the clamour for independence in the country was becoming deafening, he was appointed Norwegian prime minister in Stockholm. The issue of a Norwegian consular service appointed and run from Norway was raised and flatly rejected by the Swedes, at which point Sigurd realized the complete inevitability of the dissolution of the union. His way forward – calling for further discussions between the two governments, another general election in Norway, amendments to the Norwegian constitution that would ensure the legality of the secession and, crucially, the offer of the crown of Norway to a Bernadotte member of the Swedish royal family as a way of appeasing the Swedes – was completely at odds with the momentum for immediate action that was sweeping Norway. There was no place for him in the new Norwegian government formed in March 1905 by Christian Michelsen, and despite the valuable groundwork done by Sigurd Ibsen in arguing the need for independent foreign and consular services, he found himself pushed out into a political wilderness from which he never returned.

On 7 June 1905, the Norwegian parliament passed a unanimous resolution declaring that Oscar II was no longer King of Norway and that the union of Norway and Sweden was dissolved. In August the issue was put to the country in a referendum, in which 368,208 people voted for the dissolution and just 184 against. Women were not eligible to vote, but a quarter of a million of them signed a petition that also called for an end to the union. The Swedish Army began preparing an invasion of Norway. The Norwegians responded by sending armed forces to protect the borders in the east of the country. Russia, Sweden's only supporter among the great powers, was fatally distracted by its war with Japan and the domestic Revolution of 1905, while Great Britain warned Sweden not to attempt an invasion, sending a warship to Kristiania to guarantee the peace. Sweden was left with little option but to accept the situation, and did so formally in talks held in Karlstad in October. In a second referendum, Norwegians voted by an overwhelming majority to reject republicanism in favour of a monarchy, and the crown was offered to the Danish Prince Carl, who was given the name Håkon VII, picking up the thread Norwegian patriots and historians believed had been dropped at Kalmar in 1397, following the death in 1380 of Håkon VI, the last king of a truly independent Norway.

Sigurd Ibsen, condemned by the demands of his father's calling to be a man without roots, his patriotism real enough but insufficiently driven for the needs of his fellow countrymen, made a mournful attempt to follow in his father's footsteps and establish himself as a dramatist. His first play, *Robert Frank* (1914), was performed at the National Theatre and translated into several languages; a second, entitled *Erindringens tempel* (*The Temple of Remembrance*) in 1917 did less well. Inevitably, Sigurd was compared to his father as a dramatist and found wanting. After the First World War, he and his wife and young son spent most of their time abroad, in Italy and Germany. In 1920, he bought a villa in the southern Tyrol, not far from Gossensass, where he had lived as a boy.

Sigurd died of cancer on 14 April 1930. His son Tancred went on to become one of Norway's most outstanding film-makers. Among the twenty-four films he directed was the first Norwegian talkie, a 1931 comedy entitled *The Great Christening*. Of the two theatres at the Oslo Cinemateket in Dronningens gate, one is named 'Tancred' after him. The other commemorates his wife, 'Lillebil', an actress.

4. 'Tell me about the investiture. Did you speak to the King?'

Ibsen's (true) story of his exchange with Oscar II of Sweden-Norway on the subject of the king's preference for a lightweight early drama to the revolutionary tones of the late-period *Ghosts* sounds a faint echo of an entry in one of Søren Kierkegaard's *Journals*, in which the philosopher describes a royal reception in Copenhagen and a meeting with Queen Caroline of Denmark in the course of which she told the philosopher that she had read his '*Either and Or*' but failed to understand it. Kierkegaard gallantly accepted the blame for this failure; but he had noticed the slip and knew that the king had noticed it too, and that he was watching him. Kierkegaard wrote that Caroline's mistake was 'the kind of thing seamstresses etc. say' and carefully avoided catching the king's eye for the next few moments. Caroline would have found more exalted company than Kierkegaard's seamstresses in Ibsen who, on the basis of *Brand* and *The Wild Duck* in particular, was so often charged with having been influenced by Kierkegaard, and whose standard response was that he had read little of the Dane and understood even less. No doubt, Ibsen was being disingenuous, as great writers tend to be in regard to their influences. Michael Meyer, who was a personal friend of Graham Greene, once told me that Greene was a great admirer of Knut Hamsun's novels, *Pan* especially, and yet one searches the indexes of Greene biographies in vain for any reference to this influence.

The fame Ibsen enjoyed in his own lifetime was that of a lay monarch, a status tacitly recognized by the Swedish king. While he remained able to do so, Ibsen much enjoyed walking in the Queen's Garden, a private section of the royal palace located directly opposite his apartment in Arbiens gate. One Tuesday afternoon he and his masseur, a man named Arnt Dehli, crossed the road only to find the gate to the park locked. Ibsen had failed to realize that the queen was in residence, and that on such occasions the park gate was always kept locked. As soon as the matter was brought to the attention of the king, Oscar ordered a key to be specially cut for Ibsen so that he might come and go in the park as he pleased.

5. 'They had dressed him up in evening dress – like the doctor – top hat, morning coat, the lot.'

Jæger's story derives from an account given by Francis Bull, which Bull heard from his father Edvard, Ibsen's personal doctor during the last years of his life. A contemporary of Ibsen's, the phenomenally prolific Rudolf Muus, author of 286 novels, none of which made his fortune, tells a related story in one of his many non-fiction books, *Gamle Kristianiaminder* ('Memories of Old Kristiania'), a book about eccentrics in old Oslo. Among his subjects is a barber named Fredriksen, who worked in the Grønland district of the city and who occasionally traded on his strong resemblance to Henrik Ibsen to pretend that he actually was the great man. Muus describes one particular evening that began in a mood of reserved nostalgia but which became more and more animated as the drinking wore on, until presently Fredriksen-Ibsen was picking fights and insulting everyone in the room. Drunk themselves, the other guests responded in kind and a brawl ensued, which had to be broken up by the police. A sketch by Gustav Lærum recalls an occasion on which Fredriksen again dressed up as Ibsen and entered the bar of the Grand Hotel in central Oslo at about the time the dramatist usually showed up for his daily drink. Graciously acknowledging the greetings and curious stares of the other patrons, he took his seat and was still sitting there when the real Ibsen entered the premises. Muus tells us only that Ibsen 'looked surprised and furrowed his brows indignantly'.

I forbigaaende maalte Ibsen sin dobbeltgjænger med et over-
rasket blik og rynket brynene indignert.

6. 'Our women generally, not just members of the union but women generally, regard you as their champion.'

Ibsen's role in the creation of the widespread perception of Scandinavian societies as especially advanced in the equality of the sexes is
beyond dispute. Through female characters including Nora Helmer,
Hedda Gabler, Ellida Wangel and Fru Alving, he focused, with a
respectful insistence, on the equality of women with men at the same
time as he insisted on their difference from men. For Ibsen the sexes
were equal but different. By following the advocacy of the Danish
critic Georg Brandes, that a modern play should concern itself with
a discussion of modern problems, that it should talk about what
people are talking about and be in effect an extended exploration
of stories of everyday life that might appear in the daily newspaper,
he developed an accessible and popular form of drama that became
the structural and thematic model for some of the most important
dramatists of the twentieth century, from George Bernard Shaw to
Eugene O'Neill, Arthur Miller and Sweden's Lars Norén.

If Ibsen in many ways shaped the future development of Norwegian society through his plays, the same can hardly be said of August Strindberg, that other great nineteenth-century Scandinavian dramatist, whose influence on twentieth-century dramatists came close to rivalling that of Henrik Ibsen. From an outsider's point of view, the only thing the two had in common was that extremism that is so characteristic of the most celebrated Scandinavian artists, perhaps in itself an expression of the colossal effort it took to break free from the pressure to conform in small and what were then remote societies. (Although, on a visit last year to the Strindberg Museum at Drottninggatan 85, 'The Blue Tower', his last address in Stockholm, I was moved to see that it was Strindberg's habit to keep his pens, pencils, spectacle cases and ink bottles arranged around his blotting pad in neat and almost military formation, exactly as Henrik Ibsen did in Arbiens gate.) Strindberg found a natural opponent in Ibsen and was passionately opposed to the view of women expressed in the plays of Ibsen's later maturity, *A Doll's House* in particular: he attacked Ibsen's shattering play about a woman who leaves home and family in search of her true self in a short story *Et dockhjem* (*A Doll's House*), and tried to confound its sympathies in a five-act play of his own, *Herr Bengts hustru* (*Herr Bengt's Wife*), first published in 1882, six years after Ibsen's play.

Margit, the 'wife' of Strindberg's title, is a woman of noble birth whose parents have died and who is about to enter a convent. In the nick of time she meets and falls in love with a wealthy squire, Herr Bengt. The day after their wedding, Bengt's financial situation undergoes a dramatic change for the worse. Unwilling to burden his wife with their troubles, he says nothing to her, and concentrates on restoring their fortunes through hard work. In due course they start a family. One day Margit notices that her rose-bushes are wilting. She sends the estate workers to a distant well to fetch water for them. A storm approaches, threatening the crops, and Herr Bengt is distraught to learn that Margit has sent the workforce away on such a footling errand. They quarrel. Bengt comes close to hitting her. Margit duly petitions for a divorce. She allows a childhood friend to pay court to her. Then she learns that it was to protect her and their child that Bengt kept quiet about their money troubles. She considers suicide but at the last moment her maternal instincts take over and she realizes she cannot abandon the child. Instead she asks Bengt to forgive her and the couple resolve to make a fresh start. Strindberg had positioned friends in strategic locations around the theatre on the drama's opening night, to ensure its enthusiastic reception; but the professional critics were divided. Some complained that the dramaturgy was feeble and the final scene melodramatic, as Margit at last sees Bengt's essential nobility and decency and understands that her place is beside him. Swedish critics who hailed Strindberg's play as superior to *A Doll's House* did so on ethical rather than dramatic grounds: Strindberg's couple *talk it through*. They forgive each other and pledge themselves to a future together.

Although Ibsen and Strindberg never met they were aware of the relationship between them as polar and complementary. In 1893 Ibsen bought a portrait of August Strindberg by the Norwegian painter Christian Krohg and had it hung it on the wall of his study in Arbiens gate. Fascinated by the demonic eyes, he retitled it 'Incipient Madness' and claimed he was unable to write a line without 'that maniac' staring down at him. Late in the summer of 2015 I was invited to a breakfast at the Grand Hotel on Karl Johans gate by Christian Gjelsvik, an editor at Aschehoug publishing house, to meet some Portuguese students of Norwegian literature who were visiting Oslo. He had invited me along hoping I might say something intelligent to them about Knut Hamsun. Ivo de Figueiredo, who had recently published a biography of Henrik Ibsen, was there too. That morning there was a faint air of melancholy about the large, open dining room in which a coat-stand and a small table with a top hat resting on it have, for over a century, marked the spot where Ibsen took his daily dram after returning to Norway in 1891, for it happened to be the day before this historic establishment, so important to the cultural life of Norway, closed its doors and after 141 years submitted to a 'makeover'. At some point in the conversation about Ibsen we fell to discussing which of these two titans of the theatre we would rather

spend an evening with, Strindberg or Ibsen. When my turn came I replied, without much thought, Strindberg when young, Ibsen in my old age. But then immediately thought of Strindberg's deliriously unfettered imagination, and of how just five years before his death in 1912 he had arrived at a belief that apes are descended from humans rather than the other way round, and suddenly wasn't so sure of my choice after all.

7. 'The police handcuffed him and took him away.'

Else Sofie Jensdatter never married. While she was able to, she worked as a washerwoman, and in her later years she lived on poor relief. She died aged seventy-four, in Vestre Moland on 5 June 1892, too early to have played any part in the imagined events of this play. Her son and Ibsen's – Sigurd Ibsen's half-brother, Hans Jakob – worked as a smith. Hans Jakob's first wife, Mathilde, died of tuberculosis at the age of thirty, and the couple's only child died in infancy. He married again in 1882 but lost both this wife and his second child to a smallpox epidemic that swept Lillesand that same year. Eighteen months later, he married for a third time, to Ida Gurine Olsdatter. For most of his life, Hans Jakob struggled with alcoholism. When he fell off the wagon, he would go on a binge, taking with him what was said to be his proudest possession, his birth certificate, and show it around in the bars in the hope of being treated to a drink: he was proud of who his father was and read his plays, and, like his shadow-brother Sigurd, even wrote himself, in his case occasional verse of which one example survives, a poem in nine stanzas written especially for the Lillesand Temperance Society. As I write this now, I recall the odd fate of Henrik Ibsen's own birth certificate, which went missing, or was sold, along with the rest of his personal belongings after he emigrated to Italy in 1864 and his property was auctioned off in his absence to meet the debts he had left behind. Not long after Ibsen's return to Kristiania in 1891 his birth certificate reappeared, sent in the post to Sigurd by an inhabitant of Bergen, who explained in a covering letter that he had called in at a watchmaker's to pick up a timepiece that was being repaired, and found that the paper in which it had been wrapped for protection turned out to be the enclosed document.

Hans Jakob died of cancer in Lillesand in October 1916. Of the five children he fathered with Ida Gurine Olsdatter, three died in infancy, and of the two who survived one died of tuberculosis in 1922 at the age of twenty-seven. The other, sixteen-year-old Inga Hansine Hansen, lured like any Little Eyolf by the siren song of America, was among those who boarded the Danish emigrant ship SS *Norge* that steamed out of Copenhagen harbour on 24 June 1904. Four days later, at 8 o'clock in the morning, the vessel hit a submerged cliff off Rockall and sank within twenty minutes. There were 795 passengers and crew on board, but lifeboat places for only 250 of them. Inga was one of the 635 men, women and children who drowned that day, the largest single loss of life on one day in Norwegian history. Danes, Swedes and numerous Russian Jews were also among the dead. One of the Norwegians who made it onto a lifeboat was a young man named Herman Portaas, who later changed his name to 'Wildenvey' (*vil den vei* – 'will go this way') and became the outstanding Norwegian poet of his generation. In the oscillating trajectory of my thought, I now remember reading somewhere that his marked facial resemblance to Oscar Wilde, coupled with his choice of pen-name, led to persistent rumours in Norway that he was the illegitimate son of the author of *An Ideal Husband*.

10
The Emigrants

IN 2014, STATISTICS NORWAY PUBLISHED A LIST SHOWING
that the most common name among men and boys living in Oslo is
now 'Mohammed'. Muslims joke that one in five of them is named
Mohammed and the other four spell it differently, so it shouldn't
really have surprised me, but the speed with which the Knuts and
Håkons and Olavs of Norwegian tradition have been outnamed still
seems surreal. It led me to ponder the whole phenomenon of emigration – what it is, who and what immigrants and emigrants are – and
it was while thinking on such matters during the so-called 'migrant
crisis' that occupied the front and most of the inside pages of almost
every daily newspaper throughout 2015 that I came to recall a small
dinner gathering I attended some twenty years ago at the house of
my friend Don Nelson and his wife Ane, at which the subject of
the large-scale Scandinavian emigration to America in the nineteenth
and early twentieth centuries came up.

Don was a Canadian photographer who had, like me, married a
Norwegian and settled in Norway. A lot of his work was done as
a stills photographer in the Norwegian film industry. We met while
Don was working on Henning Carlsen's Danish-Norwegian film
version of *Pan*, actually the fourth attempt to film Hamsun's classic
story. Carlsen's version in 1966 of Hamsun's breakthrough novel

Hunger had made his name as a director and won for the Swede Per
Oscarsson the Best Actor award at the Cannes Film Festival in 1967.
My impression was that Hamsun's short and hypnotic novella had
continued to haunt Henning for much of his life and now finally he
had decided to do something about it before it was too late. He cast
the Danish actress Sofie Gråbøl in the part of Thomas Glahn's lover
Edvarda, a role she made her own so completely that when the era

of the Scandinavian noir television series came along I could never
accept her as Detective Sarah Lund in *The Killing* but was condemned
to remember her forever as Glahn's tormenting and tormented lover
in Carlsen's film. While *Pan* was still in pre-production Carlsen had
asked me to translate his screenplay into English so that it could be
sent round to potential investors in Europe. This was standard procedure for ambitious Scandinavian film-makers wanting to reach out
beyond their small linguistic communities and over the years I had
done many such screenplay translations. Most of them never acquired
three-dimensional lives as films, but *Pan* had made it to the screen.
I think it was at some kind of social get-together for the whole crew
at Filmens Hus, the National Film Theatre, to celebrate the comple-
tion of the film, that I first met Don. A piano trio had been hired for

the occasion, and at some point Don and I fell into a conversation about the uniqueness of Scandinavian jazz and its strikingly lyrical, modal and melancholic quality. I had always thought these elements arrived in Scandinavia at a quite specific point, early in the year 1964, when Bill Evans brought his trio over to Stockholm to play on Monica Zetterlund's *Waltz for Debby* album, which included Evans's arrangement of a Swedish folk song called *Jag vet en dejlig rosa*. Not so, Don informed me. According to him, that honour more likely belonged to a Swedish pianist named Jan Johansson, whose *Jazz på svenska* album, recorded a year or two before Zetterlund's, consisted entirely of arrangements of Swedish folk songs, most memorably, in Don's view, a fragile little classic called *Vi sålde våra hemman* ('We sold our home') or *Emigrantvisa* ('The Emigrant Song'), first documented in 1854 and one of the many folk songs that arose out of the Swedish emigration to America.* Don's erudition impressed me, as did the length of his grey ponytail, and we became friendly.

Don and Ane lived in Haslum, a leafy and comfortable suburb of western Oslo not too far from Filmparken, the large enclosed lot where most Norwegian film companies have their offices and rehearsal studios. The Nelsons' house was one of those large rambling homes in wine-dark timber built in the late nineteenth century, old by Norwegian standards, and surrounded by tall, sheltering horse-chestnut and pine trees. A singular feature of it was a smaller annex standing a few metres away on the further side of the gravelled yard. The Nelsons were in the habit of renting this out to visiting film technicians or actors.

On the particular occasion I was remembering their guest had been the Swedish actor Max von Sydow. He was in Norway shooting the final scenes of another of Troell's films, which happened, coincidentally, to be a biopic about Hamsun. The screenplay was by Troell's fellow-Swede P.O. Enquist and was based on *Prosessen mod Hamsun* ('The Trial of Hamsun'), a 1976 book by the eminent Danish writer Thorkild Hansen. In every sense, Troell's film was a competitor to

---

* You can see Jan Johansson play this at https://www.youtube.com/watch?v=ej4P6m7L-4U.

the recently completed dramatization of the same writer's life, in six fifty-minute episodes, produced by Norwegian State Broadcasting, which was based on a biography of Hamsun I had written some ten years earlier, *Enigma: The Life of Knut Hamsun* (*Gåten Knut Hamsun*). In an attempt to maximize financial returns, the series had also been raided to make a ninety-minute feature film for showing in cinemas. As luck would have it, the films were in production almost simultaneously, and with someone of von Sydow's eminence playing the part of the fallen writer there wasn't much doubt about which would attract the most attention. And yet I felt little tenderness for the Norwegian enterprise. I had written the six episodes that formed the basis of the series, but the director brought his own 'dramaturge' with him, who rapidly convinced the producer that our series should resemble as closely as possible a recent Swedish television dramatization of the life of August Strindberg, in which Thommy Berggren had played the great dramatist. Each episode now acquired long and tiresome scenes of marital 'conflict' between Hamsun and his wife Marie and by the time a score or so of major emendations had been made to the original scripts I hardly recognized them as my own and would have taken my name off the series altogether had I not been afraid it might oblige me to return the money already paid out to me, money which I no longer had. So my attitude towards the Norwegian film was ambivalent in the extreme, which was lucky for me, since it meant that the evening at the Nelsons was not going to be compromised by any unease at the thought that von Sydow was currently finishing work on a film that would in all likelihood consign ours to the dustbin of movie history.

I assumed that Don had invited me to dinner thinking that Max von Sydow might want to discuss aspects of Hamsun's life and personality with me, since my biography was still, at that time, the only full-length cradle-to-grave book around in any language. But almost from the moment we sat down at the table I realized that the great actor, while perfectly civil, was so completely bound up in his creative processes he would hardly say anything at all for fear of losing track of something important that, once dropped, would be so hard to pick up again that he might just as well give up altogether, pack his suitcase and return to Stockholm. Realizing this, I immediately felt under an obligation to talk about *anything but Hamsun*. The actor was the soul of courtesy and several times complimented our hostess on the excellence of the *lutefisk* she set before us – dried cod soaked in lye, with its trimmings of mushy peas and crispy diced bacon, a quivering jelly of a dish not for the fainthearted; but as far as I remember, the only time he emerged fully from his inner world was when the conversation between Don and Ane got onto the subject of the mysterious disappearance, at some point in the fifteenth century, of the Greenland colonists who had settled in the south and west of the island some four hundred years previously.

Don, who had a romantic interest in Native American history, began talking about one of the more eccentric explanations offered for their disappearance that involved a tribe of Plains Indians known as the Mandan which, prior to its extinction early in the nineteenth century after contracting smallpox from French fur traders – George Caitlin includes a heartbreaking account of their brief and furious struggle against the disease in his study *North American Indians*, Don added parenthetically – had long been an object of wonder to outside observers for the light hair and blue eyes of some of their number. According to this theory, the starving and desperate remnants of the two Greenland colonies, isolated from the Scandinavian homelands as the Medieval Warm Period ended and ice returned to Greenland's coastal waters and made access by sea impossible, crossed the Davis Straits to the North American continent where, willingly or otherwise, they were absorbed into the Mandan. The white hair and blue eyes are the genetic input of these long-vanished Greenlanders. Modern geneticists will have none of it, said Don. But a man would need a mind of stone not to find some fascination in it.

'Is there any proof of this theory?' von Sydow asked, pausing in mid-motion as he lifted a spoonful of diced bacon from the little white bowl to drip over the cod.

Don said that the Kensington Runestone was sometimes offered as proof, and began to describe how, in the summer of 1898, a Swedish immigrant farmer named Olof Ohman who was grubbing stumps on his farm at Solem, near the village of Kensington, in Douglas County, Minnesota came across one particular tree, a small, misshapen aspen, that obstinately resisted his every effort to remove it. Eventually he dug away the soil around its roots and discovered that the source of his trouble was a large flat stone lying immediately beneath the tree. The stone was held firmly between two of its thickest roots and Ohman had to be careful not to damage the blade of his axe against it as he hacked through them. He then lifted the stone out of his way and carried on digging. His ten-year-old son came by to help him. At some point the boy stopped work and began to study the stone. Its surface was smooth and flat and the boy dusted it clean with his cap. His voice raised in excitement, he called to his father to come see what he had found: across one face of the stone and along one of its edges a series of regular markings had been scratched or chiselled. They clearly formed some kind of message, but written in an unknown language. A transcription of the mysterious signs was made and sent to O.J. Breda, a professor of Scandinavian languages in Minnesota. Breda eventually produced a translation of what he identified as Old Norse runes:

> Eight Goths and 22 Norwegians on a journey of discovery from Vinland westward. We had a camp by two skerries one day's journey north from this stone.

> We were out fishing one day. When we returned home we found ten men red with blood and dead. A V M (Ave Virgo Maria), save us from evil.

A shorter row of runes carved along one side translated as:

> have ten men by the sea to look after our vessel fourteen days' journey from this island. Year 1362.

If the story on the stone was true, and these Scandinavians had wandered on the North American continent over a hundred years before Christopher Columbus arrived, said Don, then the history of the

European discovery of America would have to be rewritten. Along with accounts in two Icelandic sagas that describe the Viking Age discovery of America by Greenlanders early in the eleventh century, it appeared to provide compelling confirmation of the theory that Scandinavians had visited the North American continent at least twice before Columbus. Starting with Breda, however, a succession of scholars proceeded to dismiss the stone as a poorly executed hoax, on linguistic as well as historical grounds. Their chief objections were that the runic forms used were either unknown, obsolete at the supposed date of their appearance on the stone, or else had not yet entered the language. The use of the word *opthagelses-fardth* to mean 'journey of discovery' was considered particularly objectionable, said Don, since it could be shown that it had not entered the Scandinavian languages until the late sixteenth or early seventeenth centuries.

Once the excitement aroused by the stone's discovery had died down, Ohman began using it as a nail-straightener. He was still straightening nails on it when a true believer, a Norwegian-American immigrant named Hjalmar Holand, turned up at his farm one day and bought it from him for ten dollars. Holand subsequently dedicated his life to trying to prove the stone was genuine. For him,

the linguistic anomalies that caused scholars to dismiss it were the best proof of its authenticity. He pointed to the mixed nature of the group as described on the stone: Goths – meaning Swedes – and Norwegians; and to the lack of any notion of an ideal standardization in the language at the time; and he argued that it was quite natural that travellers in a remote part of the world would develop individual peculiarities in the way they wrote the language that were different from the norms observed by scribes in the large population centres back home. Holand's passionate faith in the stone is the main reason debate about its authenticity continues to this day.

'But to answer your question, Max,' Don continued, 'Holand's theory was based on a mention in the records of an expedition under Pål Knutsson that set out in 1355 on the orders of King Magnus of Norway and Sweden to visit Greenland and report back on the state of the colonies there and investigate rumours that the colonists had abandoned the Christian faith. Finding the two colonies deserted the expedition continued its search for them across the water in North America, travelling as far inland as Minnesota where, in 1362, they met the fate described by one of the last surviving members of the party on the Kensington Runestone.'

'Do you believe that?' asked Max.

Don wrinkled his nose doubtfully. 'I'd like to,' he said. 'But there's no proof the expedition ever even sailed. Actually, I've always thought the whole thing is more interesting if you look at it as being about status among immigrant groups at the end of the nineteenth century. Rivalry between groups low down in the pile during those decades of mass immigration at the end of the nineteenth century was fierce. Especially between Italians and Scandinavians. Think what it would have meant to be able to say that sailors from your country were the first Europeans ever to land on the North American continent. I think it was about status. Probably didn't have much to do with competition for jobs because Italians immigrants tended to settle in the big cities like New York and Boston whereas Scandinavians headed for rural areas where they could recreate the sort of communities like the ones they'd left behind in Sweden, which they found mostly in the American Midwest – pretty much the way Karl Oskar and Kristina did in your film *The Emigrants*, Max.'

Von Sydow laughed and nodded, adding that the film's idyllic lakeside settlement at Ki Chi Saga, which appeared to show the Swedish settlers in their new life in America, was actually in Sweden.* Jan Troell had trawled the Midwest with his producer and failed to find anywhere suitable that wasn't already spoilt by modernization.

'You know something I wondered about in that film,' Don went on. 'I remember I was particularly interested in the character of the rebellious priest, Danjel Andreasson. You remember how in the film he keeps getting arrested and thrown into jail for holding holy communion at home in his kitchen, without the authority of the state church and its priests. "Satan's best recruiting agents" he calls them in that scene when the official Lutheran priest bursts into the kitchen with all the local bigwigs supporting him and finds Danjel Andreasson sitting there with his congregation. "Creatures of the Devil." Of course, it was very political, his congregation was that little group of misfits, reformed prostitutes and mentally ill people, the very poorest, whom the state Church in Sweden, being such an intrinsic part of the class system in Swedish society, ignored. But do you know if Vilhelm Moberg, when he wrote the novels, based that character on Erik Jansson?'

'Who was Erik Jansson?' said Ane, pre-empting my own query by a couple of seconds.

'He was a figure from the early days of Scandinavian emigration. When it was still a lot to do with religious persecution. He was a farmer who led a cult that rejected the state Church in Sweden and turned against Lutheranism. He had hundreds of followers, preached Old Testament sermons that could last more than five hours, told his congregation that faith leads to absolution from all sin, and the priests of the state Church were the Devil's helpers, just

---

* Jan Troell's Swedish film *Utvandrarna* (*The Emigrants*), in 1971, was followed by the sequel *Nybyggarna* (*The New Land*) in 1972, both starring Max von Sydow, and both based on the four-novel *Utvandrarna* sequence published by Vilhelm Moberg in 1949–59.

like the Andreasson character in *The Emigrants*. He told them the Bible was the only book. No Luther, he rejected Luther and arranged evenings of book-burnings of Luther's works accompanied by hymn singing and the chanting of prayers. He was arrested five times by the authorities in 1844, every time violently resisting arrest and his followers trying to protect him – his own wife was once knocked unconscious. He was arrested again in 1845, and while he was being transported to the prison in Gävle his followers ambushed the wagon and freed him. From then on he went underground, travelling around and preaching, sometimes disguised as a woman.

'Eventually he made his way across into Norway and sailed with about 1,500 followers to Victoria in Illinois, southwest of Chicago, and established a colony that he named Bishop's Hill. Bishop's Hill was the new Jerusalem, the new Zion. Jansson told them that when they read the Bible prophecies about the Chosen People, those prophecies were about themselves. He was an autocrat, a dictator. Whoever despises me despises God. Two hundred left the movement in 1848, another hundred and fifty died in a cholera epidemic the following year. One of his rules was that you weren't allowed to leave the sect. Anyone who did so was required to forfeit all their property and leave their family behind. He got shot in the end. A man named John Root who was married to Jansson's cousin shot him dead when Jansson tried to stop him taking his family with him when he left the sect.'

'Doesn't sound much like the priest in the film,' said Ane when he had finished.

'No, not the way it turned out. I was thinking more of how it began, rebelling against the state Church.'

'I don't know if Moberg was thinking of Jansson,' said von Sydow. 'I think one inspiration might have been Kierkegaard and the campaign he waged against the Church in Denmark during the last few months of his life. But I don't think religious persecution was a major factor in Swedish emigration, was it?'

Don offered to top up von Sydow's aquavit glass, but the actor declined with a slight wave of his large hand over the rim of the tiny glass. Without even the formality of quizzically raised eyebrows Don then filled Ane's glass, mine and his own.

'Up to about 1850 you could say it was, all over Scandinavia,' he continued. 'Besides the Janssonists, Gustaf Unonius travelled out and started a Free Church community in Wisconsin. And the first significant emigration from Norway was certainly inspired by the desire to escape religious persecution. A handful of Norwegian seamen who had been held in Chatham during the Napoleonic Wars came under the influence of some English Quakers – I think what attracted them most was the Quakers' pacifism, their opposition to all forms of war. When they got back to Norway after the war, they started a small Quaker group in Stavanger. Norway had just got its own constitution in 1814 in which paragraph two stated specifically that the evangelical-Lutheran religion was the official religion of the state, and that people were obliged to raise their children in the faith. Jesuits and Catholic Orders weren't allowed, nor practising Jews either. Compare that with the American constitution of 1789: Congress shall not pass any law regarding the establishment of religion, or hinder the free expression of such. So as soon as the Quakers started burying their dead in unconsecrated ground and carrying out marriage ceremonies that were not recognized under Norwegian law, there was trouble. That's why a group of them headed for America. Forty-five passengers and seven crew on the *Restoration*, a little sloop of thirty-nine tons. Forty-six by the time it arrived in New York on a Sunday morning in October 1825 after three months at sea: a pregnant woman gave birth on the way. The trip included a stopover at Funchal on Madeira. Not long before they reached the harbour they fished a barrel up out of the sea that turned out to contain unspoiled Madeira wine, and by the time the ship drifted into port the barrel was empty and the crew and most of the passengers so drunk they didn't raise a flag and had to be mistaken for a plague ship and had to be warned by a passing German ship that if they didn't hoist a flag up pretty quick the harbour guns would start firing on them.

'Their arrival caused a sensation in New York. The *New York Daily Advertiser* carried a big story about how this little boat no bigger than a fishing smack had crossed the Atlantic with fifty-three people on board, wedged inside its fifteen- by five-and-a-half-metre (49 x 18 feet) hull. The sensation nearly turned out to be the undoing of them. A Federal Act of 1819 set a limit of two passengers to every five tons of tonnage in transatlantic shipping, so the minimum legal tonnage for the *Restoration* should have been a hundred and fifteen tons. The sloop was impounded, and its skipper locked up for a while; but the case attracted so much sympathetic attention that all charges were dropped and the sloop returned to its owners, so that they were able to sell it, and, along with gifts of money and clothing from sympathetic New Yorkers, continue their voyage to the home their advance man Cleng Peerson had found for them on the shores of Lake Ontario.'

'That's quite a story,' said von Sydow. 'It would make a good film.'

'Or a musical,' said Don. 'Actually, someone in the canteen in Film-parken today told me that Björn and Benny from Abba are working on a musical based on *The Emigrants.** Those novels, that quartet, or is it a trilogy, I'm never sure, are set at about the time the character of the emigration changes, from about the middle of the century onwards. Leaving aside the religious persecution angle, your character in the film, Max – Karl Oskar – I would say he was typical of the first few decades of Swedish emigration, the grinding poverty of the cotter class in Sweden and Norway too. Not a lot different from slavery, the way those two boys in the first film, Arvid and – what was the name of your brother, Karl Oskar's brother?...'

'Robert,' Max supplied.

'The way they were treated is unbelievable. Mind you, Sweden was always a more class-ridden society than Norway. A lot of the emigration from Norway was by young men in their twenties and thirties, farmers' sons who found themselves trapped by the tradition of the *odelsrett* that gave the eldest son in the family first refusal to inherit the family farm. That left any younger brothers and sisters with the choice of either heading for Kristiania or Bergen or Stavanger to look for work, or taking the chance of a new life in America with

---

* They were. *Kristian från Duvemåla* by Björn Ulvaeus and Benny Andersson had its premiere in Malmö on 7 October 1995.

their share of the buyout. You had the pull of the Homestead Act of 1862 that saw young Swedes and Norwegians spread right across the rich farming land of the Midwest to Kansas, Minnesota, Nebraska, Iowa, Wisconsin. The big farmers and construction bosses would send their agents over to Sweden and Norway with instructions to assemble a cheap workforce of hard-working young men. It led to these densely populated settlements, of Swedes and Norwegians in Chicago and Minnesota, with their own churches, clubs, schools and newspapers. In the 1860s and up to the turn of the century people really could live inside those closed communities without knowing any English at all and acting just like they'd never left the old home.'

'Like some of the elderly Pakistanis in Oslo now,' said Ane. She turned to von Sydow. 'But something I wanted to ask you, Max: did you ever meet Moberg? He killed himself, didn't he? Even though he was quite old?'

In those days I still had what the Norwegian novelist Per Petterson once called an *evighetsperspektiv,* a certainty that I had forever in which to live. The idea that a person might grow tired of life was inconceivable to me, and the suicide of people who had already attained a respectable old age a source of wonder at what could possibly have persuaded them not to wait it out until the natural end; and so I was very curious to hear what lay behind Moberg's suicide. But von Sydow, after a brief statement to the effect that Moberg had suffered from a cancer, said that all he remembered of the writer's one visit to the set of *The Emigrants* was that he had kept the film crew awake most of the night by playing his mouth organ in the corridor of the hotel at which they were all staying.

'You know something that's always puzzled me? Why all the Scandinavians were lumped together and called "Swedes" over there,' Don said into the silence that followed this singular piece of information. 'In terms of sheer numbers there were more immigrants from Norway than Sweden throughout the period up to 1915. Excuse me a moment.'

He pushed back his chair and padded across the dim, candlelit room towards the wall of bookshelves in the brown Hopi moccasins he always wore indoors, long grey ponytail swaying in a small arc across his back. Reaching up unerringly for a volume he pulled it down, turned it in his hand and puffed away a small cloud of dust from the page tops then returned with it to the table, clearing a space in front of him by pushing aside the empty bacon-dice bowl.

'This is Theodore Blegen, *Norwegian Migration to America*,' he announced, slipping on a pair of half-glasses. Silence for a few moments as he thumbed the pages in search of what he was looking for and then cleared his throat. 'Between 1851 and 1855,' he announced, 'when the emigration per 1,000 inhabitants from Norway was 2.81, the figure for Sweden was 0.63; between 1866 and 1870 the figures were 8.64 against 3.87, and between 1881 and 1885 11.05 and 6.41. Between 1836 and 1915 800,000 Norwegians had emigrated to the United States, over four-fifths of the population in 1801. In European countries the proportion is exceeded only by Ireland. The corresponding figure for Sweden over the same period is 1.25 million. By 1870 the number of Scandinavians in the American population had risen to 241,669, with Norwegian born numbering 114,243, Swedes 97,328, and Danes 30,098.'

He looked up from the book and went on to say that the huge increases that characterized the second phase of Scandinavian emigration, from about the end of the American Civil War up to the 1920s, showed how closely these peaks corresponded to crop failures back home in Norway and Sweden. Other factors apparently included the phenomenon of chain emigration, in which entire communities dissolved, emigrated and reformed in the new country. Gold mining was another draw. Negative factors included a near-doubling of the Scandinavian population over the course of the nineteenth century as a result of peace, better nutrition and better health care.

'And,' Don continued, 'Blegen even says here that alcohol was an influence. A law of 1816 that legalized home-brewing on Norwegian farms had the surprising effect of turning the whole country into an enormous public house. Farmers put all their arable land to the cultivation of potatoes, there was widespread drunkenness and demoralization, smallholders ruined, homes broken up, families ruined.

Emigration to America was for some a last desperate attempt to escape from the demon drink. Seems a bit extreme, doesn't it?' he added, looking over the top of his spectacles at me.

'Not all of the emigrants made it to America,' he continued. 'Blegen has a story about a group of gold-miners who left Trondheim on 30 September bound for San Francisco by way of Rio de Janeiro and Cape Horn but got no further than Rio. The ship's captain had spent much of the journey out arguing with the passengers and once they put in at Rio he suddenly declared his ship – the *Sophie* – no longer seaworthy and upped and sold her, leaving his passengers stranded. Hearing about a German colony already established in the Santa Catharina province some of them threw in their lot with them and instead of digging for gold in San Francisco found themselves farming exotic products like coffee, cotton, rice, lemons and bananas in Brazil. Others waited for the arrival of the next ship and continued on their way to California; still others saw all this trouble as a bad sign, abandoned the whole idea and made their way back home to Norway. But it worked out for some of them. A few years later three members of the original party who had made it all the way to San Francisco arrived back in Levanger and walked down the gangplank with enormous gold rings on their fingers, flashing breastpins, glinting tiepins, watch chains and other suchlike bling.'

Von Sydow, as though he had thought of nothing else since Don raised the matter, now looked up and remarked that the probable reason Americans called all Scandinavians 'Swedes' was that Norway was still part of the Sweden-Norway double monarchy throughout the nineteenth century. 'Although that wouldn't apply to Danes, I suppose,' he added pensively. 'Come to think of it, did any Danes actually emigrate to America at all?'

'A lot fewer than from Norway and Sweden,' said Don, consulting the book again. 'Blegen says here maybe 350,000 in the entire period between 1820 and 1920. Way less than half the number from Norway and less than a third of those from Sweden. Some of them were adventurers who were in it for gold, though according to Blegen a lot of them preferred to try their luck in Australia. And a surprising number were converts to Brigham Young's Mormon religion – Ane's grandfather was one,' he said, gesturing across the table in the direction of his wife. Ane nodded in confirmation. For a moment it looked as though she was going to add some supplementary detail about her grandfather, perhaps confirm for us that her family was originally Danish, but she had just raised a forkful of mushy peas from her plate and chose them instead.

'In the end about 2,000 of them settled in the Mormon centres in Utah,' Don went on. 'But mostly they were farmers and farmworkers, responding to the impulse that attracted so many other Scandinavians – the Homestead Act of 1862 that offered free farms of anything up to 160 acres to anyone who could pay the registration and work the land for five years. As in Norway and Sweden, the 1880s saw a big exodus from Denmark, something like 84,000 made the crossing on the Danish Thingvalla line ships operating between Copenhagen and New York.'

Don looked up from the book, frowning slightly: 'One of them was a photographer named Jacob Riis. He wrote a book called *How the Other Half Lives.* Illustrated with his photographs. With his own money Riis opened a hostel for the homeless in New York in 1901. Teddy Roosevelt named him "New York's Most Useful Citizen". I thought of making a documentary about him for a while but I never got round to it.'

'You should still do it,' said Ane, moving her hand to cover his on the table. 'It's a great idea.'

Don shrugged uneasily. 'Yeah, it's a great idea,' he said. 'Having great ideas is easy. The hard part is doing it.'

A slightly embarrassed silence followed, broken at length by von Sydow's courteously enquiring whether Riis was the man who had actually first used that title. 'It's such a famous phrase now one might almost think it was a book title from the sociology of the 1950s. *The Lonely Crowd. Generation X. How the Other Half Lives...*'

Don said he wasn't sure but he seemed to remember from the days when he knew all about Jacob Riis that the title was a quote from somebody else, Rabelais maybe. But Riis was certainly the first to make something out of it like that.

'He sounds like an interesting man,' said von Sydow, and let it go at that.

'We still have some of my grandfather's letters home somewhere,' said Ane brightly. 'We used to have, it's a long time since I've seen them. They weren't published in the newspapers like a lot of the letters. The emigrants all telling the people back home how wonderful everything was in the Promised Land. Do you know where those letters are, Don?'

Don shook his head and said that maybe her sister in Copenhagen had them, didn't she once lend them to her sister because one of her kids was doing a school project on emigration? Because if she did maybe they should think about trying to get them back. Don was obviously still annoyed at having reminded himself of his failed idea for a documentary film about Riis, and thinking to move the conversation on I broke my resolution not to talk about Knut Hamsun. I pointed out that the newspaper articles and short stories Hamsun wrote based on his own experiences of immigrant life in North

America in the 1880s were a valuable corrective to the idealizations not just of over-enthusiastic young Norwegians but of much more respectable pillars of society like Bjørnstjerne Bjørnson. And the idea of America as a land of freedom and opportunity was one even Ibsen promoted in *The Pillars of Society*.

'Hamsun's experience of America was very different from that of a famous and celebrated writer like Bjørnson,' I went on. 'In every little prairie town he arrived at, Bjørnson was met by a marching band when he stepped down off a train. Hamsun's was the poor, ordinary man's experience of the immigrant's dream of America. He has a great short story about the time he worked as a tram conductor in Chicago, how he couldn't afford warm clothing during the cold Chicago winter and adopted the tramp's habit of wearing layers of newspaper next to his skin to keep out the cold. His friends used to poke him, he said, just to hear him rustle. And then in stories like 'Zachæus' and 'On the Prairie' he wrote about what it was like working on places like Oliver Dalrymple's giant wheat farm in the Red River valley, with over a thousand fieldhands, its own general store, its own smith and wainwright, its own team of painters and chippies. The fieldhands started work on a fifteen-hour day at three-thirty in the morning. Scandinavians and Irish most of them.

'No shade to be had out there in those vast open fields, the hot, hard earth scorching their feet. He writes about a mule that collapses with sunstroke and is left to die where it lies while another one is sent for. A few minutes later, this one collapses too. And only then does the foreman order all hands to stop work and rest in the shade under the wagons until the worst of the heat has passed. The wealthy wheat-kings like Dalrymple even had their own recruiters travelling round in Scandinavia because of the reputation the Swedes and Norwegians had as workers willing to endure this kind of gruelling regime without complaint. In one of his newspaper articles he urgently advised any young men thinking of emigrating to avoid such farms at any cost. You might have heard of the 'Eight Hour Movement', he tells them, the demand of factory workers in the east for an eight-hour working day. Well, he says, the 'Eight Hour Movement' hasn't reached the Midwest yet.

'But your film isn't about Hamsun's life, is it?' I couldn't help asking von Sydow. 'It's only about the war and his trial afterwards for siding with the Germans?'

He nodded, a curt downward dip of his chiselled head, and I realized I had guessed correctly, he did not want to get into any discussion of what for him was a role, a creation, *his* Hamsun, not my Hamsun, nor Thorkild Hansen's Hamsun, nor yet the Hamsun of all those young Norwegian writers who flared up at Hansen when his book appeared in 1976 and accused him of being a fascist himself for writing a nuanced and thoughtful book about Hamsun. Looking at him I noticed that he actually seemed to bear quite a marked facial resemblance to Hamsun, and I couldn't help but wonder if this wasn't a sort of temporary illusion imposed by his acting genius. The impression that he had for the time being almost *become* Hamsun was reinforced later when I saw the film, and never more sharply than during the scene of the infamous meeting with Adolf Hitler at the Berchtesgaden in 1943, where Hamsun is urging Hitler to withdraw his *Reichskommissar* in Norway, Josef Terboven, and replace him with a Norwegian. A little girl, Albert Speer's daughter, wanders into the room and Max von Sydow's Hamsun is totally distracted. He turns away from Hitler and gives the child his full attention. It's just one of many brilliant and illuminating touches von Sydow brought to that performance.

★

While Ane gathered up the plates and took them off to the kitchen, Don returned to the subject of emigration. 'You ever hear that song "Oleanna", about Ole Bull's Norwegian colony in America?' he asked. 'It's a bit like the "Big Rock Candy Mountain", that old Burl Ives song: "Oh the buzzing of the bees in the cigarette trees, / the Big Rock Ca-a-ndy mountain." "Oleanna" mocks the way people heading out for New Norway and its capital town of Oleanna had all sorts of wild and rosy expectations about the new life they were going to.'

And then, to all our surprise, I think, and perhaps as a way of cheering himself up, Don plucked the napkin off his lap, laid it on the table, pushed back his chair and taking a couple of steps off into the room launched into a rousing rendition of the song, slapping his knees and flapping his elbows like a drunken old goldminer in a Deadwood saloon:

Ole, oleanna, ole, oleanna
ole, ole, ole, ole, ole, oleanna

Oh to be in Oleanna,
that's where I'd like to be
Than to be in Norway
and bear the chains of slavery

Little roasted piglets
rush around the city streets
Inquiring oh so politely
if a slice of ham you'd like to eat

Beer as sweet as back home
springs from the ground and flows away
The cows all like to milk themselves
And the hens lay eggs ten times a day
The women there do all the work
As round the fields they quickly go
Each one has a hickory stick
And beats herself if she works too slow

In Oleanna land is free
The wheat and corn just plant themselves
Then grow a good four feet a day
While on your bed you rest yourself

'Ole Bull thought big,' said Ane, returning with a tray of cold stewed apple crumble and whipped cream desserts that the Norwegians mysteriously refer to as *tilslørte bondepiker*, 'veiled farm-girls'. 'That's what I like about him. Everything he did he thought big.'

'The greatest violinist in the world,' said Don as he returned to his seat at the table, still panting from his song and dance. 'Shame he died before the recording era; it would have been marvellous to hear him play. But what a dream that was. A New Norway. Hundreds of Norwegian immigrants settling in the wilds of northern Pennsylvania. Everything from scratch. Five full-size towns, with churches, court-houses, hotels, schools, streets, houses, newspapers. And within two years, the whole thing – *phutt*.' He flipped his hands in an upward and outward arc to illustrate an explosion, knocking the spoon out of Ane's trifle dish, bending to pick it up from the rug without missing a beat, wiping the business end on his napkin before almost offering it to her but then changing his mind and offering her his own spoon instead.

'What happened in Oleanna?' asked Max.

'What didn't happen? There was a huge amount of clearing to do, and once they cleared it the land turned out to be not nearly as good as they thought it was when he bought it. The closest railway station was twenty-eight miles (45 km) away at Coudersport. And it turned out anyway that the agents Bull bought it off were conmen who didn't have the right to sell it to him in the first place. Bull had promised every settler-builder work and a daily wage, and for a monthly fee he would provide all the necessities of life – housing and food and suchlike. Very soon he realized he'd bitten off more than he could chew and he was having to haul back on some of his promises. He stopped visiting the colony, partly because the huge financial outlay meant he had to go on long concert tours just to cover his outgoings on it. He meant well, but the colonists began to hate the place and as soon as they were paid the money Bull owed them, they left.

'He never stopped thinking big, he didn't know any other way to think. He writes to tell his brother he's simultaneously laying out these five towns, he's got people in Philadelphia to subscribe two million dollars to the Sunbury and Erie Road which will run close by the southern limit of the colony, and he's struck another deal with New York for a branch of the Erie and New York Railroad to run from Elmira to Oleanna so that the town would be only twelve hours' travel from New York, ten from Philadelphia and so on and so on, with the building of these roads and railroads supposed to provide years of employment for thousands of Norwegian colonists. But when the scandal of the irregularities around the sale broke he deeded the land back to one of men who sold it to him and got out of it with losses estimated at around 70,000 dollars.'

'When was this, Don?' I asked.

'Winter of 1853, I think. It was all over in less than a year.'

'That would be around the same time as Bull started the National Theatre in Bergen,' I continued. 'Ole Bull was the guy who gave Ibsen his start. He made him head of the new theatre. It was all part of the drive towards Norwegian independence. The idea was they would only put on plays in Norwegian, not Dano-Norwegian they way they did in the capital. It was a fashion thing. The smart people thought Norwegian was the peasant's language. Not dignified enough for the state. Ibsen had done nothing up to that point. He was only twenty-five. *Catiline*, that's all he had written. He had the same experience in Bergen as the colonists in Pennsylvania: *where is the guy? where is Bull?* He gets people all fired up with his big ideas and then off he goes and leaves it up to them to realize them. You remember Gyntiania in *Peer Gynt*? That's taken straight from Ole Bull's adventures in North America with Oleanna. There's a lot of Ole Bull in Peer Gynt, though Bull was this fabulous violin virtuoso whereas Peer wasn't anything in particular at all. Bull was also a brilliant talent-spotter – besides Henrik Ibsen he discovered

Edvard Grieg. Bull heard him play when Grieg was just fifteen years old and persuaded his parents to send him to the conservatory at Leipzig.'

Max had retired to his inner world again. Shortly after we left the table and had seated ourselves around the glass-topped coffee table for coffee and a cognac he stood up and said he would have to leave us, he had an early start in the morning. Ane accompanied him to the front door, switching on the outside lights to help him find his way across to the annex in the dark. Don and I sat in silence for a while, enjoying the Bache-Gabrielsen cognac Don had brought to the table. Then Don stood up and padding across the room to the bookshelves again ran his eyes across his large collection of CDs, wall-to-wall and three shelves deep. As earlier with the Blegen book, he seemed to know exactly where everything was in his collection and had soon extracted a disc which he put into his CD player. Lately he had rediscovered Sixties free jazz, an enthusiasm of his youth and one that I shared with him, and I was expecting and even hoping it might be something by his current favourite Ornette Coleman, maybe the great live album *At the 'Golden Circle' Stockholm* – Ornette is another of those American musical geniuses, like George Russell, who had to come to Sweden to be understood – but the music that came flowing out into the room was very different from Ornette's urgent and thrilling bark. Instead it was warm, big-band jazz, comfortable music, redolent of a vanished age of easy self-confidence. The melody seemed familiar but I couldn't place it and while Don left the room to say his goodnights to Max I was left to puzzle over its teasing familiarity, resisting the temptation to sneak a look at the jewel case. By the time he stepped back into the room a minute or two later I thought I had it.

'This is Grieg, isn't it?'

'Yes,' he said, handing me the jewel case. 'It's Duke Ellington's arrangement of music from the *Peer Gynt Suites*. When we were talking Ole Bull and Grieg earlier I remembered this and I wondered if you knew it?'

I said I'd never heard it before, never even knew of its existence.

'Not one of his better-known pieces,' Don said. 'I guess Duke was looking for some kind of respectability, doing the classics, don't you know. As though his own music wasn't classy enough. Didn't work here, mind you; when the record was issued here back in the Sixties, Norwegian State Broadcasting banned it. Or at least, we like to say *banned*, it makes us feel heroic, as if we've triumphed over the ignorant past. They probably just didn't like it. Grieg and *Peer Gynt*, that's *nasjonal helligdom*, you know,' he said, reverting to Norwegian, which he spoke as fluently as English. 'Mustn't mess with Grieg. Those were the days, eh? When there was a *they* who knew what they were doing.'

'*Skål!*' Don lifted his glass in an ironic cheer and I raised mine too.

Obscurely embarrassed that as one of Ibsen's biographers I had failed to have picked up this nugget of information during the years spent trawling for information about him, as casually as I could I presently challenged Don to tell me if he was familiar with Harald Sæverud's music for Ibsen's play, composed after the war in 1947 for an anti-national romantic production of *Peer Gynt* performed in *nynorsk*, Norway's other official language, at Det Norske Teatret in Oslo? There was artistic courage if you like, I added in a friendly way: the leading young Norwegian composer of his generation takes on the nation's greatest composer in his greatest musical offering. Don asked me if Sæverud's music was any good, at which I affected a liking for it beyond anything I actually felt, but which later had the effect of sending me back to the recording to listen again, an experience that resulted this time in my admiration for the composition rising to the level of that earlier and pretended enthusiasm.

*

Much later, on the crowded last metro train back to Majorstua, and wedged into a six-seat section alongside five Estonians talking a language of which I understood not a word, I began thinking again about immigration and the rootlessness that comes when it doesn't work out. I was lucky. Even though I was an immigrant, I never thought of myself that way. I had chosen to come to Norway out of a deep attraction to what I knew of the culture. For me, it was and remains a peculiar sort of honour simply to be allowed to live here. I wasn't in flight from poverty or hunger or from anything more dangerous than the sheer size and noisiness of England. I thought about the story Don told me, after Max had left us and Ane had said goodnight and gone to bed – sitting in rattan armchairs as we slowly made our way down the slim bottle of Bache-Gabrielsen, with the Duke's sublime *Peer Gynt Suite* murmuring away in the background – a last chapter in the saga of the Kensington Runestone, and the life of an obscure Swedish whisky pastor named Sven Fogelblad who was long suspected of being the man behind the forgery.

Born sometime in the 1820s, Fogelblad had studied theology and classics at Uppsala. After graduating, he worked for a while as a minister in a Västergötland parish, until his drinking got out of control and he resigned his pastorate and emigrated to America, arriving in the Kensington area sometime around 1885. Links with the Lutheran mother church in the old country were not good, there was a shortage of priests, and Fogelblad was almost persuaded to resume his pastoral duties. But his drinking once again got the better of him so nothing came of the plan, and his life after that was uncertain, fragmentary and rootless.

He used his learning to take on work as an itinerant schoolmaster, staying for a few weeks at time at different farmhouses and getting paid fifty cents a month, along with his board and lodging, for each child he taught. When the seasonal demands of farm work took precedence over education and the children were called to help out in the fields, he was still allowed to quarter himself upon farmers; but he was never known to help out at harvest time, never carried a pail of water for anyone nor an armful of logs. Yet, farmers were always glad to see him because whenever he turned up he brought news of the latest births and deaths in the area along with all the latest gossip. Although he always seemed contented, people detected in him an undercurrent of melancholy, and those who knew him best said he was never happy after leaving Sweden. He spent a lot of time reminiscing about his student days, and his eyes would well up with tears when he recalled the exalted pleasures of singing Swedish folk songs along with three or four hundred other students at Uppsala. In 1895, after a year spent with a nephew in Scott County, he returned to Kensington to see some old friends. Close to the house of one of them, a priest named Andrew Anderson, he collapsed. Three days later, he died of an undiagnosed cause.

Aware of the rumours that linked Fogelblad to the markings on the Kensington Runestone, Hjalmar Holand, once he'd bought the stone from Olof Ohman, set out to discover whether or not the suspicions were justified. He conducted interviews with people who had known Fogelblad in Grant and Douglas counties, asking them all the same questions. Did you ever see or hear of his making runes on window casings, doors, or anywhere else? Did he ever speak to you of the Scandinavian discovery of America? In your opinion, could he have had anything to do with the Kensington inscription? To all of these questions, Holand reports, he received an invariable and unequivocal 'no'. Though many of these people doubted the stone's authenticity, all of them were convinced of Fogelblad's innocence. He was, they said, too honest and conscientious to have perpetrated such a fraud; he had no aptitude for practical jokes; he was too lazy to have carried out such a plan, and too garrulous to have concealed it had he done so. And learned man that he was, he was entirely ignorant of the fine runological and linguistic points involved in the inscription. Holand traced the suspicions back to the fact that at the house where Fogelblad died, a copy of an old Swedish grammar was found among his possessions, and it included two lines of runes in a chapter illustrating the evolution of written Swedish. But these two rows showed only the standard sixteen-character *futhark*, with no sign of the peculiarities and anomalies that characterized the message carved on the stone.

Don, whose taste for an unsolved mystery was another of the things I liked about him, had kept an eye on the story as arguments concerning its authenticity flitted in and out of the news over the years. He told me that, partly as a result of the enduring controversy surrounding it, the stone had recently been shipped to Sweden for an exhibition at the Historical Museum in Stockholm. The original plan was to return it to Minnesota after the exhibition, but there was particular interest in it from Hälsingland, the province in eastern Sweden from which Ohman had emigrated more than a century earlier, and the county museum in Hudiksvall was given permission to exhibit it for a few weeks before it went back to the United States.

In among all the attendant media coverage, a retired professor of linguistics named Tryggve Sköld happened to hear a radio broadcast about the exhibition. At the Centre for Dialect and Place Name Studies in Umeå he had been studying a collection of papers after Edward Larsson, a tailor and musician born in the province of Dalarna. On two documents in the Larsson Collection, one dated 1883 and the other 1885, he had come across rows of a curious crypt-runic writing which he had never seen anywhere else before. His curiosity was aroused. Checking the characters used on the stone against these cryptic runes, Sköld realized they were almost identical. Sköld surmised that the carver of the Kensington stone was himself a tailor, familiar with the same type of runes as Larsson, who had used an esoteric guild language employed by itinerant Swedish tailors to carry out an intricate and extremely successful practical joke.

But, as Don said, the durability of the controversy has given the stone a status quite independent of whether it is fake or not, and the identity of Alexandria, the town closest to where Ohman found it, has long accepted the stone as tangible proof that, in the fourteenth century, an intrepid band of Scandinavian explorers met their deaths nearby at the hands of Native Americans.

As though to cover every possible aspect of an ancient Scandinavian identity Alexandria also boasts an enormous statue of a Viking close to the town's dedicated Runestone Museum on North Broadway. Known locally as Big Ole, this colourful figure stands 28 feet tall and weighs just under 6 tons. The legend on his shield reads 'Alexandria Birthplace of America'. Upon his head he wears a magnificent winged helmet, a thing that Vikings only ever wore in the dreams of the set designers of the first productions of Wagner's *Ring* cycle at Bayreuth.

Of the rest of that remote and long ago evening in Haslum, I recall only that I had intended to ask Don whether he had ever understood why David Mamet named his play *Oleanna*, because as long and as hard as I had thought about it the connection escaped me; and that I forgot to ask. And the relief I felt, as the metro shuddered its way down the tracks from Haslum towards central Oslo, that I had managed to avoid gushing to von Sydow about how brilliant he was in those *Utvandrarna* films, how brilliant all the performances were: the Norwegian Liv Ullmann as his wife Katarina, playing as so often in her early career a Swede; Eddie Axberg as his brother Robert, whose portrayal of a man masking the pain of a constant ear-ache haunted me for many nights after watching the films; Pierre Lindstedt as Robert's friend Arvid, the simple and trusting young giant who would follow Robert to the ends of the earth, and does so, heading west for California with him in search of gold but dying along the way after drinking poisoned water; the singer Monica Zetterlund in her first acting role as the reformed whore Ulrika, who ends up marrying a Baptist pastor – had I started I would have gone on praising the films all night, for their six hours of sustained intensity, their poetry, their truth, their salutary reminder of what being an immigrant really means, the gamble taken, the suffering, the pain of loss, the disappearing roots immigrants cling to even as they gamely try to adopt the language and culture of the new land to which they have come, and in which they have placed their hopes of a better future.

It was long past midnight when I got off the train at Majorstua. Frost had settled so densely on the roofs of the carriage sheds it looked like snow in the white electric light of the station compound. Walking home beneath the bare chestnut trees along the narrow lane that divides the police training college and a health clinic I found myself wondering what I would say when my wife asked me about the evening and what Max von Sydow was like, thinking there was really nothing I could say apart from the fact that he seemed like an abstemious and a decent and hard-working man. What a crowd that was, I thought; all those actors and technicians associated with Ingmar Bergman who went on to acquire international reputations. Besides Max von Sydow there was Liv Ullmann, Erling Josephson, Bibi Andersson, Sven Nykvist.

But not Per Oscarsson, I recalled. Great actor that he was, Oscarsson was never part of the Bergman elite and his name never travelled much outside Scandinavia. I met him once, at a gathering of the Hamsun Society up in Hamarøy, in the far north of Norway. A distinguished-looking man with shoulder-length, prematurely white hair, he had been invited as a guest of honour for a showing of *Hunger* during the week-long literary festival. I knew he had made a great many films but that *Hunger* was always regarded as his finest hour. This was back in the late 1980s, in the days before Sky became a news channel and while it was still feebly attempting to be a British copy of MTV. Every Saturday night at midnight I was in the habit of watching a film slot on Sky presented by a Boris Karloff lookalike who called himself 'Deadly Ernest' and wore a long black cape to lisp an introduction to the evening's low-budget horror film. Among a host of mostly forgettable offerings, one that stood out was *Victor Frankenstein*, in which Per Oscarsson played the part of the monster so movingly that almost the first thing I did when we met in Hamarøy was to congratulate him on his performance in that film.* I shall never forget the look of profound injury that flitted across his face. I realized at once that he thought I was being sarcastic and I had to struggle for the next fifteen minutes to persuade him I most definitely was not.

The encounter was unnerving for another reason: *Hunger* must be one of the most black-and-white films ever made, and all the while I was speaking to him I couldn't get used to the missing chiaroscuro, so much so that at times I wondered whether I were not in fact dreaming the whole thing. A lifetime ago, long before I ever became an emigrant myself, I had a similarly disorientating experience. It was one night in London, back in 1968 or '69, about a week or so after I had arrived in the city for the first time. In the cathedral glow of an old public house off Shaftesbury Avenue I happened to look up from my pint of Worthington E and saw a famous English actor of the time, Leslie Phillips, relaxing at the bar with a tall drink in his hand. It took me an absurdly long moment to overcome my surprise at seeing him in colour, and not in black and white, the way I was used to seeing him on our Sobell TV set back in our old home on Windsor Road in Lytham St Annes.

---

* You can see the film online at http://www.dailymotion.com/video/x15nonw_terror-of-frankenstein-1977_shortfilms.

11
World War II:
The Scandinavian Experience

AT 4.30 ON THE MORNING OF 9 APRIL 1940, A FOURTEEN-
year-old boy named Odd Hansen was woken at his home in Gylte,
Halangspollen, two kilometres north of Drøbak, by an unearthly
roaring. The sound seemed to come from the direction of the Oslo
fjord. He sat up in bed. His younger sister Rigmor was still asleep
beside him. In the dimness on the far side of the room he saw that his
mother's bed was empty. Odd slid out of bed and was about to put on
his socks when the house was shaken by a huge crash that seemed to
come from the kitchen, on the other side of the bedroom wall. Rigmor
opened her eyes and screamed. Odd ran to the door and opened it.
A stinking ball of gas rolled towards him. The kitchen window had
been blown out. He ran barefoot across the shards of broken glass to
where his mother's body lay, almost cut in two at the waist by shrapnel.

Their father was away working nights at a tanker facility on the
fjord, halfway between Drøbak and Oslo. Though he knew at once
she was dead Odd still tried to lift his mother. Moments later, wearing
just their nightclothes, the children were running through the night,
heading for a house further up the road where an uncle lived. It was
cold. Late snow lay thick and wet on the ground. Their uncle listened
in silence to what the children told him. He then sent them back to

the house with instructions to put on their warmest clothes and then make their way down to the boats as quickly as possible. Within a matter of minutes, the inhabitants of that tiny settlement were seated in four small boats and rowing northwards up the Oslo fjord.

*

For a period of about two years, from 1987 to 1989, my wife and I lived in Maurbakken, a white wooden mansion on the sloping banks of the Oslo fjord at Drøbak that had been built to his own design in 1904 by Knut Hamsun. It was a rich man's house, but the royalties that paid for it came not from Norway, where Hamsun was still regarded as an obscure and modern writer, but from the sales of his books in Germany, where *Hunger*, *Mysteries* and *Pan* had quickly been recognized as the work of a great writer.

Hamsun's people were poor, his formal education no more than 252 days at the local travelling school. Certain of his own talent, at the age of nineteen he composed a self-consciously florid letter to Erasmus Zahl, the local squire, or *matador*, as such men were called in Nordland, in which he asked Zahl to back him in his dream of becoming a writer. Zahl summoned him to Kjerringøy for a personal interview and was sufficiently impressed with the youth's strangely intense self-belief to give him enough money to live on for several months while he wrote his novel, and to travel to Copenhagen to get it published, where it would, according to the plan, make his name and earn him enough money to pay Zahl back.

The dream failed. Among many other things, *Hunger*, written ten years later, is Hamsun's bleakly ironic account of what that failure felt like. But his dream of the style in which a rich man lives survived the rude disappointments recorded in *Hunger*, and this Drøbak mansion, with its chandeliers and its six pillars set into the walls of the main living room was a recreation of what he had seen during that brief visit to Zahl's house up in remote Kjerringøy a quarter of a century earlier.

As things turned out, the house marked the end and not the

beginning of his dream. In 1898 he had married Bergljot Bech, a wealthy upper-class divorcée, and in 1902 the couple had a daughter, Victoria. But already Hamsun had fallen out of love with Bergljot, and these three lived as a family in Maurbakken for no more than a few months before Hamsun left and moved into an apartment in Kristiania, as Oslo was still called at the time. His pencil drawings for the layout of the house, and notes on the intended uses for each room, survive in the Manuscript Collection of the National Library in Oslo. From these, which I photocopied, I saw that during the years in which my wife and I lived in Maurbakken, we slept in the same bedroom as the one in which Hamsun had slept. A connecting door – gone since his time – gave access to an adjoining bedroom which was marked 'Bergljot'. And yet I never dreamt of him, nor even met his ghost, which is a shame, because I would have liked to have talked to him.

During our time in Drøbak, in the late 1980s, a peaceful little car ferry traversed the fjord to Hurumlandet at half-hourly intervals, until it was replaced, some years ago, by a dull tunnel. Seen through the window of our front room, the sight of this little black-and-white ferry slanting across the water filled me with an inexplicable pleasure. Often, if I could think of nothing better to do, or was satisfied that I had done enough work for the day, or had given up all hope of doing any work, I would walk down narrow, twisting Vestbyveien to the ferry terminal at the foot of the hill and take the ten-minute ride across the water to Hurumlandet. There was nothing to do on the other side, only drink a cup of coffee and eat a waffle with a slice of brown goat's cheese in the almost invariably deserted terminal café. Often, seated by the window and looking back across the water at Drøbak from this unusual and distant angle, I would drift into a reverie, wondering who to thank for my fate so far, for my wife, my house, my home, for the simple fact of being alive in Norway, until it was time to go back.

Sometimes on those crossings, if the waters of the Oslo fjord were calm and the sunlight striking at the right angle, the ferry would pass through a region of oil patches in fantastic and ragged forms, like outlined countries on the map of a water world. Along with a few straggling lines of air bubbles, these patches of oil are all the visible remains of the *Blücher*, a German cruiser that was sunk by gunfire from the island fortress of Oscarsborg in the early hours of the morning of 9 April 1940 as it made its way up the fjord towards Oslo. On board were some 2,400 men, sailors and troops charged with the military subjugation of the capital as the first stage in the German occupation of Norway. Besides the *Blücher*, 'Angriffsgruppe 5' consisted of a second heavy cruiser (the *Lützow*), a light cruiser (the *Emden*), three torpedo boats (the *Möwe*, the *Albatross* and the *Kondor*), eight minesweepers and two supply ships for the minesweepers. Finished and launched in 1939, the *Blücher* displaced 12,200 tonnes, was 193 metres (633 feet) long and equipped with 40 cannons and 12 torpedo ramps. She was one of the most modern warships in the world, with her own calculating machine for its artillery and torpedo handlers, a forerunner of the modern computer.

The blacked-out flotilla, sailing without flags, had been observed entering the Oslo fjord through a misty drizzle at 23:15 the evening before by the captain of a coastal patrol boat, who radioed the information ahead to his colleagues further up the fjord. By the time the ships reached the narrow sound at Drøbak, the three cannons on the Oscarsborg fortress were all manned, as were the artillery and torpedo batteries on the eastern arm of the fjord, just past the town. At this point most of the Norwegians were convinced that these were ships that had been damaged in a sea battle and were simply taking refuge in the Oslo fjord. But as the flotilla penetrated ever further in the direction of Oslo this conviction wavered. The commander of the torpedo batteries at the northerly end of the island had been ordered to load his torpedo ramps with the detonators in place. He recalled having to pinch himself in the arm to make sure he wasn't dreaming, then called the fortress commander, Birger Eriksen, to ask whether he should actually use the torpedoes once the ships were in sight. 'Yes,' Eriksen told him, 'once they pass the fortress security line, you fire.' At this point, as Eriksen noted later, none of them knew the identity of the intruders.

And when the *Blücher* did cross the line, the first shell fired from one of the three Oscarsborg cannons struck the command tower on the port side, toppling the state-of-the-art gun-control tower into the water and leaving the *Blücher* incapable of returning directed fire. The ship's tower was hit by a second shell that took out its electrical system and destroyed the hangar and planes. Out of control, the blazing vessel drifted by the islands, guns blazing in all directions, lighting up the early morning mist with what one Norwegian gunner later likened to a horizontal snowstorm of glowing projectiles. By the light of this eerie blizzard, those on the island and those watching from the windows of their houses in Drøbak could see men on deck, and hear the terrible cries of the wounded and dying, surreally counterpointed by voices singing 'Deutschland über alles'. Two torpedoes completed the damage, and two hours and one minute after the first shell was fired the *Blücher*'s propellers and stern reared sharply into the air, were held suspended for a few seconds, then slipped down beneath the water. Almost to the last, a solitary man could be seen by those watching from the town, standing with his arm outstretched in a Nazi salute as the great ship slid away.

Something like a thousand German invaders were killed by gunfire, burned to death or drowned on that first day of the war in Norway. Three Norwegians lost their lives. In addition to Marie Hansen from Gylte, a sixteen-year-old maid working at Reenskaug's Hotel at the foot of Vestbyveien was hit as she ran up into the trees behind the hotel, and a man died in a fall from some steps in Akershusveien. A gunner in Oscarsborg sustained minor injuries.

The action had enduring consequences for Norwegian self-regard, but heroic as it was, it also had crucial consequences for the progress of the war in Norway and the nature of the German occupation. The thirty-hour delay in reaching Oslo enabled the Norwegian royal family and the government, under Prime Minister Johan Nygaardsvold, to leave the capital and start a hide-and-seek journey northwards, keeping always just a step ahead of the advancing German forces, stopping first at Hamar and then at Elverum, some 60 miles (96 km) north-east of Oslo. A motorcade carrying the nation's gold reserves also left the capital that morning on the first leg of a long and hazardous journey that ended with the reserves being shipped intact to safety in the United States.

Like Denmark and Sweden, Norway had declared itself neutral on the outbreak of war in 1939, and although the government issued the order for a general mobilization there was little that could be done at such short notice to stem the German advance. Resistance was more sustained and effective in the north of the country, where a partial mobilization had been in force since early 1940 as a consequence of the outbreak of the Finnish–Russian War, and where, with the help of hastily assembled, but inadequate, British naval forces and French and Polish soldiers, the German advance was at least hindered at Narvik. Early in June, however, these forces had to be recalled to fight in France, and on 7 June the royal family and government gave up the unequal fight and sailed for England. By a resolution passed on 9 April 1940, they would remain, for the duration of the war, the legally constituted government of Norway.

★

In the racial theories that underpinned the Nazi ideology formulated by geneticists like Alfred Rosenberg, Scandinavians were categorized as *Homo Europaeus,* popularly called 'Aryans'. Within this highest racial category, the Danes, Swedes and Norwegians were regarded as the *übergermanere*, the purest of the Aryan peoples, with the inhabitants of remote and inaccessible Norway the purest of them all. But from the moment of the sinking of the *Blücher* and the escape of the king and cabinet onwards, there was never any question of a 'model occupation' of Norway. Possession of Norway was crucial to the German war effort. German munitions factories were reliant on the supply of iron ore from Kiruna and Malmberget in Sweden, and they needed to able to protect the ore as it was shipped down the west coast of Norway from the port of Narvik on its way to Germany. Narvik was an isolated northern town with no rail links to the rest of Norway; but it possessed a line that ran cross-country eastwards into Sweden, an arrangement that made it relatively easy to secure the transport of the ore on its way to Narvik. Control of the Norwegian coastline also gave the German armed forces a base for the submarine fleets operating in the North Atlantic and airbases that would be involved in the Battle of Britain, while the occupation of Norway and Denmark jointly gave them control over access to the Baltic, isolating Sweden and, for the first three years of the war at least, enabling Germany consistently to spin Swedish neutrality in their favour.

On the afternoon of the first day of the occupation, Vidkun Quisling, leader of Nasjonal Samling (NS: National Unity), the Norwegian Nazi Party he had started in 1933, went into the studios of Norwegian State Broadcasting at Marienlyst in Oslo and announced the formation of a new government, with himself as its head. It was Quisling's infamous response to the German invasion that led to his name being, for several decades, a synonym for 'traitor'. The bleak neologism appeared for the first time in an editorial in *The Times* on the morning of 19 April 1940: 'We should all be profoundly grateful to Major Quisling,' it began. 'He has added a new word to the English language.' The writer went on to give his reasoning in detail:

To journalists and other writers, weary of racking their brains or raking the well-thumbed pages of Roget in search of alternatives, the word Quisling is a gift from the gods. If they had been ordered to invent a new word for 'traitor' and given carte blanche with the alphabet, they would hardly have hit upon a more brilliant combination of letters. Aurally, it contrives to suggest something at once slippery and tortuous. Visually, it has the supreme merit of beginning with a 'Q', which (with one august exception) had long seemed to the British mind to be a crooked, uncertain and slightly disreputable letter, suggestive of the questionable, the querulous, the quavering, of quaking quagmires and quivering quicksands, of quibbles and quarrels, of queasiness, quackery, qualms and Quilp. Quisling, then, so be it. We welcome the word as sincerely as we detest the qualities which it connotes.

The day after the invasion, Quisling rescinded the order for a general mobilization issued by the Nygaardsvold government. Five days later, the Germans established an administrative council to run the country's affairs and Quisling resigned. In the autumn of 1940, Josef Terboven, the Nazi *Reichskommissar* for Norway, dissolved the council and appointed individual ministers to run the country's internal affairs. All political activity and all parties except Quisling's Nasjonal Samling were banned.

With the keen participation of Quisling, the Nazis then set about establishing a new order for Norway. When NS interfered with the activities of the courts by trying to control the makeup of the benches, members of the Norwegian Supreme Court resigned *en masse* in December 1940, to be replaced by other judges willing to dispense the laws introduced by the new regime. All wireless sets were confiscated in August 1941. Strikes were outlawed, incurring severe penalties: on 8 September 1941, deliveries of milk to a number of work-places in Oslo were not made, and the following day some 25,000 workers in the Oslo region went on strike; two of the union leaders held responsible for the strike, Viggo Hansteen and Rolf Wickström, were arrested, tried and executed before the

sun went down on 10 September. Appointees from NS were put in charge of both the Union of Employers, and the Landsorganisasjonen, the Norwegian Trades Union Congress.

Early in 1942 Vidkun Quisling returned to power as Norway's Minister-President, answerable to Terboven, who despised him. He established a Teachers Union which would work to bring about the new order. Membership was compulsory. A local version of the Hitler Youth was established and Norwegian schoolchildren obliged to enrol. The teachers protested, and in March 1300 were arrested and over 600 deported to Kirkenes, on the Russian border in the far north. In the same spirit of protest Norwegian priests resigned from their posts and were likewise deported from the capital. After a campaign of sabotage and acts of direct military confrontation carried out by resistance fighters from Company Linge, a unit named after its early leader Martin Linge, which had been specially trained in Britain, Terboven declared a state of emergency in Trondheim in October. Ten leading citizens – who had nothing to do with the resistance – were executed as a warning, and death sentences on twenty-four partisans carried out. During the months of October and November members of Norway's pitifully small community of Jews were arrested and deported. One ship – the *Donau* – and one trip were all that was required. Five hundred and forty Jews were taken to Stettin, thence by train to Auschwitz. Only nine of them survived the war. Following a series of student arrests at the University of Oslo in 1943 protestors started a fire in the Aula. The Germans closed the university and arrested twelve hundred students and thirty teachers. Some three hundred of the most active were deported on the *Donau* to the camp at Sennheim for instruction in civic responsibilities from SS officers. Another large group were sent to Buchenwald where they received a similar education.

With signs of a German defeat becoming ever clearer from the middle of 1943 onwards, the brutality of the German occupiers and their Norwegian puppets increased. When Karl Marthinsen, the Norwegian head of state security and a prime mover behind the deportation of Norway's Jews, was assassinated in his car on 8 February 1945 in an Oslo suburb by members of Milorg, the resistance movement, twenty-nine Norwegians were shot in revenge.

The Norwegians had a hard war. Oslo was the last occupied capital in Europe to be liberated. On 8 May the Germans formally surrendered and Milorg assumed temporary control of the country until members of the government in exile returned on 13 May. King Håkon himself delayed his return until 7 June, choosing the date on which Norway had declared itself independent of Sweden forty years earlier.

*

In Denmark the constitutional position and nature of the subsequent occupation was different. Alone among the Scandinavian countries, Denmark had signed a non-aggression pact with Germany, in May 1939, and on the basis of that had reduced the size of the Danish Army from 36,000 to 14,000 by the time of the invasion. Sharing a border with Germany on the Jutland peninsula, the Danes did not enjoy the same geographical advantages in self-defence as did Norway, and in order to avoid senseless loss of life the Danish government surrendered after a few hours of scant resistance, in which just sixteen Danes were killed.

In a vividly prophetic display of Newspeak the Germans then announced they would be respecting Danish neutrality, observing a policy of non-interference in Denmark's internal affairs and allowing the king to remain in office. After a period of initial manoeuvrings and resignations a coalition of the four main Danish political parties took office in July 1940 and continued to run the country's domestic affairs for the next three and a half years. The Danes' reward for their peaceful acceptance of the occupation was to be allowed to continue as a constitutional democracy, albeit with a number of crucial restrictions. Some, such as the closing of the embassies of the Allied powers in Copenhagen and an embargo on trade relations with Britain and its Allies, created difficulties that became ever more burdensome as the war progressed. Other moves, like the outlawing of the Danish Communist Party in November 1941 which legitimized a mass arrest of party members, chimed with Danish national sentiment and were accepted without much protest.

In other crucial areas, however, Danish sympathies remained resolutely unsynchronized with the ideals of German Nazism. Of the 200 Danish ships at sea when the invasion took place, over three-quarters defied instructions from home to sail to ports outside the zone of conflict and instead headed for ports under Allied control. The overwhelming majority of Danish seamen put their services at the disposal of countries with which Germany was at war.

The government rejected all attempts by the Germans to secure representation in the Cabinet for Nazis, as it did any attempt to introduce the kind of anti-Semitic measures that were a central part of Nazi ideology. Sephardic Jews had been living in parts of Holstein since 1622 and, despite intermittent discrimination, they had been increasingly accepted as part of the native population, with all remaining discriminations removed by the constitution of 1849. Abraham Pais the biographer of Niels Bohr, describes an episode in the autumn of 1942 that shows just how foreign the notion of Jews as aliens was to the average Dane. Reacting to rumours that Bohr was among the favourites to be the new Rector of the University of Copenhagen, a Nazi-run Danish newspaper ran an article opposing his appointment, complaining that Bohr was a Jew, that the age of the Jew was over, and asking was it not possible to find a *Dane* to occupy the post? But, 'If Bohr is not Danish then who is?' asked another newspaper, ridiculing the presumption behind the italicization. As Pais points out, such a reaction would have been unthinkable in any other Nazi-occupied country.

German indulgence of Denmark's democratic traditions allowed a remarkably free General Election to take place in March 1943. All save communist parties were allowed to participate; but unease at the general level of accommodation offered to the occupiers was growing and it reached a turning-point in the autumn of that year. German military setbacks had started to cast doubt on the once widely held assumption that German victory in the war was inevitable, and as this doubt increased so did Danish resistance to the occupiers. Acts of sabotage proliferated, from ten in 1940 to more than a hundred in 1942, and to over a thousand in 1943. The occupiers demanded a ban on strikes and the execution of convicted saboteurs. When parliament declined, the Germans imposed a state of martial law on 29 August 1943, occupied military installations and interned Danish officers. The Danish government resigned, and the Germans, under Werner Best, assumed direct control of the internal affairs of the country.

These increased tensions turned out to be an immediate prelude to an attempt to deport the Danish Jews. So far they had enjoyed the same benefits of the 'model occupation' as any other Danes. Uniquely among Jews in occupied territories, they had been allowed to continue in their jobs; their civil rights were guaranteed under Danish law; and they remained free to conduct religious services. The eerie comfort of all this changed on 28 September with the issuing of an order that all Jews in Denmark were to be rounded up for deportation. The procedure was due to start three days later, on 1 October, at 9 o'clock in the evening.

On the day the order arrived, however, one of Best's closest associates, a German shipping *attaché* named Georg Ferdinand Duckwitz, took it upon himself to pass the date and time on to two leading Danish politicians, who in turn ensured that as many as possible of the country's 7,500-strong Jewish community were alerted to the danger. Two German freighters had arrived in Copenhagen on 29 September to transport the Jews to concentration camps, but by the time the round-up started on the evening of 1 October, only 284 were taken into detention. The rest had already fled their homes and taken up offers of help from ordinary Danes, going into hiding in private houses, churches and hospitals. Many were surprised to be approached by strangers in the streets offering them the keys to their apartments or their country cottages. The final number deported to the camp at Theresienstadt, in Bohemia, was only 474. What remained for the 7,000 who had gone into hiding was evacuation over the water to safety in Sweden, a drama that involved members of the Danish resistance, dozens of small fishing vessels, and the connivance of the German port commander in Copenhagen, who kept his fleet of patrol vessels resolutely in dock at a time when traffic across the sound to Sweden was at its most intense, on the pretext that his ships were unseaworthy and in need of repair.

Gestures of civil disobedience, combined with a growing realization on the part of the native population that Germany was not, after all, going to win the war meant that over the remaining eighteen months of the occupation of Denmark the last vestiges of its relatively civilized nature rapidly disappeared. Tensions between the German military and the Danish police increased. Through the early part of 1944, Nazis murdered a number of critical voices whose sudden and violent silencing was supposed to have a salutary function. The victims included Kaj Munk, a priest also famous as the leading Danish dramatist of his generation, taken from his vicarage home in Vedersø on the night of 4 January 1944 and, after a cursory hearing, shot by Danish Nazis of the so-called Schalburg Corps, who dumped his body in a roadside ditch 6 miles (10 km) away. Two days later, a doctor and local politician named Willy Vigholt was shot in his own consulting room in Slagelse. For each killing attributed to the resistance, another of these so-called 'clearing murders' would be the response. The Germans insisted that newspapers carry reports of the two incidents on adjacent pages so that the connection would be unmistakeable to readers. More than a hundred revenge murders were carried out in this way. The Germans presently turned to a more terrifying form of revenge killing, in which a pedestrian or cyclist might be shot at random in the street.

This campaign to subdue a growing and active hostility to the occupation led to one of the most well-remembered episodes in Danish war history. At 5.30 on the morning of 26 May 1944, the Gestapo knocked on the door of a house in Gråsten that was the home of Colonel Svend Paludan-Müller. Paludan-Müller was head of the Danish gendarmerie, whose duty it was to patrol the Danish–German border on the east of the Jutland peninsula, and a man whose distaste for the compromises of the occupation had led to his involvement in plans for an active military engagement against the Germans. His early-morning visitors announced that they wanted to speak to him. He replied that in that case they must return at 10 o'clock and the interview might be conducted during normal office hours. When the colonel persisted in his refusal to open his door, the Germans blew it open and entered the house. Paludan-Müller immediately shot dead the first military policeman. The Germans withdrew to gather at a safe distance and the colonel barricaded the door. What happened then is extraordinarily reminiscent of the last hours of Gunnar of Hlíðarendi, the great and noble friend of Njal in *Njal's Saga*, trapped by enemies in his own house and fighting on against overwhelming odds to the very end.

While the Germans discussed how to deal with the situation, the gendarme made it clear to his wife that he would not allow himself to be taken alive. He led her and their daughter Ragny and a house-maid down to the safety of the cellar and awaited developments. Once the Germans had taken up their positions around the small house, and with heavier artillery already on its way from Åbenrå, the local priest was given permission to try to persuade the beleaguered man to surrender. He arranged for safe passage from the house for the three women, but Paludan-Müller could not be persuaded to surrender. The priest, a man named Holst, later described the cool and fatalistic resolution with which Paludan-Müller rejected his arguments and accepted the inevitability of his death, kneeling calmly as he asked Holst to bless him in God's name.

At the head of the cellar stairs he took his leave of his wife and daughter, kissing them both and saying 'Goodbye, and God be with you.' It was then simply a matter of time. Two hours, as it turned out, during which he held out against fifty men armed with fire-bombs, hand grenades and machine-guns. By 8.30am the house was aflame and Paludan-Müller was dead, along with five German soldiers. It was late afternoon before his body was recovered from the ashes. Afraid that a local funeral might give rise to disturbances, the Germans refused to allow the ceremony to take place in Southern Jutland, and Paludan-Müller was buried in the parish church in Snesere, his childhood home. Estimates put the number of mourners in attendance at 2,500, all of them present in direct contravention of an official proclamation that the burial was illegal and prohibited.

In mid-September 1944, some 300 of a total force of 337 of Paludan-Müller's gendarmes were arrested. Most were sent to Neuengamme, an extermination-through-labour camp housing thousands, on the outskirts of Hamburg. Survivors described how the camps shower-rooms also doubled as gas-chambers, although 'only' Soviet prisoners-of-war were murdered in this way. Executions by hanging had to be carried out by the prisoners themselves, a second man hanging the first, the third the second, the fourth the third, and so on. As part of the same purge, 2,000 regular Danish policemen were arrested and sent to Buchenwald.

Despite the protests in the Danish press, Bohr did not get the job as Rector of the University of Copenhagen. Instead, he was one of the 7,000 Danish Jews who had been so effectively warned of the impending round-up. By the time it took place, Bohr, along with most of the other Jewish refugees, was in Stockholm. He and his wife Margrethe had been among a party who had gathered clandestinely at a small garden-cabin in a Copenhagen suburb, which they left late at night, at times instructed to crawl on all fours on their way to the beach, to the embarrassment of Bohr who felt all this might be a little over the top.

On the beach they were picked up by a small fishing-boat that took them out into the Öresund, where they transferred to a trawler that docked in the Swedish harbour of Limhamn in the early hours of the morning. Later that day Bohr was taken by train to Stockholm, Margrethe staying behind to await other family members who were travelling in a separate group. Bohr – being the immensely delicate and valuable package of intelligence that he was – was informed that the British wanted him delivered at once. A de Havilland Mosquito, an unarmed and very fast type of bomber converted to carry passengers, stood ready to fly him over from Stockholm's Bromma airport.

A number of delays ensued, however, and it was 5 October 1943 before the plane finally took off.

During the Nuremberg Trials after the war it emerged that the Nazis had originally planned to arrest Bohr and take him to Germany shortly after the declaration of martial law on 29 August but had decided instead to disguise his arrest as part of the next month's general detention of all Danish Jews. Bohr's biographer, Abraham Pais, provides several cheerfully surreal anecdotes of this dark and dangerous period of Bohr's life. In one, Captain Gyth, who took it upon himself to be Bohr's personal bodyguard at the private house where he was staying on the night before he was due to fly to Scotland, is sitting up in Bohr's Stockholm room in the early hours when he hears soft sounds approaching; he pulls out his host's old service revolver in one hand, picks up a heavy candlestick in the other, and tenses himself. The soft steps approach the door. The letter-box opens and a morning newspaper drops onto the carpet. Captain Gyth peers out the window a few moments later and sees the old newspaper lady shuffling away in her felt mustn't-wake-people-up outdoor slippers.

During the flight itself, later that day, the Mosquito climbed as it flew over occupied Denmark, and Bohr was told through the intercom to turn on his oxygen. As there was no response from the bomb bay at the back where Bohr was lying, the pilot saw no alternative but to descend to near sea-level for the remainder of the flight. When they landed in Scotland early on the morning of 6 October, Bohr announced that he had slept most of the way and was feeling fine. It emerged later that he had been talking the entire time he was being given his safety briefing at Bromma and, having failed to grasp the importance of what the pilot was telling him, had lapsed into unconsciousness from lack of oxygen soon after take-off.

Another former pupil of Bohr's, the physicist George Gamow, recalled how Bohr liked to relax after a day's work at the physics institute by going to a Western. The plots of these always seemed so complicated to him that he had to take one or two students along to explain things for him. After one such evening at the cinema, a discussion ensued on the relative advantages of being the good guy and the bad guy in a shootout. Bohr's view was that the edge lay with the good guy: he knows he can never shoot first, and this puts all the pressure of deciding when to draw on the bad guy. All the hero has to do is wait to see his opponent's hand move, and a conditioned reflex will ensure that his own hand moves faster. The students disagreed, and to settle the matter Gamow visited a toyshop the following morning and bought two toy guns. In a series of shootouts that followed, Bohr, as the good guy, emerged victorious every time.

One can't help wondering whether Bohr ever recalled that afternoon of harmless fun once he reached England and realized just how far advanced the Allies were in their preparations for making an atomic bomb; and whether in due course he ever felt that the preemptive use of it on Hiroshima and Nagasaki in 1945 invalidated his theory or not. As things turned out, Bohr took little active part in the work on the bomb project, although the presence of such a towering genius among the younger physicists of the British Tube Alloys nuclear weapons development team and the Americans in Los Alamos, New Mexico, where the bomb was being designed and built, must have been inspiring.

His real value to them lay in his knowledge of how far the Germans, whom they knew to be working on a similar bomb, had got in their efforts. To this end, Bohr's account of his wartime meeting with Werner Heisenberg, head of the German research team, became of crucial importance. Heisenberg had arrived in Copenhagen in the autumn of 1941 to attend a conference organized by the occupying power at the German Institute in Copenhagen. Danish physicists from Bohr's own Institute of Theoretical Physics boycotted it, obliging Heisenberg to pay a visit to the Danish institute himself in order to see Bohr, an old friend and colleague whom he greatly liked and admired. Bohr gave his account of the meeting, and based on what Heisenberg told him presumably also offered an assessment of how far the Germans had got. He would also have told the Allies what he knew of German efforts to increase the supply of heavy water being made at the Norsk Hydro plant in Rjukan, Telemark, in central Norway, following a number of sabotage actions by British and Norwegian commando units. Although his informant told him that the treated water was for 'industrial purposes only', Bohr had by this time learned to distrust such assertions. The Allies would have made particular note of Bohr's report that Heisenberg told him he had been working 'exclusively' for the previous two years on the problem of the release of atomic energy, and of Heisenberg's conviction that if the Germans, against all expectations, failed to win the war by conventional military means and it turned into a long-drawn-out affair, then its outcome would probably be settled by the use of an atom bomb.

One of the central witnesses used by the Austrian writer Robert Jungk in his 1958 *Brighter Than a Thousand Suns*, the first published account of the Manhattan Project and the German atomic bomb projects, was Werner Heisenberg. Bohr read Jungk's book in its Danish translation a couple of years later and took issue with most of what Heisenberg told Jungk. 'I have a completely different perception of what took place during the visit from the one that you express in your contribution to Jungk's book,' he wrote in response. Bohr was upset on two counts. One was professional. In the book Heisenberg recalled the silence with which Bohr greeted the news of the project he was working on, and implied that it expressed Bohr's scientific doubt that the thing was in fact possible at all. Not so, objected Bohr. His silence was the silence of horror.

The other count was personal. Reading Jungk he became aware that Heisenberg had allowed the years to corrupt his memory of what was actually said during their conversation to present his role in a more favourable historical light. He objected particularly to Heisenberg's claim to have hinted strongly to Bohr that his German team were discreetly working to *hinder* the successful outcome of the fateful research. Bohr countered that he could recall the 'quite extraordinary impression' Heisenberg's visit had made, and that he 'carefully noted every word uttered in our conversation, during which I, constantly spied upon as we were by German Police, was obliged to maintain an extreme reserve'. Under the circumstances he could not recall Heisenberg having made any reference, veiled or otherwise, to attempts to sabotage the German atom bomb project. All of these revelations are contained in a series of eleven draft letters released to the public by the Bohr Archive in 2002. None were ever sent. Bohr, a fabulously decent man, seems to have decided to let a sleeping dog lie.

*

The Swedish declaration of neutrality was the only one respected by the Nazis, marking a further extension of the position adopted by Sweden at the conclusion of the Napoleonic wars. In view of this historical association it seems paradoxical that one of Sweden's most notable sons over the hundred-and-thirty-year period was Alfred Nobel, a man who made an unearthly fortune as the inventor of dynamite. Nobel's life contrasts in many ways with that of Niels Bohr. Bohr was a happily married man and father to six children. He was open, spontaneous, warm and vague. In his youth, he kept goal for Copenhagen's Akademisk Boldklub. Nobel's health was always poor and he never married. In 1876, at the age of forty-three, he met Bertha Kinsky, a writer and peace activist and fell in love with her. He asked if 'her heart is free'. It was not, and to prove it she married a young baron, Arthur von Suttner, in the summer of the same year. That same autumn Nobel began a long and resigned career as sugar daddy to Sofie Hess, a shop assistant twenty-three years his junior. A teetotaller and non-smoker, and a man who, according to one Swedish biographer, was never heard to laugh, Nobel once described his existence as a 'pathetic half-life'. He was terrified of being buried alive. The last paragraph of his will contained instructions that his veins be opened after his death, 'and when this has been done and competent Doctors have confirmed clear signs of death, my remains shall be cremated in a so-called crematorium'.

Nobel's will included a bequest to Sofie Hess; but the document was most notable for dedicating his huge fortune to the setting up of the Nobel Prizes. With particular reference to the most celebrated of them all, the Peace Prize, many found it hard over the years to divorce the philanthropic gesture from the notion that it was dictated by a guilty conscience over a lifetime spent and a fortune amassed in the pursuit of ever more efficient means of waging war and destroying human life on the grand scale. Bohr's contemporary Albert Einstein was in no doubt about the relationship between Nobel's bequest and his work: 'He invented an explosive that was stronger than any known before – an exceedingly efficient means of destruction. In order to calm his conscience he created his Nobel Prizes.' In his 'Speech to the Swedish Nation' in 1910, August Strindberg referred to the prize money as something morally tainted: 'Nobel money – some call it dynamite money.' Ludwig Wittgenstein, looking for somewhere remote in which to explore the mysteries of logic in peace, found the perfect site in Norway on a promontory overlooking Lake Eidsvatnet in Skjolden. He had a house built there to his specifications, and probably to the great annoyance and inconvenience of the local builders insisted they use gunpowder only in blasting the foundations, citing as his reason a moral disapproval of Nobel's invention and of the vast amounts of money being made from it.

Nobel himself was well aware there were moral aspects to his innovations. Indeed they fascinated him. His assistant, Ragnar Sohlmann, recalled a conversation with him: 'Once, when we were discussing experiments with explosive armour-breaking hand grenades that would succeed in penetrating plate and exploding behind it, he said: "Well, you know, we are actually dealing with rather demonic devices. But as problems, they are so interesting, purely as technical problems – financial or commercial considerations aside – and for that reason alone worth pursuing."' And to Bertha Kinsky, now Bertha von Suttner and in 1905 the first female recipient of a Peace Prize, Nobel once volunteered: 'I should like to be able to create a substance or a machine with such a horrific capacity for mass annihilation that wars would become impossible forever.'

It seems almost as though the atom bomb, which owed so much to Niels Bohr's discoveries, was the creation Nobel had been dreaming of. For Bohr saw it in the same light, as an opportunity to make war history. The Soviet Union was aware of the goal of the Manhattan

Project. Determined not to be left behind, the Soviets joined in the macabre courtship of Bohr's mind in hopes of winning it for themselves. In April 1944, several months after arriving in Britain, he received a long-delayed letter inviting him to come to the Soviet Union. Bohr gave a non-committal response, but the invitation confirmed his sense that the invention of the atomic bomb, or 'atomic bum' as his Danish pronunciation always rendered it, had changed the world forever. As Nobel had done, Bohr felt instinctively that a 'balance of terror' was the best guarantee of world peace. To this end, he suggested during a meeting with Winston Churchill, in May 1944, that a mutual openness with the Soviets was the best policy, a view Churchill found so alien that in a letter to a third party he wrote that Bohr 'ought to be confined or at any rate made to see that he is very near the edge of mortal crimes'. Bohr then proposed the same idea to President Roosevelt, who could only suggest that Bohr go back to England to try to win British approval.

The upshot of this bizarre ping-pong was that, at a meeting between Churchill and Roosevelt at the latter's Hyde Park residence, New York, in September 1944, they decided to keep the project secret. An informal note added to the record of their conversation advised that 'enquiries should be made regarding the activities of Professor Bohr and steps taken to ensure that he is responsible for no leakage of information, particularly to the Russians'. In June 1950, with the Korean War looming, Bohr addressed an open letter to the United Nations: 'The development of technology has now reached a stage where the facilities for communication have provided the means for making all mankind a co-operating unit,' he told them:

> And where at the same time fatal consequences to civilization may ensue unless international divergences are considered as issues to be settled by consultation based on free access to all relevant information. The very fact that knowledge is in itself the basis for civilization points directly to openness as the way to overcome the present crisis. Whatever judicial and administrative international authorities may eventually have to be created in order to stabilize world affairs, it must

be realized that full mutual openness, only, can effectively promote confidence and guarantee common security.

Bohr's natural optimism is still a beautiful thing. Once, when a friend asked why he had a pair of deer's antlers mounted above the door to his study, he replied that it was for good luck. Teased about this, he admitted he didn't believe in such things, but added, with a wondering smile, that apparently they worked even if you didn't believe in them.

★

Almost inevitably, the membership of Norway's Nasjonal Samling had rocketed after the occupation of the country. There was hardly anything sinister in this – if anything, it shows how fundamentally indifferent most people are to political ideologies – for membership of the party gave better access to sugar, butter, clothing, leather shoes and the numerous other everyday commodities that were in short supply.

Knut Hamsun, Norway's pride and joy, in the opinion of Isaac Bashevis Singer the literary genius from whose coat all twentieth-century writing in the Western world was cut, was a lifelong lover of Germany as well as a committed Anglophobe who had been among the 5 per cent or so of Norwegians who supported the Germans during the First World War. To the great disappointment of his fellow-countrymen Hamsun saw no reason to change sides when the second war came along. The Germans were delighted to have him on board again, and in the course of the war invited him to Germany, where he met, among others, Josef Goebbels, a genuine lover of his novels, and Adolf Hitler, who seems to have been not much interested in them but glad of someone marginally more respectable as literary sympathizer than Louis-Ferdinand Céline and Ezra Pound to confound the Allies' propaganda machine. The Norwegians, shuffling about the streets of Oslo in their homemade fish-skin shoes, joked about it. Have you heard the news? they said. The Nazis are splitting Hamsun's authorship into two. The Germans are getting *The Growth of the Soil* and we're getting *Hunger*.

Membership of the NS had been criminalized by the government-in-exile, and with the legislation considered retrospective, more than 90,000 cases were tried after the war. So extreme was the loathing of Quisling and his team of collaborating politicians, civil servants and judges that the government feared lynch-mobs would take over if it didn't bring back the death penalty, and for the first time since 1876 judicial killings took place in Norway. Reidar Haaland and Arne Braa Saatvedt, Norwegian torturers who had worked with the Gestapo, were the first to go, executed before the winter of 1945 had set in. Vidkun Quisling, sitting in his cell in Møllergata 19 after his trial and awaiting execution, spent his last hours trying to give shape to a manuscript expounding his customized mongrel philosophy, *Universismen*. A gifted mathematician in his youth, Quisling overstretched himself now with the announcement that he was the first person able to provide *mathematical* proof of the existence of God. In some ways a pitiful figure in his catastrophic foolishness, he was shot by firing squad at 2.40 on the morning of 24 October 1945, a sheet of A4 paper pinned to his chest to help the soldiers focus their aim. His last request, not to wear a blindfold, had been rejected.

In all thirty men received the death sentence. Four were pardoned, one died in jail. The last judicial killing was that of Ragnar Skancke, Quisling's Minister for Educational and Religious Affairs, shot by firing squad in August 1948. After that, the mood of rage faded. Men who had been given life sentences found themselves free again by the early 1950s. People wanted to get on with enjoying and rebuilding their lives. The Norwegians had been an independent people for only thirty-five years before independence was so rudely taken away from them. One striking effect of the five years of German occupation was to reinforce Norwegian nationalism, a rare cocktail of passionate patriotism, pride, openness and decency that today expresses itself in the joyful and decidedly non-military celebrations of National Day, on 17 May, when the entire country seems suddenly awash with processions of small children waving flags.

The Danes too, having managed to keep a substantial hold on their democratic and institutional structures for so much of the war, could allow themselves to feel after liberation that they had at least not dishonoured those lines of the poet H.P. Holst that had been adopted almost as a national motto after Denmark's defeat in the war of 1864 and the loss of Slesvig-Holsten to Prussia, *hvad udad tabes, det maa indad vindes,** the idea that that something lost without must be restored within, a powerfully effective mantra for national self-improvement. But in Denmark, too, a degenerate hardening of the occupying forces and those who had chosen the 'wrong' side as they began to sense their own defeat after the reversals at Stalingrad in 1943 ensured a bitter reckoning once the war came to an end. Forty thousand were arrested on suspicion of collaboration, of whom about one-third received some form of punishment, in most cases a prison sentence of under four years. As in Norway, the dormant death sentence was revived and seventy-eight collaborators were sentenced to death. Forty-six sentences were carried out, the remainder commuted to terms of imprisonment.

One of the very few directly political statements in Quisling's *Universismen* is an expression of military regret that the Nazis had not completed the occupation of Scandinavia and overrun Sweden as well. It's hard to see what the advantages might have been. With Norway and Denmark occupied, Germany victorious in France and Great Britain, the Swedes, under siege, were effectively isolated. Needing food, fuel and raw materials, they were in no position to prevent the Germans defining the terms of their neutrality, and for the first three years of the war that is exactly what the Germans did. A Transit Agreement signed in July 1940 allowed German soldiers – described as medical staff – to use the Swedish rail network to move men and supplies in and out of Norway to Baltic ports; it was a flagrant breach of neutrality. In 1941, the Swedes were pressured into allowing troop divisions from Norway to pass through Sweden on their way to take part in the war in Finland. Consignments of

* For the meaning of this phrase, see the discussion on page 123.

iron ore from Kiruna and Malmberget passed across the top of the Scandinavian peninsula on their way to Narvik as Sweden promised to maintain supplies at pre-war levels, and did so for three years.

As elsewhere, Stalingrad marked the watershed. The Transit Agreement was revoked by Sweden in August 1943, and when Quisling and Hitler's other willing helpers began the arrest and deportation of Scandinavian Jews in October Sweden gave refuge to some 5,000 who made the dangerous border crossing to safety. As the balance swung ever further away from Germany, pressure from Britain and the United States began to spin Swedish neutrality their way. Deliveries to Germany of ball-bearings and other important commodities were reduced, and in the final months of the war all trade with Germany came to a standstill.

Elsewhere in occupied Europe, during the final few weeks of the war, desperate SS officers were trying to cover up the evidence of the Nazi camps and what had taken place in them. At Ravensbrück, 50 miles (80 km) north of Berlin, 6,000 women were gassed, and many more lives would have been lost had it not been for a very particular Swedish effort, the famous fleet of 'White Buses', so-called because they were painted white to distinguish them from military vehicles. These set out from Sweden on 15 March and began their tour of German concentration camps, picking up Danish and Norwegian inmates and delivering them to safety in Sweden. French, Polish and Dutch were also among the rescued. As dangerous as it undoubtedly was, the operation was only possible with the co-operation of the Germans.

On a similar errand, and under considerably more hazardous circumstances, Raoul Wallenberg, one of the great humanitarian heroes of modern Sweden, is credited with saving the lives of 120,000 Hungarian Jews in Budapest. He arrived in the city for the specific purpose of doing so in June 1944, issuing some Jews with specially designed Swedish passports and persuading the SS general in charge to spare the lives of others with the threat that the man would be held personally responsible for any final massacre of Jews in the city's ghetto and tried as a war criminal.

The mystery of Wallenberg's disappearance early in 1945 has only increased his legend. Leaving Budapest on 17 January with a Red Army escort, on his way to meet members of the Hungarian provisional government, he vanished and was not heard from again. It seems that he was arrested almost immediately on leaving Budapest and accused by the Soviets of being an American spy. A document released by the Soviet authorities on 6 February 1957, but dated 17 July 1947, asserts that he died of heart failure in the KGB's Lubianka prison in Moscow a short time previously. Other sources suggest that he was executed, by poisoning say some, shot by firing squad according to others.

*

The three very different ways in which each Scandinavian country experienced the war had repercussions once it came to an end. Sweden was inclined to turn inward and urged Denmark and Norway to join it in a defensive union of the Nordic countries. The Danes and Norwegians, with first-hand experience of how little declarations of neutrality might mean, preferred to entrust themselves to the strong arms of NATO. Sweden's partiality to Nazi Germany during the early phase of the war – the iron ore transports, troop movements and fraternizations particularly – had been a bitter disappointment to many. In wartime exile, Norway's Prime Minister Nygaardsvold had written a furious letter from London to his *attaché* in Stockholm instructing him to convey his anger to the Swedish prime minister: 'Greet him from me. Tell him there are two things I want: one is to see the Germans driven out of Norway; two, that I live long enough to let him and his entire government know exactly what I think of them.' 'There is nothing,' Nygaardsvold went on, 'nothing, nothing, nothing I hate with such passion and such abandon as Sweden.' To this day, some Norwegians believe that Sweden's role as a humanitarian superpower is driven by guilt over the country's conduct during the war, and for every refugee that arrives in Sweden the Swedes cross one more name from the list of German soldiers who had crossed the border between Norway and Sweden between 1940 and 1944.

★

Back in 2006, my wife and I drove along the coast to see a rare
screening of Viktor Sjøstrøm's 1916 silent film of Ibsen's *Terje Vigen*
at Fjæreheia, the vast open-air quarry theatre just outside Grimstad.
'Enslaved', one of the world's top death-metal bands, had been
commissioned to create a soundtrack for the film. The performance
began at 11 o'clock. It was a warm windy August night. As the film
crackled into life on the huge screen, the four young men, posing
dramatically in front of it in their ankle-length black leather coats,
waist-length hair lifting in the breeze against the darkening sky, set
up a dense wall of sound and kept it up for the duration. Their 'Goth'
aesthetic of pale skin and dark make-up reflected eerily the heavy
white facial make-up and black eye shading used by the actors in
the film to compensate for the failings of the primitive cine-cameras.

Sjøstrøm, who as well as directing the film also played the part
of Terje, was Ingmar Bergman's great idol and inspiration. Decades
later, when Sjøstrøm was seventy-eight years old, Bergman wrote
the part of Dr Borg in *Smulltronstället* (*Wild Strawberries*) for him.
Sitting there in that slightly surreal setting, watching Ibsen's tale of
the sufferings of the Norwegian people during the Napoleonic Wars,
the craggy walls of the theatre flickeringly lit by the action on the
screen as the guitar riffs swirled around them, I found myself thinking about the place's history, how this quarry was the result of Albert
Speer's plan to use its stone to build an enormous stadium on the site
of the old Zeppelin dock in Nuremberg, with seating for 400,000
people: a suitable venue for every future Olympic Games that would
be held there, once the Pan-Germanic Empire was established. During
the war, huge quantities of Fjæreheia stone were piled up on the
docks at Grimstad, ready for shipment to Germany and Nuremberg.
And with the failure of the new order there they stayed, moss grown
and studded with pale lichen, a massive and useless monument to
this absurd and cruel dream. Although not quite useless, I reflected:
the hole they made had become the theatre I was sitting in.

12
The Power of Scandinavian Women

BY WAY OF CONTEXT: BACK IN THE REMOTE 1960s, WHEN I was about eleven years old and we moved into our house in Windsor Road, in St Annes, I found during my early explorations of its nooks and crannies on a shelf at the back of the coal-cellar a pile of A5-size magazines covered in grime and neatly tied with that hairy, straw-like twine one rarely sees nowadays. The magazine was called *Lilliput*. Each of the forty or so issues was filled with black-and-white photographs of naked young women in 'tasteful' poses: kneeling, with one hand holding up the long hair to one side of the head; standing, back to the camera and looking over the shoulder, that kind of thing. I was excited by my find and routinely hid it somewhere even more inaccessible than the back of the coal-shed, where my father would never go anyway. But at the same time I was puzzled and even disappointed, for from every one of these photographs all trace of the pubic hairs and what lay beneath them had been carefully excised leaving only a faintly smudged patch of skin.

Fast-forward, as they say, to 1967 and a Swedish film called *Hugs and Kisses*. It was at a time when the British Board of Film Censors was still largely preoccupied with censoring naked human bodies out of existence, and every visit to a cinema would be preceded by

a sombre moment in which the curtains drew back to reveal a statement in white print on a black background announcing which of
three audiences the film was considered appropriate for: an 'X' certificate for over-sixteens only; an 'A' for under sixteens accompanied
by an adult; and a 'U', which meant anybody could see it. Getting
into X-rated films was a kind of holy grail for kids under sixteen,
and in Blackpool there were two cinemas in particular that were
known to be easier to get into than others. One was the New Ritz on
the Promenade, and the other the Tivoli, a little further back from
the seafront, not far from the Talbot Road Bus Station. Both were
flea-pits, scruffy, rundown and cheap. As far as I can recall, they only
ever showed X- or A-rated films. At fourteen I hadn't even started
shaving, so visits to the Tivoli and the New Ritz were things I used
to hear about from my older brother William. The word had got out
that there was a film showing at the New Ritz with a naked woman
standing in front of a mirror where you could see her pubic hair, her
breasts, her arse – *everything*, as we boys used to gasp in disbelief in
the playground.

My brother usually went to the cinema on Friday nights with
two friends from school. This Friday, for some reason, they couldn't
make it and he reluctantly ordered me to go along with him. We
caught the 11A from St Annes Square, got out and began walking
towards the cinema entrance. It wasn't raining but he had given me
his white shortie mac to wear, saying it would make me look older.
Right outside Louis Tussaud's waxworks, next door to the cinema,
just before we reached the neon glow of the foyer, he stopped,
scrutinized me, turned up the collar of the shortie, took a packet of
Embassy tipped from an inside pocket, lit one from the one he was
smoking and stuck it in my mouth, telling me quite unnecessarily
to remember to say to the ticket-seller that I was sixteen if he asked
how old I was. As it turned out the ticket-booth was manned by a
tired old pensioner who hardly even bothered to look up from his
newspaper to sell us our tickets, which is how I got in to see *Hugs
and Kisses* and for the first time in my life saw female pubic hair.
It turns out the hair belonged to an actress named Agneta Ekmanner,

now seventy-nine years old and to this day still working, according to the IMDb website. I am fascinated to note that she had a part in Suzanne Osten's *Bröderna Mozart* (*The Mozart Brothers*), the 1986 film Olof Palme went to see on the night of his murder. *Hugs and Kisses* was Swedish, and with this film I had my first experience of that legendary frankness about sexuality that has been such an important part of how the rest of the world thinks about Scandinavians; or to be more precise how the rest of the world thinks about Swedes and Danes. Norwegians and Norwegian cinema were never a part of the sexual revolution exported throughout the last decades of the twentieth century by its neighbours, and which was still being exported in the twenty-first century by the Danish director Lars von Trier in films such as *The Idiots* and *Nymphomaniac*. In the 1980s, in the days before the internet, a striking sight when crossing the border by road from Norway into Sweden was all the caravans parked up on spare farm land on the Swedish side advertising 'PORNO' for sale in huge hand-lettered writing.

*

The outside world has always found Scandinavian women exotic. An illuminating example is a story from the earliest days of Viking activity on the Iberian peninsula, told by the twelfth-century Muslim scholar and biographer Ibn Dihya al-Kalbi, based in turn on oral traditions. It concerns a diplomatic mission undertaken in about 845 by the Andalusian poet and traveller Yahya ibn-Hakam al-Bekri al-Jayyani, better known as al-Ghazali (sometimes as al-Ghazal), to the court of a Viking king in northern Europe. The trip was made on the orders of emir of Cordova, Abd-ar-Rahman II, after a fleet of eighty longships, with square brown sails that 'covered the sea like dark birds', had appeared off Lisbon in 844, in the estuary of the Tagus, and over a thirteen-day period had engaged in three sea-battles with local ships before heading further south. The harbour at Cadiz was occupied by the invaders, and while one group of Vikings made its way inland to Medina-Sidonia, the main body of the fleet sailed up the Guadalquivir River into the very heartland of al-Andalus – Moorish Spain – and established a base on an island not far from Seville.

The city was taken, seemingly without resistance, for most of the inhabitants had fled to Carmona or up into the mountains north of Seville, and for some two weeks the city was in Viking hands. The banks of the great river formed a noted centre for the breeding of horses, allowing the Vikings to range far and wide across the region in their plundering. As other ships arrived to join the occupying force, those inhabitants who had not managed to flee were massacred or taken captive. It seems that the sheer unexpectedness of the raid on Seville astounded the emir, for it was some time before he thought to order the army out against the enemy. With the help of catapult-machines, they drove the Vikings out of the city, killing some 500 and capturing four ships. In the middle of November the Vikings were again defeated, again with heavy loss of life. Thirty longships were burnt, and the corpses of Viking captives were hung from the palm trees of Seville and Talyata. In symbolic triumph, the heads of the leader and 200 of his men were sent to the Berber emir in Tangier.

Abd-ar-Rahman II's long-term response to the dreadful novelty of these raids from the sea was to build a number of warships of his own and to establish a chain of lookout posts along the Atlantic coast. Seville was restored, its defences strengthened and an arsenal established. More immediately, Ibn Dihya tells us that the emir received envoys from Turgeis (Turgesius), the Viking king behind the raid, requesting peace, and it was with his answer to this offer that al-Ghazali sailed up through the Bay of Biscay with what remained of the Viking fleet.

After a hazardous and stormy voyage they arrived in Turgeis's kingdom. The king ordered that they be given the best accommodation and sent men out to greet them. 'The Vikings thronged to look at them,' Ibn Diyha tells us, 'and wondered greatly at their appearance and their garb.' In due course, al-Ghazali was brought before the king and delivered the emir's letter. The king had the letter read to him and expressed his pleasure at its sentiments. The gifts sent by the emir were brought before him, he examined the various garments and containers and declared himself well pleased. Having got the business side of things out of the way, the cultural exchange could begin.

In Ibn Diyha's account, al-Ghazali is an immediate hit. He has already foiled Turgeis's attempt to humble him by making the doorway in to his presence so low that anyone approaching must necessarily do so on their knees, instead shuffling in on his bottom, feet first and with the soles of his shoes pointing at the king, an Arabic insult that Turgeis either chooses to ignore or fails to recognize. In contests of wit and learning, al-Ghazali has trounced the local champions, and in general made such a good impression that the king's wife, Nud, orders him to appear before her so that she can see the prodigy for herself.

The relationship that subsequently develops between these two is at the heart of Ibn Dihya's narrative. It is both a fine picture of the eternal type of the *roué*, with his awestruck and stagey silence when he sets eyes on her, and a clear expression of genuine surprise and respectful admiration for the many and profound ways in which he learns that Scandinavian women differ from the women of his own country:

Al-Ghazal greeted her when he came before her then stared at her for a long time, gazing at her as though dumbstruck. She told her interpreter to ask him why he was staring at her like that. 'Is it because he finds me very beautiful, or the opposite?'

Al-Ghazal answered: 'It is because I had not imagined there could be such a beautiful sight in all the world. In the palaces of our king I have seen women chosen for him from among all the peoples of the world, but even among them I have never seen a beauty to compare with this.'

She told her interpreter: 'Ask him if he's being serious or is he joking?'

'I am completely serious,' he replied

'Are there then no beautiful women in your country?'

Al-Ghazal asked to be shown some of the local women, so that he would be able to make the comparison. The queen ordered that local women famed for their beauty be brought before him. When they arrived al-Ghazal looked them up and down.

'They are beautiful,' he said. 'But not in the way the queen is beautiful. Her kind of beauty, the qualities that she has, these are things that cannot be appreciated by the ordinary man. Only poets can express it. If the queen wishes me to I will describe her beauty, her quality and her wisdom in a poem which will be declaimed through all our land.'

The queen was delighted to hear this and ordered that he be given a gift. Al-Ghazal refused to accept it.

'Ask him why not,' she told the interpreter. 'Is it me he dislikes or the gift?'

Al-Ghazal replied: 'She is a queen and the daughter of a king and the gift she offers is truly magnificent. To receive it from her would be a great honour. But just to see her and be received into her presence are gift enough for me and the only gift I could want. I desire only that she continues to receive me.'

And when the interpreter had conveyed these words to her the queen's joy and admiration knew no bounds.

'Let his gift be carried to his dwelling', she said. 'And if he wishes to pay me a visit let the door never be closed to him, for he is always assured of an honourable welcome from me.'

Al-Ghazal thanked her, wished her well and departed.

Tammam ibn 'Alqama said: 'I heard al-Ghazal tell this story, and I asked him: 'Was she really as extraordinarily beautiful as you told her she was?'

And al-Ghazal said, 'By your father, she had some charm. But by talking to her in this way I won her good graces and obtained from her more than I desired.'

Tammam ibn 'Alqama also said: 'One of his companions said to me: 'The wife of the king of the Vikings was infatuated with al-Ghazal and could not let a day go by without sending for him. And he would stay with her and tell her of the life of the Muslims, of their history, their countries and their neighbours. And after every visit a gift would be delivered to him as an expression of her appreciation of him – clothing or food, sometimes perfume.

It was all becoming too obvious and his companions began to get worried about it. Somebody warned al-Ghazal and for a while he adopted a more cautious policy and went to see her only every other day. She asked him why this was, and he told her of the warning he had received.

'We do not have such things in our religion,' she laughed. 'Nor do we have jealousy. Our women are with our men only from their own choice. Here a woman stays with her husband as long as it pleases her. If she gets tired of him she leaves him.'

It was the custom of the Vikings before the religion of Rome reached them that no woman refused any man, except that if a noblewoman accepted a man of humble status, she was blamed for this, and her family kept them apart.

When al-Ghazal heard her say this, he was reassured and resumed his former familiarity.

Tammam says: 'Al-Ghazal was middle-aged by this time but still a strikingly good-looking man. In his youth he had been so handsome that people gave him the nickname al-Ghazal (the Gazelle). At the time of this trip to the land of the Vikings he was about fifty and his hair was turning grey. But he was still a virile, energetic man, handsome and straight-backed. One day the king's wife asked him how old he was and for a joke he told her he was twenty.

'What youth of twenty has grey hair?' she asked him through the interpreter. 'What's so unusual about that?' he said in reply. 'Have you never seen a foal emerge grey-haired from the womb?'

The queen was delighted by his answer and she burst out laughing. On the spot al-Ghazal composed another verse:

> *You are burdened, O my heart, with a wearying passion*
> *With which you struggle as with a lion.*
> *I am in love with a Viking woman*
> *Who will not let the sun of beauty set,*
> *Who lives at the limit of God's world, where he*
> *Who goes towards her, finds no path.*
> *O Queen, O young and fair one,*
> *From whose buttons a star rises,*
> *O you, by my father, than whom I see*
> *None sweeter or pleasanter to my heart,*
> *If I should say one day that my eye has seen*
> *Any one like you, I would surely be lying.*
> *She said: 'I see that your locks have turned white'*
> *In jest, she caused me to jest also,*
> *I answered: 'By my father,*
> *The foal is born grey like this.'*

> (TRANSLATED BY W.E.D. ALLEN)

The story goes on to describe how, once the interpreter had translated the poem for her, the queen burst out laughing again and told the Gazelle that he should dye his hair. Next morning he appeared in front of her with it dyed black. She told him she thought it suited him, whereupon he recited another poem he had composed in her honour:

> *In the morning she complimented me on the blackness of my dye,*
> *It was as though it had brought me back to my youth.*
> *But I see grey hair and the dye upon it*
> *As a sun that is swathed in mist.*
> *It is hidden for a while, and then the wind uncovers it,*

And the covering begins to fade away.
Do not despise the gleam of white hair;
It is the flower of understanding and intelligence,
I have that which you lust for in the youth
As well as elegance of manner, culture and breeding.

Their mission completed, al-Ghazali and the other envoys left the court of the Viking king and headed for home by way of Shent Ya'qub (Santiago de Compostella), eventually returning to the court of Sultan Abd-ar-Rahman after an absence of twenty months.

Queen Nud's brisk dismissal of any fears that the regular audiences with her Arab visitor were anybody's business but her own is an early expression of the sexual freedom and independence that people living outside the region historically associated with Scandinavian women. The tradition of strength and independence among Scandinavian women is also reflected in the power and status accorded the female principle in Ásatru, the religion followed by most Scandinavians until its replacement by Christianity in the tenth and eleventh centuries. Polytheistic where Christianity was monotheistic, its pantheon included goddesses – Freyja, goddess of fertility, Odin's wife Frigg, Hel the goddess of the Underworld and death, Idunn the goddess of youth, as well as Thor's wife Sif, of whom little is known save that she had golden hair, from which a function as protector of fields and crops might be inferred. There were also the Valkyries: armed and byrnied like warriors themselves, these were female spirits possessed of the power of flight who hovered in flocks above battlefields, choosing who should live and who should die, and transporting the fallen heroes back to Odin in Valhalla, where they would be welcomed by other Valkyries with the ritual offer of mead from a drinking horn, for they were also the handmaidens and companions of the dead warriors. And there were Norns too, goddesses believed to appear at the birth of every child to bestow a unique fate upon it, and the *dis* and *fylgja*, female spirits who might appear to the man or woman in later life, in dreams or in visions, at moments of great and fateful personal significance.

The medieval imagination ran wild when it reached the limits of the known world. In Adam's *Gesta Hammaburgensis* we may read of the Alaner or Albanere, a race of men born with grey hair; or of an unusually long-lived tribe of pale green people, and of the dog-headed offspring of the women of a Baltic *terra feminarum* ('land of women') with heads down in their chests who communicate by barking. Adam's *terra feminarum* was neighbour to Sweden and inhabited by a ruthless and misandric tribe of women. He writes of a military expedition sent by the Swedish king across the Baltic in search of territorial gain. Upon reaching this 'land of women' the leader and all of his following are wiped out when the men-haters poison the source of their drinking water.

Belief in the existence of a land ruled by hard, wilful and dangerous women was almost certainly based on references in the sources Adam would have used and the wise heads he would have consulted in writing his history of a place in the far north of the world called *Kvenland*. Ottar, the Norwegian trader who visited King Alfred's Anglo-Saxon court in Wessex towards the end of the ninth century, mentioned it in his detailed description of Scandinavia as the area around the northernmost fringes of the Baltic. He said nothing about it being ruled by women. The word *kven* was thought to be a variant of *kvinne*, the common Scandinavian word for 'woman', an intuitive guess, intuition being the only etymological tool available to scholars a thousand years ago. Modern scholarship suggests the name meant 'low-lying land'.

It may be that the tradition of strength and independence and a historical gender equality associated with Scandinavian women owes something to the fact that until very recently Danes, Swedes and Norwegians were seafaring people, with the men of the family away at sea and absent from home for long periods, leaving the management of the home economy and the family in the hands of their wives. A scene-setting chapter in the *Saga of the Earls of Orkney* (*Orkneyinga saga*), written down early in the thirteenth century but describing life as lived there 300 years earlier, relates how the archetypal Viking Svein Ásleifarson divided his year, sowing the crops on his farm in the spring then sailing away to spend the summer raiding in the Hebrides and Ireland, returning in the late summer in time for the harvest, then heading off to resume raiding again until the coming of winter. No mention is made of who ran the farm during these long absences, but the obvious inference is that it was his wife, Ingrid.

The sagas are also rich in strong and self-willed female characters who can be fatally implacable if they feel themselves wronged. One of the most memorable scenes in *Njal's Saga* is the one in which Njal's closest friend Gunnar of Hlíðarendi meets his death. Sentenced to leave Iceland for three years as an outlaw, Gunnar sets off on horseback to join the ship that is to take him away. His brother has received the same punishment and rides down to the sea with him. On the way, Gunnar's horse stumbles and he is thrown. As he gets to his feet, he cannot resist one last lingering look at his home and his farm Hlíðarendi. The moment turns out to be fateful: 'How beautiful that slope is!' he says to his brother. 'I've never seen it looking so beautiful before, with its ripening grain and new-mown hay. I'm going back home. I'm not leaving.' And as his brother carries on alone to the waiting ship, Gunnar wheels his horse about and rides back home.

An outlaw in violation of a legally binding sentence, Gunnar knows he is fair game now for powerful enemies who are legally entitled to kill him, and that his death can only be a matter of days away. His wife Hallgerd is with him when they arrive. Hopelessly outnumbered, Gunnar nevertheless manages to kill two and wound another eight as they lay siege to his house. Although wounded, he is still confident he can overcome the odds, but then disaster strikes when the string of his bow breaks. Gunnar has an inspiration: he asks Hallgerd to cut two strands of her long hair and twine them together to make him a new string.

'Is it important?' she asks.

Gunnar tells her it's probably a matter of life and death – as long as he has a bow they'll never be able to get close enough to the house to kill him. Now Hallgerd mentions something that happened a few weeks earlier, an episode that began when she ordered a slave to steal food from another farmstead. When Gunnar found out about it he had remonstrated with her. They had argued and he had slapped her face. Hallgerd had warned him then that she would not forget it, and now she shows him that she hasn't: 'In that case let me remind you of the time you slapped me,' she says. 'It doesn't matter to me whether your life goes on or ends now.'

'We all need something to be proud of,' Gunnar tells her bitterly. 'I won't ask again.' He fights on, wounding another eight attackers before he is finally cut down.

*

Hedda Gabler, Ibsen's cold queen of haughty vengeance, could hardly have made herself any clearer than Hallgerd. I was thinking about her on the morning before I wrote this, during the regular daily walk I took up the pebbly beach from the cold little house in Winchelsea Beach, where I was staying, to the settlement at Rye Harbour; there, I bought coffee in an old-fashioned plastic tumbler, a newspaper and a bar of Cadbury's Whole Nut from the village store. It was still too early for the 'William the Conqueror' to be open so I sat and spread the newspaper out on one of the wooden picnic tables outside the pub and began leafing through it, sipping my coffee. It was a bright November morning, cold and very still. To preserve my sanity I was at the time studiously avoiding any stories, articles or letters from readers having to do with immigration, terrorism or cookery programmes and very soon found myself at the culture, a two-page section at the back. Under the headline 'The man who knew the soul of women' was an article about Ibsen's female characters by the theatre director Richard Eyre. Most of them were mentioned, those creations who have exerted such a powerful effect on our society: Nora Helmer, Hedda Gabler, Rita, fru Alving.... He might have added Ellida Wangel, Rebecca West, Dina Dorf and perhaps even Hjalmar Ekdal's extraordinary daughter Hedvig in *The Wild Duck*. Eyre's admiration was boundless for a writer with not only the empathy but the talent to invent female characters like these, as complex in their existential struggles as anyone in Shakespeare. Think of Nora slamming the door on her family, he urges the reader. And I do. I've thought often about that very thing. I recall one of the many performances of *A Doll's House* I have attended at successive annual Ibsen Festivals at Oslo's National Theatre at which the audience, admittedly young and largely female, became so involved in the goings-on that most of Nora's husband Thorvald's lines were greeted with spontaneous hissing, quite as though he were a pantomime villain. I believe it may have been then that the idea first occurred to me of how interesting it would be to see a production of *A Doll's House* in which Thorvald was instructed by the director to deliver his most outrageous characterizations of women in a frail and hesitant voice, as though he were forcing himself to play the part of a socially conventional male in which he, as an individual, did not really believe. Nora, by contrast, would be instructed to be strident.

The notion arose entirely out of a perverse irritation at the way this profound play has been turned into a cliché about heroic women and monstrous men. In that connection I have never forgotten an account I read in one of Liv Ullmann's autobiographies of a production of *A Doll's House* in New York in 1975, in which she played the lead opposite Sam Waterston. On the morning of the first performance, Waterston sprained his ankle or sustained some other injury to his leg that required him to use a stick that evening. It seems that this tiny adjustment, the sight of the bully Thorvald wincing and panting with pain as he limped about the stage supporting himself on a walking stick, played havoc with the audience's sympathies. Ullmann saw the humour in it, but it made her task very difficult. I could see the humour in it too, but I also saw the potential.

Having finished my coffee, I tossed the empty cup into a green wayside bin and continued sitting for a few minutes, watching as fifteen or twenty starlings gathered in a large puddle outside the pub doorway, splashing their wings and showering themselves in an infectious ecstasy. Eventually I tore myself away and began heading back, down the muddy lane that twists along the landward side of the enormous nature reserve running the length of the shore, from Rye Harbour to the Ridge at Winchelsea Beach. As I walked along, overstimulated by the coffee, I annoyed myself by mentally drafting a letter to Richard Eyre in which I set out in detail an idea I have been trying to realize on and off for the past fifteen years, one which would bring this marvellous play back to meaningful life *as an ethical challenge.* As though it had been waiting for a final touch since the Ullmann anecdote, the idea came to me one evening while watching the film version of Oscar Wilde's *An Ideal Husband*, with Rupert Everett as Lord Arthur Goring and Jeremy Northam, son of the late John Northam, one of England's best Ibsen scholars and translators, playing the part of Sir Robert Chiltern, the 'ideal husband' of the title. Half-way through the film, I rose from my seat in the throes of a revelation: Wilde has rewritten *A Doll's House*, I said to myself. Unhappy with the way Nora refuses to forgive the despairing and apologetic Thorvald, Wilde has given us the same situation in reverse. He shows us a wronged leading character forgiving his miscreant wife. The homosexual Wilde, with his deep knowledge of the strength of human weakness, his own as well as other people's, has offered us his own corrective to the harsh lessons of *A Doll's House*.

In the weeks that followed, I tried to interest several Norwegian theatre directors of my acquaintance in the idea. I asked Kjetil Bang-Hansen, Terje Mærli, Tom Remlov at the National Theatre on Tour. Nothing doing. 'And here you are,' I said to myself in disgust, 'here you are a decade and a half later, wasting your time yet again in composing yet another long and useless letter suggesting that these two great plays be performed on successive evenings as part of the same double-bill, with the same cast for both. Theatregoers would buy a ticket for both plays, and after each rotation a passionate debate would ensue. People wouldn't want to leave. By the end of the evening the staff would be pleading with the audience to leave...'

I shook my head wearily and through an act of will that did not come easily, given the strength of the coffee I had recently drunk, I forced the idea to leave me and instead began to consider a mild and more positive thought about *A Doll's House,* this time on the explosive power this play retains among audiences in societies not yet fully irrigated by Ibsen's passionate demands on behalf of women. The Muslim world, for example, where Nora's difficulties are heart-rendingly caught by the Iranian director Dariush Mehrjui in his 1993 film version of Ibsen's play, under the title *Sara.* Here everything is different, and yet thanks to the skill with which the original drama has been filtered through the screenwriter-director's own cultural prism, all is recognizable. Mehrjui's modernized reading achieves a social relevance, deriving from its Islamic cultural environment, that no Western version, addressing itself to a society that has long since embraced a gospel of self-realization and in which more than 50 per cent of marriages end in separation and divorce, could possibly hope to achieve. In place of what – to a modern audience – are now almost unplayably naive scenes, such as the secret and transgressive nibbling of macaroons, Mehrjui's Nora is a secret smoker. The equally difficult tarantella scene is simply hinted at, with music to which Sara/Nora sadly and abstractedly moves her head from side to side in close-up, a moving, intimate and subtly filmic substitute for the wild physicality of the original dance. Thorvald's illness becomes cancer, the twentieth- and twenty-first-century plague, a life-threatening illness that can be cured, but only by an expensive trip to Switzerland which they cannot afford. Ibsen's story unfolds against a social, religious and cultural context that makes its message effortlessly relevant. With great and natural self-confidence Mehrjui introduces the bank as a second theatre of activity, turning the Krogstad letter element into an exciting taxi chase through cross-town traffic and a race through the bank's corridors to intercept Thorvald's mail.

Mehrjui's small changes to the plot are entirely in Ibsen's spirit, and his ending takes the radicalism of the original one step further when Sara/Nora leaves home and takes her infant child with her. The detail both overcomes one of the persistent ethical objections to Ibsen's concluding scene, in which Nora abandons her innocent children, and gains a revolutionary resonance within Islamic culture, where custody of the children of a failed marriage invariably goes to the father. In an inspired last touch, Ibsen's famous final stage direction, 'The sound of a door closing', becomes the slamming of the car door as Sara/Nora, clutching the sleeping child, gets into the taxi that will drive her away from her life with Hessam/Thorvald.*

★

Henrik Ibsen was the great chronicler of the inner lives of Scandinavian women. The huge success of his later plays, especially following his breakthrough in the English-speaking world in the 1890s (some fifteen years after German audiences had recognized his universal genius), with their unbroken line of leading female characters, created an image of Scandinavian womanhood that audiences outside Scandinavia still take as authoritative. Within Norway itself, his Noras, Rebeccas, Ellidas and Heddas gave Norwegian women something to live up to and helped shape a female Norwegian national identity that was a powerful complement to the image of the Norwegian man as a tough and fearless adventurer in the mould of Fridtjof Nansen. These strong and clearly articulated individuals played an important role in persuading the outside world that the Norwegians had an identity all their own, quite separate from that of the Swedes to whom they were joined in the double monarchy, and were fully able to stand on their own two feet as an independent nation. Even so, Norwegian women were not eligible to vote in the referendum in 1905 that by an overwhelming majority led to Norwegian independence. That right was obtained in 1913, two years before women achieved it in Denmark and eight before women in Sweden. To date, Sweden has never had a woman as prime minister, and Denmark only briefly in 2014–15. But Norway's first woman prime minister, the Labour Party leader Gro Harlem Brundtland, held the office on three separate occasions, heading a minority

---

* Another unusual creative adaptation for the screen of an Ibsen play is Satjayit Ray's *Ganashatru,* based on *An Enemy of the People,* in which Ibsen's spa waters become Ray's temple waters.

government for almost nine months in 1981 before being ousted by the Conservatives' Kåre Willoch. After the social democratic Labour Party returned to power in 1986 Brundtland nominated a Cabinet of eighteen that included eight women, at that time the highest proportion of female members of a Cabinet anywhere in the world. The event itself, and the very striking accompanying photograph, went around the world and brought about a transformation in the make-up of governments followed in most other European countries. In a way, it was the long-delayed fruition of a thought Ibsen had noted down while working on the first draft of *A Doll's House* in Rome, back in 1878. 'A woman cannot be herself in modern society,' he wrote, 'because it is an exclusively male society, with laws made by men, and with prosecutors and judges who judge feminine conduct from a masculine standpoint.' Well, now she could.

*

The subsequent change in the image of Scandinavian women that resulted from the concentrated feminism of the 1970s and 1980s remains, to some extent, an internal perception, not least because one of the most visible results of the new gender equality has been in winter sports, a field of no special interest to countries like the United Kingdom which are not actively engaged in them, or at least not in the blue riband distance skiing events. In Norway and Sweden, the names of successful cross-country skiers such as Marit Bjørgen, Therese Johaug and Charlotte Kalla are among the most celebrated and feted in the whole pantheon of national celebrities, yet they are almost unknown outside the winter-sport countries. Well before women's football became popular in the UK, Sweden and Norway were pioneers of the sport. Both countries have won the UEFA Women's World Cup.

Scandinavian women very naturally tend to assume that others see them more or less as they see themselves. They suppose that they are thought of as feisty, sports-loving outdoor types. I remember when I first came to live in Oslo in the early 1980s, and on my visits to Stockholm and Copenhagen too, noticing a fashion among women of all ages for wearing the hair short, with little visible facial makeup, while around the neck was draped a large lightweight shawl-like scarf in black-and-white or red-and-white, known as a 'Palestinasjerf', in imitation of the headgear ostentatiously adopted by Yasser Arafat. It was so widespread as to be almost a feminist uniform and I assumed it was a politically inspired fashion, a pointed rejection of glamour. But fashions change, and over the years the more traditionally feminine styles, with long hair, make-up and feminine clothing have made a comeback among younger women, though without a reversion to the status of women that their mothers and grandmothers fought so hard to reform. The gains are now a given.

Among casual outside observers, an older image of Scandinavian womanhood persists alongside this new one. This is the one created by a century of film and television depictions of Scandinavian women as strikingly beautiful, complex, erotic, emotional, haughty, enigmatic, troubled and sensual, a cliché about as valid as the one so many Scandinavians still fondly cling to of the typical Englishman as a habitual wearer of brown brogues and three-piece tweed suits whose response to any situation is invariably an understatement delivered in an Oxbridge drawl. The first and probably greatest exponent of this 'other' type of Scandinavian woman was the Swedish actress Greta Garbo. Between 1925 and 1941, when she retired at the age of thirty-five after making twenty-eight films, Garbo was the biggest female star in Hollywood. Her subsequent life as a recluse gave an especial poignancy to one particular line from *Grand Hotel*, the 1932 film in which she starred with John Barrymore, Joan Crawford and a Danish actor with the deceptively French-sounding name of Jean Hersholt. Garbo plays the part of a Russian ballet dancer, Grasinskaya, brilliant but riddled with self-doubt, afraid that her talent is deserting her along with her audience. Grasinskaya has just failed to make a scheduled performance. We are in a hotel room. A middle-aged woman in a dark coat and hat is speaking in a Russian accent on the telephone. She's clutching the black receiver with both hands. 'She's gone,' the woman wails into the mouthpiece. 'No, she isn't here.'

An officious man bustles through the open door. He walks up to her and grabs the receiver from her hands. He's wearing a bowler hat.

'Ingvar?' he barks into the mouthpiece. 'What's happening? No, I haven't found her. Who's dancing? Dupres? Oh. Well, how was it? Good. Alright. You keep the show going.'

He slams the phone down. The conversation has lasted no more than ten seconds. He turns to the woman whimpering quietly in the centre of the room.

'This little trick is going to cost madam a suit for breach of contract.'

'Madame is ill,' the woman implores. 'Her *nerves*!'

The man won't have any of it. 'Her nerves? What about *my* nerves? Who is she? Where does she think she is? Russia?'

Garbo appears in the doorway just in time to hear this. She's wearing a tutu that seems to shroud her body in a diaphanous haze. She stops. She leans back, pressing her shoulders against the jamb, her lovely head drooping.

The officious man glares at her. He takes two quick paces across the room and confronts her, doffing his bowler as he does so.

'Well?'

'*I want to be alone*,' Garbo says.

'Where have you been? I suppose I could cancel any other contract'.

'*I just want to be alone.*'*

I just want to be alone.

Garbo's last film was *Two-Faced Woman*, a romantic comedy of modern manners directed by George Cukor. She played Karin Borg, a ski-instructor who impulsively marries a fashion journalist and regrets it almost immediately as she realizes she is expected to play the dutiful wife at the expense of her independence. They separate. He returns to New York and takes up with an old flame. In an oddly theatrical and old-fashioned twist, Garbo arrives in town and pretends to be Karin's twin sister, a hard-drinking, rumba-dancing man-eater who sets about seducing her 'sister's' husband. The theatrical trailer shows how self-consciously Cukor and Metro-Goldwyn-Mayer were trying to re-invent Garbo in this film. A white-lettered 'Who' does somersaults on the screen as it teases the audience with a series of questions:

* The *Grand Hotel* scene is on Youtube at https://www.youtube.com/watch?v=tojjWQvlPN8.

Who... is the screen's new Rhumba Queen?
Who... is still your Top-Ranking Star?
Who... doesn't 'want to be alone' anymore?

And then the revelation:

Garbo, that's who... and how.

By the strict standards of the time, Garbo's character was a deeply amoral woman and the film itself seen as a flippant and cynical attack on marriage. Following protests from the National League of Decency and the Catholic Church, several scenes were rewritten and reshot before it was eventually released in January 1942. The critics were dismayed. Of Garbo, who was thirty-six at the time but looks older, *Time* magazine wrote that to see her playing a lush was 'almost as shocking as seeing your mother drunk'. The public weren't keen either, their mood not helped by what must have seemed an unfairly sharp contrast between the frivolity of the film and the horror of the Japanese bombing of Pearl Harbor three weeks before its release. Garbo was the most revered actress in Hollywood at the time, but the poor reviews effectively ended her career, as she chose to reject the studio's suggestion that she 'didn't want to be alone any-more' and began her long life in inner exile.

In the same year as Hollywood effectively killed off Garbo by trying to turn her into a typically 'modern' American woman, the mantle of the world's favourite Swedish beauty passed to Ingrid Bergman, whose unearthly beauty and obvious intelligence, along with an aura of extraordinary decency and niceness which was at the same time sexy, were such an important part of the success of *Casablanca*. The film turned her into a world star, and for the remainder of the 1940s she made almost a film a year and was nominated for an Academy Award for Best Actress four times, winning the award for the first time in 1943, for *Gaslight*.

In 1950 she added another layer to the outside world's perception of Swedish womanhood when she fell in love with the Italian film

director Roberto Rossellini while filming *Stromboli* with him, and became pregnant with Rossellini's child while still married to her first husband, a Swedish dentist, with whom she already had a daughter. What shocked Middle America was that Ingrid Bergman showed no shame in the matter. She was quite open and natural about what had happened and so, for the next few years, found herself on one of Hollywood's ethical blacklists. Her untroubled acceptance of the break-up of her marriage and indifference to the moral outcry raised against her was probably as influential as anything else in fostering the idea that was such a central part of the perception of Scandinavian women during the second half of the twentieth century, among American and Britons particularly, that Swedes were unusually free from artificially induced guilt in matters to do with sex.

Bergman divorced her husband and married Rossellini shortly after the birth of their son. In due course her career revived and she won a second Oscar for her performance as *Anastasia* in Anatole Litvak's 1956 film about the life of the Romanov imposter 'princess'. Her penultimate film, before she died from breast cancer in 1982 at the age of sixty-seven, was Ingmar Bergman's *Autumn Sonata*, made in 1978, in which she played the part of a celebrated concert pianist whose success has come at the expense of a normal and stable family life. Throughout, her life and career had described a remarkably clear trajectory of the way those outside Scandinavia thought about Swedish women: the enigmatic love-object becoming the liberated female lover, becoming in turn a woman tormented by the tensions between the demands of motherhood and the urge to self-realization by way of a career. Throughout the 1960s and 1970s Ingmar Bergman had been refining and deepening this latest instalment in the story of Swedish womanhood, conducting an exploration and a portrayal of the female psyche as penetrating and illuminating as Henrik Ibsen's a century before him. Almost incidentally, films such as *Persona* and *Autumn Sonata* were schooling foreign audiences in a particular view of what Swedish women were like. And though they don't have the same depth or seriousness of purpose as Bergman's films, some of the most successful manifestations of the marketing trend known as 'Nordic noir', such as Stieg Larsson's 'Millennium' novels or the Swedish-Danish television series *The Bridge* (*Broen/Bron*), represent a continuation and development of this ongoing series of portraits. Sofia Helin as the Swedish detective Saga Norén ticks many of the traditional boxes: austerely beautiful, mysterious, strong, independent, highly intelligent in a flawed and possibly even pathological way.

In a pre-series promotional interview in 2015 with Helin a British journalist brought up the tricky question of a possible divide along sexual lines in the nature of viewers' interest in Saga Norén: how did Helin feel about the large numbers of men following the series who apparently saw her character as a sex symbol? Helin said she wasn't too happy about it: 'I heard she's a feminist icon and that's something I want to hear,' she replied. 'Some students at a Q and A in London said she is now a feminist icon and that made me really happy.' It's hard to imagine Garbo and Bergman – not to speak of Anita Ekberg – responding in quite the same way.

13

Dagny Juel and the
Invention of Melancholy

IN THE SUMMER OF 2013, A JOURNALIST FROM A DAILY newspaper in London telephoned me at my apartment in Oslo. The Legatum Institute in London had just published its Prosperity Index, a survey that claimed to offer 'the world's only assessment of factors that lead to higher levels of material wealth and subjective well-being', and the reporter wanted to talk to me about it. From the Institute's analysis of a total of eighty-nine variables, it had placed Norway at the top of a league-table of happy people living in happy countries. Great Britain was in thirteenth place of the 110 countries included in the survey. Zimbabwe, where the life expectancy of the average adult is forty-four, was bottom of the list. North Korea wasn't even on it. Factors included in the survey and identified as 'pillars of prosperity' ranged from purely economic indicators to abstract quantities such as social capital, personal freedom, and safety and security. Figures on rates of marriage and divorce, religious attendance, statistics about the numbers of citizens taking part in voluntary work, and surveys showing how much citizens trust each other were also included.

The journalist wanted to know whether I, as a long-time British resident of Norway, had any comments to make on the result.

A thousand responses flashed through my head, all of them positive. This is a very open society, I might have told her. It's not punitive. There's a strong sense among the people that the government will always respond to public concern. It's one of the most advanced countries in the world in terms of equality of opportunity and equality in rights between men and women. Up to 75 per cent of women are in employment, and the men often work in child-care roles. This is a society built on trust and faith in human nature. When a Norwegian does well in the outside world the whole country celebrates. It's as if a favourite son or daughter has brought honour on the family. Everyone shares in the achievement and feels a collective pride. There's very little backbiting. The country's two most popular tabloids – *Dagbladet* and *VG* – regularly carry book reviews. You'd never get that in the *Daily Mirror* or *The Sun*. Here, reputations are preserved for generations. The Nasjonalbiblioteket (National Library) in Oslo is currently running a twenty-five-year retrospective on the band a-ha, the Norwegian trio who had a string of hits in the 1980s and '90s. At one point in the 1990s, after Norway did quite well in the World Cup, there were some thirty or forty Norwegians playing for English Premier League clubs. One reason the managers liked them so much was because they were almost uniformly clean-living and decent people who trained hard and showed respect. You'd never get a Gazza or a George Best in Norway.

All of this I would gladly have said to her, but as luck would have it I was on my way out to pick up my father-in-law and drive him to a dental appointment and I was late already. When she asked if I could suggest another source I thought of my old friend Birger Rønning, a translator working from English into Norwegian who had spent many years of his childhood and schooldays in England, where his mother worked as a lecturer at the University of East Anglia. She thanked me and hung up, and I thought no more about it until an evening some months later when I met Birger at a Translators' Union social in Rådhus gata and in the course of our conversation remembered that phone call. I asked if the journalist had telephoned him.

'Yes, she called alright, but I don't think she used what I told her.'

'What did you tell her?'

'That I didn't believe a word of it. As if you could measure something like that. They're as bad as Jehovah's Witnesses, these rationalists. Religious faith, human love, human happiness – they think if they shine the light of reason on it all will be illuminated. I told her my truth, Robert. That people here aren't any happier than they are anywhere else. It wasn't what she wanted to hear. I expect she went to some know-all professor of sociology instead. Opinions on everything. He'd tell her what she wanted to hear.'

'So what did you tell her? You gave her the melancholy narrative instead?'

He groaned. 'That's the other end of the same cliché.' He already knew I intended to write a study of Scandinavian culture and made some disparaging remark about how he hoped I wouldn't be putting that in my book, that Scandinavians are gloomy and mentally unstable melancholics.

I protested. 'Come on, Birger. The Brits are funny but not very good at sex. The Italians are good at sex but not very funny. The French are intellectual. The Germans always wait for the green man before crossing. And when they're not knocking out high-quality furniture and committing suicide the Scandinavians sit in the darkness and think about doing it. They might not be the whole truth but these national characteristics are a useful shorthand guide.'

I was hoping to wind him up. Ever since the idea of writing a book about the history of Scandinavian culture first came to me I had assumed it would have a title with an allusion to melancholy in it. 'The Narrow Road to the Dark North' was one I thought of. Or 'Thirteen Types of Melancholy', something like that. But the further I got into the book the less faith I had in the truth of the idea.

Birger was suitably provoked. 'Scandinavian melancholy is a literary illusion,' he said as he put his glass of white wine down on a low table next to an untouched bowl of Twiglets. 'It's an artistic myth. Listen: Saga literature. August Strindberg. Edvard Munch's obsession with death. Ingmar Bergman's obsession with the failure to communicate.' He held a bunched hand up in front of him and with each name unfolded another finger. 'For a hundred years that's all the outside world ever knew about the Scandinavians. We were appointed official purveyors of melancholy to the rest of Europe. Anything that didn't fit the cliché, they didn't want to know about it. You remember Edward Said's *Orientalism*? The imposition of a cultural definition from outside? Well, this is Nordicism. We should sue somebody.'

I said it was an interesting theory but I wasn't convinced. What about *Inferno*, Strindberg's harrowing account of his descent into madness? And how did his theory square with Henrik Ibsen's famous remarks about the secluded and remote valleys and long dark nights of the winters turning every Norwegian inhabitant into a brooding philosopher?

Birger eased down into an armchair beside his wine glass and drained it. 'Ibsen was a professional Norwegian,' he said derisively. 'What did Ibsen know? He lived in bloody Italy most of his life. As for Strindberg, he's misunderstood. Strindberg was a joker. He's even funnier than Samuel Beckett. Listen. I'll tell you a Strindberg joke. After he asked Frida Uhl to marry him she told him she needed time to think about it. They arranged to meet on a certain date in the Red Room and she would give him her answer. When she gets there Strindberg is already sitting at his usual table. Near the back, in the shadow of the staircase, away from the light. He couldn't stand the light. It was one of the first things he told her. Something she had to know about him if the marriage was going to have any future at all. One of the first things he *impressed upon her*. Frida comes in. He doesn't look up but she can tell that he's registered her arrival. She shakes the wet snow from her frilly black umbrella, furls it and hangs it by its bone handle over the back of the chair next to his. She takes off her coat and sits down beside him. She's had all night to think about things and now here she is, ready to give him her reply. Strindberg looks as though he hasn't slept at all. His high, delicate cheekbones are flushed pink, the whites of his blue eyes are flecked with red as they flick restlessly around the red walls of the bar. Now and then they pass across her and she can almost feel her skin burning. Then, suddenly sitting upright in his chair, he reaches into the inside top pocket of the heavy black overcoat he's still wearing. He seems to feel about for something. But when he brings his hand out again it's empty. Now he erupts in a fit of dry coughing that almost doubles him over. Once he's recovered he straightens up again, eyes glinting feverishly. He shakes his head violently, as though to clear it. He rubs his lips hard with his fingertips, presses the waxed wings of his moustache upwards with the tips of his forefinger and thumb four or five times. Then, finally, his gaze fixes on her. She knows this is it, he's not going to look away until he has had her answer.

She takes a deep breath. Then a second, even deeper. And then: 'Yes, August,' she says. 'My answer is yes.'

She sees the tension drain from Strindberg's body. His shoulders sink down inside the black overcoat, the lapels and fur collar stand up from his chest. Again he reaches down into the inside pocket of the coat. This time, when his hand emerges, he's holding a slender-barrelled black pistol. Delicately, almost soundlessly, he places it on the table in front of him.

'Oh my God, August!' Frida whispers in horror. 'Would you have shot yourself if I'd said no?'

He looks at her in astonishment, his blue eyes wide. 'No,' he says, 'I would have shot you.'

Birger rose to his feet to bellow out the punch line, and heads turned, wondering what we were talking about. He ended by giving me a friendly pat on the shoulder, as though he hadn't enjoyed shattering my illusions, and admitted he had once read an interview with Strindberg, on the occasion of the Swede's sixtieth birthday, in which he revealed that he had first thought of killing himself at the age of seven.

'Although perhaps even that was a joke,' he added, half to himself.

I persisted. I said it was beyond the bounds of coincidence that every great Scandinavian writer, painter and film-maker should have concerned himself with an art that concentrated on the darkest and most painful aspects of human existence. Sickness. Death. The failure of love. I invoked the crop of *Dogme* films from Denmark, about incest, insanity, child abuse, the imminent end of the world. Surely, I said, you can't ignore thematic content as consistent as that?

Birger would have none of it. 'Those are all art films you're talking about. All those von Trier and Thomas Vinterberg films. And Ingmar Bergman. Art films are the only Scandinavian films foreigners ever see. Show them a film about the Olsen gang or one of those silly *selskapreise films*, those Lasse Åberg and Jon Skolmen films about idiots on package tours, and they'd walk out complaining that it wasn't the real Scandinavia. Or let them read Triztán Vindtorn's poetry instead of all this "Nordic noir" crap. Now there's a case of coals to Newmarket if I ever heard one.'

Birger's command of English was excellent, but some of the gaps in his grasp of idiom could still surprise me. He once told me he had commissioned a friend of ours, Erling Jonsrud, to paint a *self-portrait* of his dog Gunstein, the long-legged, sad-eyed poodle with whom he shared the house in Ljabru he had inherited on the death of his mother. On another occasion he gave me a harrowing description of the time Gunstein had been menaced in Frogner Park by an enormous black *ascension* dog. The films about the Olsen gang he was referring to were a series of films from the 1960s and '70s, about a gang of badly dressed and incompetent Norwegian criminals, farcical in tone and not unlike the *Carry On* films in spirit. Vindtorn was a surrealist Norwegian poet who, at the age of sixty-two, changed his name from Kjell Erik to Triztán.

I accused Birger of wilfully not seeing my point. He glared huffily at his empty glass and then disappeared through the crowd to replenish it. As so often happens at these dos I got into conversation with someone else almost immediately, a young woman with fragrant hair who wanted to pick my English brain for the meaning of a phrase in an English novel she was translating for Gyldendal, to 'push the envelope': what does it mean when you say someone is 'pushing the envelope'? I hadn't the faintest idea. Perhaps it had something to do with a bribe being offered? Money being pushed across a table in a fat envelope? But I failed to convince myself and in the end could only suggest she ask an American.

Later, as I was leaving, I passed Birger on the steps. He was talking to a chubby youth in a check shirt with red cheeks and a bushy beard, both of them smoking, the youth listening intently as Birger told his Alan Bates story, a story I had heard many times, but always late on in the evening, so that I never quite felt I had got the full gist of it, other than that he had once met the actor Alan Bates, or once for some reason spoken to him on the telephone around the time Bates was filming *Gosford Park*, and that Bates, imperfectly remembering his name, had addressed him throughout their conversation as 'Mr Trotting'. It was an inconsequential story, but the pleasure Birger derived from re-telling it was infectious. It had led him to develop a sort of obsession with Alan Bates, which, it has only recently occurred to me, may have had something to do with their sharing a faint facial resemblance, a phenomenon I have noticed before among certain of my friends as providing a credible explanation for an otherwise inexplicable passion. Without really breaking the thread of his tale he turned as I walked past on my way down the steps into the courtyard, tapped me on the shoulder and announced that he could not stand idly by and allow me to perpetuate the illusion of a congenital Scandinavian melancholy and ordered me to ring him and arrange a meeting at which he would demonstrate his theory of the artificial origin of the illusion irre*vo*cably, as he put it, dropping into English, as though no Norwegian word could possibly convey the absolute finality of what he was proposing to offer me, and jabbing my shoulder with his finger for emphasis. I said I would.

*

'I'm going to talk to you about what I call the Golden Age of Scandinavian melancholy,' he began in the familiar didactic manner that was one of the reasons I found his company so relaxing. It was the same whenever we met. Birger would do the talking, I would respond with a series of nods and hums and grunts, which every few minutes would turn into a whole sentence intended usually to encourage or provoke him into continuing. 'I'm going to prove to you that it is not a national characteristic unchanging down through the centuries. That it had its definite beginnings in a definite artistic environment and that it is the legacy of this quite specific artistic environment that leads directly to the films of Ingmar Bergman, the plays of Jon Fosse, and most strikingly to the school of "Scandinavian noir" novels that have become so popular recently in your country. That thanks to the lifestyles and creations of a handful of Scandinavian artists around the turn of the nineteenth century the rest of us have been cast in the role of experts on melancholy and madness and there is little we can do about it.'

It was mid-December. We had arranged to meet at Majorstua station and take the metro out to Skøyenåsen in the eastern suburbs of Oslo and then embark on a point-to-point stroll around Østensjø lake and on up past Rustadsaga to Skullerud, where we would pick up the metro or 74 bus back into Oslo. Leaving the station at Skøyenåsen we skirted the lower part of the lake and then took the forest path that leads up past an indoor ice-hockey stadium before descending along the open eastern side of the water. A faint humming sound came from a yellow Portakabin involved in some small lakeside clearing project. Periodically we glimpsed it as we climbed through the trees.

*

'Once upon a time there was a woman named Dagny Juel,' he began. 'She was born in Kongsvinger in 1867, into one of the leading families in Norway – in the days of the Sweden-Norway union her uncle Otto Blehr was the Norwegian prime minister in Stockholm. Her parents were enlightened people, modern people. The family was musical. Her sister was a fine singer. Edvard Munch painted the two of them at the piano once, Dagny with her back to us at the piano, Ragnhild facing us, singing. Very unmelancholic painting. Dagny wanted to be a writer. I know all this because I'm translating a new book about her. By an American academic. Dagny spent two years at some kind of finishing school in Erfurt, in Germany, where she became fluent in German. After that, she returned to Norway and a few years later moved to Kristiania to study music. In Kristiania she got to know a lot of artists and novelists and poets, people like Vilhelm Krag, Sigbjørn Obstfelder. She also got to know Edvard Munch. In February 1893 she went to Berlin to continue her music studies. She hooked up with Munch again and he introduced her to the crowd that hung out at a bar called Zum Schwarzen Ferkel, where all the exiled Scandinavian artists congregated. Strindberg, for example. Plus a smattering of men from other countries. Poles. Like Stanislaw Pryszbyszewski. Actually it wasn't called The Black Pig at all. Its real name was *Das Kloster*, but Strindberg thought the leather wineskins that hung above the door looked like three black pigs.'

We had reached the footbridge at the top of Østensjøvatnet, where the ducks congregate. Birger, already pale and panting from the exertions of the walk, though it had all been flat once we crested the forested knoll at the foot of the lake, took the opportunity to rest, leaning both arms on the wooden railing and affecting a keen interest in the mallards circling in the water below us and quacking for bread.

'I saw Woody Allen on a French television show once,' he said after a few moments. 'The interviewer asked him what he would like to come back as if he could choose. A sponge, he said. The interviewer laughed and asked why. He thought he was joking. Because a sponge is alive, said Woody Allen. It's alive but it's incapable of suffering.'

'And how would Woody Allen know that?'

Birger shrugged. 'Guessed, I suppose. Anyway. Dagny fell for

Pryszbyszewski, known as 'Stachu'. He was one year younger than her but living with a woman who already had three children by him. Pryszbyszewski was a hell-raiser. You know the type: he comes round to your house, drinks all your booze and is sick all over your carpet. He was a writer and a self-taught pianist, a wild man at the piano, jumping up and down on the stool while he played Schumann and Chopin. They were a musical crowd at The Black Pig. Strindberg used to take his guitar along sometimes and accompany himself in a special tuning of his own devising while he sang folk songs and ballads. Sigbjørn Obstfelder carried his violin about with him and played Grieg, Svendsen and Bach. Women are funny, aren't they? What they'll fall for. Dagny being a pianist herself I'm guessing it was Stachu's playing she fell for. He carried on seeing his old love but in August of that same year, 1893, he and Dagny got married.

'I'm trying to paint you a picture of a certain kind of environment, in which the two most famous names were Edvard Munch and August Strindberg. Strindberg was the oldest man in the group, over forty at this time. He was secretly engaged to an Austrian woman half his age, an actress named Frida Uhl. According to Strindberg, while Frida was away from Berlin he was Dagny's lover for three weeks and then, in his own gallant phrase, he *handed her over* to a young Swedish scholar named Bengt Lidforss. After that he embarked on a campaign of hatred of her. He writes a letter about her to a friend: she's rented a room in a red-light district, he says. The woman is a moral imbecile. Any day now the police are going to arrest her. It's like a bloody novel, he says. She breaks up happy homes and ruins talented men, drives them to leave their wives, their homes, their jobs, their responsibilities. Mind you, it's none of my business, he adds, she's someone else's mistress now. But for her own sake, and the sake of her family, he says in this letter, get someone to fetch her home.'

We had walked on now, under the flyover, and crossed to the other side of the lake and were ambling in the direction of Rustadsaga, where we planned to stop for a waffle and a cup of coffee. I remarked that his story showed yet again the great difference in personality between Strindberg and Henrik Ibsen.

'The author of the book I'm translating thinks these expressions of hatred for Dagny and horror at her destructive force can be explained by the fact that he was about to enter a binding relationship with Frida Uhl that would inevitably, to his way of looking at things, emasculate and enfeeble him. He needed a woman as a scapegoat. Dagny was handy.'

'Is that what you believe?'

He shrugged and scuffed the cindered path with the toe of his dirty white trainers.

'Possibly. Or perhaps she competed with him. He hated competition. I remember in your Hamsun biography, when Hamsun and Strindberg were in Paris, how he didn't like being around Hamsun because he said his personality was too strong. Dagny was strong. She had an easy, confident strength that maddened him. She wrote a play in 1895 called *Den sterkere* ["The Stronger"]. Strindberg had written a play six years before that was called *Den starkare* ["The Stronger"]. Well, there's only one thing stronger than the stronger, and that's the one that comes after it. I think she did it deliberately. She just didn't buy into his bullshit. Inventing a new tuning for the guitar. Discovering a new planet all by himself. And why not? It's hilarious. Of course it is – if you look *with* Strindberg. It doesn't work if you look *at* him. I think Dagny looked *at* him, and he couldn't take it.'

Birger stopped again, panting heavily, as the path rose slightly, heading away from the football fields at the northern end of the lake. Struggling to get his breath back he glared at the grass on either side of the footpath and made some obviously diversionary remark about how worrying it was that there was no snow yet. Nearly Christmas and still no snow. As I knew he hadn't the slightest interest in climate change I let this pass, and once he'd recovered we carried on at the same easy shuffle as he resumed his attempts to prove to me *irrevocably* that Scandinavian melancholy was either a myth, a piece of pernicious Nordicism, or even a commercial construction.

'Of course, Strindberg's hatred of Dagny may have been merely an artistic convenience. For the purposes of his writing he needed someone to hate. It could have been anyone, but it happened to be her. He wrote about her. Dagny was his dark muse. His Aspasia in *Inferno* and *Svarta fanor*, his Henriette in *Brott och Brott*, his Laïs in *Klostret* and *Karantänmästarns andra berättelse*. Edvard Munch used her in his paintings and lithographs too. Dagny was his orgasmic *Madonna*. His *Vampyr*. He used her in *Sjalusi, Aske, Kyss*. She wasn't beautiful. She must have been what people call attractive. You had to *be* there to get it. Look at any photograph of her, then look at Munch's *Madonna*. Look at the eyes. She was everyone's model. Stachu used her in his first novel, *Totenmesse*.* He used her again in *Overbord*. He used her over and over again. What a life. Everybody's muse. It must have worn her out. Stachu used Munch in *Overbord* too, the first part of his *Homo Sapiens* trilogy. About a writer who steals a woman from his painter friend. So Munch used him. Again and again. The haunted, white-faced goat-boy staring out at us from paintings like *Jealousy* or *Red Virginia Creeper*, that is Stachu.'

'Was this before or after Munch painted *Scream*?'†

'Munch painted *Scream* for the first time in 1893, so this was right in the middle. Late in 1895 Dagny gave birth to a boy, Zenon. Stachu was still seeing the woman he'd left for Dagny, a woman named Martha Foerder.' Birger sighed. 'You read about these people and you wonder how they had the stamina. Some didn't. In June 1896 Martha killed herself. Stachu was arrested on suspicion of being involved with her death and held in jail for two weeks before being released without charge. In the winter of 1897 Dagny gave birth to their second child, a daughter christened Iwa. Stachu was starting to make his name in native Poland and he was offered the job as editor of *Zycie*, a literary magazine published in Cracow,

---

* These works by Strindberg have appeared in English as *Black Banners* (*Svarta fanor*), *Crimes and Crimes* (*Brott och Brott*), *The Cloister* (*Klostret*) and *The Quarantine Master's Second Story* (*Karantänmästarns andra berättelse*). Munch's paintings, in English, are *Jealousy* (*Sjalusi*), *Ashes* (*Aske*) and *Kiss* (*Kyss*). Stachu's *Totenmesse* translates as 'Requiem'.

† Munch's title is *Skrik*, 'scream'. English usually adds a definite article, calling it *The Scream*.

so in 1898 the family moved to Poland. A few months later Dagny's father died. She wasn't able to get home for the funeral. Her husband was an alcoholic and a serial adulterer. She had two young kids. She couldn't speak a word of the language. So there she was, trapped in Poland with this mediocre, flashy shit.' He said this last with such venom that I glanced at him and wondered fleetingly if, in the course of translating her biography, he might have fallen in love with Dagny himself. But his round, owlish face betrayed nothing.

'So she left him. Left Poland and the children and spent most of 1900 travelling around. She was in Berlin, Prague, Paris, back home in Kongsvinger, Stockholm. And then she decided to give Stachu another chance. Because of the children I suppose. So it turns out she wasn't Nora Helmer after all. Stachu said he was willing.'

We had passed under the railway bridge that carries the metro's Line 3 and were clambering up the steep rise that the brown footpath takes before it enters the dense forests of the Østmarka. It had started drizzling and the track was lightly coated with mud and slippery. Birger must have stopped five times in the course of the short climb, right hand flat against his heaving chest, face pale and glinting with a combination of rain and sweat, the wispy brown hair sticking to his forehead. I found myself wondering what to do if he collapsed, but he made it to the top after a couple more stops and a few minutes later we were sitting inside the café at Rustadsaga.

It's a typically Norwegian ramblers' café of the type that are dotted throughout the forests of the *marka*, cocooned in a 1950s atmosphere with wooden walls adorned with fly-specked black-and-white photographs of the innocent people of that time, in their heavyweight anoraks and ancient wooden skis. Rustadsaga was a place to sit and stare out of the window at the trees and through them catch blue glimpses of the waters of Lake Nøklevann while munching on a warm golden waffle folded over a few thin slices of sweet-tasting Norwegian brown cheese. If they really wanted to find out why Norwegians seemed so content, I thought to myself, all the people at the Legatum Institute needed to do was take a walk up here and spend half an hour over a coffee and waffle at Rustadsaga.

Although we had spoken of quite other things for the past fifteen minutes, Birger resumed his narrative, after returning to the table with a second cup of coffee, as though he had only just left off.

'They had a friend who hung out at The Black Pig, a young Pole in his early twenties named Wladislav Emeryk. Known as the Dog on account of his slavish devotion to Stachu. His father was a millionaire industrialist and Emeryk had invited them to stay at the family home near Tbilisi. I imagine poor Dagny thought Stachu might have grown up and turned over a new leaf now that he'd made his name in Poland. And he could write a love letter. Listen to this.'

Birger picked up his rucksack, unfastened the straps and pulled out an iPad. He tapped the screen a couple of times, pulled up his translation and began to read from it:

Min Ducha, [...] Now, only now do I realise that I love you [...]
I remember [...] how you put up with me when I was drunk, how
you have suffered and rejoiced with me, I see your lovely, refined,
aristocratic cheek and feel your delicate, silky panther skin in my
hands [...] I want you to know that it is you who have made me, and I
want to possess you as I have never before possessed you: your naked,
quivering soul, your naked and quivering thoughts [...] A nature such
as mine can only exist in you, because you alone are my absolute,
highest, most intimate ideal [...] I will write the most wonderful
things, I will tower through the skies, I will do everything, everything,
everything. But I must know that you love me.

He looked up from the screen: '*Ducha*, that means "soul" in Polish.
It's what he called her. So of course, she goes to the station with
Zenon and their suitcases and everything. And Emeryk is there, and
they wait for Stachu. And he never turns up. At the last moment, he
sent a telegram saying he was delayed and they should go ahead,
he would join them with Iwa as soon as he could. So in April
1901 these three left Warsaw and began the long rail journey to
the Caucasus.

In mid-May they reached Tbilisi. Emeryk booked them in at
the Grand Hotel, pretending to be Dagny's brother. Nothing from
Stachu. Not a word, not a letter, not a note. He has her passport. As
the days pass her despair and bewilderment increase.'

Birger cleared his throat, adjusted his glasses and read from the
screen again:

My mind is frozen. A month, and not one single word from you. I
have telegraphed Cracow, Lvov and Warsaw – no answer. Okay then!
Tomorrow we leave Tbilisi for Emeryk's place in the countryside by
the Black Sea. I cannot, of course, make any further arrangements
until I have heard from you. My address remains Grand Hotel, Tbilisi.
Very important: you must immediately send a passport for me and
Zenon. It could cause me great difficulties if you don't. You promised
to send the passport after two days! I'm begging you: do it now.

'The same day she wrote this,' Birger went on, 'Emeryk came into the hotel room where she was dozing in a chair. She had her back to the door. Zenon was sitting on the floor with a colouring book. He looked up as Emeryk entered. Emeryk put a finger to his lips, admonishing silence, and held out his hand to the boy. Zenon took it and Emeryk walked him in silence down the corridor and into a room where a friend of his was staying. He kissed him, then returned to Dagny's room and shot her through the back of the head at close range. He lifted her body out of the chair and arranged it on the bed. Then he shot himself. Five days earlier at the hotel he had written and sealed a number of letters that showed the murder was long premeditated. One was to Stachu. Stachu, he wrote, I'm killing her for her own sake. Another was to Zenon. On the front of the sealed envelope he wrote that it was to be given to the boy on his twentieth birthday:

> My dearest Zenon! I am taking your mother from you. You will hear the strangest things about her, but literature – both what has been written and what will surely be written – will not give you […] the truth. For she was not of this world […] That she was the only one of the absolute Almighty's incarnations, that she was God, you will hear from others. I wish only to say, to express myself in an earthly way, that she was holy. She was Goodness itself, she had a royal goodness which came from contempt. You alone were everything for her […] She believed that her goal, that her reason for being sent here – was to give birth to you. I am taking her from you. I am doing you a terrible, boundless wrong. Maybe your life will be ruined by it. I cannot do anything else, I cannot do anything else out of concern for her. In eternity, when we meet …

'I think a lot about this murder,' Birger said, closing the screen, slipping the iPad back into his rucksack. 'Perhaps I shouldn't do. But it keeps me awake at night. The papers were full of it. Apparently it was all her fault. She was this *femme fatale*, this home-wrecker, heartbreaker, etcetera, etcetera. A French paper even managed to get the two Strindbergs mixed up, writing that August had been in love with

Dagny, and when she rejected him in despair he signed up for Andrée's balloon expedition to go to the North Pole and was never heard from again. And the whole extraordinary rumour mill started grinding. To this day there are people who believe Stachu was behind it, that Stachu had asked the Dog to clear up a messy situation for him.'

'That was the only reason Emeryk gave for killing her? That insane babble about how ethereal she was?'

He nodded. 'And yet, this pointless and unspeakably cruel murder came about only because this quite normal woman was sufficiently grown up to be able to think of men as friends, a feat of the imagination that appears to have been beyond the reach of these sex-obsessed geniuses, these men-children she found herself among. In my view the story encapsulates the whole myth of Scandinavian melancholy, though that's hardly the right word, Scandinavian melancholy, mental disturbance, sexual darkness, insanity, whatever. It can stand as an unmasking of the whole sorry myth. It spread through Scandinavian art. It penetrated everywhere. Like water. Edvard Munch was convinced that Irene in Ibsen's last play *When We Dead Awaken* was

based on Dagny – you remember how in that play Irene was the sculptor Professor Rubeck's model, his muse?'

'Do we know if Zenon ever read that letter?'

'I don't know. But a friend of mine told me a curious story concerning him. My friend was a conscientious objector and he opted to do *samfunnstjeneste** instead of military service and found himself working as an attendant at the Munch Museum in Tøyen. He told me that one day

---

* This is a community service, an alternative to military service in Norway.

a rather sad and defeated-looking elderly Swedish man arrived at the museum accompanied by his wife. My friend said he asked to be directed to 'Munch's portrait of my mother'. He said he had seen reproductions of it but never the original painting. As luck would have it the painting wasn't on display at that time – they don't have room for everything on the walls. The head of the museum was called – I think it might have been Arne Eggen – and when the Swedish gentleman explained who he was, he was allowed down into the basement. Eggen went down with him, to show him where to find the painting and to set it up for him, and then he found a chair for him to sit on, placed it in front of the portrait and left him alone. His wife waited upstairs for him in the cafeteria. He spent a long time down there, just looking at Munch's portrait of his mother. Half an hour at least. And when he came back up again, my friend said, he seemed like another man. He said you would hardly have recognised him. The experience had transfigured him.'

Birger drank the last of his coffee, stood up and shouldered his rucksack. 'Come on, or we'll never get to Skullerud.'

What did Birger think he had proved? That it was these painters and writers, living this particular kind of life and creating this particular kind of art, who had *created* the national trope of the Scandinavian that so much of the rest of the world responds to even today? That *The Bridge*, Mankell, all of this is gloomy merely because it comes from Scandinavia, where everybody makes gloomy art because gloom was what they inherited from their nineteenth-century forefathers? Absurd. And what about Henrik Ibsen? Apart from the illegitimate child he fathered from his days at the chemist's shop in Grimstad, Ibsen led a life that makes Trollope look like Henry Miller. But surely it was Ibsen more than any of those alcoholic bohemians, with his enormous fame, with his Brands and his Gregers Werle, his fru Alvings and his Osvalds, his Hedvigs and his Rebecca Wests, the incest, the syphilis, the blindness, the suicide, surely he was the one who had schooled the rest of Europe in this perception of Scandinavians? No. Birger's 'Nordicism' argument was unduly cynical. Kierkegaard thought the way he did, Ibsen wrote the way he did, Strindberg wrote and painted the way he did, Munch painted and wrote the way he did, Bergman made the films he made because they *could not do otherwise*. And if this were not the case, where was the Swedish Oscar Wilde? The Danish Noel Coward? The Norwegian Tom Stoppard? No, Ibsen was naturally attracted to darkness. Scandinavians are naturally attracted to the shadows.

I argued this to Birger all the way as we followed the twisting path through the trees towards Skullerud. I half-expected him to mount a renewed defence of his theory about how a handful of drink-sodden bohemians, entirely untypical of the average Scandinavian, were responsible for the whole image outsiders have of them. But he seemed to have wearied of the discussion and instead started talking about how important Ibsen had been to the writers of Nordic noir. With a wave of the hand he reeled off a few names: Jo Nesbø, Liza Marklund, Peter Høeg, Stieg Larsson....

Concerned not to let him duck what seemed to me a clear flaw in his train of thought, I protested that their inspirations were rather American, such as Raymond Chandler, Joseph Wambaugh, Elmore Leonard, Michael Connelly, and that while Ibsen was certainly responsible for the creation of the modern theatre, with his revolutionary idea of dramatizing the lives and problems of his own contemporaries, the crime novel as a genre was actually the invention of another American, Edgar Allan Poe.

'A sad case of cultural imperialism,' he replied obdurately. 'Nothing has been invented until it has been invented by an American or an Englishman. Or in the case of James Joyce and the stream of consciousness, an Irishman, since that was discovered and first used by our own Knut Hamsun in *Mysteries*, published back in 1894. No, the modern crime novel was actually the invention of an obscure nineteenth-century Norwegian writer named Mauritz Christoffer Hansen, born on July 5th 1794 in Modum. His novella *Mordet på Maskinbygger Roolfsen* ["The Murder of Engineer Roolfsen"] was published in 1839, a full eighteen months before Poe's *Murders on the Rue Morgue* appeared. It has all the hallmarks of the classically structured crime novel as we know it today. It is focused throughout on the investigation of a crime committed by a person or persons unknown. There is a detective, a lawyer and a police chief who interview suspects and witnesses in a slow and methodical attempt to create a complete picture of the actual train of events. Among the clues that emerge, one provides an early example of the use of forensics.

Putting all his information together, Barth, the investigator, arrives at a surprise double-solution. One is that the guilty party is the city's most powerful man, the person who has pressed most strongly for a quick and successful resolution of the case. The other is that Roolfsen hasn't been murdered at all, but disappears in such a fashion that everybody thought he had been. In contrast to his literary descendents like Arsène Lupin, Sherlock Holmes and Hercule Poirot, Johannes Barth is a realistic, everyday character, even to the point of having a strong weakness: the main suspect's mother was the love of his young life. She wouldn't have him, because he came from a lower social class, but his feelings for her have never died.

Hansen never made much money from his writing and sustained himself mainly by teaching and writing textbooks of grammar. He died at the age of forty-eight, three years after the publication of *The Murder of Engineer Roolfsen*. He left no school behind him and his books were soon forgotten. He did have one famous pupil, though. Henrik Ibsen was notoriously cagey about his influences, but in an autobiography he began writing but never finished Mauritz Hansen is one of the few names he mentions as being among his early reading. The retrospective technique Ibsen used in his plays from contemporary life, where the secrets of the past are slowly stripped away, layer by layer, until the truth of a present situation is laid bare, is the very essence of all crime writing, and owes much to what he learned from books like *The Murder of Engineer Roolfsen*.

After I had listened to Birger's deconstruction of the myth of Scandinavian gloom, with which I thought he seemed overly satisfied, we walked on in silence, heading for the metro station at Skullerud to catch a train back to the centre of Oslo. I was feeling obscurely defeated, as if I hadn't worked hard enough to defend a point of view I instinctively felt to be true.

Outside a Narvesen newspaper kiosk at the head of the station I stopped in my tracks: 'What about *Hamlet*?' I crowed. 'Where does *that* come from?'

'Hamlet wasn't a real person,' he countered implacably, walking on, turning down the station slope. He was right, of course, and there was no more to be said about it.

On the train into town Birger spent a lot of time looking out the window, frowning at his reflection in the glass, shaking his head now and then, as though conducting an inner debate. It occurred to me that he might consider his victory a mere technical knockout. Encouraged by the thought, I decided to take another crack at it.

'Well alright then, leaving aside the fact that in Saxo Grammaticus's history Hamlet is a real person, explain to me where Shakespeare got the characteristics from? The madness? The intensity? The endless and futile philosophizing? Hamlet had to be a Scandinavian *because only Scandinavians are like Hamlet*. Hamlet was an Elizabethan cliché. A high-class one, yes, but still a cliché.'

Birger snorted. 'Nonsense,' he said. 'He got it from John Dowland. Dowland was in Denmark at precisely the period when Shakespeare was writing *Hamlet*.* He was member number 140 of Det Kongelige Kapel at King Christian IV's court at Elsinore.'

'Dowland had a *number*?'

'They all had numbers. The Danish Royal Orchestra is the oldest functioning orchestra in the world. Founded in 1448 and still going strong. They had to keep track of them somehow. Or maybe Shakespeare got it from number fifty-six, William Kempe. Kempe was also a member of the Chamberlains' Men at the same time as Shakespeare and Richard Burbage. Carl Nielsen, the great Danish symphonist, was number six hundred and fifty-seven.'

Brushing aside a sudden fear that he might be about to give me the names and numbers of everyone who had ever joined the orchestra I asked him whether there was any proof of Dowland and Shakespeare even knowing each other, never mind swapping influences?

---

* Dowland was in Denmark between 1598 and 1606, and the writing of *Hamlet* is usually dated to a time between 1599 and 1602.

Birger paused a moment before responding. He removed his spectacles in their heavy black frames and stared at them with a dazed frown, as if he'd never seen them before. He huffed on each lens in turn before polishing them on a corner of the faded black T-shirt that was hidden beneath his oatmeal-coloured pullover and that I knew from experience carried an image of Henrik Ibsen and lines from *Brand* which I had always thought particularly appropriate for my intransigent friend: *Det som du er, vær/ fullt og helt/ og ikke stykkevis og delt* – 'Be what you are with all your heart, not now and then, and just in part'. Then, with a peculiar, twisting lunge, he wedged his face back inside the spectacles.

'It's unthinkable that they did not know each other,' he asserted with a weary patience. 'In all likelihood they were friends. Probably very good friends. I see them in the corner of some dark tavern. Let's say The Boar's Head in Eastcheap. Shakespeare is working on *Hamlet*. He's picking Dowland's brains over a pint of ale. What are the Danes like, John? How would you describe them? "A sad and troubled people, William," says Dowland. "They think too much." "Just give me a few key words," says Shakespeare. "Melancholy," says Dowland. "Sorrow. Trouble. Gloom." But you know what Dowland was doing, don't you?' Birger went on. 'He was projecting his own melancholy onto the Danes. Dowland was describing himself. If he'd been at Versailles, and talking about the French, he would have said exactly the same things. I do it. You do it. We *all* do it.

With this QED, Birger sat back in the seat, folded his arms and stared out the window again. As the train slowed to stop at Høyenhallen station he sat up, suddenly very alert, shading his eyes as he stared out the window.

'See that house there?' he said, without turning to look at me, pointing down across the roof of a school to a house standing on its own in a wintry garden. There was a strange, tight excitement in his voice, as though the sight of the house both frightened and exhilarated him. I leaned forward to look. A low white picket fence ran along either side of a muddied driveway leading up past the front of the house. The roof was tiled in black. A thin bare tree stood guard outside the entrance, and the single most striking thing about the house was the brilliant red Virginia creeper that covered almost its entire front. 'I used to live there when I first got married,' he said. 'We had the ground floor.'

I was astounded. I had known him for twenty years and never heard him even mention a wife. 'I didn't know you were ever married, Birger,' I said. 'How long were you married for?'

'Nine days,' he said as the train pulled into the station. 'She ran off with —.' And here he named of one of Norway's most famous novelists. 'She was pregnant at the time.'

'So you're a father?' I said, even more surprised.

'No,' he said, turning his head away with such finality that I asked no further questions.

⋆

We said goodbye to each other at the National Theatre, and I exited up the pedestrian ramp into the street behind the theatre, past the two Roma musicians who had claimed the ramp as their own for the past few weeks. With Christmas just a couple of weeks away they were singing a full-throated version of 'Jingle Bells' that mysteriously segued into 'La Bamba' before returning to 'Jingle Bells' again. I crossed Stortingsgata to buy an English paper at the Narvesen opposite the station, the most well-stocked kiosk in town because of its proximity to the Continental Hotel, forgetting yet again that they had recently and permanently ceased to stock any English dailies, apart from the *Financial Times*. Apparently the importer no longer found it profitable. The curse of the internet.

Thwarted in my plan to spend an hour in some quiet booth in Burns' with an English newspaper, a beer and an aquavit I decided go to the National Museum and take another look at Munch's *Scream*. I crossed back over the road and slanted across the cobbled open ground in front of the National Theatre, passing Sinding's two huge statues of Ibsen and Bjørnson on their cylindered plinths, Ibsen with hands clasped behind his back and head bowed, to my eyes obviously brooding and inward, Bjørnstjerne Bjørnson the very image of the self-assured chieftain he was in life, his chest puffed out, arms akimbo and head tilted back looking, Ibsen once remarked, as though he were taking part in a spitting contest.

Crossing by the Hard Rock Café on the corner of Karl Johan I made my way up Universitets gate to the National Gallery. I can never climb the steps to the gallery without thinking of the time *Scream* was stolen back in the 1990s, while the attention of the whole country and its police force was focused on the opening ceremony of the Winter Olympics at Lillehammer, two hours away from Oslo by car. The thief was a small-time gangster from Tveita named Pål Enger. In his youth Enger had been a talented footballer, good enough to play a few games for Vålerenga, the biggest club in Oslo, until they had to let him go after he was caught going through his team-mates' pockets in the dressing-room.

Birger had mentioned the Olsen gang films. Well, the way Enger stole the *Scream* could have come straight out of one of those old Olsen gang caper-films. At seven-thirty on the morning of 12 February 1994 he had propped a ladder up against the gallery wall just in front of the steps, climbed up it, fallen down it, climbed up it

again, smashed a window, jumped inside, grabbed the painting off the wall and climbed back down the ladder with it, hopped into the stolen Mazda Estate that was waiting at the kerb and driven off. The whole thing was caught on CCTV cameras, though the definition wasn't good enough to enable an identification. As soon as Enger jumped down onto the gallery floor a motion sensor set off an alarm in the guard room. The security guard on duty looked up from his book, turned it off, and went back to his reading. As for the ladder, Enger and an accomplice, both dressed in black, had carried it through the streets of Oslo late the night before without being challenged, and with a quick left-right-left-again glance up and down Universitetsgata hidden it behind the bushes against the gallery wall. People must have seen them but assumed their behaviour had a reasonable explanation. It made me think of the Legatum Report, and the top score Norwegians got for trusting each other.

Enger was arrested, tried and sentenced in 1996 to six years in jail for the theft. When sentence was handed down, he leapt onto a courtroom table, smashed a water jug and had to be restrained by the police. 'I am innocent!' he shouted as he was dragged away. Enger continued to deny it until 2008, when he was serving a one-year sentence for the theft of some duvets from an abandoned caravan, and two pairs of socks from a Kiwi supermarket. As part of an art project that consisted of photographs of prisoners accompanied by personal statements, Enger offered, as his contribution, a written confession: he had kept Munch's painting hidden in a specially concealed compartment in a relative's kitchen table.

Standing in front of the gallery's version of Munch's extraordinary foetal image – one of the five different versions he painted – I recalled another thread in the strange history of this painting. How, in the media frenzy and chaos of theories that followed the theft, the anti-abortion priests Børre Knudsen and Ludvig Nessa had requisitioned the event for their own cause, hinting at their involvement in it as part of their long and lonely campaign against Norway's liberal abortion laws. They published a sketch showing a hand closed firmly around the defenceless subject of *Scream*: 'Which is more valuable?'

went the caption, 'A painting or a child?' Police with plexiglass riot shields had to protect Knudsen from the spitting and stone-throwing of the Anti-Nazi League supporters in the crowd when he took the stage at an anti-abortion rally held at Spikersuppa in central Oslo and enacted his impression of *Scream* as part of the same campaign.

14
Malexander

SEVERAL DECADES AGO A STORY APPEARED IN A NUMBER of English newspapers about a man named Frank Mitchell, an associate of the Kray brothers known to the press as 'the Mad Axeman'. Mitchell was serving a jail sentence in Dartmoor at the time but was allowed out now and then to take a pint in the village local. On this one occasion it was pouring with rain by the time he got back to the jail. He was soaking wet and then had to stand outside hammering on the gates and ringing the bell for five minutes before a warder eventually appeared. 'What kept you?' he roared when the prison gates were finally opened, 'I'm fucking drenched!'

I thought of that story earlier this year while reading Elisabeth Åsbrink's book about the murders that took place, in 1999, in the sleepy Östergötland village of Malexander, in the south of Sweden. In a general review of the liberal regimes in Swedish prisons, she describes an occasion in 1975 when Gunnar Engström, governor of Umeå prison in the north of Sweden, received so many requests from girlfriends and mothers of prisoners that in the end he gave up and decided to let them all go home for the Christmas weekend. The press got wind of the incredible story, a journalist called to verify it. Engström made some excuse and asked the journalist to call him back in ten minutes. Then he rang round the various wings to find out if everyone had returned. Don't worry, he was told, they're all back, although Tärna-Johan is still pretty much legless. A few minutes later, when the journalist rang back as instructed, Engström was able tell him that yes, it was true, and that the venture had been a complete success. The story of the empty jail went round the world, offering further confirmation of the fact that the Swedes appeared to be living on a different and more advanced planet than the rest of us when it came to the treatment of prisoners, and even seemed to be making it work.

It's hard to place exactly when Sweden's reputation for a radical willingness to question conventional wisdom on issues such as the best way to treat criminals and the most practical way to harmonize the sexual instinct with the need for an ordered society arose. Watching Delmer Daves' 1959 film *A Summer Place* recently, I noticed how Helen Jorgenson, played by Constance Ford, in the furious and bitter tirade she levels at her film husband Ken (Richard Egan), blames his tolerant attitude towards the relationship between their daughter Molly and local boy Johnny Hunter on Ken's Swedish roots. 'Sweden,' she snarls, 'with its *trial marriages*.' It was a reminder of how surprisingly venerable this reputation is.

Of course, experiments such as Engström's at the Umeå prison don't always work out, and when they don't the Swedes themselves are the first to laugh. In April 1985, the theatre director Jan Jönson was working on a production of Samuel Beckett's *Waiting for Godot* with five inmates of Kumla prison. Hoping it might lead to a further rehabilitation of his actor-prisoners, all of whom were serving long sentences for drug offences, he arranged to give the play a public performance at Gothenburg City Theatre. Minutes before the curtain went up four of the five actors slipped out the emergency exit and made their escape. Beckett was told the story and got a good laugh out of it, and in 1999 the Swedish director Daniel Lind Lagerlöf made it the basis of his comedy *Vägen ut* ('Way Out'). But in the year Lagerlöf's film appeared, another idealistic experiment with similar farcical potential led instead to tragedy and a film of a very different kind.

At the time of this particular experiment, ten prisoners in the '7:3' category were being held in the maximum security wing of Tidaholm prison in Västra Götaland county. The categorization derived from a sub-section of the 1974 penal code outlining the treatment of men considered most likely to try to escape – men most deeply committed to the path of criminality, those with the greatest resistance to any attempt to rehabilitate them. Prisoners in this category were held in individual cells of about the same size and standard of comfort as the student accommodation found in any Scandinavian student village, the differences being the bars on the windows and the reinforced steel doors with peephole. Knives in the communal kitchen were anchored to heavy blocks by steel wires to prevent their being removed. Outside the wing was a small grassy compound, in which the inmates paced up and down, or round and round, as the mood took them. Time hung heavy in such a place. There was little for the men to do except watch the television each had facing him at the end of his bed, and to pump iron endlessly in the prison gymnasium.

The idea of theatre as therapy is an ancient one, and one day the prison governor suggested the men form a theatre group. It would help pass the time, she suggested, and might give them greater self-insight. Of the four who expressed an interest one dropped out almost immediately. The three who remained were:

Carl Thunberg, aged thirty-two, leader of a gang of armed robbers known in the Swedish press as the 'Military League' for the precision of their planning and efficiency of their operations. Thunberg was serving a fourteen-year sentence for robbing some ten or twelve banks.

Tony Olsson, aged twenty-five, convicted of numerous offences of theft and currently serving a six-year sentence for conspiracy to commit murder.

Mats Nilsson, aged twenty-two, serving a five-year sentence for assaulting a police officer and robbing a cash transport.

Unsure how to proceed with their plans, the three men decided to write to Lars Norén, a dramatist of almost legendary status, widely recognized as Sweden's greatest since August Strindberg, though his early influences were more the American chroniclers of dysfunctional family life like Eugene O'Neill and Tennessee Williams. Norén was regarded by many as the conscience of the liberal middle class and enjoyed a moral authority and a degree of adulation that has no direct parallel among contemporary British or American writers. Carl Thunberg wrote the letter in March 1998. He told Norén who and where they were, and that they wanted to start a theatre group. He asked whether Norén had a play with parts for four men that they could rehearse and perform. They scarcely even expected a reply and were astonished not only to receive one, but to read that Norén wanted to visit Tidaholm himself and meet them.

Norén duly turned up at the prison one day accompanied by Isa Sternberg from Riksteatern, the National Touring Theatre of Sweden. Norén was artistic leader of the company, Sternberg a producer who had worked closely with him on numerous projects. They met and talked with the prisoners. They drank coffee and munched buns together. They got on well. Isa Sternberg wrote in her diary that the men were 'relaxed, nice and amusing' as well as being 'articulate, intelligent and well-read'. The plight of these young men touched them and they determined to do something to help them. The prisoners were initially disappointed to hear that Norén could not offer them a play that matched their specific requirements, but delighted when he offered them something even better: a play written especially for them.

Norén had recorded those first conversations, and when he and Sternberg returned to Tidaholm on 20 April he showed them a draft first act of the new play. It turned out to be closely based on their earlier conversations. The prisoners were distinctly underwhelmed but remained flattered and proud to have attracted the attention of such a celebrated and admired figure as Norén, and they decided to continue with the project. This became the pattern of all subsequent meetings. What the four of them argued about, laughed about, raged

about – all of it was recorded and laboriously transcribed by Isa
Sternberg, who then handed it over to Norén for shaping. Gradually,
the three men realized that what Norén wanted was for them to
play themselves. Disgusted with the falsity and pretensions of conventional theatre, he wanted now to write a play that could hardly
be described as a play at all and yet defied every attempt to prove
that it wasn't a play. He wanted his prisoner-actors to *be* themselves,
to express their views on anything and everything under the sun
in a wholly free and uncensored way. And since they were neither
delivering lines nor pretending, like real actors, to be who they were
not, Norén gave them their own names in the play. They were Mats,
Tony and Carl playing Mats, Tony and Carl. The only exception
to this strict realism was the fourth member of the cast, the writer
himself, whose name was not Lars but 'John'. Rehearsals consisted
of learning as 'lines' things they themselves had previously said in
the course of discussion, debate and argument. Norén gave them
full access to the script as it developed and encouraged them to take
issue with anything he had written that they found problematical.
If they felt passionately enough about it Norén removed the
offending lines, even where this went counter to his better artistic
judgement. In due course Norén brought in a professional actor
from Riksteatern to play his part, the part of the writer sitting in one
of the four chairs and urging Mats, Tony and Carl to open up to him.
'John' was played by Reine Brynjolfsson, one of Sweden's leading
actors and well known to Swedish audiences, especially from his role
as the vicar in *Änglegård* ('House of Angels'), a feel-good hippy film
directed by the Swedish-based British director Colin Nutley, which
was a huge box-office success in Sweden in the early 1990s.

The meetings-cum-rehearsals came to a halt over the summer and
resumed in the autumn. Norén's brooding passion for the project
was contagious. At the end of October he had a meeting with
Gunnar Engström, the governor who had so successfully emptied
Umeå over twenty years earlier and who was now administrative
head of the prison service in Stockholm. Engström gave Lars Norén's
project his enthusiastic backing and promised his support all the

way to the premiere – because this had gone so far by now that it had been decided an essential part of the therapeutic aim of the process must be to take the play outside the walls of the prison and perform it in front of a paying audience. That meant parole for the actor-prisoners, days out, lots of them, socializing, enjoying the status their association with Lars Norén gave them, roaming the corridors of the Riksteatern's premises, hanging out with the theatre's elite, riding the cutting edge of advanced thought in Sweden. The prisoner-actors found themselves enjoying most of the privileges of free men. Over the fifteen or so months of his association with the project, Tony Olsson was given ninety days' home leave, sometimes with an overnight stay thrown in.

As the winter drew on and rehearsals progressed it became apparent that Isa Sternberg had developed what seemed, to the regional prison governor Birgitta Göransson, an over-intense identification with the three personable young inmates. Her mothering instincts appeared to have come into play. Worried, Göransson asked all four of them to a meeting at which she stressed the importance of keeping things professional. The drama group was therapy, occupational and psychological. That was as far as it went. But the warning came a little too late. As Olsson's designated contact, Isa Sternberg had arranged for him to stay at her house on his overnight paroles; but she was an indulgent minder and on many occasions had no idea where he *actually* spent the night. Her commitment to the project was so complete, her unwillingness to keep a buffer space between herself and her charges so fully realized – particularly as regards Olsson – that on one occasion she complained to a friend she'd been kicked out of her own apartment 'because Tony wants to have a meeting with his Nazi friends'. On another occasion, as she was leaving the house for the drive to the prison, she grabbed a plain brown envelope and told the friend with her that inside it were magazines devoted to weapons and gun culture that Tony and the others had asked her to buy: 'It's illegal, but what can I do?' she offered helplessly. One of Olsson's friends even took over her duties as the prisoners' chauffeur, driving them to and from the theatre for rehearsals and, in due course, actual performances. Andreas Axelsson's appointment was entirely informal. He was never vetted by anyone from the prison service, and the fact that he, the driver, was also editor of a neo-Nazi newspaper remained unknown. As Birgitta Göransson had suspected, Isa Sternberg's faculty of empathy was out of control.

Even knowing the basic method Norén was following, the three prisoners remained sceptical about the artistic value of it. Privately, they found the whole idea outlandish: *Va' är det här for skit?* ('What kind of crap is this?'), Mats Nilsson imagined audiences asking themselves. He found it hard to believe anyone would enjoy listening to them ramble on about themselves and their opinions through an entire evening, harder still that people would pay to do so. Mostly they kept their doubts to themselves. At one point Carl Thunberg, the most self-assured of the three, their letter-writer and the only one whom Norén confessed he actually feared, suggested that what they were offering their audiences was social pornography. Norén assured him nothing could be further from the case.

Another thing: over the summer break an hour of the dialogue had been edited out. According to Mats Nilsson most of it was nuanced stuff about right and wrong and about what distinguishes the sick from the healthy mind. He particularly regretted the disappearance of a scene in which the three had done their best to respond to a request from Norén that they describe the happiest times they had known in their lives. With that gone, it seemed to him, the play had tipped over into an exercise in darkness. But in this, as in other matters that dismayed them – Norén calling the play 7:3, for example, as well as his insistence on an opening scene in which the prisoners were encountered for the first time as the lights went up, muscles rippling beneath tight-fitting t-shirts, pumping furious push-ups to the accompaniment of off-stage counting, until Carl and then Tony drop out leaving Mats pumping away alone. Norén assured them that audiences would laugh, and they deferred to his dramatic insight.

By the end of November 7:3 had reached its final form and all of those involved enjoyed a celebratory dinner at Sternberg's apartment in Östermalm. Some weeks later, on 6 February 1999, amid enormous public curiosity that was in equal parts a fascination for anything Lars Norén did and simple social voyeurism, the premiere of 7:3 took place in Umeå Folkets Hus, the town's cultural centre. It was the first of what would eventually be twenty-two performances of the play in front of a paying audience. The run ended on 27 May and Tony Olsson was driven back to spend the night in Österåker prison. He had already been granted seventy-two hours leave from 1 o'clock the following day, from Friday 28 May to Sunday 30 May. As a sort of grand finale to the whole thing he, Mats Nilsson, Andreas Axelsson and Lars Norén had arranged to go to a Metallica concert in Stockholm on the Friday evening. But back at Österåker he asked to be allowed to leave at eight the following morning instead. He still hoped to make the Metallica concert, but there was something else he had to do first. Permission was granted.

*

In view of what was to transpire, Lars Norén has never allowed the script of 7:3 to be published. Almost from the start, however, a documentary film team had been allowed into the prison and given complete access to the rehearsals, the discussions, the arguments that arose along the way. The documentary was interspersed with images of the prisoners' daily life: pumping iron; lying on the beds; tramping up and down in the exercise compound. An edited version of this material was released as a ninety-minute film entitled *Repetitioner* (*Rehearsals*) in 2005.

The film of the rehearsals makes a strange parallel to the play. More even than the play itself it looks like the slice of almost unreconstructed reality that Norén was aiming to create. It is pure Andy Warhol. There is no building tension, no dramatic development, little evidence of artificial control over the material. It is a four-pronged extrusion, cut to a length. A number of extracts from actual performances of the play are included. Typically, four chairs and corner lighting illuminate a stage about the size of a boxing ring. As at a boxing match, the audience surrounds the platform on all sides, the front rows close enough to lean forward and touch the performers. Apart from Reine Brynjolfsson's 'John', the acting is as amateur as one might expect. The dialogue is forcibly but not convincingly delivered.

The first sensational moment comes late on in proceedings, during Scene 9, when Tony Olsson volunteers the following: 'I am personally anti-Semitic. To me the Jews are an alien presence among us. They don't belong here because they fracture our culture and our sense of community. They leech upon us...' In the filmed version of the scene, a few whistles of disapproval can be heard before the dialogue moves on. And when it's over the three prisoners and the professional actor are rewarded with a typical Scandinavian *trampeklapp*, an ovation in which spontaneous applause evolves into a thunderous unison of clapping, accompanied by foot stomping. The players line up and bow, just like professional actors. They are presented with bouquets of flowers. Their exhilaration is palpable. What might have been a disastrous exercise in radical chic seems after all to have justified itself.

But what was the audience applauding? Was it, like the applause that hails a monkey for riding around the circus ring on a fairy cycle, not so much for a thing well done as for a thing done at all? Was what they had just seen a play, or was it real? Should the performers be regarded as actors speaking lines or as real people voicing their own views? Erik Sidenbladh, a journalist on *Svenska Dagbladet*, was in no doubt about the answer. Nor was Tony Olsson. Sidenbladh's response to Olsson's proclaimed anti-Semitism went further than a few discrete whistles. During a public performance in Hallunda he rose to his feet and shouted: *Vad i helvete är det du säger!* ('What the hell are you saying!'), to which Olsson ad-libbed from the stage: *Du där borta ska hålla käften! Vi uttrycker våra åsikter* ('You over there shut your mouth! We're expressing our views.') Sidenbladh found himself thwarted by lawyers when he tried to bring a prosecution against two of the actors under a Swedish law that forbids incitement to racial hatred. He was told that Olsson's words enjoyed the protection the law offered where the words or views expressed were an integral part of a work of art.

The original rehearsal-cum-conversation scene is included in *Rehearsals*. There, Lars Norén assumes that Olsson and Nilsson are Holocaust deniers and is initially puzzled by the fact that they are not. They explain their position to him: what the Nazis did in Germany has no application to Sweden and Swedish anti-Semitism. It was a German thing. What they are talking about is a specifically Swedish National Socialism. As the discussion proceeds Norén suggests to them the absolute naturalness of applying oneself to becoming a professional success in a society as a way of protecting oneself against the kind of prejudice that Jews have been exposed to over the centuries in Europe. *They don't belong here because they break down our culture and our sense of togetherness*, Olsson complains in the play. Norén might have asked him to explain how a mere 15,000 Swedes of Jewish descent could have such a catastrophic effect on a nation of over 9.5 million non-Jewish Swedes. But he allows the expression of anti-Semitism to stand, determined to censor nothing in the name of a confessional truth that he firmly believes will lead to an expansion of empathy and understanding for prisoners and audience alike, as well as achieve a new and unprecedented level of onstage reality. As the rehearsal discussion proceeds, it emerges that both Olsson and Nilsson are white separatists and as such implacably opposed to multi-culturalism in Sweden. Nilsson talks about his experiences in a prison wing known as 'the Gaza Strip' because of the number of inmates of North African origin. Apart from a paedophile, with whom he disdained to talk, he was the only white Swedish-speaking prisoner on the wing.

Norén works to keep the exchange conversational. To counter the anti-Semitism, he suggests a line for 'John' in which John tells them there is a synagogue in Israel where the name of every Jewish victim of the concentration-camps is read aloud, for as long as it takes, until every death has been noted. He encounters ferocious opposition to the line from Tony, who so objects to being objected to that he throws down the script and storms out of the room in an infantile rage and swears he will have nothing more to do with the project. Moments later, Lars Norén gets up, puts his script down on his seat and quietly follows him out into the corridor, determined to keep him on board.

*

Norén knew that two of the three prisoners he was working with on 7:3 were neo-Nazis. The enigmatic and highly intelligent Carl Thunberg, who at one point remarks that when the Military League dressed up in their black masks and black clothing before robbing a bank it was like entering into character, playing a role, becoming someone else for a while, displays a thinly disguised contempt for the ideology; but Mats Nilsson and in particular Tony Olsson are open about their enthusiasm and passionately defensive of it. In that opening scene with the three of them showing off the bulging body-builder muscles beneath the tight T-shirts, Mats and Tony's tattooed swastikas are in-your-face evident as they engage in that strangely threatening – because performed with such naïve pride – display of physical strength. The audience realizes at once that these men have spent most of their time in prison turning their bodies into killing machines. No professional actor, Norén insisted, could have achieved that same effect. It was all part of his idea of the kind of thing he wanted to put on stage at Umeå.

But, what exactly *was* his idea?

Even before the events that would unfold had radically limited the kinds of things it became possible for Norén to say about 7:3, he had offered a number of reasons for wanting to write this particular play in this particular form for this particular set of people, and why he had chosen to more or less 'absent' himself as a shaping dramatic consciousness or even the censor of the material. In a way that is unfamiliar to newspaper readers and public figures in Britain and elsewhere in the world, the culture of public debate is deeply rooted in Swedish, Norwegian and Danish society. Long before the advent of the internet, such debate was considered essential to a healthy and functioning democracy. It was one of Norén's aims, as a responsible citizen, to start a media debate on the dehumanizing effect of prison and prison regimes on inmates; and though he always insisted 7:3 was a work of art and not a therapeutic exercise, he also believed that immersion in the world of drama would help prison inmates generally in their effort to reintegrate into society once they had served their time.

Not everyone shared his optimism. Norén hoped that the chaplain at Österåker prison would become part of the project and invited him to attend a preview of 7:3. Having seen the preview the chaplain declined to be involved, saying he thought it was a potentially disastrous undertaking and that in his view what Norén was doing would reinforce the criminals' ideas of themselves as criminals rather than liberate them from it. Norén's response was that he wanted to 'investigate evil, find out what evil is'. Professionally he was also trying something new, and for the same reason that Samuel Beckett in his time rejected traditional dramatic form: he was, as Beckett once said, 'turning from it in disgust, weary of puny exploits, weary of pretending to be able, of being able, of doing a little better the same old thing, of going a little further along a dreary road'. In an interview with the American journalist Stan Schwartz Norén said that he was 'so tired of watching theatre. I wanted to pick up the language of the streets, the things you don't normally hear in the theatre. I wanted to break down the barrier between the theatre and the world. Scenic reality can be every bit as concentrated as the analyses of psychotherapy.' He spoke of the dangers of being inarticulate and unable to express oneself and of how this would inevitably lead to violence.

Rehearsals shows Norén willing to share some of his own darkest and most enigmatic secrets and fears as he works to create the confessional atmosphere he wants for the prison conversations. With an almost religious intensity he pursues an artistic credo that was perhaps most clearly expressed by the Norwegian novelist Hans Jæger, figurehead of the Kristiania bohemians in the 1890s, in the first of his nine bohemian 'commandments': *Du skal skrive dit eget liv*

('You shall write your own life'). Its single outstanding characteristic is an insistence that the only art of any literary or therapeutic worth is confessional art. In Scandinavian literature, Hamsun's *Hunger* and *Mysteries* are outstanding examples of this. In our own time, the six volumes of Karl Ove Knausgård's *Min Kamp* ('My Struggle') are another. In Denmark, some of its most outstanding exponents have been Tom Kristensen and Suzanne Brøgger. In Sweden, August Strindberg and Ingmar Bergman upheld the tradition, though rarely with as little retouching as Norén offered in *7:3*. Henry Miller, Jack Kerouac, Charles Bukowski and Raymond Carver are examples familiar to English-language readers. Norén's faith in the redemptive power of confession was the motor behind the prison project, the almost religious belief that change is possible only when that which lurks deepest inside us is forced up to the surface and out into the light.

*

'The subtext,' Norén told Stan Schwartz in that newspaper interview, 'it's the subtext that is the heart of theatre.' Providing he knew what a subtext was, Tony Olsson would surely have agreed with him. Almost throughout the year of his association with the project, Olsson had been assiduously creating a subtext of his own to Norén's *7:3*. You might call it *NRA*. The initials stand for the Nationella Revolutionera Armé (the National Revolutionary Army), an association of kindred spirits to which he had been devoting all of his energies that did not go into the theatre project. The model for this 'army', which was never more than a three-way cell, was the IRA – the Irish Republican Army – and specifically the ways in which the IRA considered itself a valid military entity, with a valid political aim, and funded its political operations through bank robberies and other forms of criminal activity. The NRA's aim was to sponsor its activities in promoting Swedish neo-Nazism the same way.

During breaks from rehearsals for *7:3* and while on some of his numerous seventy-two-hour unsupervised leaves from prison, Olsson had been taking part in rehearsals of a very different kind: a series of robberies – of post-offices, supermarkets and state off-licences – in remote Swedish towns, specially chosen for their distance from the nearest manned police stations. Along with Olsson and Axelsson the third member of the gang was Jackie Arklöv. Arklöv was a former mercenary who had fought in the Balkans in the 1990s and afterwards been arrested, tried and sentenced in a Bosnian court to thirteen years in jail for crimes against civilians. Only months into his sentence, he had been released as part of a prisoner swap and in due course arrived back in Sweden, where he resumed life as a free man after a brief period of detention by the Swedish authorities (for which he was later awarded 60,000 kronor for wrongful detention). Half Liberian and half Swedish, Arklöv had dark skin and justified the apparent and even surreal anomaly of his enthusiasm for Adolf Hitler's views by telling people that Hitler's army had included a special corps of black African Nazis. As someone who had experienced real war and who had killed several times Jackie Arklöv was a hero to Tony Olsson, and while in jail Olsson began a correspondence with Arklöv that led in time to the development of a profound bond between the two men. As part of his developing dream of a Nazi revolution in Sweden Olsson appointed Arklöv military commander of the NRA.

The choice of targets, routes and alternative routes, and of where to abandon the first getaway car and transfer to a second, were all the responsibility, meticulously carried out, of Olsson's prison driver Andreas Axelsson. In the brief series of raids carried out by these three men in the early spring of 1999, in the countryside around the city of Linköping in Sweden's south-east, the violence and degree of threat used was out of all proportion to the modest proceeds of the robberies. The money was not the object of these exercises, however. The real aim was to habituate the robbers to the use of violence.

*

In the early afternoon of Friday 29 May Kenneth Eklund was officer on duty at the police station in Kisa, a community of under 4,000 inhabitants some 30 miles (50 km) due south of Linköping, when a member of the public called in with information that a robbery appeared to be taking place in Malexander, at the Östgöta Enskilda Bank, on the high street. Eklund jumped into his car and headed in the direction of the bank, pulling up some distance away to observe. What he saw was a man standing on the pavement outside the bank, next to a green Saab 3000. The man was dressed in black, wearing a black hood with eyehole slits and cradling an automatic weapon in his arms. Eklund parked his black and white patrol car behind a group of trees a couple of hundred metres away. Following standard instructions, he made no attempt to interfere in the robbery but kept watch as the banality of evil unfolded at a leisurely pace. Periodically he stepped out into the road to keep track of what was happening. The hooded man guarding the bank entrance noticed Eklund's presence, and each time the policemen peered out the raider levelled his weapon in Eklund's direction and shouted a warning not to come any closer. Cars passing by slowed down to see what was happening. A tourist bus stopped to let passengers take photographs of the masked man with his Uzi. Only when he aimed his weapon at the driver did the bus move on. An elderly man crossed the road and strolled down the pavement, heading straight for the guard. The guard gestured with the gun, indicating to the man to go back. The man kept on walking. Finally the guard aimed the weapon at his chest and shouted at him to stop, turn around, go back.

'Why?' asked the man.

'Because this is a robbery,' said the gunman. 'Can't you see?'

'Yes,' protested the man. 'But I live here.'

Finally, he agreed to turn round and headed back up the street at the same leisurely pace.

After some fifteen minutes and several other surreal encounters of this sort, two men, also hooded, wearing overalls and carrying automatic weapons, came running through the bank door carrying bank boxes and a rucksack heavy with money, and jumped into the Saab. The driver turned the car around and headed up the wrong side of the street at high speed. Eklund saw it at the last moment, saw the gun barrels sticking out of the windows and ducked down behind his car as the Saab flashed by no more than 4 or 5 metres (13 to 16 feet) away to head on out of Kisa. He then jumped into his patrol car and followed. His intention was simply to try to stay on their tail until back-up arrived. The drama that would unfold developed in a rather different way…

*

Rounding the first curve of an S-bend, after a mile, Eklund discovers the Saab has come to a halt midway through the second curve. All three occupants are out of the car and ranged around it with their weapons raised. They open fire. Eklund brakes, throws the gearbox into reverse and stamps down on the accelerator as hard as he can. The three robbers jump back into their car and speed off. Eklund follows. As he bounces through the narrow, twisting curves of the E34 the needle on his speedometer hovers around the 150-kilometre mark, close to 100 miles an hour.

A minute or two later the robbers repeat their manoeuvre, stopping around a bend and opening fire on Eklund's patrol car as it comes into sight. Again he slams on the brakes, struggling to control the wheel as the car screeches to a sideways sliding halt. By the time it stops the distance between the two vehicles is no more than twenty-five metres. They continue shooting, and Eklund again tries to throw his vehicle into reverse. But the engine has been shot out, the motor's dead. He lies prone across the passenger seat for a few moments, hoping they'll get back into the Saab and drive on. Silence for a few seconds. Thinking they might have gone, Eklund sits up. What he sees is the men halfway towards his car. The only thought in his mind is that he does not want to die in the car. He opens the door, dives out and sets off running as hard as he can for the scrubby marsh that runs along his side of the road. He hears the rattling crack of the automatics, followed by explosive roars as two hand-grenades explode just a few metres behind him. Racing on through the trees he spies an upturned white rowboat and dives behind it for cover.

He stays there for fifteen minutes. When at last he thinks it might be safe to stand up he sees a man approaching through the trees. He's carrying what looks like a gun. Certain it's one of the robbers Eklund levels his service pistol at him and shouts that he's a police officer, stop or I'll shoot. The man shouts back that he's a journalist. Eklund lowers his gun. As the journalist approaches, Eklund realizes that what he took to be a gun is a camera.

Meanwhile two other officers have responded to the alarm that came in just as they were clocking on for the afternoon shift. They work the Mjølby police district and are based at Motala. Malexander is not actually their patch but Robert Karlström and Olle Borén radio in that they're heading into the Boxholm area as they suspect this may be the route the robbers have taken. They park up on the E34 and watch the traffic. A passing motorcyclist attracts their attention and they signal him over to check his papers. As luck would have it this same motorcyclist just a few minutes earlier rode his bike directly across the line of fire as the robbers chased after Eklund into the scrubland, and at the very moment one of the two hand grenades exploded. As the policeman check out his papers he describes what just happened, how he felt the jolt as he rode through the shock wave. Questioned about the interview later, he says he noticed at the time that the police were more interested in checking his papers and didn't seem to take in what he was saying. They send him on his way and continue to follow the traffic. This, plus the fact that news of the attempted murder of Kenneth Eklund is broadcast only on his own home Linköping wavelength and not relayed on the Mjølby band, means that Karlström and Borén have no real idea of the sort of men they are looking for.

Suddenly a white Toyota appears. The driving is fast and erratic and their suspicions are aroused. The driver seems to be alone in the car. It might be stolen, the driver might be drunk. Olle Borén rings in the licence plate on his mobile phone and pulls out after the Toyota. The duty officer back at Motala has just arrived for his shift and needs to log on to the computer before he can give them an answer. Borén has left the line open as the police Volvo moves up to sit on the tail of the Toyota and the blue flashing 'pull-over' light goes on. As the duty officer in Motala is about to tell Borén that the car is a hire from a Statoil petrol station in Stockholm he hears one of the two officers say something. Then there's the sound of automatic gunfire.

For a third time the robbers have used the tactic of coming to a sudden and unexpected halt in the middle of a bend. This time it's just past a lay-by with a grey metal crash barrier lining its far side. Borén makes an emergency stop and the patrol car ends up six or seven metres behind the Toyota. A man who must have been lying down in the back seat of the Toyota now sits up and immediately fires off two rounds of six or seven bursts each through the rear window. Borén and Karlström roll out of their respective doors and return fire with their service pistols. A third man who has been hunched in the passenger seat footwell kicks open the front door and using the door as a shield begins shooting. The two policemen are hopelessly outgunned. Karlström goes down at the back of the patrol car, Borén makes a break for cover on the far side of the road, is shot and collapses face down in the roadside ditch. Crime-scene investigators later count fourteen bullet holes into or through the coupé, twenty-six points of impact on the outside of the car and nineteen on the inside.

The robbers get back into the white Toyota and drive away, leaving two dead policemen behind them. Axelsson is badly wounded in the chest and stomach, and not long after the shootings Olsson and Arklöv stop a passing motorist and give him a cock-and-bull story about a serious road accident. They persuade him to drive Axelsson to the Boxholm district health centre while they say they will return to the scene of the accident to see what help they can offer. The driver does not believe a word of it but can see the man is wounded and in need of treatment. Meanwhile, Olsson and Arklöv dump the Toyota in the empty barn of a deserted farmhouse and take to the woods on foot, carrying a rucksack full of money and as many weapons as they can.

*

All police leave in Sweden was cancelled as a massive manhunt got under way. Going through Axelsson's diary, the police found Tony Olsson's name, and from the man who had driven Axelsson to the clinic they knew that the third member of the gang was dark-skinned. Arklöv had been incredibly reckless. At one point during the bank raid, he had raised his mask to scratch his face. While persuading the motorist to take Axelsson to hospital he wasn't even wearing it. It all seems part of the shadowy incompetence that surrounded the whole robbery, the dreamlike infantilism of the violence. Under the circumstances a dark-skinned man speaking Swedish like a native and wanted in connection with the murder of two policemen and the attempted murder of a third while robbing a bank of more than 2.5 million kronor had little chance of evading capture. After a brief gun battle, in which he was wounded, Jackie Arklöv was arrested on 31 May 1999 outside Andreas Axelsson's flat in Tyresö. Tony Olsson, helped by his girlfriend Lena, managed to evade the huge police dragnet before crossing into Germany, from where he caught a flight to Costa Rica. Acting on a tip-off, his rented apartment was surrounded by local police on 5 June and he surrendered without a struggle. After a few weeks in a Costa Rican jail, he was flown back to Sweden.

At their trial in November 1999 all three were found guilty of murder, attempted murder, the bank robbery at Kisa and the rehearsal robberies at the post office, the supermarket and the off-licence. All three were given life sentences. Mats Nilsson, a free man by the time of the robbery, got a one-year sentence for handling stolen money. A few years into his sentence Jackie Arklöv was tried in a Swedish court and found guilty of crimes committed as a mercenary in Bosnia in the 1990s, including torture and murder. It made him the first Swede ever to be convicted as a war criminal.

Throughout the trial, the robbers consistently refused to reveal who it was that had fired the fatal shots that killed Olle Borén and Robert Karlström. The general view among both police and journalists was that it was most likely Tony Olsson, the only one of the three diagnosed as a psychopath. Interviewed following his recovery from his wounds, Andreas Axelsson also implied that Olsson was the culprit. Olsson himself would neither confirm nor deny the supposition. The truth emerged two years later, following a showing of Folke Rydén's documentary film *Vägen til Malexander* ('The Road to Malexander') on Swedish television. After watching it, Jackie Arklöv requested a formal meeting with two senior police officers. In the presence of his lawyer, he gave a full account of what had actually happened two years earlier. How they stopped the car on a bend in the road next to a crash barrier. How he opened the passenger door, squatted down and began firing. How, after a few seconds without return of fire, he stood up straight. How the Toyota was too close to the crash barrier for the door to open properly, so that he had to step directly over it and onto the sloping ground beyond. How he then walked around to the back of the blue and white patrol car where he saw Robert Karlström lying on the ground, blood pumping from his nose and mouth and pooling on the asphalt below his head. How he picked up Karlström's service revolver, which lay nearby, and crossed the road to where Olle Borén lay face down in a shallow ditch on the other side. Borén had only flesh wounds, from which he would undoubtedly have recovered had not Arklöv leant forward and shot him through the back of the head with Karlström's pistol. Arklöv then picked up Borén's gun, returned to the back of the Volvo, and, from a distance of about 10 centimetres, put a bullet through Karlström's forehead.

★

Did Lars Norén in any way share the anti-Semitic views of two of his three prisoner-actors? To the contrary. In his old age Henrik Ibsen once expressed a mild envy of the Jews for their freedom from the burden of nationhood. Norén, during a televised interview with a man who had been a prisoner in Auschwitz with Primo Levi – one of Norén's literary idols – expressed the same envy even more vigorously, saying he wished he *were* a Jew, he had always felt like a Jew. As the echoes of the murders at Malexander fade, it becomes possible to look again at what he was trying to do with 7:3.

An aspect of the play that has been little discussed is the light it sheds on the conditions of free speech in Sweden, and the status and position of the socially conservative Right in general in Swedish political life. In recent years Norway's Fremskrittspartiet (FrP; the Progress Party) has been part of the country's Centre-Right coalition government. In Denmark, the Dansk Folkeparti (DF; the Danish People's Party) received more than 20 per cent of the vote in the 2015 General Election and has seats in the Danish Cabinet. The sister party to both FrP and DF in Sweden is Sverigedemokraterna (SD; Swedish Democrats). All three parties are conservative on the subject of immigration and multiculturalism, and they distinguish their position absolutely from racism. At the General Election held late in 2014, the SD's share of the vote made them third largest of the eight parties that won seats in the Swedish Riksdag; but a *cordon sanitaire* was put in place around the party since it first gained representation in the Swedish parliament in 2010, and rather than break it and allow the party a voice in government the six other parties represented in the Riksdag formed a coalition under Social Democrat leader Stefan Löfven, in which the determination to deny the SD a voice was the only genuine common ground.

The Swedish arrangement made a nonsense of the virtues of proportional representation, since it entailed the disenfranchisement of the large section of the Swedish electorate who had voted for the party. In effect, it was as though they had never voted. The migrant crisis of the 2010s and the Paris massacres of 2015 only increased the SD's popularity at the polls, and at the point at which the crisis threatened to overwhelm Sweden in the first weeks of 2016, the coalition resorted to every measure of control that the SD had been advocating for some time: closing borders, checking trains and ferries and cars crossing the Öresund Bridge, and suggesting that as many as 80,000 of those who had recently arrived in the country, seeking asylum, would have their applications refused and face deportation as illegal immigrants.

The chaotic situation in which the country found itself illuminates another aspect of Sweden's commitment to a boundlessly radical humanism, and that is an almost pathological fear of socially conservative views and a demonization of those who hold them. To call the attitude 'political correctness' misses the point. Sweden's cultural and political elite have internalized the core values of a social democracy that entails the active promotion of multiculturalism and of feminism as a political philosophy, and pursue the dream of a globalized culture so passionately that at times it seems prepared to contemplate the abrogation of the nation-state. Perhaps the driven and infinitely well-meant tolerance of an Isa Sternberg in the face of the needs of men like Tony Olsson and Mats Nilsson reflected, at the individual level, an attitude of mind that is characteristic of Sweden's intellectual and cultural elite as a whole, for whom Sweden is a country whose natural form of government *must* reflect the values of social democracy, regardless of the views of ordinary people. For spirits like these, opposition to such a view is regarded as at best wrong-headed and at worst sinful.

Some of the stories of the *cordon sanitaire* created around the SD following their electoral success in 2014 suggest moral vanity. The arrival of the SD in the Riksdag occasioned a change in the seating arrangement in the committee rooms. In place of the traditional two rows of seating, one for the government and one for the opposition, a third row was created especially for the SD. The explanation was that other opposition parties did not wish SD members to know where they stood on various issues in case they decided to vote with them. The fear of moral taint became absurd in the more recent story of a member of the ruling coalition who was scheduled to appear on a television programme with someone from the SD but refused to enter the make-up room as long as the SD representative was being made-up in there.

It seems a paradox that the Swedes, with their reputation for an openness that challenges society's most deeply rooted taboos, who seem to challenge the whole idea of invoking taboos at all, should cling so hard to this one, with its intolerable suggestion that ours might not, after all, be a perfect world. In wondering why Lars Norén gave Olsson and Nilsson a platform in *7:3* from which to air their anti-Semitic views, I have sometimes wondered whether he instinctively understood the pressure-cooker-type dangers that can arise when the articulation of views that may be ugly and disturbing is overtly or covertly suppressed; and that his unease on this score was part of the subtext of 7:3. Was he trying to remind his audiences that, no matter how little he or they might like it, the views held by people like Olsson, Larsen and Arklöv really existed and that, as he noted himself, violence was the likely consequence where such views were censored out of existence? Did he sense that the well-meaning censorship of crude and unpleasant words and ideas may not be the best way to counter them? That it may actually drive those prevented from voicing them into a smouldering and resentful underground existence from which, in due course, they explode in what looks like a sudden and apparently inexplicable orgy of violence? Among its other subtexts, was 7:3 a contribution to the debate on the subject of freedom of expression in Sweden?

★

There's a twenty-minute YouTube video of an interview with Jackie Arklöv that was made in 2013. The television interviewer talks to him across a table. Arklöv is wearing a prison blue jacket over his pale blue T-shirt. He's a handsome, healthy-looking man. Later in the interview, when he removes the jacket, you can see he has the same prison work-out muscles as Tony Olsson, Mats Larsson and Carl Thunberg in *Rehearsals*. His manner is mild, shy even. He seems articulate. Thoughtful. They talk about Malexander and about the confession he made in 2001. He confirms that his decision to tell the truth about what happened that day was motivated by something said by someone still mourning the loss of the two policemen. As the conversation goes on, he relaxes. 'What is your identity now?' 'Who are you now?' the interviewer asks. After a long pause Arklöv says: 'I'm the person I should have been. Before all this happened.'

They talk about Norway's mass killer, Anders Breivik. The interviewer asks if he can understand how it was possible for Breivik to do what he did. Arklöv thinks long and hard about it and then comes up with a metaphor. A man is driving along in his car, he says, and he realizes there's something wrong with the engine. He gets out, opens the bonnet and finds the problem is a faulty spark plug. He tosses the useless plug away. In the same way that man doesn't hate the spark plug, he says, Breivik didn't hate his victims. In both instances it was a case of diagnosing the cause of a problem and dealing with it. Nothing personal. Arklöv recalls science-fiction films in which space ships land and disgorge aliens, beings that may look exactly like us but are in fact not like us at all. The first time he saw Breivik's image, he says, he thought he looked like such an alien. Arklöv smiles briefly across the table as he offers this analogy. It's a natural, head-shaking smile of mild disbelief, as though inviting the interviewer to share in his sad puzzlement over the mystery of such a man. 'But this is the way many people think about you,' the interviewer at once reminds him. Arklöv nods. His smile fades and in that moment, in spite of yourself, knowing what he did, knowing the untold suffering he caused, still your heart aches for him. You recall an argument Norman Mailer used while campaigning for the release of Jack Henry Abbot from the Utah prison cell where Abbot was serving a nineteen-year sentence for manslaughter and robbery, that it is just too harsh to judge a man on the single worst moment of his entire life. Then you think of what happened after Abbot was released. Of the waiter he stabbed to death fourteen days later for refusing to let him use the staff toilet in a restaurant. You think of Jackie Arklöv again, and reflect that his worst moment seemed to go on an awfully long time. And then, like the interviewer, you shake his hand and leave the room, closing the door behind you.

15
Oslo 2016

ABOUT TWO YEARS BEFORE HE DIED, I WENT WITH MY old friend Erling to a Cinemateket showing in Dronningens gate to see Tom Cruise in *Minority Report*. It's one of those rare, overtly commercial films that turn out to be thought-provoking. Based on Philip K. Dick's short story of the same title, it is set in a future in which certain kinds of people called 'Precogs' have developed the power to dream the murders of the future, and by using their foreknowledge the police are able to intervene so successfully that no murders are committed and the murder rate in New York (or wherever the film is set) drops to zero. The would-be killers are then kept in a state of cryonic arrest in giant test-tubes in some kind of vast underground prison vault. The point of the film is the ethical problem raised by the fact that they never actually committed the crimes for which they are now being held in this state of permanent vegetation.

As Erling and I headed toward Karl Johan along Dronningens gate I tried to communicate my excitement about the film to him. He kept stopping in his tracks and seemed to be trying to respond, his eyes wild, his fingers clasping the top of his head as though he felt his brain was about to explode. Thinking back on it now I realize this performance had nothing to do with the ethical problem raised by the film. It was simply that his alcoholism had left him pitifully vulnerable to the sensory assault of any American film, that it was the loud background music, the explosions and banging that had distressed him so much and which he was still, fifteen minutes later, trying to claw out of his shattered head.

We parted company in Egertorget, and I took the westbound metro. As soon as we boarded I noticed the young man. He was blonde-haired, in his early thirties, and casually but smartly dressed. With almost palpable absorption, he was reading a paperback. What other people read on trains always interests me. Glancing at the cover I saw that the book was in English and written by Bruce Bawer, an American writer living in Norway. I knew Bruce. As expats and writers of roughly the same generation, we shared the same frame of reference, and the many evenings we had gone out for a beer, usually to Eilefs Landhandleri on Kristian IVs gate, were oases of rich and allusive and flowing conversation in my otherwise quiet life. It was the first time I had ever had the experience of seeing a complete stranger reading a book by someone I knew, and I thought for a moment about informing the young man that the author of the book he was reading actually lived here, right here in Oslo. But Egertorget to Majorstua is just two stops, and I let the moment pass.

Bruce is a married gay man. One of his earlier books was *Stealing Jesus*, an attack on the fundamentalist Christian churches in America for the cynical way they ignore the true gospel message of inclusion and selfless love. The book the young man on the metro was reading was *While Europe Slept*. It's another expression of Bruce's distaste for religions that foster hatred and exclusivity, in particular expressing his fear that social tensions arising from the sudden arrival of large numbers of Muslims in secular and largely atheist Europe might provoke the need for an accommodation between religious and secular communities, and that the first to feel the effects of any such accommodation would almost certainly be gay men, whose hard-won and fledgling social liberties might be considered negotiable in an emergency.

As I got off the metro at Majorstua I was still thinking how pleased Bruce would be when I told him about the incident but soon forgot all about that intently reading young man until the July day a few months later when he dressed up as a policeman, murdered seventy-seven people, seriously injured a great many others and tried to blow up the government buildings in central Oslo. Among my more trivial reflections on the events of that day, I thought back to *Minority Report*, and imagined a world in which Tom Cruise came crashing feet first through the carriage window and slapped the handcuffs on Anders Breivik before he could even get started on his rampage. And yet even in that world there is one thing I feel sure of: neither the Norwegians, nor the Swedes nor the Danes would have put him under cryonic arrest in some underground vault and thrown away the key.

In March 2016, Breivik's case against the Norwegian state, for the violation of his human rights in keeping him in solitary confinement for much of the preceding five years, came up. For security reasons, the hearing took place at Telemark prison, Skien, in a prison gymnasium specially converted for the purpose. The international press was there in force. *The New York Times* report opened with a paragraph about prison life in Skien, how Breivik served his sentence in a three-room suite, with windows, that was about 340 feet square (31.5 sq m); that he had his own workout equipment, his own fridge, a DVD player, a Sony PlayStation and a desk with a typewriter; that he'd been taking a correspondence course at Oslo University, had access to television, radio and newspapers; that he was allowed to make his own food and entered the prison's Christmas gingerbread-house-baking contest last year. Most of the other, non-Scandinavian, reports conveyed the same sense of quiet disbelief at this treatment of one of the worst mass murderers of recent times. The feeling did not diminish when in due course the court found for Breivik and against the state.

My instinct on the day it happened was that the police should have shot him and dropped his body into the sea like any bin Laden. In line with those Norwegians in 1945 who revived the long-dormant death penalty and executed Quisling and his Nazi associates and collaborators, it seemed to me that this was a crime so heinous, so exceptional, that it demanded an exceptional response. And I had thought, once the trial started, that there was little to discuss. Breivik had confessed, the evidence against him was overwhelming, the whole thing would be over in a week or two.

It went on for months, with the killing and wounding of each individual treated as a separate crime and requiring its own full and separate investigation and verdict. As the weeks passed, I slowly came to realize that the trial was not about Breivik at all, that at the heart of the long and painstaking process lay a profound respect for each and every single individual life lost on that unspeakable day. Knowing that the maximum sentence Breivik faced was twenty-one years,* I still felt, as many of my Norwegian friends did, that a prison term of four months per victim could never be thought adequate for a crime that had plumbed new depths of human degradation. Yet my reaction when the maximum sentence was duly handed down was one of speechless admiration rather than outrage. The law had won. As it says in the laws of the Trøndelag Frostating, the oldest extant Norwegian legal code, written down in the eleventh and twelfth centuries, *med lov skal landet bygges*: 'our country shall be built on the law'. They meant it then, and they mean it now.

The same fidelity to the sanctity of law, come what may, was seen in Sweden in 1988 when Christer Pettersson, a psychopathic drifter who had already murdered one complete stranger and narrowly failed to kill another, was found guilty and sentenced to life imprisonment for the shooting of the Swedish prime minister, Olof Palme, two years earlier. On appeal, he was freed on a technicality later the same year and awarded 300,000 Swedish crowns in damages for wrongful imprisonment. On the day of his release, he became an instant celebrity. Press photographs showed him heading out to celebrate with two bottles of gin and a bottle of Bailey's under his

---

* Under the terms of a preventative detention known as *forvaring* the state has the option to extend a maximum sentence indefinitely if it considers the prisoner still poses a danger to society.

arm, cigarette in mouth. That same evening Stockholm's bartenders were offering a gin and Bailey's cocktail to their customers. They called it *dräperen* ('the killer').

Palme and his wife Lisbet had been to the cinema alone that night. Palme had told his bodyguards he wouldn't be needing them. The couple had originally planned to see Lasse Hallström's *My Life as a Dog,* but when their son Mårten rang and told them he and his girlfriend were going to Suzanne Olsen's *Brødrene Mozart* (*The Mozart Brothers*) at the Ritz on Sveagatan, they changed their minds and joined them. Several months earlier, Suzanne Olsen had contacted Palme to offer him a cameo role in her film. She described it as a farce, pointing out the connections with the Marx brothers' *A Night at the Opera*; but it didn't take him long to reject the idea, amusing as it might have been. He was curious, however, to see how the film had turned out, and how the actor who had finally been cast in 'his' role performed. Leaving the cinema after the showing the couple set off to walk home. They crossed Sveagatan to a store where Lisbet wanted to window-shop. As they walked on, at the corner of Sveagatan, a busy main street, and Tunnelgatan, a narrow old city cut that turned into stone steps running up the walls on each side of it, 50 metres in, Lisbet Palme heard a loud bang. She thought it was children playing with firecrackers. She turned to say something to her husband and saw him lying face down on the pavement. There was a second crack as the gunman fired at her. The shot went through her coat. As she knelt over Palme's body, a witness heard her scream something which he thought was in a foreign language. Another who heard the same wail of anguish thought she heard 'My God, what have you done?' The killer jogged away along Tunnelgatan and up the steps.

The enquiry into the murder of Olof Palme remains open, with a permanent group of five officers still attached to the investigation. It has grown into the largest murder investigation in history, exceeding even the man hours and documentation of the Kennedy assassination. The overwhelming majority of Swedes, including those with close knowledge of the case, remain convinced that Pettersson was the killer. When he died in 2008, from head injuries sustained during an attack of epilepsy, his body remained unclaimed in the mortuary for almost five months. Finally, a funeral service was arranged at Sollentuna Church, with music and singing provided by members of the Maranata sect, a fundamentalist Christian group to which Pettersson had grown attracted during the last months of his life. Sollentuna council paid the costs of the burial.

The whole complex of personalities and events surrounding Palme's murder is an unmitigated tragedy – for his family, who have to live with the knowledge that his murderer will never be brought to justice, and more generally for the Swedish people, who pay the price of trauma for their heartbreaking fidelity to the values that have created and sustained and illumined their gentle society for so long. Anna Lindh, the Swedish Minister for Foreign Affairs and a woman tipped by many as a future leader of the Social Democrats and the country's first female prime minister, was one of Palme's protégées. She was insisting on those values the day she entered the NK shopping mall in central Stockholm, without bodyguards, in 2003 and was stabbed to death in full view of other shoppers. Anna Lindh was forty-six years old. The killer was found within days. At his trial, Mijailo Mijailovic was sentenced to life imprisonment. For Swedes, the 'Open-Unsolved' nature of Palme's murder makes it the worst crime novel ever written. A generation of Swedish crime-writers have been trying to put things right ever since, writing book after book after book in which the murderer always gets caught.

★

The relationship between the three members of the Scandinavian tribe was always contentious. In 1971, the British writer Roland Huntford, for many years the *Daily Telegraph's* man in Stockholm, published *The New Totalitarians*, a book in which he expressed his reservations about the strongly authoritarian nature of Sweden's social democracy. In terms of negative characterization of a society, it was comprehensively trumped in 1983 by *Tilfaeldet Sverige* ('The Case of Sweden'), by the Danish journalist Mogens Berendt, in which he damned

Sweden as a land in which 'everything is forbidden and nothing is permitted'.

The Swedes in turn passed the accusation of totalitarian socialism on to the Norwegians. In a television news broadcast in September 1999, in what he thought was an off-mike moment, the Swedish Industry Minister Björn Rosengren vented his exasperation at negotiations with his Norwegian counterpart in a telecommunications merger involving Swedish Telia and Norwegian Telenor. He was heard complaining that *Norrmännen är ju egentligen den sista Sovjetstaten. De är så oerhört nationalistiskt... allt är politik* – 'Norwegians are actually the last Soviet state in Europe. They are so unbelievably nationalistic... Everything is politics.' Confronted with the remarks, Rosenberg tried to explain that it was a joke, but someone had forgotten to tell him that politicians aren't allowed to make jokes, and in deference to the media fashion of the times he eventually had to offer the usual meaningless 'apology' to the entire Norwegian nation.

Beneath these brittle exchanges one sees clear traces of the traditional Scandinavian tribal pecking order and the thousand-year dominance of the Danes, briefly interrupted in the seventeenth century by Sweden's Age of Greatness, with Norway permanently cast as the kid brother, told what to do, now by the Danes and now by the Swedes, and with that last outburst from the Swedish minister a poorly disguised irritation at the Norwegians' temerity in suddenly overtaking both of them on the back of their oil wealth.

It's a long time now since different branches of the tribe actually fought against one another. Both Sweden and Denmark-Norway had been bit-players during the upheavals of the Napoleonic Wars, with Denmark-Norway on the French side, the Swedes on the side of the British and their allies. Sweden's king, Karl Johan, a Frenchman by birth, had been expected by those who had offered him the crown in 1810 to solicit Napoleon's help in recovering Finland, which Sweden had lost to Russia the year before. But Karl Johan was more interested in acquiring Norway from Denmark as compensation for the loss. By the terms of the Treaty of Kiel in January 1814, Sweden was given Norway as a spoil of war. This was an arrangement to which the Norwegians objected. At a gathering of the country's leading men at Eidsvoll on 17 May, a constitution was drawn up and the serving Danish regent in Norway, Prince Christian Frederik, was elected the new King of Norway. The move put the onus on the Swedes to claim their prize by force, and this they presently set about, putting an army of 45,000 up against the 30,000 Norwegians mustered to resist them. In the brief weeks of fighting that followed, a last deadly battle was fought at the Kjølberg Bridge, near Fredrikstad in southern Norway, on 9 August 1814.

A captain on the Norwegian side, Jens Christian Blich, has left a detailed account of a skirmish in which he was personally involved that day. The fighting started early, at about 4 o'clock in the morning. Torrential rain was falling. Blich had divided his force of 200 men into a left and a right flank and was about to attack a Swedish position at the top of a slight rise. Leading his men on the left through a forest, he began shouting orders. Soldiers on both sides were wearing identical cylindrical hats, visibility was poor, the heavy rain left the smoke from the muskets trapped in the lower branches of the trees. Suddenly he realized that the men he was shouting to were Swedes. They, in the general confusion, assumed that Blich and those around him were Swedes too, and at once began moving towards them to join forces.

Blich called on to his own men to charge and led the way himself. All save one of the Swedes fled. Blich shouldered his musket and took aim, but the drenching rain had soaked his powder and the gun misfired. The Swede, seeing that Blich was in trouble, levelled his bayonet and charged at Blich, lunging ferociously. By an extraordinary piece of luck, as Blich relates, he was carrying a wallet in the inside pocket of his jacket, and it was this that took the full force of the blade. Blich then parried the bayonet with his left hand and with his right drew his sword and struck the Swede so fiercely across the face that the sword's guard was shattered and the weapon rendered useless. The wounded Swede fell to his knees but managed to hold on to his rifle. His comrades, meanwhile, realizing that their pursuer was a solitary Norwegian, were running back to help him. At this point, writes Blich, a second Norwegian arrived on the scene and hit the Swede with the butt of his rifle. As he toppled to the ground, Blich snatched the gun from his hands and stabbed him to death with his bayonet. As several more Norwegians now began arriving the outnumbered Swedes again fell back through the trees, and for the remainder of the morning the fighting continued in this demented and confused manner.

A ceasefire was called the next day, 5 August 1814, the day that marks the official beginning of Sweden's 200 years of neutrality. The skirmish did nothing to change the terms of the Treaty of Kiel. The sheer size of the Swedish Army forced Prince Christian Frederik to relinquish his claim to Norway and hand over power to Karl Johan. Or nearly: the handover was not formally to the Swedish king but to the Norwegian government, on the understanding that Norway would govern itself until the Storting reassembled and formally ratified the new reality. Karl Johan also promised to honour the constitution of 17 May, with the necessary amendments that a union with Sweden would entail. Whether it was an act of generosity or a lack of political foresight, Karl Johan's decision astonishes historians to this day. It meant that once the terms of settlement were accepted, the Swedish Crown took possession of a Norway that was very different from the one it had been awarded at Kiel. Far from being a simple Swedish dependency, Norway was now a country with a constitution of its own and a national assembly and government of its own. It lacked only independent consular representation and a foreign minister. The next hundred years saw an inexorable rise in the demand for both of these national facilities and, in 1905, their eventual satisfaction in the Norwegian declaration of independence.

*

Of the 400 years or so between the beginning of the Kalmar Union in 1397, which joined the Scandinavian tribes into one 'loving union', and the Treaty of Kiel in 1814, Sweden and the kingdom of Denmark-Norway had spent 134 of them waging war on each other. That's counting only the formal declarations. The statistic easily exceeds the corresponding one for hostilities between England and Scotland over the same period.

The struggle for bragging rights in the region never quite comes to an end. Football, being the continuation of hostilities by other means, witnessed the first international between newly independent Norway and a Sweden still smarting from the humiliation of the loss as early as 1908, in Gothenburg, in front of a crowd of 3,000. Organized sport in Scandinavia was still in its infancy. The Danes were the first to start a club, the Kjøbenhavn Boldklub, a sports club founded in 1876. Among the summer activities of the club was *kricket* (sic), and to give the *kricketers* something to do in the winter a football team was started. Other Danish *kricket* clubs followed suit, and in 1889 the Dansk Boldspil-Union (DBU) was established to put things on an organized footing. League football wasn't introduced to Sweden until 1910, and then as a private initiative, which it remained until the establishment of the Allsvenskan series in 1924.

In all three countries football remained an amateur sport until the 1960s, leaving those Scandinavian players keen enough on the idea of playing professionally no option but to try their luck abroad. One was Carl 'the Shoemaker' Hansen, a Danish centre-forward who signed for Glasgow Rangers in 1921 and went on to win three Scottish championship medals with them. In footballing terms, the Danes always considered themselves the big brother of the three and found it natural to measure themselves against Germany or England rather than their Scandinavian neighbours. They won the silver medal at the 1908 Olympics, losing 2–0 to England in the final after beating France 17–1 in the semis. Harald Bohr, brother of the great physicist Niels, led the forward line.

The 1908 game in Gothenburg, coming just three years after the break-up of the union, marked the start of a long and difficult period in which Swedes and Norwegians had to adjust their status *vis à vis* each another. The Norwegians fielded several players from the Kristiania (Oslo) club Mercantile FK, including a Belgian engineer who simply happened to be working in Norway at the time. The Norwegians got off to a sensational start when their outside-right, Tryggve Gran, another Mercantile player, set off on a mazy run in the first minute of the game, jinxing his way past two Swedes, body-swerving and wrong-footing a third before hitting a perfectly judged cross for the centre-forward Ole 'Minotti' Bøhn to nod into the back of the Swedish net. Briefly the Gothenburg crowd was stunned. But by half-time the Swedes had recovered to lead 5–3 and in the end they ran out easy winners 11–3. Near the end of the game, a group of Swedes lowered the Norwegian flag to half-mast, a gesture that so incensed the patriotic Gran he left the pitch with play still in progress and personally raised it again.

It turned out to be Gran's only cap. But he was also one of Norway's top skiers, and three years after the Gothenburg game, on the advice of his friend Fridtjof Nansen, Captain Robert Scott invited Gran to join his expedition to the South Pole so that he could teach other members of the team how to improve their skiing. Gran was a member of the search party that set out to look for Scott, Oates, Wilson, Bowers and Evans after the Pole group failed to return. When the buried tent was found, and the snow and ice cleared away, he was the first to enter. In a letter to his mother he described the sight that met his eyes: the three dead men, Scott, Wilson and Bowers, with Scott in the middle sitting up, half out of his sleeping bag, as though in a grotesque attempt to greet them. Gran noted how the extreme cold had given the skin of the three men an eerie, glassy sheen beneath which their blue veins glowed. It was, he said, like looking at a geological cross-section of the human body. For the remainder of his life, he said, he was haunted by sound of Scott's arm snapping off as someone retrieved the journal wedged beneath it. A brittle, whip-like crack. Before leaving the site, Gran took off his skis and fastened them above the tent in the form of a cross, as a memorial and a marker in the landscape. Then, in a gesture of great tenderness, he strapped on Scott's own skis so that, as he put it, they at least would complete the journey.

On the day after that 11–3 trouncing, the players from Sweden and

Norway ate breakfast and drank schnapps together before parting on the best of terms, and for most of the next ten years Norway continued to lose football matches to the Swedes with a good grace. Winter sports were different. The first in what the Swedes hoped would be a series of winter games had been held in Kristiania in 1903. Two years later, when the next Nordiska Spelen were due to be held in Stockholm, the Norwegian team stayed away, explaining their absence as the result of a 'profound depression' brought on by Sweden's negative reaction to the demand for independence. The Swedes were outraged by the deliberate mixing of politics and sport. By the time of the 1907 games, sporting relations between the countries remained sour and the Norwegians arranged a games of their own in Trondheim. Foreigners were invited to take part, but none attended. Formal winter-sports relations were resumed by 1909, but the Swedish hosts had to endure the Norwegian flag being raised and Rikard Nordraak's lovely national anthem being played four times as the great Oscar Mathison from Oslo won skating gold at all four of the classic distances.

The end of the Second World War brought a revival of sporting tensions between the neighbours. Their experiences had been so different, Norway's five years of harsh occupation in such sharp contrast to Sweden's neutrality. Certain aspects of the way Sweden had managed its neutrality had left many Norwegians feeling bitter. During the early years of the war Sweden had arranged winter games to which both the Germans and the Italians were invited. So when the time came for the first Holmenkollen meeting – a Norwegian winter-sports event held around the ski jump on the northern outskirts of Oslo that had become a national tradition – the Norwegians invoked a technicality to declare the race open to domestic competitors only. Their skiers were national heroes, and after five undernourished and humiliating years they did not want to court further humiliation by seeing the heroes beaten by the next-door neighbours. The same technicality was not deemed applicable to the ski-jumping, however, and five Swedes and two Danes were among those allowed to launch themselves into the empty air above Oslo, in the certain knowledge that none of them would end up anywhere near the podium. As for the *femmilla*, the classic 50-kilometre (30-mile) ski race that is the blue riband event of the games, the Danes would probably not even have bothered to enter anyway. For simple geographical reasons they don't do winter sport.

The sea-change in the status of football that came about in the 1990s means that people the world over are more likely to know the name of Sweden's Zlatan Ibrahimović than that of Ingmar Bergman, to recognize a photo of Norway's Ole Gunnar Solskjær but stare in puzzlement at one of Edvard Munch. Most of us are more familiar with Scandinavia's footballing heroes than its artists or politicians, and our associations and memories from the recent history of Denmark, Norway and Sweden are more likely to be sporting ones than social and political ones of ultimately much greater significance: Sweden reaching the World Cup Finals in 1958, the year of the Brazilian revelation, and losing 5–2; Zlatan's four goals for Sweden against England in 2012, including that wonderful bicycle kick from near the half-way line that sailed over Joe Hart's head and into the empty net; Zlatan the irritable genius, who was so annoyed at coming second to tennis's Björn Borg in a Swedish sports journalists' poll to find the country's greatest-ever sports star; Solskjær's toe-poke lunge in the last seconds of the Champions' League Final against Bayern Munich that won the trophy for Manchester United in 1999; Denmark getting a wild card entry to the European Championships in 1992, after the break-up of Yugoslavia meant it couldn't compete, reaching the final and beating Germany 2–0 (a game I listened to on the car radio driving back from Tønsberg to Oslo, so desperate for the Danes to win I had to pull in at the petrol station at Sande for the last fifteen minutes to make *absolutely sure they did*); Paul Gascoigne in the same year saying 'Fuck off Norway' when asked by a friendly journalist if he had a message for the Norwegian people ahead of an England–Norway game; or the urbane and stylishly-dressed Swede Sven-Göran Eriksson, one the best and most successful England managers of recent years, and his affairs with the glamorous Nancy Dell'Olio and Farah Alam which so fascinated the English tabloid press and which gave the Swedish people their first shocked insight into the true nature of redtop journalism in England; or the less urbane and stylishly dressed Egil 'Drillo' Olsen, who twice took little Norway to the World Cup Finals in the 1990s, who habitually wore wellington boots in the dugout and was for many years a card-carrying member of the Norwegian Communist Party.

Olsen always said that his two favourite teams were the Brazil of almost any era and the Wimbledon of the Joe Kinnear 'crazy gang' era, and he went on to endure a short and unsuccessful spell as manager of the club; but his finest hour came as manager of the national team that had to beat Brazil to proceed from the group stage of the 1996 finals and did so, thanks to Kjetil Rekdal's penalty kick. I watched that game in a hotel room in Park Lane with Hallstein Laupsa, a man whom I had never met before, the boss of the publishing firm where my wife worked. He happened to be in London at the time on business and staying at the Hilton. I called on him, looking for some company in which to watch the game, and the two of us sat on his hotel bed and emptied the mini-bar as the minutes ticked by and when the final whistle blew embraced each other like madmen. It was as if Norway had landed a man on the moon. Hallstein and I left the hotel after the game to celebrate, first at the 12 Bar, a little folk and blues club on Denmark Street, then on to Ronnie Scott's in Frith Street. Every so often we would stop talking, grab each other by the lapels and stare into each other's eyes, shouting in wild and ecstatic disbelief *We beat Brazil!*

For many Norwegians, the 2–1 victory over England at Ullevål Stadium in 1981 was a still more astounding achievement. The game has been immortalized by the bi-lingual ravings of the Norwegian commentator Bjørge Lillelien as the final whistle sounded:

Norway has beaten England 2–1! We are best in the world! We are best in the world! This is incredible! We have beaten England, birthplace of giants. Lord Nelson, Lord Beaverbrook, Sir Winston Churchill, Sir Anthony Eden, Clement Attlee, Henry Cooper, Lady Diana, we have beaten the lot of them, we have beaten the lot of them! Maggie

Thatcher, can you hear me? Maggie Thatcher, I have a message for you in the middle of our election campaign, I have a message for you: we have knocked England out of the football World Cup! Maggie Thatcher, as they say in your language in the boxing bars around Madison Square Gardens in New York, your boys took a hell of a beating! Your boys took a hell of a beating, Maggie Thatcher! Norway has beaten England at football! We are best in the world!

Even now, almost forty years on, one's reaction remains poised between delight at the surreal charm of the rant and dismay at its utter silliness. I remember how England dominated the game completely, and how I surprised myself by greeting each of the three goals with the same howl of delight and fist-pumping jump into the air. Many years later I was in Haugesund, on the west coast of Norway, to give a talk on Ibsen in connection with an exhibition at the city's art gallery of paintings inspired by his plays. I was having a drink afterwards with the curator, an Englishman who had recently moved to Norway to take up the post, and in trying to convey to him the joys of immersing oneself completely in the culture of another country I described that evening in 1981 and the joy with which I had greeted all three goals. I remember him replying, almost with a shudder, that he hoped that would never happen to him. Then as now, however, it seemed to me a case of loyalties doubled rather than divided.

*

I watched that game on my mother's black-and-white TV in the front room of her little pebble-dashed council house in Edenfield, near Bury. It was the year after I had graduated from University College London with a degree in Scandinavian Studies. I was thirty-three years old. My only reason for taking the course had been so that I could read Knut Hamsun's novels in the original. Other than to get closer to unravelling the secrets of Hamsun's mysterious style I had no further notion of where the study might take me, and indeed no particular expectation that it would take me anywhere at all. That night, as I lay in bed listening on a Walkman to Olafr Havrevold's legendary reading of *Hunger* from 1959, I began to hear the novel, with its intense and compelling introversion, as outstanding material for a radio play. On the train back to London the next day I drafted a few scenes for an adaptation, and a few days later sent them to Richard Imison at the BBC Radio Drama department. He liked them enough to commission a play, and a few months later the adaptation was broadcast.

One of those who heard it was Torbjørn Støverud, a former Norwegian cultural attaché in London. I met him not long afterwards in the cafeteria at my old college, where I had called in to return a library book I thought I'd lost – I remember now that it was Axel Sandemose's novel *En flyktning krysser sitt spor* (*A Fugitive Crosses His Tracks*). In those far-off days, before cheap air travel and the advent of the internet, one still met the kind of Englishman I had once been, who thought polar bears padded the streets of Oslo, and that Stockholm was the capital of Norway, and anyone exhibiting even a minor obsession with their remote community was actively encouraged by Norwegians to pursue that interest. Støverud urged me to apply for a government scholarship that would allow me to spend a full year in Norway. Few prospects could have been more appealing to me, and I did so. In late October of 1983 I left England in a van driven by a man from Reading about whom I knew almost nothing save that he owned a van. We travelled on the overnight ferry from Harwich to Gothenburg and then on up the E6 to Oslo. In the back of the van I had everything I owned, everything I valued, everything I would need to start a new life: four cardboard boxes of LPs, a record-player and a suitcase full of clothes.

I stayed on after my year was up.

A Scandinavian Timeline

c.AD 400–800 Creation of the Gotland picture-stones, Sweden.

c.550–790 The era of Swedish culture known as the 'Vendel Period'.

793 The attack on Lindisfarne, on England's north-east coast, signals the start of the Viking Age.

813 The *Carolingian Chronicles* mention a punitive Danish raid on Norwegian Vestfold.

839 The *Annals of St-Bertin* contain the first written reference to Swedish Vikings known as 'Rus'.

865 The largely Danish 'Great Heathen Army', as the Anglo-Saxons describe it, invades England, beginning 120 years of conquest.

870–930 Settlers from Western Norway arrive in Iceland.

c.880 Ottar, a trader from the north of Norway, visits Wessex and provides King Alfred's courtiers with a clear account of his own way of life, and of the distribution of power in Scandinavia between Danes, Swedes and Norwegians.

921 Arab traveller Ibn Fadlan witnesses a funeral ceremony on the banks of the Volga enacted by Swedish Rus travellers and leaves a memorable description.

930 The Icelandic assembly, the Alþingi (Althing), is established. There is no king; instead, a code of law known as Ulfljot's Law is adopted as the instrument of rule.

c.970	The Danes adopt Christianity, and Harald Bluetooth raises the Jelling Stone, in south-east Jutland, to mark the religious conversion.
986	Erik the Red leads the settlement of Greenland from Iceland. Two colonies are established.
999/1000	The Icelanders adopt Christianity.
c.1000–1020	Attempts made from Greenland to establish settlements in North America fail when they come under attack from Native Americans. The two *Vinland Sagas* give lightly fictionalized accounts of the venture.
1013	The Danish king Sven Forkbeard conquers England and establishes the Jelling dynasty. He dies a few weeks into his reign and is succeeded by his son, Cnut (Canute).
1018–1035	The North Sea empire of King Cnut I embraces England, Denmark and Norway; but the Jelling dynasty in England comes to an end with his death.
c.1024	Olav Haraldsson brings Christianity to Norway.
c.1100	After long opposition, the Swedes finally adopt Christianity.
1103/4	The first archbishopric in Scandinavia is established, at Lund, in Skåne, at that time part of Denmark.
1122-1132	The Icelandic priest Ari the Wise writes *Íslendingabók*, a history of the settlement of Iceland from 870.
c.1208–1218	Saxo Grammaticus compiles his *Gesta Danorum*, a history of the Danes.
Before 1241	The Icelandic chieftain, poet and historian Snorri Sturluson writes *Heimskringla*, chronicling the reigns of Norse kings.
1262–3	Dynastic feuding brings the Icelandic Commonwealth to an end and it becomes part of Norway.
1349	The Black Death reaches Scandinavia. As much as a third of the population perishes from its ravages in the following decades.

1397	Beginning of the Kalmar Union, in which Denmark, Sweden and Norway are united under one crown. Denmark remains the dominant power for the next 120 years.
1420s	Danish King Erik VII builds the first castle at Elsinore, which will become the setting for Shakespeare's *Hamlet*.
c.1500	Final failure of the Greenland settlements.
1517	Martin Luther's publicizing of his 'Ninety-Five Theses' heralds the beginning of the Reformation in Europe.
1520	Danish King Christian II invades Sweden to uphold the Kalmar Union in the face of popular opposition led by Sten Sture the Younger. More than eighty leading Swedish opponents, including some bishops, are executed for 'heresy' during a few days in November: the so-called 'Stockholm Bloodbath'.
1523	Christian II is deposed, to be succeeded by his uncle, the pro-Lutheran Frederik I. Swedish independence from Denmark, under Gustav I Vasa, means the effective end of the Kalmar Union.
1536	The Danish Church passes into state control, adopting a Lutheran direction. The changes to doctrine and practice are applied also in Norway, which is downgraded to provincial status, beginning centuries of subservience to its Scandinavian neighbours.
1541	The 'Gustav Vasa Bible', translated into Swedish, appears.
1550	Christian III's Bible, translated into Danish, is published.
1563–70	The Northern Seven Years' War, waged between Denmark-Norway and Sweden, brings Swedish territorial expansion.
1611	Sweden's 'Great Power Era' begins – the period of the Swedish Empire, which lasts until 1718, beginning with the reign of Gustavus Adolphus (1611–32).

1611 (contd.)	Denmark-Norway and Sweden fight the Kalmar War (until 1613).
1625	Denmark enters the conflagration of Europe's Thirty Years' War.
1627	In the so-called 'Turkish Raid', Barbary pirates make an attack on Iceland.
1628	The Swedish warship *Vasa* sinks on her maiden voyage.
1630	Sweden enters the Thirty Years' War.
1644–54	Queen Kristina reigns in Sweden, until she abdicates and converts to Roman Catholicism.
1658	Karl X Gustav leads a Swedish army across the frozen Belts to Själland. With the Peace of Roskilde, Sweden gains Skåne, Halland, Blekinge and Bohuslän from Denmark-Norway, establishing the boundaries of modern Sweden.
1660	Denmark adopts an absolute monarchy.
1679	Olof Rudbeck begins publication of his magnum opus *Atlantica*, which situates the lost civilization of Atlantis in Sweden.
1682	In Sweden there is the effective adoption of absolute monarchy.
1700–21	In the Great Northern War, an alliance of states led by Russia (and often including Denmark-Norway) fights the Swedish Empire under Charles XII. Swedish defeat signals the end of empire and absolute monarchy.
1719–72	The Instrument of Government inaugurates Sweden's 'Age of Liberty': power shifts from the monarchy to the Riksdag of the Estates and the competing 'Hat' and 'Cap' political groupings.
1770	The royal physician, effective regent and lover of the queen Dr Johann Heinrich Struensee, attempts to impose Enlightenment ideas in Denmark. He introduces freedom of speech – a first in Europe. The Danish navy undertakes its largest-ever action:

the bombardment of Algiers, as part of an effort to combat North African piracy.

1772   In Denmark, Struensee is executed.

In Sweden, King Gustav III (r.1771–92) restores monarchical authority in a royal coup.

1807   Fearing that Napoleon might appropriate the Danish fleet, British naval warships bombard Copenhagen and confiscate the Danish navy.

A British blockade of Norway begins, lasting seven years and bringing famine in the south and east.

1809   Jørgen Jørgensen declares Iceland (briefly) independent from Denmark.

Defeat in the Finnish War (1808–9) forces Sweden to cede Finland to Russia and produces a revolution: Sweden's King Gustav IV Adolf abdicates, and a new Instrument of Government decisively restores power to the Riksdag.

1814   By the terms of the Treaty of Kiel, Sweden acquires a reluctant Norway from Denmark as compensation for the loss of Finland to Russia. Denmark retains Iceland as a dependency.

Norwegian defeat at the Battle of Kjølberg Bridge confirms Swedish control; but Norway is granted its own constitution and national assembly.

The enduring era of Swedish neutrality and avoidance of international pacts and alliances begins.

1818   The former French general Jean-Baptiste Bernadotte becomes King Karl Johan (Charles XIV) of Sweden-Norway, establishing the extant Bernadotte dynasty on the Swedish throne.

1837   Hans Christian Andersen publishes the first volume of his *Fairy Tales,* including 'The Little Mermaid' and 'The Emperor's New Clothes'.

1843   Søren Kierkegaard's *Either/Or* and *Fear and Trembling* are published, both under pseudonyms.

1844	Kierkegaard publishes *The Concept of Anxiety*.
1848–63	The Danish rule of the archaeologically inclined King Frederik VII.
1848–51	Denmark (and Sweden) fight with Prussia over entitlement to the ethnically and linguistically mixed Jutland duchies of Slesvig-Holsten (Schleswig-Holstein) and Saxe-Lauenburg.
1849	A new constitution signals the end of absolute monarchy in Denmark.
1864	In the Second Slesvig-Holsten War, Prussian and Austrian forces defeat the Danes at the Battle of Dybbøl, and acquire sovereignty over the Jutland provinces, drastically reducing Denmark's size and extent. North Schleswig is eventually returned to Denmark following a plebiscite in 1920.
1865	Henrik Ibsen writes the verse-play *Brand*.
1867	Ibsen writes *Peer Gynt*, another verse-play.
1868	Edvard Grieg composes his Piano Concerto in A Minor.
1876	Denmark's Social Democratic Party is founded. The first organized football club in Scandinavia is founded, as part of the Kjøbenhavn Boldklub. Ibsen writes *A Doll's House*. The first performance of a version of *Peer Gynt* adapted for the stage takes place at the Christiania Theatre, Oslo. The incidental music by Edvard Grieg includes 'In the Hall of the Mountain King' and 'Morning Mood'.
1880–1900	These two decades witness the most intense period of Scandinavian emigration to the United States.
1887	Norway's Labour Party is founded. August Strindberg writes *The Father*.
1888	Strindberg writes *Miss Julie*.
1889	Sweden's Social Democratic Party is founded.
1890	Knut Hamsun's influential novel *Hunger* is published.

1891	Anna Månsdotter is executed in Sweden for the murder of her daughter-in-law; her co-accused was her son and lover. By 1910, all of Scandinavia has abandoned the death penalty (briefly revived in Norway and Denmark for Nazi collaborators).
1894	Edvard Munch paints *Scream*.
1897	The Swede Salomon August Andrée mounts an ill-fated attempt to fly a hydrogen balloon to the North Pole. His remains, and those of his companions, are discovered thirty-three years later.
1898	Strindberg's quasi-autobiographical prose work *Inferno* is published.
1901	Dagny Juel, Norwegian writer, bohemian and muse to Munch (and others), is murdered in Tblisi, Georgia. Strindberg writes *A Dreamplay*, which is not performed until 1907. The first Nobel Prizes are awarded, the legacy of the Swedish industrialist and inventor of dynamite, Alfred Nobel (1833–96).
1903	Sigurd Ibsen, son of Henrik, is appointed Norway's prime minister within the Swedish-Norwegian union.
1905	Norway, having already largely achieved autonomy in internal affairs, declares independence from Sweden. A referendum is overwhelmingly in favour of restoring the Norwegian monarchy. A Danish prince takes the throne as Håkon VII, the first Norwegian king in more than 500 years.
1911	Norwegian explorer Roald Amundsen reaches the South Pole.
1913	Norwegian women win the right to vote. Denmark follows suit in 1915.
1914–18	The Scandinavian countries remain neutral during the First World War, but trade and communications are affected by the British naval blockade of Germany and by German sea mines. Germany's telegrams to

the Americas are routed through neutral Sweden (but are not secure: Britain is able to read them). Norway, especially, loses shipping when Germany institutes unrestricted submarine warfare. In 1916, the war's largest sea battle, between the British and German navies, takes place in waters off the coast of Jutland.

1917   The Swede Viktor Sjöström, Ingmar Bergman's first cinematic idol, directs and stars in a film version of Ibsen's *Terje Vigen.*

1921   Women in Sweden win the franchise.

1922   The Nobel Prize for Physics is awarded to the Dane Niels Bohr.

First performance, in Copenhagen, of Carl Nielsen's Symphony No. 5.

1925   The Norwegian capital, known as Kristiania since 1624, reverts to its former name of Oslo.

1929   The first Social Democratic government takes power in Denmark.

1932   Sweden experiences its first Social Democratic government; it is effectively in office for the next forty-four years.

In the Hollywood film *Grand Hotel,* its star, Swedish screen goddess Greta Garbo, utters her memorable line: 'I want to be alone.'

1935   Norway has its first Labour Party government.

1940   Forces of Nazi Germany invade both Norway and Denmark (9 April), beginning occupations of both countries. Norwegian guns manage to sink the German warship *Blücher* in the Oslo fjord, and Britain and its Allies attempt an intervention at Narvik, but to no avail. Norway's king and government have time to escape, but occupation allows the rise of Vidkun Quisling and his collaborationist National Unity party. Sweden remains formally neutral during the war, at first geopolitically locked into trade with the Axis powers, but later providing a refuge for Danish Jews. British forces take control in Iceland.

1941 Norwegian union leaders Viggo Hansteen and Rolf Wickström are executed after strikes and civil disobedience. German *Reichskommissar* Josef Terboven declares a state of emergency.

1942 Swedish actress Ingrid Bergman stars opposite Humphrey Bogart in the Hollywood wartime classic *Casablanca*. She later stars in the Hitchcock films *Spellbound* (1945) and *Notorious* (1946).

1943 Quisling becomes Norway's 'Minister-President', under Terboven.

The Danish government resigns, and Germany takes direct control of the country. The vast majority of Denmark's Jews escape transportation to Nazi camps by finding exile in Sweden, aided by the Danish populace.

1944 The Republic of Iceland is established, independent of Denmark.

The efforts of Swede Raoul Wallenberg save the lives of around 120,000 Hungarian Jews, mainly by issuing them with Swedish passports.

1945 The Swedish 'White Buses' manage to extricate Danish, Norwegian and some European inmates from German concentration camps.

Liberation from Nazi occupation for Denmark and Norway. Quisling and other leading Scandinavian Nazis and collaborators are executed.

1949 As the Cold War blocs take shape, Denmark and Norway join NATO. Sweden remains neutral.

1951 In Sweden, the first IKEA furniture catalogue is issued.

1957 Ingmar Bergman's films *The Seventh Seal*, starring Max von Sydow, and *Wild Strawberries*, starring Victor Sjöström and Bibi Andersson, are released.

1958	Sweden reach the World Cup Final, losing 5–2 to Brazil.
1959	The Swedish boxer Ingemar Johansson defeats Floyd Patterson to become World Heavyweight Champion.
1959	The European Free Trade Area (EFTA) Treaty is signed in Stockholm.
1961	Dag Hammarskjöld, the Swedish Secretary-General of the United Nations, dies in a mysterious plane crash over Africa during the crisis surrounding Congo's independence.
1964	Jan Johansson releases the *Jazz på Svenska* LP, which gives birth to a uniquely Scandinavian form of jazz.
1966	Norway starts drilling for North Sea oil. The first strike is in 1969.
	Ingmar Bergman's film *Persona* is released, starring the Norwegian actress Liv Ullmann.
1967	The Dane Henning Carlsen's film of *Hunger* is released. Its star Per Oscarsson wins Best Actor Award at the Cannes Film Festival.
1969	Denmark legalizes all types of pornography but with a restriction on selling to minors. A decade later further restrictions are introduced concerning child pornography.
1971	Jan Troell's film *Utvandrarna* (*The Emigrants*) appears, based on Vilhelm Moberg's *Utvandrarna* quartet of novels. Its stars include Max von Sydow and Liv Ullmann.
1972	Norwegian voters reject membership of Europe's Common Market; but Danish voters choose to join.
1974	Abba's song 'Waterloo' wins the Eurovision Song Contest, launching a durable international pop stardom for the four-member band.
1976	Iceland obtains an internationally recognized exclusive fishing zone in its territorial waters, and the

intermittent Cod Wars with British trawlers and naval vessels come to an end.

Swedish tennis player Björn Borg defeats his rival Ilie Nastase to win the first of five consecutive Men's Singles titles at Wimbledon.

1978　　　Ingmar Bergman's film *Autumn Sonata* is released, featuring Ingrid Bergman, Liv Ullmann and Lena Nyman.

In Paris, the Norwegian entry 'Mil etter Mil' ('Mile after Mile') sung by Jahn Teigen becomes the most famous Eurovision song to earn *nul points* during the judging – though it is by no means the first or the last to do so in Eurovision history.

1981　　　Gro Harlem Brundtland becomes Norway's first female prime minister. In her second Cabinet (1986–9) eight of her eighteen ministers are women, the highest proportion of women in any Cabinet in the world to that point.

Norway's national football team beats England 2–1. Norwegian commentator Bjørge Lillelien screams: 'Maggie Thatcher... Your boys took a hell of a beating.'

1982　　　Ingmar Bergman's epic family drama *Fanny and Alexander* is released.

1983　　　*The Wild Market Place* (*Det vilda Torget*), Tomas Tranströmer's ninth book of poetry, is published.

1986　　　Sweden's former prime minister, Olof Palme, is assassinated in Stockholm.

1990　　　The Norwegian Oil Fund is established.

1991　　　*Faceless Killers*, the first crime novel by Swede Henning Mankell to feature Detective Inspector Kurt Wallander, is published.

1992　　　Denmark's football team beats Germany 2–0 in the final of the European Championship.

1993　　　There is an assassination attempt on William

Nygaard, the Norwegian publisher of a translation of Salman Rushdie's *The Satanic Verses*.

1994   Norway joins the European Economic Union and signs the Schengen Agreement, whereby member states allow travel without passports across their border. But Norwegian voters reject *full* membership of the European Union in a second referendum.

Munch's *Scream* is stolen from the National Gallery, Oslo. It is recovered two years later.

1995   Danish film directors Lars von Trier and Thomas Vinterberg publish the 'Dogme 95 Manifesto' for filmmakers, advocating an emphasis on narrative, eschewal of special effects and other devices.

1998   In the Football World Cup, Norway beats Brazil 2–1.

1999   In a notorious incident at Malexander, Sweden, two police officers are murdered by a group of bank robbers, including the neo-Nazi prisoner-actor Tony Olsson.

2000   Formal separation between Church and state is introduced in Sweden.

2003   The Swedish foreign minister, Anna Lindh, is stabbed to death in a Stockholm shopping centre.

2005   The first of Swede Stieg Larsson's *Millennium* trilogy of crime novels, *The Girl With the Dragon Tattoo*, is published, posthumously.

2007   The first series of the Danish police drama *The Killing* is aired, starring Sofie Gråbøl as Detective Inspector Sarah Lund.

2009   The first book of Karl Ove Knausgård's multi-volume autobiographical novel *My Struggle* is published.

2011   In Norway, Anders Behring Breivik kills seventy-seven people in an attack on the ideals of multi-culturalism. Most are young people attending a Norwegian Labour Party summer camp. Breivik is sentenced to twenty-one years' preventive detention.

2011	The Swedish poet Tomas Tranströmer wins the Nobel Prize for Literature.
2012	The Lutheran Church of Norway is formally separated from the state after 400 years. Operative from 2017.
	The first series of the Dano-Swedish television crime drama *The Bridge* is aired, starring Sofia Helin as Detective Saga Norén.
2016	Breivik wins a case against the Norwegian state for keeping him in solitary confinement for the first five years of his sentence.
	Swedish golfer Henrik Stenson wins the Open Championship at Royal Troon.

For Further Interest

PRELUDE. A SEASON IN HELL: COPENHAGEN 1969

Heimskringla: History of the Kings of Norway, From the Icelandic of Snorri Sturlason, translated by Samuel Laing (1844). Freely available online.

Letters Written During a Short Residence in Sweden, Norway and Denmark by Mary Wollstonecraft, edited by Richard Holmes (1987).

Northbound: Travel, Encounters and Constructions, 1700–1830, edited by Karen Klitgaard Povlsen (2007).

English Historical Documents, Volume I, c.500–1042, edited by Dorothy Whitelock, general editor, David C. Douglas (1979).

CHAPTER 1: STONES

Stones, Ships, and Symbols: The Picture Stones of Gotland, From the Viking Age and Before by Erik Nylen and Jan Peder Lamm (1988).

The Saga of the Jomsvikings, translated and introduced by Lee M. Hollander (1988).

Norwegian Maritime Explorers and Expeditions Over the Past Thousand Years, edited by O. K. Johansen, translated by Dahlia Pfeffer, Veronica Harrington Hansen and Richard Lawson (1999). Includes an English translation of Ottar's account at the Wessex court of King Alfred.

The Annals of St-Bertin, edited by Janet Nelson (1991).

Ibn Fadlan and the Land of Darkness: Arab Travellers in the Far North, edited and translated by Caroline Stone and Paul Lunde (2011).

Eaters of the Dead: The Manuscript of Ibn Fadlan Relating His Experiences with the Northmen in AD 922, novel by Michael Crichton (1976). Filmed in 1997 as The 13th Warrior.

CHAPTER 2: THE CONVERSION OF THE ICELANDERS

Íslendingabók and Kristni Saga, edited and translated by Siân Grønlie (2006).

History of the Archbishops of Hamburg-Bremen, by Adam of Bremen, translated by Francis J. Tschan (2005).

Sturlunga Saga, translated by George R. Thomas and Julia H. McGrew (1970).

What Price Cod? A Tugmaster's View of the Cod Wars, by Norman Storey (1992).

The Royal Navy in The Cod Wars: Britain and Iceland in Conflict 1958–1976, by Andrew Welch (2006).

The Norse Atlantic Saga, edited and translated by Gwyn Jones (1986). This includes translations of *The Book of the Icelanders, The Book of the Settlements, The Saga of the Greenlanders, Eirik the Red's Saga, Karlsefni's Voyage to Vinland* and *The Story of Einar Sokkason*.

CHAPTER 3: AMLETH, LUTHER AND THE LAST PRIEST: THE REFORMATION IN SCANDINAVIA

Saxo Grammaticus: The History of the Danes, Books I–IX, Volume I, *English Text*, Volume II, Commentary, translated and annotated by Hilda Ellis Davidson and Peter Fisher (2002).

Edda, by Snorri Sturluson, translated and edited by Anthony Faulkes (1987).

Hamlet (The Arden Shakespeare), by William Shakespeare, edited by Ann Thompson and Neil Taylor (2016, 2nd revised edition).

The Essential Anatomy of Melancholy, by Robert Burton (2002). A well-abridged edition, from Dover Books.

CHAPTER 4: THE KING OF THE PAST: FREDERIK VII OF DENMARK

The Poetic Edda, translated by Carolyne Larrington (2014). Includes a translation of *The Sayings of the High One*.

Carolingian Chronicles: Royal Frankish Annals and Nithard's Histories, edited by Bernhard Walter Scholz (1970).

The Saga of Grettir the Strong, translated by George Hight, edited and introduced by Peter Foote (1970).

Defying Napoleon: How Britain Bombarded Copenhagen and Seized the Danish Fleet in 1807, by Thomas Munch-Petersen (2007).

Terje Vigen, by Henrik Ibsen, translated by John Northam. Online at http://ibsen.nb.no/id/27224.0. This is the best Ibsen website there is, most of it available in both English and Norwegian. John Northam's translations of all of Ibsen's major poems are included.

The English Dane, From King of Iceland to Tasmanian Convict: A Story of Empire and Adventure, by Sarah Bakewell (2006). On Jørgen Jørgensen's remarkable life.

Journey to the Centre of the Earth, by Jules Verne.

Sundes verden – De Beste (2 CDs) by Øystein Sunde. His greatest hits.

CHAPTER 5: THE *VASA* SHIP: SWEDEN'S AGE OF GREATNESS

Descartes: The Life of René Descartes and Its Place in His Times, by A.C. Grayling (2006). Includes a chapter on Descartes' fatal sojourn in Sweden.

Queen Christina (DVD of 1933 film), directed by Rouben Mamoulian, starring Greta Garbo and John Gilbert.

Finding Atlantis: A True Story of Genius, Madness, and an Extraordinary Quest for a Lost World, by David King (2006). A full and sympathetic account of Rudbeck's life and career.

The Vasa: The Royal Ship, by Lars-Ake Kvarning and Bengt Ohrelius, translated by Joan Tate (1998). A comprehensive account in English of the sinking, re-discovery, recovery and restoration of the great ship.

CHAPTER 6: ABDUCTIONS: THE WAR BETWEEN THE DANES AND ALGERIANS

Drakenberg, verdens eldste bloffmaker, by Geir Hasle (2004). In Norwegian.

1001 Natt. Den ukjente historien om to Norske slaver i Alger, by Vetle Lid Larssen (2013). A journalist traces the fate of two individual Norwegians enslaved in Algiers. In Norwegian.

The Pirate Queen: In search of Grace O'Malley and Other Legendary Women of the Sea, by Barbara Sjoholm (2004). Includes a chapter on the abductions from Reykjavik and the Vestmannaeyjar (Westman Islands).

CHAPTER 7: THE SHORT SWEET RULE OF JOHANN FRIEDRICH STRUENSEE

Festen (DVD of 2008 film), directed by Thomas Vinterberg. Featuring Ulrich Thomsen, Henning Moritzen and Thomas Bo Larsen.

A Royal Affair (DVD of 2012 film), directed by Nikolaj Arsel. Featuring Alicia Vikander, Mads Mikkelsen and Mikkel Boe Folsgaard.

The Visit of the Royal Physician, by P. O. Enkvist, translated by Tiina Nunnally (2003). A historical novel about the Struensee years.

Hvem skjøt William Nygaard? by Odd Isungset (2010). In Norwegian. A fascinating account of the still-unsolved case of the attempted murder of Rushdie's Norwegian publisher William Nygaard (2010).

CHAPTER 8: TAKING GOD AT HIS WORD: SØREN KIERKEGAARD AND OLAV FISKVIK

Fear and Trembling, by Søren Kierkegaard, translated by Alastair Hannay (2005). Penguin Classics edition.

Papers and Journals: A Selection, by Søren Kierkegaard, translated and edited by Alistair Hannay (1996). This is an excellent place to start reading Kierkegaard.

Encounters with Kierkegaard: A Life as Seen by His Contemporaries, collected, edited and annotated by Bruce H. Kirmsee, translated by Kirmsee and Virginia R. Laursen (1996). A fascinating collection of reminiscences.

Søren Kierkegaards Skrifter [Søren Kierkegaard's Writings]. Online at http://sks.dk/forside/indhold.asp. A website, in Danish, containing all of Kierkegaard's published and unpublished writings, journals and papers, and letters.

Mordernes forventninger, by Erling Sandmo (1998). An essay in Norwegian on the history of changing attitudes towards insanity and murder.

On Overgrown Paths, by Knut Hamsun. Translated by by Sverre Lyngstad (2003). Written at the age of 87, this is Hamsun's own account of his detention, psychiatric examination and trial after the Second World War.

CHAPTER 9: THE LONELINESS OF THE LONG-DISTANCE EXPLORER

The Expedition: Solving the Mystery of a Polar Tragedy, by Bea Uusma (2015). A complete account of the Andreé expedition.

Flight of the Eagle (feature film, in Swedish), directed by Jan Troell (1982). With Max von Sydow, Sverre Anker Ousdal and Göran Stangertz. Available on YouTube, without subtitles, but worth seeing for the beautiful imagery.

En frusen dröm (DVD of 1997 film), directed by Jan Troell. This documentary tells the story of the Andrée expedition, with English subtitles.

Strindberg's Star, by Jan Wallentin (2012). A Dan-Brown style novel with characters based on members of the Andrée expedition.

INTERLUDE: *IBSEN'S GHOSTS*

A History of Modern Norway: 1814–1972, by T. K. Derry (1973).

The Three Ibsens: Memories of Henrik Ibsen, Suzannah Ibsen and Sigurd Ibsen, by Bergljot Ibsen (1951). A memoir written by Sigurd Ibsen's wife.

CHAPTER 10: THE EMIGRANTS

Hamsun Samleboks (DVD box, 2009). Five filmed versions of Hamsun's novels, including Hunger; the early silent The Growth of the Soil from 1921; and Henning Carlsen's Pan from 1995. The box also includes Jan Troell's fine 1996 biopic Hamsun, starring Max von Sydow and Ghita Nørby. All subtitled in English.

Norwegian Migration to America 1825–1860, by Theodore C. Blegen (1969).

Norwegians and Swedes in the United States: Friends and Neighbors, edited by Philip J. Anderson and Dag Blanck (2011).

Norse Discoveries and Explorations in America, 982–1362: Leif Erikson to the Kensington Stone, by Hjalmar R. Holand (1968).

CHAPTER 11: WORLD WAR II: THE SCANDINAVIAN EXPERIENCE

Krysseren Blücher, by Alf R. Jacobsen (2010). In Norwegian. A detailed account of the sinking of the Blücher.

Niels Bohr's Times: In Physics, Philosophy and Polity, by Abraham Pais (1994).

Ibsen on Screen (DVD box, 2006). Three Norwegian/Swedish film versions of Ibsen's plays, including Victor Sjöström's *Terje Vigen* from 1917, all with English subtitles.

Den rettspsykiatriske erklæringen om Knut Hamsun (The psychiatric report on Knut Hamsun). This is the full text of the examination of Knut Hamsun undertaken in 1945/46 by two psychiatrists, Gabriel Langfeldt and Ørnulv Ødegaard, at the request of the authorities, to determine whether or not Hamsun was fit to stand trial for his wartime newspaper articles and radio broadcasts urging Norwegians not to resist the Nazi invasion of Norway in 1940. Published in 1976. A fascinating document. In Norwegian.

CHAPTER 12: THE POWER OF SCANDINAVIAN WOMEN

The Poet and the Spae-Wife: An Attempt to Reconstruct al-Ghazal's Embassy to the Vikings, translated and edited by W.E.D. Allen (1960). A translation and discussion of this story. Also online as PDF file: http://vsnrweb-publications.org.uk/Poet%20and%20 Spae-wife.pdf

Njals Saga, translated and edited by Magnus Magnusson and Hermann Palsson (1970).

Four Major Plays: Doll's House, Ghosts, Hedda Gabler and The Master Builder, by Henrik Ibsen, translated by James McFarlane and Jens Arup (2008).

A Doll's House (DVD of 1973 film), directed by Patrick Garland and starring Claire Bloom, Anthony Hopkins and Ralph Richardson.

An Ideal Husband (DVD of 1999 film), based on play by Oscar Wilde, directed and screenplay by Oliver Parker. Featuring Rupert Everett, Minnie Driver, Jeremy Northam and Cate Blanchett.

Casablanca (DVD of 1942 film), directed by Michael Curtiz. Featuring Ingrid Bergman and Humphrey Bogart. Ingrid Bergman's character in the film, Ilsa Lund, is supposed to be a Norwegian.

Ingmar Bergman. The Masterpiece Collection (DVD box). Ten films spanning Bergman's career from Summer with Monika (1953) to Fanny and Alexander (1982) In Swedish, with English subtitles.

CHAPTER 13: DAGNY JUEL AND THE INVENTION OF MELANCHOLY

Melankoliska Rum, by Karin Johannisson (2009). A well-written and thoughtful study of changing ideas of what melancholy is, and how – and whether – it should be treated. In Swedish.

Suicide and Scandinavia, by Herbert Hendin (1965). Addressing a Republican National Committee breakfast in Chicago in the summer of 1960 President Eisenhower informed his audience that Sweden 'has a tremendous record for socialistic operation following a socialistic philosophy. And the record shows that their rate of suicide has gone up almost unbelievably and I think they were almost the lowest nation in the world before that.

Now they have more than twice our rate.' As statistics of the time show, Swedes came no higher than fifth in that melancholy listing. Eisenhower apologized in due course, but by then the damage had been done and within five years Hendin's influential book-length study had appeared, to compound what was already an ancient stereotype.

Edvard Munch (DVD of 1974 film). Peter Watkins's intricate biopic, almost three hours long and acted by a cast of Norwegian amateurs. English subtitles.

CHAPTER 14: MALEXANDER

Smärtpunkten, by Elisabeth Åsbrink (2009). A full account of events leading up to the tragedy by a Swedish journalist. In Swedish.

Chockvågor, by Tony Olsson (2011). Olsson's autobiography. In Swedish. The proceeds from Olsson's book go to the Malexander victims' families.

Repetitioner: en film om brott och straff (DVD of 2005 film), by Michal Leszczylowski and Gunnar Källström with Lars Norén (2005). In Swedish, with English subtitles.

CHAPTER 15: OSLO 2016

Hjertet mot steinen, by Adrian Pracon (2012). Pracon came face to face with Breivik during Breivik's rampage on Utøya. This is a survivor's account of the attack. In Norwegian.

One of Us: The Story of a Massacre and Its Aftermath, by Åsne Seirstad (2016). A full account of the events of 22 July 2011.

Offret & Gärningsmannen: en essä om mordet på Olof Palme, by Hans Hederberg (2010). In Swedish. An essay on the murder of Olof Palme with a revealing biographical study of Christer Pettersson.

Bjørge Lillelien's victory rant: You can hear this in all its glory on several Youtube sites.

List of Illustrations

Page 80: Frederik VII with Master Engineer Møller at Jelling, 1861. Drawing by Kornerup. National Museum of Denmark.

Page 92: The opening of Queen Kristina's grave in Rome, in 1965. Photograph Hjalmar Gustavsson/Lund University Archives.

Page 100: The diving bell used in the salvage of the *Vasa* ship. Author's collection.

Page 103: A reconstruction of the working methods used by divers in the salvage of the *Vasa* ship. Wikimedia Commons.

Page 133: The execution of Johan Struensee in 1771. Wikimedia Commons.

Page 148: The botanical gardens in Visby. Author's collection.

Page 156: The heads and partitioned bodies of Johan Struensee and Enevold Brandt. The Royal Library, Copenhagen, Denmark.

Page 159: Søren Kierkegaard. After a sketch done by his nephew Niels Christian Kierkegaard. SZ Photo/Bridgeman Images.

Page 170: The execution of Anna Månsdotter, 1890. Wikimedia Commons.

Page 190: Andrée's balloon drops towards the sea shortly after take-off from Danskøya, Svalbard. Historical image collection by Bildagentur-online/Alamy Stock Photo.

Page 193: Members of Andrée's expedition ponder their fate after the *Eagle* comes down on the ice. Photo: Nils Strindberg/Wikimedia Commons.

Page 194: Cutlery improvised by members of the Andrée expedition. Photo: Nils Strindberg/Wikimedia Commons.

Page 197: The Andrée expedition on the ice with tent and boat. Photo: Nils Strindberg/Grenna Museum, The Andrée Expedition Polar Centre.

Page 203: Hjalmar Johansen, the only man who travelled with both Nansen and Amundsen. Wikimedia Commons.

Page 210: Nils Strindberg's remains. Grenna Museum, The Andrée Expedition Polar Centre.

Page 218: Ibsen in his study in Arbiens gate. Ibsen Museum, Oslo.

Page 256: The harbour at Grimstad, *c.* 1850. A painting attributed to Henrik Ibsen. Ibsen Museum, Oslo.

Page 259: Sigurd Ibsen. Wikimedia Commons.

Page 263: Henrik Ibsen glares at his impersonator, the barber Fredriksen, in this drawing of their close encounter at Grand Hotel, Oslo sometime in the 1890s. From Rudolf Muus' *Gamle Kristianiaminder*.

Page 266: Portrait of August Strindberg, by Christian Krohg, 1893. Private Collection/© O. Vaering/Bridgeman Images.

Page 268: Herman Wildenvey and Oscar Wilde. Wikimedia Commons.

Page 270: Sofie Gråbøl as Edvarda and Lasse Kolsrud as Glahn in Henning Carlsen's 1995 film version of Knut Hamsun's novel *Pan*.

Page 275: Olof Ohman, discoverer of the Kensington Runestone in 1898, posing with his find in about 1929. Minnesota Historical Society.

Page 284: Immigrants in New York *c.* 1890, photographed by the Danish photographer Jacob Riis for his book *How the other half lives: Studies among the tenements of New York.* Granger Historical Picture Archive/Alamy Stock Photo.

Page 289: The Norwegian violin virtuoso Ole Bull. Wikimedia Commons.

Page 296: Statue of 'Big Ole' in Alexandria, Minnesota, created to accompany the Kensington Runestone to the New York World's Fair in 1965. Wikimedia Commons.

Page 303: The *Blücher* sinks in the Oslo fjord, Drøbak, on 9 April 1940. Wikimedia Commons.

Page 307: German soldiers marching on Karl Johans gate, Oslo after the invasion of Norway on 9 April 1940. The palace is in the background, the old university to the right in the picture. Universal History Archive/UIG/Getty Images.

Page 308: Norwegian children celebrating the liberation of the country, 8 May 1945.

Page 329: A still from Jonas Cornell's 1967 film *Puss og kram (Hugs and Kisses).*

Page 343: Gro Harlem Brundtland with her cabinet of 1986. Thorberg, Erik/Scanpix Norway/Press Association Images.

Page 346: Greta Garbo, from the 1932 film *Grand Hotel.*

Page 348: Ingrid Bergman. Getty Images.

Page 353: The last known photograph of August Strindberg, taken on 9 April 1912. He died of cancer the following month. Adocphotos/Corbis/Getty Images.

Acknowledgements

IT IS A PLEASURE TO ACKNOWLEDGE THE HELP I RECEIVED while writing this book from two genuine scandophiles, my agent David Miller and my editor Richard Milbank – their steady encouragement and judicious advice was much appreciated. I would also like to thank the novelist Henrik Andersen for his help with questions on matters of Danish culture and language. I have been lucky over the years to have the support of Erik Henning Edvardsen, head of the Ibsen Museum in Oslo, whose knowledge of Ibsen and Ibseniana is unparalleled. My visits to Gotland over the last fifteen years have been among the real joys of my life, and I would like to thank the people of Gotland for making these possible through their generosity in funding the Baltic Centre for Writers and Translators, in Visby. My thanks also to the Centre's head, Lena Pasternak, for her unfailingly warm welcome. My thanks are also due to the National Library in Oslo for the use of a desk in Forskersal 6 during the last two years.

For permission to quote from W. E. D. Allen's translation of *The Poet and the Spae Wife* I am grateful to the Viking Society for Northern Research, which published Allen's study of al-Ghazal's journey in Saga Book XV, no. 3, 1960. The translations are the copyright of the estate of W. E. D. Allen.

Index